CW01237862

DAVID TRIMBLE

Advance Praise for *David Trimble: Peacemaker*

'Without David Trimble there would be no Good Friday Agreement. Stephen Walker's superb book details his strength, leadership and courage. A carefully crafted biography of a political giant.'

Bertie Ahern, Former Taoiseach

'The story of a complex, sometimes brittle, man who staked his leadership on a risky peace deal. Stephen Walker's intimate portrait benefits greatly from the insights of those who knew him best, particularly the Trimble family who reveal what the Nobel Prize winner was like away from the political spotlight.'

Mark Devenport, Former BBC Ireland Correspondent

'This overdue assessment charts David Trimble's fascinating journey from academia to a lengthy hiatus on the also-ran fringes of unionism, and onto his legacy as the most consequential Unionist leader of his generation; without whom the 1998 peace agreement would probably not have been possible. This is thorough, detailed and well measured: the perfect companion piece to Walker's biography of John Hume.'

Alex Kane, Writer and Columnist. *Belfast Telegraph* and *Irish News*

'The fascinating story of one of unionism's most compellingly consequential leaders, and its most complex. Stephen Walker's hallmark is his fairness – he allows the reader to settle for themselves many of the biggest questions about Trimble, based on the accounts of those who were with him at key junctures.'

Sam McBride, Northern Ireland Editor, *Belfast Telegraph*

'Stephen Walker has captured the remarkable story of David Trimble perfectly. He has spent hours talking to those who knew the Nobel laureate best, to create a revealing, nuanced account of a complex man who took risks for peace and who made his mark on history. A political page turner from start to finish.'

Freya McClements, Northern Editor, *Irish Times*

'From the firebrand of the Vanguard movement to the angst-ridden leader of Ulster Unionism whose support of the Good Friday Agreement was so crucial to peace in Northern Ireland, Stephen Walker's David Trimble is a man of principle and contradiction, a man of peace and division, a man of ambition and doubt who inspired deep loyalty and even deeper loathing. With great skill Walker captures Trimble's brittleness and power, his cunning and naivety, his highs and lows, his glory and tribulations. This is the brilliantly told story of a man whose character, with all its strengths and flaws, was central to peace in Northern Ireland.'

Gary Murphy, Professor of Politics (DCU) and Author

DAVID TRIMBLE

PEACEMAKER

STEPHEN WALKER

GILL BOOKS

Gill Books
Hume Avenue
Park West
Dublin 12
www.gillbooks.ie

Irish Writers Centre
Áras Scríbhneoirí na hÉireann

Gill Books is an imprint of M.H. Gill and Co.

© Stephen Walker 2025

9781804581926

Design origination by Liz White Designs
Edited by Neil Burkey
Proofread by Ruairí Ó Brógáin
Printed and bound in Great Britain by Clays Ltd, Elcograf S.p.A.
This book is typeset in Minion Pro by Typo•glyphix.

The paper used in this book comes from the wood pulp of sustainably managed forests.

All rights reserved.
No part of this publication may be copied, reproduced or transmitted in any form or by any means, without written permission of the publishers.

To the best of our knowledge, this book complies in full with the requirements of the General Product Safety Regulation (GPSR). For further information and help with any safety queries, please contact us at productsafety@gill.ie.

A CIP catalogue record for this book is available from the British Library.

5 4 3 2 1

MIX
Paper | Supporting responsible forestry
FSC® C018072

For Katrin, Grace, Jack and Gabriel.

CONTENTS

Prologue ix
1. Bangor boy 1
2. First among equals 19
3. Vote Trimble 39
4. Bringing down the house 53
5. Breaking the Convention 61
6. Hello, Daphne 71
7. To have and to hold 85
8. Murder in the morning 99
9. The wilderness years 111
10. Goodbye, Queen's 127
11. Snowballs and secret talks 145
12. Stalking and walking 157
13. Follow the leader 173
14. New Labour, new ideas 193
15. The final countdown 211
16. Deal or no deal 227
17. Just say yes 245
18. From Omagh to Oslo 263
19. Guns and government 283
20. Stop start Stormont 303
21. Hearts and minds 321
22. Spies, splits and suspensions 339
23. A good innings 357
24. The final days 373
25. Portrait of a peacemaker 391

Acknowledgements 411
Sources 415
Bibliography 419
Endnotes 421
Index 437

PROLOGUE

Castle Buildings, Stormont Estate, Belfast
Good Friday, 10 April 1998

The door was locked. No one was coming in and no one was leaving.

For David Trimble and his party, it was decision time. The Ulster Unionist Party leader and his inner circle had much to discuss.

In the cramped, airless room, there was a groundbreaking deal to be considered. The pressure was intense.

Hours before, in the grounds of Stormont, there had been raised voices from Ian Paisley's Democratic Unionist Party, who believed a sell-out was on the cards. Paisley, Ulster's 'Dr No', so long the voice of uncompromising unionism, opposed power-sharing and had boycotted this round of talks.

He and his supporters had branded Trimble a traitor, while others had used the term 'Lundy' – a reference to Robert Lundy, who famously betrayed Protestants during the Siege of Derry in 1689.

As the talks process entered its final stages, Paisley had turned up to protest and demand that his main unionist rival should walk away.

Trimble was going nowhere.

Over the past 24 hours there had been no shortage of advice for the UUP leader, and calls to his mobile phone were constant. Prime Minister Tony Blair and Taoiseach Bertie Ahern had urged him to endorse what was on the table. They told him it was a good deal, and the agreement would deliver what he wanted. The two premiers argued that it was a historic agreement that could end Northern Ireland's long-running political stalemate, cement Northern Ireland's place in the UK, create a new cross-community government and change British and Irish relations.

It was a compromise, and Trimble was being urged to say yes. He knew what the deal could potentially deliver. This was an opportunity for peace. It was not perfect, and there was still much detail to be confirmed, but he believed it represented a fresh start. For the first time in a quarter of a century, politicians with different identities would share power at Stormont. The figureheads of this new administration would be a unionist and a nationalist.

On a personal level, Trimble knew that if this deal was endorsed by voters, he would become Northern Ireland's inaugural first minister. He also knew it presented the opportunity to become the most important unionist leader since the creation of Northern Ireland in 1921. A student of the past, Trimble knew all that. Yet, he was not interested in making history for history's sake. He wanted the agreement to be the best he could reach, and he felt it required improvements.

With the clock ticking, he needed some space and did not want to be disturbed or distracted. Away from the spin and the high-pressure sales talk, he had to gauge what his colleagues really felt.

The deadline had expired.

The former US senator George Mitchell, the American talks chairman, had made it clear that there would be no extra time. These were the final minutes. After 700 days of talking, the negotiating was over. Trimble's team, like those of the other parties, were exhausted.

Some had slept on floors and chairs in adjoining offices as they read and re-read the deal. Some had no sleep at all. Trimble needed to get them to focus.

Key questions remained for unionists. Did the deal enhance and protect the union with the rest of the UK? Was the union stronger than when Trimble and his team began to negotiate? There were other big issues to consider. What would the unionist community make of the reforms to policing, the early release of prisoners and the issue of decommissioning?

As Good Friday wore on, the UUP leader desperately needed one more thing. Trimble said he would go back to the UK government on a single issue and asked his colleagues what that should be. They all agreed there must be a stronger link between the decommissioning of paramilitary weapons and Sinn Féin's participation in a power-sharing government.

For the rest of the afternoon, Trimble and his colleagues shuttled between meetings with Tony Blair and his advisers. They made it clear to Blair that without a stronger commitment on decommissioning the Ulster Unionists could not support the deal. By that time, the other parties were getting restless and became aware of the UUP's difficulty. A novel plan was then hatched by the British government. Blair agreed that he would write Trimble a letter to reassure him that he would support the exclusion of Sinn Féin from government if there had not been any weapons decommissioning. Downing Street also asked Bill Clinton to help, and the US president rang the UUP leader and urged him to endorse the agreement.

As Trimble and his colleagues continued their deliberations, Blair's chief of staff, Jonathan Powell, finished typing the letter on his laptop and went in search of the Ulster Unionist leader.

When Powell arrived at the UUP room he could not get in as it was locked. He quickly managed to attract the attention of a young unionist near the door and, once he was inside, the letter was passed to Trimble.

The UUP leader opened the envelope and read Blair's words, with John Taylor, the former Stormont home affairs minister, looking anxiously over his shoulder. Taylor was quick to finish reading the short message and then declared, 'That is fine, we can run with that.' It was now game on.

At 4.46 p.m., Trimble lifted the phone to Mitchell. He told the talks chairman, 'We're ready to do the business.' Trimble was now able to do something that no unionist had ever done: to agree to a multi-party administration at Stormont that involved unionists, nationalists and republicans.

For Trimble, it represented another remarkable step in his political journey. Having been a hard-line street protestor who opposed the last attempt at cross-community government at Sunningdale, he was about to endorse power-sharing. As an outspoken Orangeman, he had once walked hand in hand with Ian Paisley in Portadown. Yet now, he was plotting his own course. When he was at Queen's University, he had missed out on promotion three times. Now, he was the front-runner for the most powerful job in Northern Ireland, and within months he would become a Nobel laureate.

As he prepared to make his decision public, the media were waiting. For days they had chronicled the twists and turns of a process that at times seemed pointless and ready to collapse. Wasn't that always the narrative? In the reportage of Northern Ireland, the words 'talks' and 'failure' were often part of the same sentence. Amongst the pockets of seasoned reporters were many who had covered Northern Ireland's bloodied past. Days painfully etched in their memory – anniversaries that were synonymous with pain. Bloody Sunday, Bloody Friday, the Poppy Day bombing in Enniskillen, Halloween night in Greysteel. The list was long and filled with heartache.

So, was all that about to change? Was Northern Ireland about to witness a new chapter? Were the leaders of unionism and nationalism really committed to sharing power – nearly a quarter of a century after the last attempt?

Beyond the perimeter fence amidst the television satellite trucks and temporary buildings the word had spread that an announcement was coming.

The deal was done and reporters and producers readied themselves for interviews. It had been a most unusual day in so many ways.

Even the weather was defying predictions. The sun had shone, it had rained and now it was trying to snow. Northern Ireland in April. Four seasons in one day.

Inside Castle Buildings, 53-year-old William David Trimble was about to make history and say he was ready to preside over a new form of power-sharing government. He began the negotiations as an MP and party leader, but he was about to get a new title: first minister.

For the politician and peacemaker, life would never be the same again.

1
BANGOR BOY

'His work is dirty, carelessly set out and his compositions are so full of ridiculous mistakes that often it is not worth marking.'
David Trimble school report, 1955

David Trimble was running for his life. His would-be attacker was armed with a hatchet and seemed pretty intent on causing him harm. David had the advantage of being a few paces ahead of his assailant and knew if he could just reach the sanctuary of his house, he would be safe. He sprinted and made a beeline for the glass-panelled back door, which was at the side of his house.

In the summer months it was used all the time and was normally kept wide open. As David reached the house, he quickly pushed his body forward.

On this occasion the door was surprisingly shut, and the momentum resulted in his arm going straight through the glass. There was a scream, followed by blood and tears. Pandemonium broke out. It was not meant to end like this. His pursuer was none other than his younger brother Iain. He and his sister Rosemary had been playing in the back garden of their Bangor home when David had surprised them and had tried to frighten them by pretending to be a scary monster. Iain's decision to fight back ended badly, leaving his brother with scars that he would carry for the rest of his life. Their parents were understandably furious that an innocuous bit of fun had ended in such a horrific way. Iain was told that he had behaved badly and recalls that he was punished for his behaviour and remembers being 'in the doghouse for ages'.[1]

The incident did not damage his relationship with his brother, however. In later years, often over a glass of wine, the two men would make light of that dramatic day. David would be characteristically blunt: 'Iain, do you remember the day you tried to kill me with a hatchet?'[2]

Iain may have been the villain on that occasion, but there were other times when David's temper got the better of him. David recalled getting cross on one occasion:

> I do remember when I was aged about five having an argument with another person and he got me so angry that I put my head down and ran at him. The other lad of course did the smart thing and stepped to one side, and I ran straight into a wall.[3]

This may be the first time the famous Trimble temper was aired in public. However, it was something his brother Iain would become well used to. The two boys were born four years apart. David was older, having been born in Belfast on 15 October 1944, while Iain was born on 14 December 1948 in Bangor. They got on well together, so much so that Iain was David's best man when he married Daphne Orr in 1978. Yet, the two brothers were very different. David was shy, awkward and bookish, with no interest in sport. He was the more intellectual of the two:

> I remember a teacher saying, 'You're David's brother, aren't you?' And I said, 'Yes.' 'Oh,' came the reply. And then there is an expectation which I could never fulfil because I am not that bright.[4]

Iain clearly looked up to his older brother. While they played together as kids, it was clear David was perfectly happy in his own company.

> He had a room of his own, you never saw him, except for meals. He was in his room reading. He got told off time and time again for reading in the middle of the night by candlelight.⁵

Rosemary, the eldest, was born on 8 April 1943 in a private nursing home in Belfast. She got on well with her brothers:

> We had plenty of room. We had a big garden at the back and a garden at the front. There was grass and fruit bushes, raspberries and gooseberries. We had lots of fun, chasing each other and playing all sorts of games. It was idyllic.⁶

Like Iain, Rosemary remembers David would disappear and often go and sit alone. She recalls how he was happy in his own company, but if he was missing he would be easy to locate. 'If you could not find David, you would find him with his nose in a book.'⁷

Their parents were Billy and Ivy, although Ivy was not her original name. She was going to be called Annie Margaret Elizabeth, which were the names of three great aunts. Her mother, David's grandmother, could not decide which name to use, so she decided to call her Ivy, which, according to Iain, was 'the name of the heroine of the book she was reading at the time'.⁸

Ivy was born on 4 November 1911 and met Billy Trimble while they were working as civil servants for the Ministry of Labour in their home city of Londonderry. That was how the Trimbles referred to Northern Ireland's second city. Others preferred to call it Derry, but Ivy and Billy used the longer title. The name of the city has always been controversial and cuts to the core of Northern Ireland's identity battle. Unionists have traditionally called it Londonderry, which was the name given to it by the trade guilds from London during the Plantation of Ulster. Nationalists generally regard the 'London' prefix as colonial appropriation and therefore refer to the city simply as Derry.

Beyond the name linking it to the UK, there are other reasons why unionists see the 'Maiden City' as a special place. The old streets and the world-famous walls close to the River Foyle are all part of the Ulster Protestant psyche. Those of a unionist tradition in a majority nationalist city often felt outnumbered and talked about being 'under siege' politically. It was here where the loyalist battle cry 'No surrender' was first heard, and it was home to Robert Lundy, who sought to negotiate a surrender. The name Lundy became synonymous with being a traitor to Protestantism. It was a term of abuse often hurled in David Trimble's direction when he backed the Good Friday Agreement.

The city of Derry is an important part of the Trimble story and helps to explain how he got some of his politics and beliefs. In later life, he often talked about his parents growing up there. Beyond his mother and father, the young Trimble was influenced by Captain William Jack and his wife, Ida, who were his maternal grandparents. Grandfather Jack worked in a timber merchants' firm and was then employed in the building company Robert Colhoun Ltd, which was run by his wife's family.

His politics were unionist, and, like many, he signed the Ulster Covenant in 1912, which was part of the campaign to oppose Home Rule. The outbreak of the First World War in August 1914 changed everything. The Home Rule Crisis was postponed and thousands of men signed up to fight and help Britain's war effort. William Jack was one of the many Ulstermen who went off to war, and he initially served with the Royal Inniskilling Fusiliers.

He later transferred to the Royal Irish Regiment and eventually ended the war in Egypt. He returned to Derry and settled back into a normal routine, and for the rest of his life lived with Ida. After he died, Ida came to live with the Trimbles in Bangor. She needed some care and support at this stage, as she was elderly and confined to a wheelchair. However, she quickly fitted into family life, and a bedroom was made for her in the dining room.

Even though Ida was physically limited, she was mentally sharp and had a strong influence on young David, as he recalled:

> I remember one year when school was off because it was a polling station. I remember coming down a little bit later because I did not have to go to school to find that Grandmother was up and out of bed and in her wheelchair. She was rattling her stick saying, 'Where is David to take me up to the polling station?' She grew up in Londonderry, where every vote counted.[9]

Trimble's use of the name 'Londonderry' illustrates the division over the city's name perfectly. It was a term he most likely heard from his relatives, like Ida. David's sister Rosemary says it was clear there was a special bond between David and Ida, and she observed that the 'two of them really seemed to hit it off'.[10]

As a child, David enjoyed hearing Granny Ida's recollections and was particularly fascinated to learn that he may have had ancestors who played a role in the Siege of Derry. Ida was not the only figure who helped to influence his political thinking. A cousin of his mother's was Jack Colhoun, who was known affectionately as Uncle Jack. He was well known in Derry and was a former politician who ran a construction firm and helped to build the city's Altnagelvin Hospital. David held him in high esteem and often had political conversations with him at family gatherings. So, when stories emerged about discriminatory practices in the city against Catholics as the civil rights campaign began in the 1960s, David questioned whether the claims were valid:

> When we had first of all street disorders associated with a movement calling itself the Civil Rights Association … this was in 1968, I was 24 … it came to me as quite a shock. And what I found most difficult to cope with in that shock is all the things that were being said about discrimination in Londonderry, the city of Londonderry. And it just so happened that my mother came from Londonderry, and a close relative of hers who we refer to as Uncle Jack. Uncle Jack was Mayor of Londonderry. He

was active politically and he was Mayor of Londonderry for three or four years in the late '50s and early '60s. And these allegations were being made about quite reprehensible behaviour, and I knew Uncle Jack. And I knew him to be a person of personally irreproachable character, and this did not figure.[11]

For David it was personal. How could unacceptable things be happening in a city where Uncle Jack was a leading figure? It was an example of how David thought and shows how his politics came to be shaped by relatives and friends. Aside from roots in the northwest corner of Ireland, the Trimble family can also be traced back to County Longford, where David's grandfather, George David Trimble, was born in 1874. Employment was limited, and, instead of farming like many of his neighbours, he joined the Royal Irish Constabulary (RIC) in 1895. He liked the career in uniform and was stationed in a variety of places, including Tyrone, Sligo and Armagh. He married Sarah Jane Sparks from County Armagh in 1903, and the pair had three children. The youngest was Billy, David Trimble's father. He was born in 1908. There were two other boys, the eldest being Norman, who emigrated to America, and Stanley, who continued the family tradition of policing and joined the Royal Ulster Constabulary (RUC). George arrived in Belfast in 1909 and would gain much experience dealing with the city's sectarian tensions and rioting.

Policing in Belfast before and after the Great War was tough, and George often found himself at the heart of the trouble. In the 1920s, there was much rioting and violence in the city. At over six foot tall and well built, he was an imposing figure and was clearly well regarded by his superiors. After the partition of Ireland and the creation of Northern Ireland, he also joined the RUC, rising to the rank of Head Constable. He left the force in 1931 and died in 1962, aged 87.

George spent most of his life north of the border, but the family connection to the Irish Republic has not been completely forgotten. In 2023, a bust of David Trimble was unveiled in the Dáil to mark his contribution to Irish history and the peace process. The sculpture by John Sherlock sits near a bust of John Hume, Trimble's fellow laureate. At the ceremony in Leinster House, Daphne Trimble was reminded of her husband's links south of the border. She was presented with a piece of stone from the original Trimble homestead, which was situated in the townland of Sheeroe, in County Longford, north of Edgeworthstown.

David's parents, Billy and Ivy, began their lives together in Derry, and got married at the city's Great James Street Presbyterian Church on 7 December 1940. Billy was christened William, but he never used that name. Instead, he was universally known as Billy. When David was born, Billy kept up the family tradition and gave his first son the name William David. However, to distinguish him from his father, he was known as David.

An opportunity arose within the civil service, and the Trimbles moved from Derry to Belfast, where Billy was offered a management role at the labour exchange in the city centre. It was a good move, but rather than make their home in Belfast, they decided to settle in Bangor, a pretty seaside resort along the County Down coast. It seemed like a good choice for family life. There was a direct rail line to Belfast, and the town had an excellent mix of shops and good schools. Add to this the access to beaches and the sea, and for the Trimble children it provided the backdrop to an idyllic childhood.

The family's first home was a terraced house in King Street which was close to the town centre and a short walk to the railway station. They did not remain there long, though, and when David was four years old, the Trimbles moved a short distance to better accommodation in Victoria Road. One of David's neighbours in Bangor was David Montgomery. He was younger than David and, like many boys who passed the 11-plus examination, would also go to Bangor Grammar School. Montgomery would eventually leave Northern Ireland and carve out a very successful career in the media. As chief executive of Mirror Group Newspapers in the 1990s, he would help Trimble make connections with Labour politicians, including Tony Blair:

> The Trimble family were very familiar because they stood out because of their red hair, which was unusual. And they were right at the end of the drive that I lived in. We lived in a terraced house and the Trimbles lived in a semi-detached. In those days, there was a sort of social pecking order. Those people in semi-detached or detached houses would be seen as somewhat grander than the ones in terraced houses. Everybody was very conscious of their status in life.[12]

The family were now settled into life in Bangor, and schooling was top of the agenda for Billy and Ivy. David initially went to Central Primary School close to the town centre and later transferred to the bigger Ballyholme Primary School, which was nearer the family home. Life at school for the young pupil was mixed. It is clear from his school reports that he struggled in certain subjects, and there were some lessons that he found particularly difficult. His work was not always neat, and some teachers had great difficulty reading his handwriting. At Ballyholme Primary School, Miss Martin recorded that 10-year-old David was very bright and able, but the presentation of his work needed to improve:

> David is probably one of the most intelligent in the class yet this report rates him just very average – halfway down. So long as progress is made by written examinations he will remain in this category. Unless he makes a real effort to overcome his indifference and write legibly and intelligently. His work is dirty, carelessly set out and his compositions so full of ridiculous mistakes that often it is not worth marking. Very often he can't decipher his own figures. Look at his accuracy marks. Five out of ten.[13]

On the question of whether David might get into grammar school, Miss Martin issued this strong warning: 'There is not the slightest hope of David getting the scholarship next year unless he eradicates this gross carelessness.'[14]

David's parents desperately wanted their son to get a scholarship so he could go to grammar school, which meant that the report from Ballyholme Primary School must have been particularly difficult to accept. Other remarks from Miss Martin showed that David was intellectually capable but was not responsive to the efforts of teachers. In 1955, she wrote: 'Received little cooperation this year. A pity to make so little use of a good mind.'[15]

In the months that followed, Trimble's school work clearly improved, and Miss Martin's prediction of failure did not come to pass. Much to the relief of his parents, David passed the 11-plus exam and was accepted into Bangor Grammar School. He would be the only Trimble child to pass the test, as both Rosemary and Iain failed.

The Trimbles were naturally delighted that David had secured a place at the local school, which was just a minute's walk from the family home in Victoria Road. So, in the autumn of 1956, David went through the doors of Bangor Grammar School for the first time. He was a shy, awkward 11-year-old and felt like he did not belong. The early years were difficult, and as with his time at Ballyholme Primary School, his experience at the grammar school would be mixed. Bangor Grammar School was an all-boys school where pupils were streamed, and David was placed in the B stream – a decision based on a test he sat when he arrived at the school. Before he was admitted, he was interviewed by the headmaster, Randall Clarke.

Clarke had only been in charge for a couple years but had already established a reputation as a formidable figure. It soon became clear that he and David were not going to get on.

Clarke had previously taught at Campbell College in Belfast, which had a reputation for being one of Northern Ireland's leading grammar schools. It was fee-paying, had a boarding department and attracted many pupils from an affluent background.

When he was appointed to Bangor in 1954, the expectation was that Clarke would mimic the ethos and style of his previous school.

Ken Hambly, who was in David's year, says after the new headmaster's arrival the school was jokingly called 'Little Campbell by the sea'.[16]

He also recalls how some boys at Bangor Grammar were teased by pupils from other schools for being 'Bangor snobs'.[17] Trevor Low, another contemporary of Trimble's, says Clarke clearly aspired to turn Bangor Grammar into one of Northern Ireland's poshest schools: 'While he was from Northern Ireland himself, he sounded more as if he would really prefer to be the headmaster of Eton or Harrow.'[18]

Headmaster Clarke had plans for Bangor Grammar and wanted to make the school the first choice for the most able pupils in North Down. He was viewed by the boys and staff as autocratic, and he was not averse to using corporal punishment. He would routinely discipline those who stepped out of line, and he famously expelled several pupils after they kidnapped the Head Boy, roughed him up and abandoned him in the countryside. Clarke wanted his pupils to conduct themselves in a certain way, as Low recalls:

> There was a school rule whereby you had to wear your school cap and your school uniform downtown all the time, and that included Saturdays and Sundays. So, you didn't come home from school and change into casual wear and then go downtown to go shopping or something. You had to wear your school uniform all the time.[19]

Ken Hambly says it would be wrong to portray Bangor Grammar as elitist, and, in his experience, he thought it was 'a perfectly ordinary regional school'.[20] What is clear is that Clarke's tenure helped to define the ethos of the school and in turn that influenced how pupils behaved and learned. Terry Neill, another Bangor Grammar School old boy, who was at school at the same time as David, recalls the influence that Clarke had on the pupils:

> He had a great respect for academic excellence and prowess and was encouraging. He was a bit humourless. He was stern, a sort of a disciplinarian.[21]

Trimble clearly experienced Clarke's stern side, and the headmaster regarded him as academically challenged. The personality clash between Trimble and Clarke may partly explain why he did not look back at his days in Bangor Grammar with much fondness. Marion Smith, who served as a local UUP councillor in Bangor, and was mayor of North Down, remembers being asked by Trimble, when he was an MP, to deputise for him and attend an event at Bangor Grammar School. Trimble had been invited as a guest speaker but did not attend.

Smith got the distinct impression it was simply because Trimble's schooldays were not happy ones. Much of his unhappiness may be linked to his poor relationship with Clarke who, as well as being the headmaster, taught Trimble history:

> There were only seven of us in that class and I disliked Randall intensely as a person because he was fussy and was reluctant to let me in. For the first months of that course, he kept telling me how lucky I was to be in it.[22]

David made a slow start to life at Bangor Grammar. In his first few years his results were average, and he made little academic progress. An early report showed that in a class of 47 boys he was placed 32nd. For David's parents it must have seemed like history was repeating itself. Their son's spelling was regarded as disappointing and, as with his time at primary school, the staff found his work 'too often untidy'. The concluding remarks suggested that he had potential but needed to work harder. The teacher's analysis read: 'Quite a good report. He has definite capabilities which too often he does not use to the full.'[23]

A theme was beginning to emerge about David's approach to schoolwork. He was clearly bright and a good thinker, but his written work was messy and careless, which resulted in him not reaching his academic potential. What is also clear from his early days at the grammar school is that he did not take things seriously. Iain remembers one incident when David's tomfoolery had serious consequences:

> He was misbehaving somewhat in class and decided for whatever reason he was going to run down the length of the classroom on top of the desks. So, he is leaping from desk to desk and he hit his head on one of the beams and knocked himself out.[24]

It is not known if the young Trimble was disciplined for his desk walking, nor is there any suggestion that the bang on the head did any major damage. There are other reports of David allegedly misbehaving at the school. A fellow pupil claims the future politician was part of a group of boys who bullied him during his time at Bangor Grammar. He claims David was 'not vicious compared to other boys in the gang' but says he was humiliated by him.[25]

The victim decided to take revenge and, according to the journalist and biographer Henry McDonald, he went to a Bangor gunsmith and purchased an old rifle and then made his own ammunition. His intention was to go to school and frighten or shoot David. According to McDonald, the plan was thwarted by a teacher, who handed the would-be gunman over to the RUC.

Away from the classroom there was much to occupy the mind of the young teenager. David was interested in the Royal Air Force (RAF), and at one stage it was thought he might join. His brother Iain did join, aged 16, and had a very successful career in the force, but David's prospects always seemed limited, as he had poor eyesight. Despite this, he enrolled with the RAF 825 Squadron of the Air Training Corps (ATC) in Bangor and threw himself into the group's activities.

He quickly became enthusiastic about the opportunities the ATC offered, and his spare time was spent on training nights, exercises and trips across Northern Ireland and in Great Britain.

The summer camps presented lots of fun for David and his friends. They learned about handling weapons, had glider training and were taught map-reading skills. At night in the barracks, they would play cards, or they would sneak off to the local pub in the hope that the bar staff would not question their ages. It was a formative time for David and helped him mature and learn valuable life lessons. It was there he met Leslie Cree, who would become a lifelong friend and would have a strong influence on Trimble's decision-making.

The two had similar interests and would both end up joining the Orange Order and the UUP. Cree would later serve as a Member of the Legislative Assembly at Stormont when Trimble was party leader. He remembers that, when he met David for the first time as a schoolboy, he thought he was 'shy, timid and a bit of a boffin'.[26]

He also recalls that David enjoyed learning to shoot:

> He was a bit short-sighted, but you know at a 25-yard range with a .22 rifle it was not a problem. He liked that. That was a big interest we had in common. I was mad keen on shooting too.[27]

Iain was also an ATC member and would often accompany him on trips and at training camps. He remembers one occasion when brotherly love was forgotten, and David failed to look out for him:

> We had gone to RAF Cosford, which is an RAF training camp in the Midlands, on the ATC summer camp. And during the night there was a fire practice, so everybody got up and went outside to line up, except me who was fast asleep. And my brother didn't even come back to wake me up.[28]

Home life for David was pretty settled. He had school during the day and the ATC at night and at weekends. Going to church was part of the family routine and they worshipped at Trinity Presbyterian Church in Bangor, as Iain recalls:

> We went to church every Sunday. We sat in the same pew and that was that. We went to Sunday School and there was Bible Class later and church in the evenings and things like that. So, it was typically a standard Irish Presbyterian upbringing.[29]

David clearly enjoyed church life, and as he got older, he began to get more involved in helping at church services. On Sundays, as Iain recalls, he 'took over controlling the volume of the loudspeakers which were at the back of the church and up in the gallery'.[30]

David's faith was a constant in his life, and when he got married and had children, his own family followed a similar routine to the traditional Sunday he experienced in his youth. As a child in Bangor, David and his siblings enjoyed modest family holidays, often in Scotland and across Ireland. They went cycling and travelled on a budget, frequently staying in youth hostels.

It was a happy home, although David's relationship with his parents appears at times to have been strained. Rosemary says it was their mother who ran the household: 'Mummy could have been strict. Father was easier going.'[31]

Ivy Trimble was clearly class-conscious and wanted her children to socialise with other children from similar backgrounds. According to David, she viewed herself as 'very middle class'.[32]

Billy Trimble enjoyed a drink and was a smoker. Iain remembers how his father would often come home from work, eat his evening meal, listen to the news and then go off into Bangor for a few drinks. He says during his teenage years David rarely spent time with his father and 'would stay out of his way in his bedroom with a book'.[33]

David was very happy in his own company as a child:

> I have always been fairly independent. At an early age my mother complained that I'd always do things in my own way.[34]

While he was at school, he began to take an interest in pop music, and particularly Elvis Presley. The American singer was a worldwide sensation. His good looks, charm and unique voice brought him global fame. David was fascinated by him and regularly bought his records, and even went to the cinema in Bangor and Belfast to watch his films. It was the start of a lifelong fascination. Rosemary remembers her brother's obsession:

> He had quite a collection of Elvis Presley records. He had most of the hit records. I can remember him going upstairs to study and go to his room. Then a few minutes later the music came down as well. He was always playing those records, over and over again. Everyone was well used to hearing Elvis. Mum and Dad just put up with it and shrugged their shoulders.[35]

A job as a barman in the Queen's Court Hotel in Bangor helped the young music fan subsidise his record buying. If he wasn't saving up for Elvis records, he was frequenting bookshops and purchasing history books. By his mid-teens, his results at Bangor Grammar began to improve and his reports started to reflect that he was maturing and showing a greater commitment to his schoolwork.

By the summer term of 1959, it was clear he was trying hard, and several teachers praised his efforts, although the old Trimble academic trait of 'careless errors' still popped up in the comments section.

When the Easter term of 1960 arrived, David's schoolwork had improved even further. He was first in the class in geography, scored well in history and performed better than expected in arithmetic, algebra and geometry, but his German teacher, unsurprisingly, noted that his work was 'far too careless and untidy'.[36] Aside from the need to smarten up his presentation of essays and coursework, it is clear he was now becoming a more confident student and beginning to develop opinions and ideas.

David did well in his exams and successfully entered sixth form with much confidence. His end-of-term reports got better, his work was tidier and he was starting to get glowing references from his teachers. He studied Geography, Ancient History and Modern History at A level and was at last living up to his academic potential.

He was also interested in learning to drive, and he promptly went out and with his earnings bought himself a Rover car. However, on the first day he took his new purchase out on the road it all went horribly wrong, as Iain recalls:

> He bought a car when he was still relatively young, and his first lesson was when we were living in Clifton Road. He came along Clifton Road towards the crossroads at the top of High Street and he turned left. He forgot to straighten out and he ran straight into the lamppost.[37]

Ivy was furious when she heard about the accident and gave her son a telling-off for his carelessness. In contrast, David's siblings and friends in the ATC found the episode highly amusing and routinely teased him about his inability to drive. The accident had quite the effect on him. It ended his driving career for years, and he did not proceed with any more lessons.

The crash had put him off driving, and for the next two decades he relied on public transport and lifts from other people. He only learned to drive later when he was married with children.

David had also started to become interested in the Orange Order, and while he was away at ATC camps, he began to have conversations with Leslie Cree, who was already a member. There were a number of active lodges in Bangor, and Cree was a member of Bangor Abbey lodge, also known as Loyal Orange Lodge 726. Cree remembers chatting to David one night about joining:

> I talked about it and the history to do with it, how it had been involved in politics and world affairs ... And

he was interested. He asked me lots of questions about how it works, and I explained to him the structure and all that [this was a private lodge]. He also knew that another six or eight of the boys [in the ATC] were members of it too.[38]

Trimble's decision to join the Orange Order is worth examining.

He was aware of its exclusive membership criteria and knew that it excluded Catholics. This obviously meant his Catholic friends at Bangor Grammar and the ATC could not join. He would have also been mindful that it was viewed by some as a bigoted and extreme organisation. Yet, that did not seem to be a barrier to him. On the face it, for a middle-class grammar schoolboy, joining the Orange Order might seem like an odd thing to do. There was no expectation within the Trimble household that he would become involved, although he did have family connections to the Order.

He later told the BBC that one of his grandfathers was in the Order, and Thomas Trimble, his grand-uncle, who lived in County Longford, was Worshipful Master of the Kilglass Loyal Orange Lodge.

Interestingly, his parents Billy and Ivy were not members, although his brother Iain did join. In the 1950s and 1960s, the Orange Order was an influential body in Northern Ireland and was linked to the Unionist Party. Most of its MPs were members and party meetings were often held in Orange halls. The Order was seen by many as an integral part of the state of Northern Ireland, and Orange culture often set the narrative for unionist rule at Stormont. David would have known about the Order's influence as a student of history and current affairs. However, his desire to join may have been based on social reasons rather than careerist motives.

Once a member, he became active in the lodge, attending meetings, often with Leslie Cree at his side, and taking part in parades, including the traditional 12 July demonstration that commemorates King William's victory at the Battle of the Boyne in 1690. This was another extracurricular activity for David, which meant outside school he was very busy with his bar job, church, the ATC and now his membership of Loyal Orange Lodge 726.

However, as he approached his A levels, he knew studying had to take priority.

2

FIRST AMONG EQUALS

'William David Trimble, 39 Clifton Road, Bangor, gained the Bachelor of Law with First Class Honours. The only Queen's student to do so for the past three years.'
County Down Spectator, 5 July 1968

By the start of summer 1963, David Trimble was on track to do well in his final exams at Bangor Grammar. His teachers, some of whom had been very critical, now had high hopes for him. His ancient history teacher wrote that he was 'a keen pupil and has worked well throughout the year'. His House Master was also complimentary and commented that 'he has shown remarkable improvement and a maturity of thought'.[1]

There was still concern amongst the teaching staff as Trimble prepared to leave. In his final report, one teacher wrote of the future Nobel laureate, 'this boy has a lively mind which sometimes leads him into irrelevance which can be disastrous in examination answers'.[2]

However, the expectation was that Trimble was on course to perform well. Even his severest critic, the stern headmaster Randall Clarke, was upbeat. He said that Trimble had achieved 'a most creditable report. He has improved very considerably this year in every respect.'[3]

Clarke's assessment was light years away from his earlier comments, when he suggested that Trimble was lucky just to be in his history class. As Trimble's time at Bangor Grammar ended, it was clear he had defied expectations and was beginning to shine academically. He was also developing quite an interest in politics.

He was well read, probably better than most of his peers, and he was well informed on world events. Trevor Low remembers their final days together at Bangor Grammar School:

> In our last year of school, we had a current affairs class and David and I actually sat right next to each other. And back in those days the main subject of conversation was probably communism with all the trouble between Cuba and Nikita Khrushchev as the Russian leader. JFK was the American leader, and that last year of school was probably one of the main topics of conversation. And David was always very interested in the political situation and the world situation. He always struck me as being a very serious-minded boy. Yes, he had a sense of humour, but he was not one of the lads.[4]

Even though Bangor Grammar School had quite a sporting pedigree, it did little to excite Trimble the teenager. He had no interest in playing cricket or rugby and preferred the library to the games pitch. He continued to devour books and, with his growing knowledge of current affairs, was able to hold his own in debates and discussions. Even though he was naturally shy, there were times when he felt confident to challenge the opinions of strangers. Leslie Cree remembers being at an ATC camp in England when he and Trimble wandered into a nearby town centre:

> We were walking along, and this guy was on a street corner pontificating about something and there was a crowd around him. And we stopped to listen. And before you could say, 'Jack Robinson', David was saying, 'No, that is not correct'. And the rest of us just looked at him.[5]

Near the end of Trimble's time at school, he started to have conversations with his parents about what he should do next. His father was keen on his son taking a job rather than going to university, and he encouraged David to think about a career in banking or the civil service.

When his exam results came in, they were excellent. He performed well in modern and ancient history, and geography. Trimble loved history and clearly had an aptitude for it. His desire was to study it at Queen's University. However, he had been told by a teacher at Bangor Grammar that to be a history student with honours at Queen's he needed a Latin qualification. Trimble didn't have one, and because of the guidance he was given he did not apply. It transpired that the information from the careers master was incorrect – and Trimble could have applied for his dream course.

By the end of summer of 1963, it was too late to reapply, so he had to think of an alternative option.

Not surprisingly, Billy Trimble continued to talk to his son about the possibility of other careers. The idea of joining a local bank was mooted, as was the prospect of applying to the Northern Ireland Civil Service, which would have meant following in his father's footsteps. Billy was keen on this option and firmly believed that a role with a government ministry would provide a decent salary and job security for his son. As luck would have it, an advert seeking staff for the Northern Ireland Civil Service appeared, and within days the 18-year-old was a candidate. Trimble's application was successful, and in September 1963 he began life as a civil servant and found himself working as a clerk in the Land Registry offices in Belfast, where title deeds were stored. His job involved recording the details of property transactions and in particular changes of ownership.

It was dull work and involved much laborious form-filling, which Trimble disliked. However, the ambitious Trimble had a cunning plan, one that he hoped would take him away from the boredom. His employer had recently introduced a scheme to offer staff members legal training, as the civil service was experiencing a skills shortage. Trimble recalled what happened next:

> The civil service was having difficulty retaining people in two legal branches, Land Registry and the Estate Duty Office. So, they were going to send civil servants to take

a law degree, guarantee them promotion up to a certain level if they did so. So, after a year in the civil service, I started doing this course.[6]

In 1964, the Northern Ireland Civil Service awarded two places to Land Registry staff to allow them to study law degrees on a part-time basis. They would keep their jobs and combine studying with working, and once they were legally qualified they would hopefully advance up the career ladder. Trimble was delighted to be selected. He had finally arrived at Queen's University – albeit via a circuitous route. He had become the first member of his family to go to university. The civil service scheme was very competitive, and he was awarded a place alongside Herb Wallace, who, like Trimble, had not long joined the department. The two men became friends and would later become colleagues at Queen's University. Wallace remembers being introduced to Trimble in the Land Registry office and first noticed 'his really red hair'.[7]

He would get to know Trimble very well:

> I think he was an odd man in many ways, but he was very principled. You know some people are like that and David was the kind of person who could never tell a lie to anybody. He would not think that was appropriate at all. And I think that was woven throughout his career. Sometimes, I think he hurt people because he just told them the truth.[8]

Wallace was a little like Trimble. He was shy, ambitious and keen to make a success of the opportunity at Queen's. They went to classes together, shared lecture notes and began to spend a lot of time in each other's company. Wallace was impressed with Trimble's grasp of current affairs and the two would often chat about what was in the news:

> We would both have been supporters of the Ulster Unionist Party, although I think David was slightly more interested in politics than I was. We wouldn't have disagreed with

anything politically and we worked very closely together in our studies. We helped each other with studies and so on. There was actually no rivalry between us, certainly at that stage. I regarded him as a fairly close friend.⁹

The two men were part of the second phase of civil servants who went to Queen's as part of the scheme. Sam Beattie, who was also employed in Land Registry, had gone the year before:

> We were trained in the civil service, and we tended to treat it with respect. If we had a lecture from ten to eleven, we were back in the office at half eleven. If you had a lecture in the afternoon, you attended it and went back into the office. So, you were up and down the University Road a lot. Trimble and Wallace followed us in and realised very quickly that there was room for manoeuvre here. So, they didn't come back into the office as sharply as they might have done.¹⁰

Staff from Land Registry on the degree scheme were allowed to leave the office to attend classes at Queen's but were expected to return to work promptly after the end of a lecture or tutorial. However, Trimble and Wallace got a little crafty with the way they combined work with their studies. They quickly realised that they could choose the timings of their tutorial groups, and if they planned things carefully, they could stay away from work for a bit longer and maximise their time at Queen's. Both men coordinated their timetables, so questions were never raised by their superiors.

Trimble and Wallace threw themselves into the course at Queen's and impressed the teaching staff with their ability and coursework. As they approached their final year, they were invited to a meeting by two senior lecturers, William Twining and Lee Sheridan, to discuss their future. The Queen's professors rated the two students and had a suggestion for them. Wallace remembers what happened:

David and I were invited together to a meeting with these two guys, and they said, 'We think you are both candidates for a first-class honours degree. They said they were 'not sure you can achieve it if you are only part-time students, spending a lot of time in the Land Registry. So, would you consider becoming full-time students for your final year?' At that stage, I had a wife, a mortgage and a child that was due to be born within weeks. I decided I just could not afford to do that. David, on the other hand, at that stage, did not have any encumbrances like that. He decided to go full-time for his final year.[11]

Trimble jumped at the leave of absence from Land Registry for the concluding year of his degree and became a full-time student. By that time, the Trimble family were living in a bigger house in Clifton Road in Bangor. It meant the three children could have a room each and Trimble stayed at home and travelled to Belfast every day. Iain Trimble remembers that he saw little of his brother. He recalls that most days he 'came home, had his meal and disappeared upstairs or occasionally he would disappear with some of his friends'.[12]

Home life was not without its difficulties. Billy Trimble was not well. He had been diagnosed with lung cancer and initially doctors thought they could operate and prolong his life.

However, it became clear that his condition was advanced, and surgery was not an option. He only had a short time to live, and as his son's final year at Queen's progressed, he became gravely ill.

Trimble threw himself into his studies in the summer of 1968, and was awarded first-class honours. It was an outstanding achievement, as the awarding of such honours was rare. He was also the recipient of the McKane Medal for Jurisprudence. Trimble's decision to step away from his civil service role had paid off, and he had delivered what his professors said he was capable of. Wallace says Trimble's success was impressive:

A first-class degree never went to more than one person from the year, and in some years, nobody got a first ... we graduated in 1968, and I know in 1967 there were no first-class honours afforded. So, it was a big thing, and it was a big achievement for him.[13]

Sam Beattie says Trimble's triumph was richly deserved and he was by far the best student in his year, as he was 'well read, well informed and able to argue well'. News of the success reached the offices of Trimble's local paper in Bangor, and on 5 July 1968 the *County Down Spectator* ran a story on its front page.

At this time of year, it gives us pleasure, if also a headache, trying to follow the fortunes of the many local students at Queen's to record academic successes as they become known. In the Faculty of Law, William David Trimble, 39 Clifton Road, Bangor, gained the Bachelor of Law with First Class Honours. The only Queen's student to do so for the past three years. David achieved this while studying part-time and working in the civil service.[14]

The article was accompanied by a photograph of the successful graduate. Trimble was featured looking smart, with short hair and his trademark thick glasses. He did not recall reading the article at the time, but in a BBC interview he was presented with a copy of the article and read it out on air. He told the interviewer, John Wilson, that he recalled the summer of 1968 for a variety of reasons:

I was certainly proud of the result. I don't remember seeing that [the newspaper article]. The other thing I have to say was that my father was fatally ill at the time and died the night before graduation.[15]

Billy Trimble's final days were difficult. He had fallen and broken his leg at the family home in Clifton Road and had been admitted to hospital. The lung cancer at this stage was well advanced, and in the days after his fall he declined rapidly. Iain, who was serving with the RAF in Cyprus, was given compassionate leave to come home. He arrived back in Bangor for his father's last days and was also able to attend David's graduation. Understandably, Billy's death rocked the family. As David graduated, on what should have been a joyous occasion, he was having to deal with the realisation of his father's death. It was a poignant and bittersweet moment.

By being admitted to university and then being awarded a degree he had done something that no other member of his family had ever experienced. He had defied the odds and proved teachers at Bangor Grammar School wrong. Unlike during his early days at school, he had found something that sparked his imagination, and he had triumphed in style. For Trimble, 1968 was life-changing. On the strength of his success at Queen's, he was offered a teaching post at the university, which was quite rare.

He became an assistant lecturer in the Law Faculty with the responsibility to teach land law and equity. It meant his days in the civil service were over. The new job was only part of a fresh beginning.

In September 1968, a few weeks shy of his 24th birthday, Trimble married Heather McCombe at Donaghadee Parish Church. The pair had begun a relationship when they worked together at the Land Registry offices. It was Trimble's first serious love affair, and their union and subsequent marriage surprised many of his friends. Herb Wallace remembers that the first time he saw the pair together was at the office Christmas party in 1967, and he was taken aback to discover they had started dating. A few of Trimble's friends and family members thought they were an unusual match, although they kept their thoughts private.

Trimble and his wife had contrasting personalities. He was introverted and awkward, whereas Heather was an extrovert, outgoing and popular. Despite their differences, the couple were in love, enjoyed each other's company and began planning a life together. After their wedding in County Down, they honeymooned in County Wicklow and then set up home together.

Life for David Trimble was changing at a dramatic pace. He had graduated, lost his father, got a new job and become a married man, all in the space of a few months. By the autumn of 1968, he was getting used to teaching undergraduates at Queen's – some of whom were just a few years younger than he was.

At the same time, Northern Ireland was now making world headlines. A civil rights campaign highlighting discrimination against Catholics was gaining momentum and attracting media interest.

On 5 October, a protest march was held in Derry and rioting broke out after a confrontation between protesters and the RUC. It had begun peacefully but ended in chaos, and by nightfall, television pictures were beamed across the world showing police officers using batons on protesters. The black-and-white footage of marchers being attacked at Duke Street was dramatic and shocked viewers in Britain and beyond. It showed that Northern Ireland was descending into violent chaos and highlighted the fact that the RUC was having difficulty imposing law and order. It marked a watershed.

To many watching, that was the day the Troubles began. At Queen's University, Trimble was experiencing a new world. It was a place of discussion and debate and unlike his largely sheltered upbringing in Bangor. He found himself surrounded by people from a range of backgrounds whose politics and ideas were radically different from his. Yet, it is clear he was confident in what he believed. First and foremost, he was a unionist and passionately felt that Northern Ireland's best interests were served by being part of the UK. He was born into a unionist-supporting family. His parents voted unionist just as his grandparents had done.

To Trimble, being a unionist was the natural political order. Unionism was the party of the state of Northern Ireland and had exercised power from Stormont since the partition of Ireland. Trimble was comfortable with his Britishness; after all, he had once contemplated a career in the British armed services. His ATC experiences had introduced him to large parts of England and Scotland, and he felt a bond to Britain. Like many unionists, he viewed the Irish Republic as a neighbouring foreign country, heavily influenced by the Catholic Church. As a practising Presbyterian and an Orangeman, he was also steadfast in his religious beliefs. Faith was as important to him as an adult as it had been when he was a child. It was all part of what made his identity, which he talked about with the Welsh broadcaster John Humphrys during a BBC Radio 4 interview in 2005:

> How do you acquire a national identity? Why do you regard yourself as Welsh or British? It is something you don't even think about. And people in Northern Ireland are like that too. At a very early age they absorb a national identity. They get that from their family, from their parents, from the wider family circle, from their immediate social contacts, even before they are thinking seriously about it. They then find themselves in a rather unusual situation in that their identity is not either fully recognised or legitimated or is under threat one way or another. That is because they are living in an area where the population is not naturally homogeneous.[16]

As Trimble began his teaching career, Northern Ireland was at breaking point. Like many unionists at the time, he had little sympathy for those campaigning under the Northern Ireland Civil Rights Association (NICRA) banner. He was cynical about the motives of NICRA and saw their marches and activity as overtly political and a direct attack on the unionist establishment. He suspected that republicans were manipulating the organisation behind the scenes. He saw the NICRA campaign as a direct attempt to destabilise Northern Ireland, undermine the credibility and authority of Stormont and attack the forces of law and order.

Before the outbreak of the Troubles in the late 1960s, Trimble had limited experience of sectarian or political violence. His childhood in largely Protestant Bangor had been quiet and free from trouble. He had Catholic friends at school and in the ATC, but most of his friendship group would have been Protestant. He was aware of the Irish Republican Army (IRA) border campaign from the late 1950s, but his part of County Down was largely untouched by the IRA's attacks.

As Trimble watched events unfold in Belfast as an interested observer, a young man started to gain prominence in Derry. Like many in Northern Ireland's second city, John Hume had been drawn to the civil rights campaign and had recently helped form a non-violent group called the Derry Citizens Action Committee, which lobbied for fair elections and demanded housing and employment rights for all. Hume was part of a growing new breed of activists who felt they were being ignored by Stormont's unionist government.

By early November 1968, the British government felt compelled to intervene. Northern Ireland's prime minister, Terence O'Neill, together with fellow ministers Bill Craig and Brian Faulkner, travelled to Downing Street for a key meeting with the Labour administration. Prime Minister Harold Wilson and Home Secretary Jim Callaghan were in no mood for excuses from their guests. Both men were uncompromising and told their visitors that the status quo could not prevail and life in Northern Ireland had to change. They called for reforms to the way public housing was managed and homes were allocated. They both insisted on a fairer and more democratic voting system and changes to security legislation.

After O'Neill returned to Belfast, his officials began to work on a series of changes. While people like John Hume and others in the civil rights movement saw it as a move in the right direction, some unionists viewed it as a betrayal, including Bill Craig, the minister for home affairs, who had travelled to London to listen to the prime minister. Craig opposed the reform plan and, rather than back his party leader, he went in the opposite direction and instead called for tougher action against civil rights demonstrators. It put O'Neill and Craig on a collision course, and in December 1968, O'Neill made a bold political move and sacked Craig.

The departure was a seminal moment for O'Neill and also for unionism. Craig would remain a critic within the party and continued to voice his strident opinions about law and order and how Northern Ireland should be governed. His speeches and suggestions were often at odds with the party leadership. Trimble watched all this as an interested observer, as he was not involved politically. From a distance, he was attracted to Craig's analysis and philosophy, and in time, Craig would become Trimble's mentor.

In his first few years as a lecturer at Queen's, Trimble concentrated on his work and home life. Judith Eve, who would later become dean of the Queen's law faculty, was one of his early students:

> I first encountered him in my second year at Queen's. He was excellent as a lecturer and a teacher. All we knew about him was that he had got a first-class honours and there had not been a first-class honours awarded for a couple of years. So here in front of us was a home-grown guy, who had done the degree, the same we were doing, and he got top marks in it. So, we were all rather in awe of him.[17]

Trimble approached his job at Queen's in the same way he had tackled his degree. He read voraciously and prepared his lectures meticulously. He taught land law and equity and knew the subjects intimately. Many of his students found his lectures necessary but somewhat boring. Mary McAleese, who would later go on to be elected Irish president, says Trimble had the misfortune to teach a 'dull subject'. She found his lectures hard work and says many did not find him a warm individual.

> He was not the kind of person who hung out with students or engaged in discussions with them unnecessarily. He was actually quite private, quite closed off.[18]

James Cooper studied under Trimble at the same time as McAleese. He would later have his own legal practice in County Fermanagh and became chairman of the UUP when Trimble was leader. Cooper says Trimble's specialised legal subject was dry and a 'pretty esoteric section of the law and most students thought it was a terrible bore'.

Away from the lecture hall, Trimble would often be spotted enjoying a smoke break, and Cooper recalls that he had 'a penchant for French cigarettes'. To Cooper, that just added to Trimble's image: 'I would not call him eccentric but [thought of him] as someone who was slightly apart.'[19]

Anne Logue was another undergraduate who attended Trimble's lectures and found him distant. She was impressed with his knowledge and thought he had a brilliant mind. However, like McAleese, she recalls that he would not engage with students in the way other lecturers would:

> He would deliver his lecture on the podium or wherever he was standing. Then basically without much ado he just left and went out again. I don't think he was very good at connecting with students.[20]

Despite his reputation for being private and sometimes aloof, there was a caring element to Trimble's teaching. Mary Madden remembers being in his lectures and recalls his lecturing style and manner. On one occasion Trimble showed her great kindness and support:

> He could tell from my essay that I was struggling. I was not a natural and he was very helpful. I have to be honest he was very helpful in giving me guidance and encouragement and telling me I [would] be able to pass it. You know, like saying, 'Don't be fretting'. He never only gave you corrections, but he gave you some sort of support and counselling in his own style.[21]

Trimble enjoyed his early days at Queen's and settled into academic life very quickly. He kept his career options open when he was called to the Bar in both Belfast and London.

He became a qualified barrister, but after some consideration he decided to stay in academia and was never set on becoming a full-time practising lawyer. Nonetheless, being called to the Bar was a goal he had set himself, and as with securing first-class honours, he was determined to see it through. He was called to the Bar in 1969.

So, why did he choose lecturing over practising as a barrister? It is likely that Trimble thought he would feel more comfortable in a classroom than he would in a courtroom and sensed that opportunities in academia would soon present themselves. The university had a traditional hierarchical structure and Trimble clearly hoped he could get promotion relatively quickly and move towards becoming a professor. Becoming known as Professor Trimble was something he was keen to achieve.

As Trimble settled into his first year on the teaching staff, the political unrest in Northern Ireland continued. Members of the People's Democracy, including many Queen's students, were attacked by loyalists as they marched to Derry in January 1969. They were set upon in the countryside at Burntollet Bridge, and the television images of protesters with bloodied heads and bruised faces and of their attackers holding cudgels went around the world. It was like a repeat of the scenes some months earlier in Derry and the footage represented another PR disaster for the unionist government. The Unionist Party was now experiencing serious internal tensions, and O'Neill's leadership was being questioned by some of his senior colleagues.

In February, the problems for unionism continued in the Stormont election which had been called by O'Neill. It was a gamble by the under-pressure unionist leader – a reaction to the ongoing violence and an attempt to quell party disunity. A number of backbenchers had signed a petition calling for his removal, so O'Neill was using the election as a 'back me or sack me' operation.

The poll became known as the 'crossroads election', after O'Neill's seminal broadcast in December 1968, when he memorably declared that 'Ulster stands at the crossroads'. The election also gave Trimble the opportunity to get involved. He was asked to help with the campaign of Basil McIvor, who was a moderate unionist and a strong supporter of O'Neill. Trimble knew McIvor's wife, Jill, who worked with him at Queen's, and he was happy to lend a hand. He joined McIvor's canvass team and went door to door in the new seat of Larkfield, which took in both unionist and nationalist areas. The constituency included Andersonstown, which Trimble duly visited. In the 1960s it was a more mixed area but over time it would become a stronghold for Sinn Féin. Trimble was no fan of O'Neill's political style or leadership, but he helped out because of the personal connection.

McIvor was elected with a majority of 6,115, but for O'Neill, the campaign and the result were both disasters.. The unionist vote splintered, with voters backing pro- and anti-O'Neill candidates. The Unionist leader managed to stay in power, but only with a slender majority. It highlighted the depth of division within unionism and signalled the end of the Unionist Party as a monolithic power. The election also saw the arrival of John Hume on the political scene.

After coming to prominence in the campaign for civil rights in Derry, he stood as an Independent and won a seat. It marked the start of a political career that would last for decades. Hume, who had been a teacher, would be a central figure in Northern Ireland politics for the next 30 years and would become the voice of nationalism.

Back in 1969, the idea of a political accommodation was simply not on the agenda; instead, the year became known for violence and division. A series of bombings that disrupted electricity and water supplies deepened Northern Ireland's political crisis. On 28 April, Terence O'Neill realised he was unable to carry the support of his party, and he stood down as unionist leader and prime minister. Consequently, on 1 May, he was succeeded by James Chichester-Clark, who had previously been chief whip and minister for agriculture. He beat Brian Faulkner by 17 votes to 16 in a poll amongst the party's Stormont MPs. The violence continued over the summer and it looked like Northern Ireland was on the verge of civil war.

In London, Prime Minister Harold Wilson watched the television pictures with horror and fear. In August 1969, British troops arrived on the streets of Northern Ireland. It was a defining moment in British and Irish history. What began as a temporary arrangement would become permanent. Life was about to change and not for the better.

The year 1970 saw the arrival of not one but two local parties on Northern Ireland's political scene. In April, the Alliance Party was formed and aimed to attract members and supporters from both Protestant and Catholic communities.

The new group also appealed to liberal-minded unionists who had previously backed O'Neill but did not like the direction of the party under Chichester-Clark. In August, another new movement was added to Northern Ireland's ever-growing list of political parties: the Social Democratic and Labour Party (SDLP) was formed, with John Hume as one of its founding members. It was a broad coalition and absorbed supporters and members of the Nationalist Party, the Northern Ireland Labour Party, the National Democratic Party and others who were not aligned politically.

In a slightly different way, Trimble was also dipping his toe in the political water. After his experience campaigning the previous year for Basil McIvor, he decided to join the Unionist Party. However, his attempt to become a party member did not go according to plan. According to the author Dean Godson, when the young academic wrote to party headquarters in Glengall Street in Belfast, his application was ignored, and he did not even receive a reply. There is nothing to suggest that Trimble's application was deliberately blocked. The failure to reply may just be down to simple administrative incompetence.

With his political involvement effectively frozen, Trimble continued to build his reputation at Queen's. As the months passed, his career started to progress, and in 1971, he was appointed to the post of lecturer. He was delighted with the promotion, and he hoped it could be the first step to other jobs at the university.

He was really enjoying academic life and was building up a reputation as a conscientious and hard-working member of staff. He was now living in a flat in Kansas Avenue, which was close to the Antrim Road in North Belfast. In the 1970s, this was one of the most dangerous places to live in Northern Ireland. There was a nasty atmosphere of fear, and the television news bulletins were filled every evening with the images and sounds of violence.

Once again, the security situation impacted on the politics of the Unionist Party. As leader, Chichester-Clark went to London for talks with Prime Minister Edward Heath with a demand for extra soldiers on the streets. He secured an additional 1,300 troops but, when the Unionist leader returned to Belfast, he was told by party colleagues that this figure was derisory. Two days later, the pressure simply got too much, and he decided to resign.

Chichester-Clark's premiership had lasted less than two years, and unionism faced another leadership battle. Northern Ireland's security crisis was tearing the country apart and was also creating fault lines in its largest political party. Not surprisingly, Bill Craig threw his hat into the ring to become leader. He was ambitious but was regarded by many as a maverick and had little support amongst the party's MPs at Stormont.

His rival for the job was Brian Faulkner, who was viewed as very able, articulate and media-friendly and was seen in the press as Chichester-Clark's natural successor. He had much ministerial experience, having overseen various departments including Commerce, Development and Home Affairs. Now, after a series of failed attempts to secure the leadership, his time had arrived. The result when it came was not a surprise.

On 23 March, Unionist Party MPs made their choice and backed Faulkner by 26 votes to 4, making him Northern Ireland's third prime minister in two years. After he was voted in, Faulkner had little time to enjoy a honeymoon period.

As ever, the issue of security dominated the political agenda. By the summer of 1971, calls to introduce internment were getting louder. The bombings and shootings showed no sign of abating and there was a sense of frustration amongst unionists that action had to be taken to quell the violence. Inside the Unionist Party, there were endless discussions on whether its introduction would be effective. Finally, a decision was made that would have long-lasting repercussions. Faulkner agreed that the conditions now existed for detention without trial to be introduced.

On 9 August, internment began across Northern Ireland. In the early hours, the operation codenamed 'Operation Demetrius' was rolled out, and in the first swoops 342 people were arrested. Republicans, nationalists, civil rights supporters and suspected IRA men were the targets. Quickly it became clear that the operation was flawed, as much of the information regarding the arrests was out of date, or just wrong. If the move was intended to reduce the trouble, it ended up doing the opposite.

Like everyone in Northern Ireland, the onset of the Troubles impacted the working lives of Heather and David Trimble. As the security situation worsened, Heather took a decision that would change her life. She joined the Ulster Defence Regiment (UDR), which was a locally raised unit within the British Army structure. Many like Heather joined up because they wanted to play a role in helping to defend Northern Ireland.

There was a strong feeling within the unionist community that the best way to defeat the paramilitaries was to put more military personnel on the ground and to bring in tougher security legislation.

Heather's role in the UDR meant she was often away from home, and it also resulted in her having to take her personal security seriously. UDR members were often targeted by the IRA when they were off duty, and Heather had to be careful driving home and being in the house at night. The ongoing violence and continuation of internment also affected Trimble's working life.

Belfast often felt like a city under siege. There were troops on the street, roadblocks, security alerts and bomb scares. As internment continued, several of Trimble's students were arrested by the security forces, which meant they could not attend lectures and seminars. As their lecturer, he realised they would not get the education others were experiencing, and he felt he should help. Herb Wallace was aware of Trimble's prison visits:

> I mean these people were interned because they were believed to be republican terrorists and David thought it was his duty to meet them. Because they had not been convicted of any crime, he thought it was his duty to make sure they did not miss out on their studies.[22]

Trimble's politics could not have been more different from many of the students he was reaching out to help. As an Orangeman and a unionist, he was assisting people who were suspected of trying to destroy the state he believed in. For Trimble it was simply part of his job, and his personal views had to remain just that – personal. One former internee recalled how Trimble helped him:

> Trimble went to the governor and raised the issue with him. He said I needed somewhere private to study as you were sharing a hut or cage with lots of other prisoners and there was no peace. Eventually they agreed to let me use the medical hut in the central reservation of the camp.[23]

The Long Kesh detention centre was an ugly complex with watch-towers and armed officers, rudimentary huts, barbed wire and corrugated iron fences. Situated on a sprawling site in the Lagan Valley on the outskirts of Lisburn, it was a dismal and depressing place. Trimble took his duties seriously and, after getting permission from his superiors, he routinely made the journey on public transport from the Queen's campus to the prison.

His new life was far removed from his office-bound civil service days in Land Registry. Yet Trimble did not forget his old pals and remained in touch with his former colleagues. They would meet up regularly to have a meal and a few drinks. By that time, he was also becoming quite knowledgeable about wine and was able to talk to colleagues about the different grapes and vineyards. When the boys from Land Registry had a get-together, Trimble always selected the wine for the table. As Sam Beattie recalls, that did not stop Trimble from being teased:

> He was the wine expert. And invariably, we said to him 'You pick the wines, you know the wines'. In his way he picked the wines. And invariably we would all say, 'David, why did you pick that? That was rubbish?' And he knew we were only just winding him up.[24]

Beattie says the lunches and dinners with Trimble were always good fun. They generally did not talk politics, but if Trimble did put forward a view that Beattie disagreed with, he would challenge him:

> We got on fine. You know there was no animosity, but if I thought he was getting carried away with something I would have said, 'David, that is rubbish, I don't agree with you.' And he did not like that. You could have seen the colour coming out of his face. Well, let us just say, that was David. David was hot-tempered, but he mellowed as the years went on.[25]

As 1971 ended, Trimble continued to follow the politics of Northern Ireland through the newspapers and on the television news. Soon, he would switch from being more than just an interested observer.

3

VOTE TRIMBLE

*'You see he was nakedly sectarian, you know,
back in those days. He was.'*
Mary McAleese on David Trimble

A Sunday in January 1972 marked one of the blackest days of the Troubles.

On the penultimate day of the month, thousands of civil rights demonstrators took to the streets of Derry. They had gathered to protest the continued use of internment, and the atmosphere in the city was tense. A week earlier, the British Army had fired CS gas at protesters as they walked along Magilligan Strand. There were real fears that the soldiers, members of the Parachute Regiment, would use the same force on the streets of Derry.

In mid-afternoon the march began, and the plan was to take the crowd to the Guildhall in the city centre. The protest, like the one days before, had been banned by the Stormont government, and there was a heavy presence of soldiers and police officers. The protesters' route was blocked by the security forces and the marchers were pushed back towards Free Derry Corner in the Bogside. After skirmishes between local youths and the army, soldiers moved in to make arrests. Shortly afterwards, members of the Parachute Regiment began to open fire. Many of those shot or wounded were trying to flee from the soldiers, and others were hurt as they helped the injured. By the time the shooting stopped, 13 people had been killed, and another died later.

The events of the day became known as 'Bloody Sunday', and the long-term effects of the killings in Derry would be profound. The British

Army claimed they had been fired on and said their soldiers had been under threat. To the nationalist community this was seen as cold-blooded murder and an example of a military force ruthlessly killing unarmed men and children. That night the IRA was inundated with people who wanted to join.

Most unionists saw things differently and accepted the British Army's version of events – even though it was being questioned. Northern Ireland Prime Minister Brian Faulkner said those who organised the march had a responsibility for what happened. Harrowing television images of the dead and the dying went around the world. It seemed Northern Ireland was at a tipping point. To many people watching in Britain, this was unfathomable. How could this be going on in their own country? This divided corner of the United Kingdom now seemed ungovernable, and there was condemnation of Faulkner's government from all parts of the globe.

The next day, Trimble, as normal, made his way to Queen's University. There was only one topic of conversation on campus – the shootings in Derry. Law student Mary McAleese remembers that Monday very well. In an interview for this book, she recalls meeting Trimble that day:

> I travelled over to the university that day as I did many a morning on the bus with a man who is now a retired High Court judge, Catholic and a very fine fellow, very fine brain. And we were walking down the avenue towards the library when David Trimble came towards us and with a huge smile. And said words to the effect 'Isn't it a wonderful day'. And I was a bit taken aback precisely because he wasn't the kind of person who ever greeted you. You know, he didn't. If he met you in the street he wouldn't have greeted you. He wouldn't have known who we were, certainly at the very beginning of our academic careers in Queen's. But he never was a person to engage in conversation. But on that day, he was very, very friendly, and you know the Pollyanna in me

thought, 'Oh gosh, this is remarkable, what's happened to him, he's become so friendly.' And when my friend said nothing until we got into the library, and there were little groups of people standing around to whom he had done the same thing. And they said that he was actually going up and down the road looking for Catholics, to whom he could say, wasn't it a wonderful day, which wasn't a reference actually to the day at all but a reference to the day before.[1]

McAleese is convinced that Trimble was talking about the shootings in Derry the day before and says the remarks were obvious to everyone he made them to:

You see he was nakedly sectarian, you know, back in those days. He was. Now, I had not experienced that side of him, I have to say, until that day, no direct experience of it. I was stunned when it was brought to my attention.[2]

McAleese's observations are worth exploring. Was Trimble really gloating over the deaths of Catholic civilians in Derry? She is in no doubt what her lecturer was referring to when he greeted students on that January morning. As other students have previously pointed out, Trimble rarely engaged in much social conversation before and after class. He was quiet and reserved, which meant that encounters with him were limited and often formal – which makes his behaviour after Bloody Sunday stand out.

Since being appointed to the staff at Queen's, he had kept his politics out of the classroom, but on this occasion, McAleese suggests that his thoughts shone through, and they were deeply unsettling. She also insists that Trimble's remarks, the day after the shootings, were not a one-off. She recalls a story of Trimble being at a dinner at Queen's and using 'naked sectarian language' to describe Catholics, and how a diner sitting close to Trimble was 'absolutely shocked'.[3]

Others who met Trimble at Queen's in the 1970s say he kept his political views private. Alban Maginness was a student of Trimble's and shared his lecturer's love of politics and current affairs. Maginness would go on to join the SDLP and become the first Catholic to hold the position of lord mayor of Belfast. He says Trimble was 'very professional, very good, very thorough and explained things very well'.[4]

He said there was never any chat about politics or the ongoing violence. He was aware of Trimble's political leanings, but says it was 'strictly law in the lecture room'. He recalls that when it came to the student–teacher divide, 'he respected us, and we respected him'.[5]

The events of January 1972 would have a lasting impact on the history of Northern Ireland. The original investigation by Lord Widgery in April 1972, in the aftermath of the shootings, exonerated the soldiers. The Widgery report was heavily criticised by the families of the dead, who believed it was fundamentally flawed, and they condemned it as a 'whitewash'. Relatives believed the original report failed to hold anyone accountable for the killings. For years campaigners called for a fresh investigation, and in 1998, after much political pressure, a new inquiry, chaired by Lord Saville of Newdigate, was established by Prime Minister Tony Blair. At the time, Trimble said any hopes that a fresh inquiry would help the healing process were 'misplaced'.[6]

He added that the 'basic facts of the situation are known and not open to dispute'. He did state publicly that the killings in Derry were wrong, but he opposed the establishment of a fresh inquiry into Bloody Sunday.

McAleese believes that the Trimble she first encountered in the 1970s evolved into a different man who would ultimately become a worthy Nobel laureate. She says his views and attitude changed, and he matured as a person over the years – a change she asserts has much to do with the influence of Daphne Orr, a contemporary of McAleese, who would become Trimble's second wife in 1978. McAleese says Daphne was 'utterly instrumental' in changing David's perceptions and thinking.[7]

McAleese, like Trimble, would eventually move from being a graduate to joining the staff at Queen's University. In 1987, when she was working at Trinity College in Dublin, she was appointed director of the Institute of Professional Legal Studies at Queen's – a job that Trimble had also applied for but did not get.

The killings in Derry effectively sealed the fate of Faulkner's unionist government at Stormont. A day of national mourning for the dead was held in the Irish Republic, and an estimated 30,000 people marched to the British Embassy in Dublin and burned it down. In Belfast, Faulkner's administration seemed to be on borrowed time, and unionism was in a state of flux – unsure what was going to happen next. Naturally, the different unionist groupings all had contrasting ideas on where the future lay.

Even though Faulkner was Unionist Party leader and prime minister, it was Ian Paisley who had become unionism's best-known face. A firebrand preacher with a booming voice, he was charismatic and media-savvy. Paisley was a fierce critic of Faulkner's, routinely accusing him of cowardice and political weakness. Some months earlier, in September 1971, Paisley had set up the Democratic Unionist Party (DUP) with barrister Dessie Boal, who had been expelled from the Unionist Party.

The other unionist figure attracting much interest in 1972 was Bill Craig, who had unsuccessfully run to be leader of the Unionist Party the year before. He increasingly felt there needed to be a more militant unionist grouping and a stronger approach to security by both the London government and the Stormont administration. Like Paisley, he was a critic of Faulkner's and found his party leader's approach weak and too conservative.

Craig formed his own grouping and called it Ulster Vanguard – although in time it was shortened to simply Vanguard. Craig had led a fascinating life before he entered politics. He had flown with the RAF during the Second World War as a rear gunner in Lancaster bombers. He later went to Queen's University and practised in County Armagh as a solicitor. He was first elected to Stormont in 1960, and as a rising star quickly became Unionist Party chief whip. He later served as a minister in various departments, including Health, Local Government and Home Affairs. It was in Home Affairs where he became a household name after he banned the civil rights march in Derry in 1968 – a move which resulted in the trouble in Duke Street. That was where RUC officers had drawn batons and used water cannons on protesters.

Craig's politics appealed to a broad coalition of loyalists and unionists, including members of the loyal orders, the Loyalist Association of Workers, the Ulster Special Constabulary Association and the Ulster Loyalist Association.

By that time, Northern Ireland had a menacing underworld inhabited by both republican and loyalist paramilitaries. The largest loyalist grouping was the Ulster Defence Association (UDA), which was formed in September 1971, and it included the Ulster Freedom Fighters (UFF), a cover name used for bombings and shootings. The UDA boasted a large membership in loyalist working-class areas across Northern Ireland, and routinely brought thousands of men onto the streets sporting camouflage jackets and berets. Craig hoped his new grouping could build an alliance with working-class loyalists in the paramilitaries.

Trimble observed Vanguard's growth and was impressed by what he had witnessed. He had admired Craig from afar and had listened to his speeches. He felt that, of all the local political leaders, Craig 'had the best brain', and he decided to join him:

> The only person who seemed to be talking sense was Bill Craig, who had been a leading member of the Ulster Unionist Party, Minister of Home Affairs and Minister for Development. He then formed this Vanguard movement and left the Ulster Unionist Party to form a separate party. And that ... seemed to me to have the best approach to the situation and that is where I went.[8]

After launching the new movement in February 1972, Craig set about holding large-scale public rallies across Northern Ireland. He held one at Castle Park in Trimble's hometown of Bangor, which Trimble attended. Around 6,500 people turned up, and they represented all shades of unionism and loyalism – an alliance of Orangemen, unionist party members, loyalists, security force veterans and paramilitaries. Some in the crowd even wore Vanguard armbands, and there was a military feel to parts of the event.

The rally in Bangor was soon followed by a much bigger affair at Belfast's Ormeau Park. This time an estimated crowd of 70,000 people turned up to hear Craig speak. On Saturday 18 March, they heard the Vanguard leader issue this ominous threat:

> We must build up a dossier of the men and the women who are a menace to this country, because one day, ladies and gentlemen, when the politicians fail us, it may be our job, to liquidate the enemy.[9]

Craig's chilling message and the use of the phrase 'liquidate the enemy' came as music to the ears of militant loyalists. He was speaking their language. His speech managed to increase the political temperature, which was already close to boiling point. With growing unrest, the Unionist Party leader, Brian Faulkner, was summoned to London to see Prime Minister Edward Heath. The Conservative leader had run out of patience, and had concluded that Stormont could not be reformed by unionists. In stark terms, Heath informed Faulkner that he was going to take control of Northern Ireland's security and phase out internment, and that he wanted to introduce power-sharing.

Faulkner left Downing Street shell-shocked and returned home to consider Heath's plans. He could not accept them, and after hours of discussions, Faulkner and his colleagues resigned, claiming that the transfer of security powers to London could not be justified. Unionists were not ready for power-sharing and made that clear to London, but Heath would not accept their position. Direct rule duly arrived, and Northern Ireland no longer had a government of its own. Fifty years of unionist domination had been halted at the hands of a British prime minister. Majority rule was finished, and Northern Ireland's one-party state was consigned to the past.

On Tuesday 28 March, thousands of unionists and loyalists gathered on the Stormont Estate to mark the final sitting of the Northern Ireland parliament. Faulkner appeared on the first-floor balcony of the building and addressed the massive crowd, estimated at around 100,000 people, which stretched out from the steps of the building to the statue of Sir Edward Carson and down the mile-long Prince of Wales Avenue towards the Upper Newtownards Road.

Trimble was in the crowd, and fired up by what he was witnessing. He was keen to get more involved in the activities of Vanguard:

> Like many unionists I expected direct rule to be followed by major constitutional change imposed by London and many feared that London's aim was to drive us in the direction of a united Ireland.[10]

One of those who had come to the same conclusions as Trimble was David Burnside, an ambitious, articulate young unionist who had been involved with politics at Queen's. Burnside was impressed with Trimble's intellect and his ability to analyse political problems:

> He was a bright, good thinker, articulate but not in a rabble-rousing way. He understood constitutional matters extremely well, which was important with the fall of Stormont. He was prepared to be as militant as was necessary in those days, which was necessary in the first Tory collapse of Stormont in March 1972. He was a good thinker who got on very well with Bill Craig, who was good on constitutional matters as well.[11]

By that time, Trimble and Heather were able to save enough funds together to buy a house, and they moved to Bangor. It gave Trimble the opportunity to reconnect with old friends in the Orange Order and he was able to attend meetings at the Bangor Abbey lodge. It was through the Order that he got to know George Green, who, as with Bill Craig, would have a big influence on his early political career. Like Trimble, he was an enthusiastic supporter of Craig and was becoming one of Vanguard's best-known names in North Down.

Green encouraged the young academic to sign up, as Trimble recalled:

> I became fully involved in Northern Ireland politics in the winter of 1972/73 off the back of the worst year of the Troubles when some 500 people were killed. I had watched the situation deteriorate over a number of years with growing concern. But it was the prorogation of Stormont and the imposition of direct rule that threatened to destabilise society.[12]

Trimble would start to forge numerous friendships that would last decades. One of those he met was Reg Empey, who, like Trimble, was a graduate of Queen's University and had cut his political teeth with the Young Unionists. Their relationship in unionist politics would stretch over the next 40 years. Speaking of Trimble, Empey remarked:

> I didn't regard him as terribly right wing by any means, and he certainly never came across to me as sectarian. But he was very much focused on the constitutional issue, and I think that was the point that set him apart from people. He was good at analysing that sort of thing.[13]

Another person who encountered Trimble was Jim Rodgers, who went on to have a long career in unionist politics in local government, including two stints as lord mayor of Belfast. Rodgers would also serve as honorary secretary of the UUP during Trimble's leadership of the party – and at times he would be quite critical. He, like Trimble, was attracted to the ideals of Vanguard:

> David knew where these people were coming from, but I have got to say those who were working-class loyalists

in those days, nobody talked about forming an illegal organisation. They were just hard-working people, some who worked in the shipyards, some worked in Shorts [Belfast aerospace company], some worked in Mackie's [Belfast engineering firm], some worked in offices. We had long hours of discussions on various issues. And I always knew David was a brainbox, no question about that. Some people would say that David would never make a politician, but they were proved wrong.[14]

By 1973, Trimble would get his first chance to show people that he could be a politician, and he would get an opportunity to run for office. The UK government published a White Paper entitled *Northern Ireland Constitutional Proposals*. It was a major move to restart the political process and recommended a 78-seat Assembly at Stormont, which would be elected by proportional representation. It would replace the suspended Stormont parliament, and there would also be a new power-sharing Executive which would have powers currently held by London, such as agriculture and education.

This new body would run Northern Ireland, and it would be cross-party, which meant that both nationalists and unionists would be in government. Power-sharing was the price unionists were going to have to accept.

The package of ideas put forward by London also included a new body that would work with Dublin. This would be called the Council of Ireland, which would be made up of members of the Assembly and the Dáil in a consultative role. Downing Street knew this body would get the support of the SDLP and the Irish government, and hoped it would improve Anglo-Irish relations.

Understandably, it was this part of the plan that caused the most problems for unionism.

Faulkner considered the government's plans and felt there was more to support than oppose. However, the government's plans needed to be considered by the Unionist Party's decision-makers. So, on 27 March 1973 the UUC met and, by 381 votes to 231, voted to accept the White Paper. It was a victory for Faulkner, but it came at a cost.

For Bill Craig and his supporters in Vanguard it was time to act. They opposed the idea of compulsory power-sharing and rejected the plans for the Council of Ireland. The rebels broke away from the Unionist Party and decided to form their own party. So, the Vanguard Unionist Progressive Party was born with Craig at its head. The White Paper was predictably endorsed by MPs at Westminster and elections to the new Assembly were called for Thursday 28 June.

Trimble had a decision to make. Was now the right time to enter the political arena and become a candidate in North Down? After some thought, he put his name forward and was selected and joined George Green and Ken Leckey on the three-man Vanguard slate. Trimble was very much the rookie candidate and quickly got to work on his election address.

He made several drafts, and a handwritten version still survives in the archives stored at Queen's University. In it he says he wanted to see 'fundamental rights restored to the Ulster people – the right to democratic government, the right to decide their own future; the right to security and the opportunity to work for harmony and prosperity'. Interestingly, he referred to himself in a formal way, as 'W.D. Trimble', and at this stage of his career, he does not use the name David.

On the campaign trail, Trimble and his colleagues made Faulkner and the Unionist Party their main targets. Their election literature poked fun at Faulkner, and they attempted to paint him as a weak unionist. Back in the summer of 1973, the inter-unionist fight was predictably intense and at times bitter. Michael McGimpsey, who would later go on to be a Stormont minister, and a colleague of Trimble's, remembers it well. As a young activist in the North Down Unionist Association, he vividly recalls campaigning against Trimble:

> When it came to election time, I have to say David was a thorn in our flesh. I was only in the Young Unionists, and I was not running for office or anything. But David was

very much a thorn in the flesh of unionism in Bangor and North Down. He was so prominent and so adamant and so vehement about Vanguard. 'Vote for Vanguard'. They ran candidates against us and all the rest of it. And you know how bitter the internecine war gets.[15]

Even though some in the Faulkner camp were spooked by the arrival of Vanguard on the ballot paper, their initial fears in North Down were misplaced. In his first electoral battle, it was an uphill struggle for Trimble. It soon became clear he was an unknown candidate up against a better and more organised team of rivals in the Unionist Party, Ian Paisley's Democratic Unionists and the Alliance Party. While Trimble hoped being a hometown boy from Bangor might aid his campaign, he and his Vanguard colleagues struggled to get unionist voters to switch.

When counting got underway, it soon became clear that the more established figures were well ahead and there would be no political shocks. North Down returned seven seats, with four going to the official unionist candidates, including Jim Kilfedder, who topped the poll with over 20,000 votes. Charles Poots won a seat for Paisley's party, and the Alliance Party took two seats. None of the Vanguard candidates got elected in North Down, and Trimble finished last with a final figure of 446 votes. It was a poor showing and a brutal introduction to electoral politics.

One of the successful candidates did have some words of comfort for him. He declared, 'You have done yourself a world of good in this campaign.'[16] Trimble initially thought that his rival was being patronising, but he later came to realise that the comments were well meant. Across Northern Ireland, Vanguard did pick up support, and when all the constituencies were declared, Craig's party managed to pick up seven seats and 10.5 per cent of the vote.

The overall political picture was complicated. Unionism was fractured in different directions, and if the British government had hoped for a simple, straightforward result, they were disappointed. A majority of the unionists elected to Stormont rejected Faulkner's approach. It meant he did not have majority support amongst unionists and was leading a bitterly divided party. Vanguard was now part of the political landscape, and even though Trimble had failed to get elected to Stormont, his enthusiasm for the party remained high.

In the autumn of 1973, he became chairman of Vanguard's North Down Association. He was now meeting Craig regularly, and they had a good relationship with a mutual admiration. Clifford Smyth, who would later get elected to the Assembly and the Convention, says Craig was an unusual politician in many ways:

> Craig was different from other leaders. He had an ability to encourage people and use their talents. He was very good at identifying younger people with potential – like Trimble.[17]

If Trimble's political and professional life was providing happiness, his personal life was not. His relationship with Heather was in difficulty. They had drifted apart. He was preoccupied with politics and Queen's, and she was busy with the UDR. They had also hoped to start a family, and Heather became pregnant with twins. However, the babies were stillborn. Judith Eve, who was now working with Trimble at Queen's University, recalls hearing that the pregnancies had failed:

> What I do remember about David and Heather was the tragedy when they lost both the twins. I mean all of us at work were upset. David had been so excited that they were coming and then they lost them and everybody at work knew, and it was one of those where you just did not know what to say.[18]

As time went on, David and Heather's relationship continued to be strained, and they grew further apart. Herb Wallace remembers when they decided to separate:

> I think he was cross when he told me about it. He told me on a Monday that he and Heather had been locked in discussions all that Sunday and that she had now left the house. They lived round in Henderson Drive in Bangor at that stage, and I think he was more cross than sad.[19]

Eve says there was a lot of sympathy for the couple when the separation occurred:

> There were a couple of years where things just did not go well for them. And I don't think we were surprised that the marriage broke up, because it was just a lot to cope with. It really was tragic.[20]

As 1973 ended, Northern Ireland was about to witness a political experiment that had been months in the making. Representatives of the British and Irish governments met at the Civil Service Staff College in Sunningdale in Berkshire. They were joined by unionists supportive of Faulkner, the SDLP and the Alliance Party. The aim was to finalise plans for a new power-sharing administration and to formalise the working arrangements for the Council of Ireland. After days of discussions, a deal was finally hammered out, and it became known as the 'Sunningdale Agreement'.

Faulkner insisted he had secured a good deal by getting a new government in place, and he claimed the Irish government had recognised Northern Ireland's constitutional status. He argued that Sunningdale would 'go down in history as a unionist victory'.[21]

The year 1974 looked like it could be one of political hope, but not everyone agreed with the new deal. Its opponents included a young academic from Queen's University.

4

BRINGING DOWN THE HOUSE

*'Something is going to happen,
and I can't give you anything but watch this space'.*
David Trimble on the imminent collapse of the
Northern Ireland Executive

David Trimble was convinced he was about to be harmed. There was someone outside his Bangor home, which was worrying. He was not expecting visitors. First, he heard the rap on the door. Then he heard it again. The knocking got louder and louder. Whoever wanted to see him was determined. Trimble had no idea who it was, and it was clear his uninvited guests were not going to go away.

Like many figures involved in Northern Irish politics, he had a personal protection weapon. It was a handgun, and for Trimble it seemed like a necessary precaution in dangerous times. There had been several attacks on politicians, and Trimble's membership of Vanguard meant he was viewed by the IRA as a 'legitimate target'. He quickly got used to carrying his gun around.

Whenever he left the house, he was always armed. However, on this occasion, as he hung his washing out in his back garden, his handgun was sitting 20 yards away on the coffee table in the front room. Soon, the knocking stopped.

Trimble sensed his unexpected visitors were coming in his direction. He had three options. He could try to get back into the house and retrieve his gun. He could get out of the garden and run. Or he could stay and hide. He chose to remain. Moments later, his mystery callers arrived in the garden. They found Trimble up against the wall, fearing the worst. If he seemed startled, then so too were his brother Iain and his mother, who had popped round unannounced.

They all laughed off the incident, but the episode illustrated the tension that Trimble was living with. He was only a minor political figure at this stage, but he had to take his personal security seriously. By 1974, Trimble was enjoying his work at Queen's during the day, and at night and weekends he was heavily involved in campaigning for Vanguard. It was a happy mix, and he had much to keep himself busy. He was energised politically and was a critical observer of those in power.

The target of his ire was the new cross-community Northern Ireland Executive, which had taken office on New Year's Day in 1974. It had the Unionist Party leader Brian Faulkner as chief executive, with Gerry Fitt of the SDLP as his deputy. The other ministers included unionists, nationalists and members of the Alliance Party. The SDLP had key figures alongside party leader Gerry Fitt. The party's deputy, John Hume, an articulate former teacher who had made his name during street protests in Derry, was minister for commerce.

Austin Currie, a streetwise former Nationalist Party MP, was the new housing minister. The Alliance Party leader, Oliver Napier, was also at the Executive table, as head of the Office of Law Reform. The new multi-party administration was seen by the world's press as historic and groundbreaking.

However, there was widespread opposition from many in the unionist community to the new political arrangements. Unionism was deeply divided. Some unionists supported the idea of power-sharing and wanted to give the new arrangements a fair wind. Others, used to decades of majority rule, were vehemently opposed to it. There was also a large body of unionists deeply troubled with the Council of Ireland, believing that this was a precursor to the reunification of Ireland.

Faulkner also had his own personal difficulties, and as the Executive began its work, his position as Unionist Party leader was precarious. Three days after the Executive was established, the strains within unionism were evident when Unionist Party members gathered to debate the

Council of Ireland. The Ulster Unionist Council (UUC), the party's governing body, rejected the all-island body by 427 to 374 votes – a result which signalled the end of Faulkner's reign in the UUP.

On 7 January, he resigned as Unionist Party leader. His 28-year membership came to an end, but he remained at the head of the Executive. It was a morale boost for the anti-Sunningdale unionists, who felt that the power-sharing institutions were living on borrowed time. The Faulkner resignation galvanised his opponents. Bill Craig of Vanguard and Ian Paisley of the DUP were the chief critics of power-sharing at this stage and would soon be joined by Harry West, who succeeded Faulkner as UUP leader.

By early February 1974, the political atmosphere intensified when Prime Minister Edward Heath called a general election for the last Thursday of that month. It gave the anti-Sunningdale unionists a golden opportunity to come together and, after meeting at Stormont, they selected joint candidates. DUP, Vanguard, anti-Faulkner unionists and independent unionists formed the UUUC (United Ulster Unionist Council). Sometimes called the Unionist Coalition, the group's aim was simple. They wanted to use the election as a referendum on power-sharing and the Council of Ireland.

Trimble was now meeting Craig regularly, and the Vanguard leader found the young academic's legal and political advice useful. He was becoming a key backroom figure with a shrewd ability to write policy papers and suggest tactics for Craig. Trimble was not a candidate; instead he assisted Craig in East Belfast, where the Vanguard leader was challenging the sitting unionist MP, Stanley McMaster.

The UUUC secured 11 of Northern Ireland's 12 Westminster seats, including a big victory in East Belfast for Craig. The only pro-Sunningdale MP returned was Fitt, the leader of the SDLP. The UUUC success was masterminded jointly by Paisley, West and Craig, who were all now members of the House of Commons. Their victories emboldened their coalition and meant they could now denounce the Executive, power-sharing and the Council of Ireland with a degree of authority.

Faulkner's candidates performed extremely badly and polled just 94,000 votes in contrast to the 360,000 for the UUUC. It showed that

Faulkner did not speak for most unionists. The credibility of the power-sharing administration was being questioned and its future appeared short-lived. In the weeks ahead, the pressure on Faulkner intensified.

On Saturday 9 March, supporters of the UUUC went to Stormont and called for an end to the Executive. At the end of the month, a more militant group, the Ulster Workers' Council (UWC), threatened civil disobedience unless Faulkner stepped down and the power-sharing administration was dissolved. The UWC was a coalition of loyalists who were opposed to Sunningdale. It had the political support of elected unionists and also the backing of prominent loyalist paramilitaries. The role of the UWC ended up being the game-changer which accelerated Faulkner's departure.

Trimble was very busy at Queen's, organising lectures and tutorials, and in his spare time he was throwing himself into his political work. He continued to be heavily involved in the background of the Vanguard operation and was regularly attending meetings and writing speeches for Craig.

While Trimble tried to keep his academic life and his political activity separate, most people who knew him at Queen's were aware of his views. Alban Maginness says his lecturer never discussed or divulged his politics. He says he was surprised about where Trimble's political sympathies lay:

> It did bother me, in the sense that I regarded Vanguard as a fairly sinister political party because it seemed to align itself very overtly with paramilitaries. And it was a bit surprising for ... [an] academic lawyer of that standing to be associated with a shadowy political organisation which was led by a very extreme (in my opinion) unionist at that stage, Bill Craig.[1]

Trimble was clearly unfazed by what people thought of his political views, and simply felt the power-sharing administration had to end. He was in favour of a strike and felt loyalists had enough economic muscle to organise and sustain a successful stoppage.

On 14 May, matters came to a head at Stormont. Members of the Assembly who were opposed to power-sharing secured a vote on the future of the cross-party administration and the Council of Ireland. After a tetchy and at times heated debate, Faulkner and the pro-Sunningdale members won the day by 44 votes to 28. That result lit the blue touchpaper; the UWC sprang into action and, as expected, called a strike. The next day, the stoppage began to take hold, with factory closures and power cuts.

Trimble wanted to be involved, so he went to the strike headquarters at Hawthornden Road in East Belfast and put his academic skills to good use. He helped to draft a daily news sheet that detailed how the stoppages were impacting on life in Northern Ireland. Trimble's publication was called simply the *Bulletin,* and it was useful to journalists, as it detailed what roads were blocked and where the pickets were active. The publication also acted as a morale booster to strike supporters, who could see how the stoppages were working.

By that time, a large coordinating committee had been formed to run the strike, including political leaders like Ian Paisley, Bill Craig, Harry West and Assembly member and UDA leader, Glenn Barr. Trimble got a buzz from working in strike headquarters, where there was a sense of momentum – like running an election campaign – except this was about bringing down a government. His organisational skills were being appreciated, and he was being recognised by the strike organisers as an important backroom adviser.

Trimble had by this point established himself as a political thinker, and he was starting to get noticed within unionist circles. Ulster Unionist Arnold Hatch remembers his early impressions:

> He was a young, intelligent man who talked a lot of sense. You could see, though, he was far-sighted, and he could see the dangers of Sunningdale.[2]

Herb Wallace, a friend of Trimble's and a colleague at Queen's, recalls how Trimble would spend a lot of time at strike headquarters and clearly enjoyed being involved:

I do remember that he was rarely around the Law Faculty except when he absolutely needed to be at the time. And he was a great admirer of Glenn Barr. I think David, I suppose like all of us, was sometimes flattered when other people were sort of nice to him. And he told me that Glenn Barr said, 'When we are in charge, I'll make you Minister for Law Reform.'[3]

As the days wore on, every corner of Northern Ireland was affected. Workers at Harland & Wolff downed tools, and there was a series of barricades across major roads. Soon, supplies at petrol stations were rationed and both the postal service and the telephone network were disrupted. Cars and buses were routinely hijacked and set alight, and those who refused to close their businesses were threatened. A back-to-work march organised by the Trades Union Congress (TUC) was a flop and, as the days wore on, it became clear that Northern Ireland was at crisis point.

On 24 May, as the situation worsened, Prime Minster Harold Wilson met Brian Faulkner to discuss the strike. The next day, Wilson made a television address in which he attacked the strikers as 'thugs and bullies' and said that British taxpayers and parents had seen their 'sons vilified, spat upon and murdered'. He then added a jaw-dropping line that would get the most publicity. He attacked those who were defying Westminster, accusing them of 'sponging' on Westminster and British democracy and then acting to 'systematically assault democratic methods. Who do these people think they are?'[4]

Wilson's 'spongers' speech infuriated the supporters of the strike and ultimately backfired. His broadcast simply reinforced the strikers' view that this was a battle – and if the prime minister was paying them this kind of attention, they were clearly making an impact. It heightened tension and in truth galvanised some who thought the strike would not succeed. With power cuts, petrol rationing, food shortages and roads blocked by masked men, Northern Ireland looked ungovernable. There had also been violence on the streets throughout the strike and a series of car bombs in Dublin and Monaghan, killing 34 people, including an unborn child. Loyalists were blamed for the attacks, and to this day there are allegations that British military personnel were in some way linked to the bombings.

As the stoppages continued in May 1974, Trimble continued to move between the strike headquarters in East Belfast and the campus at Queen's University. By the final week of May, the Executive was on the brink of collapse. In his own small way, Trimble had played his part in a rebellion against the British establishment, the most effective act of resistance unionists had been involved in since the Home Rule Crisis of 1912. In Trimble's eyes, he and his colleagues had taken on two big opponents: the government in London and the political leadership at Stormont. The UWC had effectively outflanked them both.

Trimble must have sensed that the strike he had supported was about to deliver. His excitement at what was about to happen became obvious. Mary Madden, one of his students, remembers being in a tutorial with him at Queen's, just hours before the Executive fell:

> David came in and there was a top table and a chair. That sort of thing. This was a man who had come in animated, excited, with a big grin on his face. You knew he really was in a euphoric state. And clearly something had happened. Everybody was anxious to hear what it was. What would he say? And he said, 'Something is going to happen, and I can't give you anything but watch this space'. And he clearly wanted to say what it was that was coming out into the public domain. But he wasn't able to breach the confidentiality of it at that time. That was in the morning, and everyone was sort of saying, 'What on earth is going on?' And he could hardly take the tutorial because he was animated about this and so excited about this. And it made a lasting impression.[5]

Trimble was ecstatic, and his joy was becoming publicly obvious. As the lights flickered across the homes of Northern Ireland, power ebbed away from Stormont. It was not a surprise when Faulkner finally resigned on 28 May; and with his resignation, the Executive collapsed. The consequences of Faulkner's departure kicked in immediately.

Direct rule resumed from London, and the UWC called off its strike. Northern Ireland was back in the land of political limbo. People in loyalist areas took to the streets to celebrate. They had defied the wishes of a local administration which they felt was pushing them into a united Ireland. That sense of euphoria and relief contrasted with the disappointment and anger others felt. Supporters of Sunningdale regarded this as a missed opportunity, and felt Northern Ireland had squandered a historic chance to move forward. It was now back to the drawing board.

5
BREAKING THE CONVENTION

*'He was diehard and focused and wanted to break free
from Harry West and the unionists.'*
Hugh Logue on David Trimble

The photographer was trying hard to get David Trimble to relax, but it was proving difficult. The academic was standing beside one of his students as he posed for a picture for the newspaper. This was not a traditional story of a lecturer bestowing congratulations on a successful student: this was an image of political rivalry – albeit with a twist.

Northern Ireland was once again experiencing election fatigue – the sixth poll in two years. This time voters were going to polling stations to elect members to a new body called the Constitutional Convention, which had been set up by the British government to try to break the political impasse. The Convention was to be chaired by Sir Robert Lowry, and his task was to come up with a form of government in Northern Ireland that commanded political support. The new body was to have 78 members elected by proportional representation, rather like the old Assembly, which had dramatically collapsed a year before.

All the major parties were contesting the seats, which were based on the 12 Westminster constituencies. Just as they had done earlier, the UUUC put forward a joint slate of candidates from the UUP, DUP, Vanguard and Independents. The coalition of unionists led by Harry West, Ian Paisley and Bill Craig was campaigning on the grounds that any new government in Northern Ireland should be based on majority rule. For them, it was a tried and tested position.

In contrast, the SDLP, Alliance and the Unionist Party of Northern Ireland (UPNI – pro-Faulkner unionists) argued that there should be a return to power-sharing. For the watching electorate it all seemed very familiar. The politicians were going to enter a new arena, but voters were witnessing old arguments.

Trimble decided to give his political career another shot, after his poor showing in 1973 in the Assembly election poll in North Down. He was again standing for Vanguard, but he had moved constituencies and was now running in South Belfast. The young man joining him for the newspaper photograph was Alban Maginness, who was running in the election for the SDLP in East Belfast. The news that a lecturer and his student were political rivals intrigued journalists, and a photo shoot was organised, which Trimble agreed to.

Maginness was enthusiastic about getting some coverage:

> The press knew that I was a student at Queen's, and I was standing in a hopeless place called East Belfast – well, hopeless [electorally] for the SDLP. He was standing in South Belfast, and he was on a high because he was going to be elected. At least you would have thought that. So, we had our photograph taken together, me and himself. I think the press found this funny, a lecturer and a student standing against each other, albeit in different constituencies for different parties ... I think he was a bit uncomfortable about it. I wasn't, because any publicity was good publicity as far as I was concerned.[1]

Maginness knew his election chances in East Belfast were poor. It was not SDLP territory, and he sensed that the victors would be predominantly unionist, with the remaining seats probably going to Alliance and the Northern Ireland Labour Party. Trimble's situation was very different. He was running in South Belfast, where there was a strong UUUC presence. It was fertile territory for those unionists who, like Trimble, had opposed the Sunningdale deal. As ever in a proportional representation election, vote management would be the key to success.

When counting began, it was clear that the UUUC was on course to do well in South Belfast. The unionist vote had come out, and it seemed likely that four of the six seats would go to the UUUC, with the remaining two going to the Alliance Party. A well-known Orangeman, the Reverend Martin Smyth, was running in his first election for the UUUC, and he was polling particularly well. He would eventually top the poll.

Trimble was way behind, and as he watched the counting, he had an agonising few hours' wait. The vagaries of the single transferable vote system meant that the transfer of votes was time-consuming and at times hard to predict. Trimble and his supporters did the number crunching and watched as his tally slowly rose at each count.

Finally, on the ninth count, he reached the quota and was deemed elected. William David Trimble's political career had begun in earnest in May 1975, as he joined the large band of successful UUUC candidates across Northern Ireland. In total, UUUC candidates secured 47 of the 78 seats, with 55 per cent of the vote. It was an impressive result and showed that most unionists were uncompromising.

Under the UUUC banner, Harry West's UUP took 19 seats, Bill Craig's Vanguard won 14 and Ian Paisley's DUP secured 12. It was bad news for Brian Faulkner's UPNI, which could only muster 5 seats and less than 8 per cent of the vote. The former prime minister's political slump was continuing, and his future in politics looked bleak. In contrast, Trimble's political career was just beginning, and his election to the Convention presented fresh opportunities and new experiences. He was introduced to parliamentary procedures and the rules of debating and speaking, all of which he appeared to take in his stride.

Trimble's political apprenticeship was in full swing, and his stature in the party rose. Within a matter of months, he was viewed as a talented and thoughtful speaker in the Convention and also seen as a good performer on TV and on radio. As a valued and trusted lieutenant of Bill Craig, he was now a key figure in discussions Vanguard had with other UUUC parties. Significantly, Trimble was also involved in talks with the pro-Sunningdale parties, particularly the SDLP. It was those discussions which would change the future of the UUUC, and Craig and Trimble.

In the summer of 1975, the two men talked privately about how they could change the political atmosphere and bring about some form of multi-party government that was not full-blown power-sharing. Trimble and Craig wanted to include a minority partner in government, but knew an accommodation along the lines of the Sunningdale deal would not be acceptable to the UUUC. Their conversations produced the idea of a 'voluntary coalition' with the SDLP.

This coalition would see SDLP members coming into a unionist-dominated cabinet, and the system of government would mirror that of the emergency-style government Britain experienced during the Second World War. The SDLP would have a place in government, over a period of time, but there would be no attached Council of Ireland – which Craig and Trimble argued had effectively destroyed Faulkner's chances of staying in office.

The idea of a voluntary coalition appealed to both Craig and Trimble as a way of breaking Northern Ireland's political impasse. Both men knew they had to proceed slowly and carefully, and they were savvy enough to see that their idea could easily be misinterpreted. They understood that they had to bring the UUUC with them and were aware that the proposal had to be handled sensitively.

Behind the scenes, Trimble embarked on a series of meetings with fellow members of the UUUC and had detailed meetings with the SDLP to discuss the proposal. Trimble also had discussions with Sir Robert Lowry, who was the independent chairman of the Constitutional Convention. It was Lowry's job to meet with the parties and try to establish if there was a form of government that would garner political support.

Lowry was very interested in the Vanguard proposal. He felt that anything that involved unionist and nationalist cooperation deserved to be explored. On 4 September 1975, he drew up a document entitled 'The Voluntary Coalition Solution'. It was an attempt to outline how such a plan might work in practice, and he hoped it would kick-start negotiations between the parties.

Lowry's document was a discussion paper which outlined the areas that the parties would have to consider if a voluntary coalition was agreed. Trimble and Craig hoped that Lowry's succinct and business-like report could win over those unionists who were wedded to the idea of majority rule.

After discussions with members of the UUUC, Bill Craig was convinced that the idea had the backing of his fellow unionists in Harry West's UUP and Ian Paisley's DUP. This is where the narrative becomes contested by other members of the UUUC. Craig insists that the DUP was constantly kept informed about the dialogue with the SDLP. He gave this interview in 1976:

> His party [Ian Paisley's DUP] was represented at every stage of the negotiation with the SDLP, and the Reverend [William] Beattie, who represented his party [the DUP], was very enthusiastic in supporting the idea of a voluntary coalition. And when we reported back that an agreement seemed possible along those lines, Dr Paisley himself personally said yes, it was the only way forward. In fact, he shook hands with me on it. That was a Friday and by Monday he had completely somersaulted. I think it was largely due to the fact that he ran into trouble not so much in his party, but in his church, who warned him if this sort of thing was underway, he would be putting the unity of the church at risk.[2]

Paisley was not just an influential unionist politician and the leader of the DUP. He was also the moderator (leader) of the Free Presbyterian Church, an evangelical Protestant church which was part of the reformed fundamentalist movement. Paisley's church members were no strangers to organising protests and commentating on public issues. Members had strong views on Sunday observance and homosexuality, and Paisley was a regular critic of the teachings of the Catholic Church in his sermons and public statements.

Craig believed Paisley's church colleagues influenced his thinking on a voluntary coalition during that weekend in September, resulting in the DUP leader backtracking. On Monday 8 September, senior members of the UUUC met to discuss Craig's plan of forming a voluntary coalition with Gerry Fitt's SDLP. It soon became clear that Craig was well and truly outnumbered, and his plan had little support.

The meeting was dominated by Paisley, and there was a strong contribution from Enoch Powell, the former Conservative MP, who was now a senior figure in the Ulster Unionists. Powell had been sacked from Edward Heath's shadow cabinet after a speech he made on immigration was denounced for being racist. Powell and Paisley rejected Craig's coalition idea, which meant the Vanguard politician was now isolated. His humiliation was complete when an option barring the SDLP from government was passed by 37 votes to 1. The result ended the idea of voluntary coalition.

Vanguard was thrown into crisis, and Craig had little option but to stand down as party leader. Paisley had outflanked his unionist rival, and if he saw Craig as a threat, he had now neutralised his importance. Vanguard may have secured more seats in the Convention, but it was Paisley who was now unionism's loudest and most charismatic voice. Trimble blamed Paisley, but he would later say that Powell had a major role in persuading fellow unionists to reject the idea of a voluntary coalition:

> He was the one who deluded the unionist leadership, particularly people at the top, into thinking the best way forward was full integration inside the UK. That was a shame because, from a unionist point of view, the voluntary coalition was a much better arrangement than Sunningdale.[3]

Vanguard Convention members met to consider Craig's resignation, and after discussing matters for eight hours, they concluded that he should withdraw his resignation. They also decided that Vanguard should remain part of the UUUC, and they could not see any circumstances in which a coalition with the SDLP would happen. They agreed that future talks or discussions on working together with other parties must be based on UUUC policy.

The voluntary coalition episode was personally disappointing for both Craig and Trimble. Trimble's decision to back the idea of working with a nationalist partner is revealing. It indicated that he believed Northern Ireland could no longer be governed by one party. It was a break from traditional unionist thinking, and he was prepared to support the idea of a coalition publicly, even though he knew it would attract criticism.

It was the first sign that Trimble was on a political journey. It was an indication that he was prepared to support ideas because he believed they were right, rather than simply back traditional unionist positions. For a unionist who had been reared in the politics of majority rule and who had opposed Sunningdale, the contemplation of coalition government was revolutionary.

Some who witnessed Trimble in the corridors at Stormont in those days say he was prepared to challenge unionist orthodoxy – something he would later repeat as UUP leader. Hugh Logue, an SDLP Convention member, says he found Trimble 'more thoughtful' compared to other unionists. He says he was 'diehard and focused and wanted to break free from Harry West and the unionists. [He was] much more in tune with that and much more radical.'[4]

Back in 1975, Craig's decision to support a voluntary coalition with the SDLP surprised many of his colleagues. Reg Empey, who was a Vanguard Convention member for East Belfast, remembers the debate well. He feels that Craig failed to prepare the party grassroots and that meant his move was bound to fail:

> The problem with Bill [Craig] was Bill didn't tell any of us. And this came out of the blue. Most of us knew nothing about it. We didn't know what he was negotiating and then he comes out with this idea. Which in retrospect was not bad. But no one was prepared for it and that created the

trouble. Had Bill told us, I think he could have sold it to us, but it just appeared as an idea without any of us being aware. And that did shock people.[5]

David Burnside was another Vanguard member who remembers the events of 1975 with shock and surprise. He thinks with hindsight that the prospect of a voluntary coalition could have transformed Northern Ireland politics:

> It would have been a good stable government with support from the SDLP. Paisley blew it. Paisley blew everything all his life, until he got to the top of the pile ... That was a big, missed opportunity when David was clever enough to see it there. But once again, you know, Paisley blew the opportunity of getting a good deal; that really was a big, missed opportunity.[6]

So the question remains, would the SDLP have accepted the offer to work with unionists under the banner of a voluntary coalition? Would an SDLP–UUUC coalition, for a time-limited period, have delivered political stability and progress? Was this plan, as Trimble would later argue, Northern Ireland's lost opportunity?

The idea seemed attractive to some in the SDLP, but to others it was full of problems. Some in the party argued that anything less than full power-sharing should be rejected. Others compared it to Sunningdale and claimed that any deal without an 'Irish dimension' was not worth considering.

The SDLP deputy leader, John Hume, thought the idea had some merit:

> While he [Craig] was not arguing for fixed and permanent power-sharing, he was talking about a voluntary coalition. And given the right wing he was coming from, to me that looked like a beginning in the change of opinion on the unionist side and a beginning of new thinking and thinking that was going in our direction.[7]

In September 1975, Craig backtracked on his resignation and stayed on as Vanguard leader, but he was now in charge of a much-diminished party in the Convention. A series of leading figures, including Ernest Baird, deserted Craig and aligned themselves with Paisley and other unionists. Unionism was now turning in on itself. Just as it was fractured during the days of Sunningdale, it was now divided during the days of its successor – the Convention.

There were now three distinct camps within the unionist family. One was Faulkner's tiny group, which went under the banner of UPNI; another was Craig's group, including Trimble, which supported a voluntary coalition; and then there was the larger block of unionists in the UUUC that opposed it. This block included Paisley of the DUP, West of the Ulster Unionists and now Baird and the Vanguard rebels.

There were also two very different narratives being played out in the press on what had happened surrounding the talks about a voluntary coalition plan. Trimble and Craig continued to insist that Paisley had initially supported the idea and then changed his mind after pressure from his church. However, Paisley insisted that he had never consented to the idea of unionists going into coalition with the SDLP. He said that Craig had acted alone and had been on a solo run.

For his part, Craig continued to fight his corner, and although he won a crucial vote at the party's central council backing his position, he had lost the support of the majority of his elected members at the Convention. The UUUC moved against Craig, Trimble and George Green, and they were initially suspended from the UUUC, before being thrown out. Craig was also expelled from the UUUC's parliamentary party at Westminster. Vanguard as a political entity was damaged and looked weak, and Craig's political future looked seriously in doubt. He had once been tipped to become the leader of unionism, but now he looked like a man whose political moment had come and gone.

Trimble stayed loyal to Craig, still believing that his party leader's analysis and vision were correct. For the young politician, the last six months had been a whirlwind, and he had learned a lot about public life and witnessed much drama. He had experienced the ups and downs of running for office again, this time having the thrill of being elected. At Stormont, he had been given a ringside seat at negotiations and tried with his colleagues to find a political breakthrough.

As 1975 ended, Trimble seemed content professionally despite the endless battles that unionist politics seemed to produce. After the end of his marriage, he was in the process of getting divorced. He had met somebody new, and life was about to take a very different turn.

6

HELLO, DAPHNE

'I started looking at him as more than just a person but with a more romantic involvement.'
Daphne Orr on her future husband, David Trimble

For the Queen's University class of 1975, graduation day was their big moment. This was what it had all been about. After the endless essays, the long tutorials, the lectures and the exams, it was all finally over. This was now their chance to unwind and celebrate in the company of family and friends. Dressed in their hired robes, they could at last call themselves graduates and put those coveted letters, LLB, after their names.

Daphne Orr, from Warrenpoint, a small border town in County Down on the shores of Carlingford Lough, was enjoying the post-ceremony strawberries and cream with her parents, Gerry and Barbara. It was a red-letter day for the couple, who ran a jewellery business in Newry. They were naturally proud of Daphne, and, apart from celebrating her achievement, the trip to Belfast gave the Orrs an opportunity to meet their daughter's friends.

As was tradition, students and staff joined in the refreshments, and it was a relaxed and jovial atmosphere. As a key figure in the Law Department, David Trimble was there too. It was the first time the Orrs had encountered him. They quickly spotted him and, turning to their daughter, wanted to know who he was. Daphne remembers her parents' exact words. They were brief and to the point: 'Who is this fellow hanging around?'[1]

Daphne explained that the slightly older man in a suit, gown and glasses was her lecturer, but she was reluctant to go into much detail.

There was a reason for her evasiveness. Now that her course had ended, she and David had just started dating: 'I would never have mentioned that to my parents at that point. There was not a whole lot to our relationship. At that stage we had been on a few dates.'[2]

Daphne first got an indication that David was interested in her romantically when students and staff came together for the annual cricket match. After the game, the players and a few spectators went to an East Belfast hotel that was owned by the family of one of the students. As the evening wore on, Daphne and David got chatting:

> Everybody went back there for a few drinks as well, for a bit of a party in the evening. And that was where I started looking at him as more than just a person but with a more romantic involvement. Then over the summer he asked me out and it sort of went from there.[3]

David and Daphne quickly realised they enjoyed spending time together. They naturally shared an interest in law but also had a mutual liking for socialising and music. They spent their first date just chatting and a few nights out followed, including some evenings spent close to Daphne's family home in Warrenpoint.

Life in this part of Northern Ireland, close to the border, was a world away from the hustle and bustle of Belfast. On several occasions, the couple visited Rostrevor, a pretty village some three miles away along the coast. One evening, David and Daphne went into the Old Corner House pub, unaware that it was run by the father of Mary McAleese, who David had taught. Paddy Leneghan had bought the pub recently after moving down from Belfast, where he had previously run a bar. If Daphne and David were hoping to have a quiet drink and keep their relationship under wraps, they were in for a shock.

Mary McAleese, then Mary Leneghan, had invited some friends, old law students of Trimble's, down for the weekend to help decorate the family premises. She remembers the night very well:

> A bunch of them were down helping us to paint the place because we were actually living over the pub for the first time in our lives. We were living in a little tiny place above the pub. I can still remember the surprise registering on their faces when, from behind the counter, half of his land law class came out. They were good humoured about it and so were we.[4]

Daphne Orr had begun her law degree at Queen's University in the autumn of 1971 and had plans to become a solicitor. Trimble had taught her land law and property law. When she first encountered him in the lecture hall, romance and a relationship were far from her mind:

> My first contact with him was sitting in a lecture room quietly. He was pontificating at the front about either land law or equity. I think at that stage it could have been either. It was a four-year course at Queen's. After your second year you had to choose at that time which honours school you went into. I went into the honours school of property law, which was very much David's field, so he was taking tutorials with me. And you know at that stage he was just one of the staff. He was one of the lecturers. Yes, I thought, he is good.[5]

Born in 1953, Daphne was the second of four daughters to Gerry and Barbara Orr. Gerry had taken over his father's jewellery business at the end of the Second World War and ran it out of Hill Street in Newry. He was the fourth of five children, and the family lived above the shop. He travelled to England to learn about the jewellery business, and while he was there, he was called up to join the services. Gerry served in the war with the 'Fighting Wessex Wyverns', which was the name given to the 43rd Wessex Infantry Division. Most of his military service was in the UK, but he did see action in France when he was part of the Normandy landings.

Daphne's mother, Barbara was from the northeast of Scotland, where her parents were tenant farmers. A bright, adventurous woman, she had a can-do attitude and went to Aberdeen University – becoming the first from her family to enter third-level education. Fluent in French and German, she travelled extensively across Europe before the war and had a spell working as an au pair in France. Back in her native Scotland, she became a modern languages teacher and got a job at Kirkwall Grammar School in Orkney.

It was in Orkney that she met Gerry, who was one of the many servicemen stationed there. They started going out and got married in June 1945, months before the Second World War ended. Only a few weeks after they got married, the new Mr and Mrs Orr came to live in Newry to run the family jewellers out of the premises on the High Street.

Their first child, Geraldine, was born in May 1948 and then Daphne was born some five years later. Daphne was given the middle name Elizabeth, which was very common for girls at that time, as it was the year when Queen Elizabeth was crowned, and she recalls that her first name was arrived at in rather unusual circumstances:

> I was to have been called Fred after my grandfather, but it wasn't to be. They were stumped for a name. But when they were sitting in Granny Orr's garden with me and the Daphne bush caught their eyes and that was that. The twins, Caroline and Judy, were born five years later.[6]

The Orrs gave their two-storey house in Warrenpoint the name of Wyvern, after the Flying Wessex Wyverns. The property had three bedrooms, and was set in garden of around a quarter of an acre and was located about half a mile away from the town centre.

The family were comfortable and would have been viewed as middle class. The four girls had a happy childhood, and the spacious home and grounds meant they were never short of somewhere to go and play. Summer holidays for the family would often be spent at the caravan site at Cranfield, which was around 12 miles away along the coast. If the weather was good, the Orr girls would be on the beach, or they would end up in an open-air swimming pool close to home.

In September 1957, aged just four, Daphne went to a local primary school. Even though she was younger than her classmates, she was clearly ready for school. She was bright, could read very well and, thanks to her parents, had a big interest in books. The education system in Northern Ireland in the 1950s was divided on religious lines (as it is largely today, although since the 1980s there has been a growth in the integrated sector), and this meant that Daphne mainly mixed with Protestant children during her early years:

> It was the only controlled [meaning Protestant] primary school in Warrenpoint; all the others were maintained [meaning Catholic]. The key distinction was that was where Protestant children went. Catholic children all went to the Catholic schools.[7]

After primary school, Daphne transferred to the preparatory department of Newry Grammar School and, not surprisingly, she passed the 11-plus examination with ease, which meant she got a place in the 'big school'. During Daphne's time there, the grammar school merged with Ashgrove Secondary School and was renamed Newry High School. She quickly established a reputation for being academically gifted:

> I was considered one of the class swots, but partly this was due to considerable encouragement and interest from home, also a natural inclination to conform. I would never have come into school without my homework done. My exam marks were always the best in the year. This made it difficult for me to choose whether to go down the arts or science route when it came to choosing subjects for O level, and I ended up compromising by doing 10 O levels, including physics and chemistry and giving up history. I was the only one in the class to do 10 O levels, and I felt

that my O level year was the hardest work I had ever done, regularly studying to nearly midnight with little opportunity to relax.[8]

Games at school were compulsory, and Daphne played for the hockey team, largely due to her dad's encouragement. Away from school, there was much to keep the Orr girls occupied. Carlingford Lough, which was on their doorstep, became an integral part of their lives as the family got involved in sailing. Faith was particularly important in the Orr family home as well. They were Methodists and worshipped regularly at Warrenpoint Methodist Church, where David and Daphne would get married in 1978.

Gerry and Barbara Orr were interested in politics but were not drawn to the unionist parties. They joined the New Ulster Movement, which emerged in 1969 and argued for non-sectarianism in politics. The group wanted the much-criticised Ulster Special Constabulary to be abolished and lobbied for reforms to the housing system to stop discrimination. Members of the group believed in power-sharing at Stormont, and in the early 1970s many left to help form the Alliance Party. Although the Orrs were members of the New Ulster Movement, they were not particularly active. Daphne does not think her parents 'ever actually went to a meeting'.[9]

The Orrs were well known in Newry because of their jewellery shop, and, like many business owners, they had witnessed countless IRA bombings in the early 1970s. The IRA targeted towns across Northern Ireland, often planting car bombs outside shops; they also frequently placed small firebombs inside premises. Daphne remembers the strain the bombings placed on her parents:

> It became an almost nightly occurrence for key holders to be called back to their premises to ensure they were safe. One by one shops were firebombed and burned down, until one day it was the turn of Radcliffe's, a large draper's shop in the next building to ours. As usual, Mum and Dad were

called out late at night and could do nothing but watch it burn. Our own building suffered only smoke damage.[10]

In her final year at school, Daphne started to think more and more about going to university. She considered a course in England, before deciding she would study for a law degree in Northern Ireland:

> I wanted something that had a clear career. Uncle Arthur was a solicitor and seemed to have made a good living, so I thought I would try law. I was briefly encouraged by school to consider Oxford or Cambridge, but I didn't feel brave enough to try. Queen's was the obvious university to contemplate.[11]

Back in 1971, student life for Daphne offered new perspectives. She was well used to the security situation at home through her parents' experience as shopkeepers in Newry, but living and studying in Belfast during the Troubles was a different prospect completely:

> In the evenings and at night sound travelled, and nights were punctuated by the regular sound of dustbin lids being banged in Andersonstown and the sound of gunfire. The city centre was not somewhere you would willingly go. There were large security gates at every entrance to the city centre, where handbags were searched and bodies patted down. This was before the era of X-ray machines and electronic devices for body searches and each person was patted down no matter who you were. Further handbag searches were carried out on entering every shop. The gates were closed at six o'clock and the city centre became a dangerous empty space.[12]

Life for Daphne was very different from her home life; she was in student accommodation and, on her student grant of £50 per year, had to deal with the issues and pressures that shared living presented. It was also an opportunity to become more independent and experience things she had not had the chance to do while at school.

During her first week at Queen's, she was presented with a long list of clubs and societies to join, but she gravitated towards an old favourite:

> When I went to Queen's I joined two clubs on Freshers' Day: the Alliance Party and the sailing club. I went to one meeting of the Alliance Party, listened to Bob Cooper [Alliance Party founder], felt instinctively that he was wrong and never went back. I felt right at home in the sailing club. Right through university I spent all my leisure time sailing.[13]

So, the Alliance Party's loss was the Queen's sailing club's gain, as Daphne stayed well clear of politics. Little did she know that, by the time she would graduate, she would be starting a relationship with a leading unionist politician.

Throughout the closing months of 1975 and into the early part of 1976, David Trimble and Bill Craig continued to work together. Away from politics, David's relationship with Daphne was going well, and his colleagues noticed that he seemed happy and content. The famous Trimble short temper was still evident, but friends of Daphne's, like Mary Madden, noticed that Daphne was influencing David:

> His nature was that he would get very excited about something very quickly. And then it would take him a while to calm down. That is why I think Daphne was so good for him and his type of personality, because she steadied the ship. But there were so many times, you know, where he just blew up on things. And you would have to give him space to calm down before you got things back on track.[14]

In the early months of 1976, the UK government still held out hopes that a political formula could be found that would see the restoration of devolution at Stormont. It was an unrealistic goal. In truth, there was little chance of the local parties finding common ground. Talks took place between the UUUC and the SDLP, but no agreement could be reached on the role of the SDLP in a coalition government.

The Constitutional Convention as a political vehicle had run its course. It sat for a final time on 3 March 1976, and Trimble decided to use the occasion to defend his position regarding the voluntary coalition idea. He wanted to criticise those unionists who had not been prepared to support it. It was an opportunity to settle some old scores. The DUP leader, Ian Paisley, was in his sights: 'In 1972, he [Paisley] was not prepared to exert himself to defend Stormont and in 1976 he does not seem to be prepared to exert himself to restore it.'[15]

Trimble then went on to allude to Aleksandr Solzhenitsyn, the Nobel Prize-winning Russian author whose work *The Gulag Archipelago* (1973) became a bestseller outside the Soviet Union. He came to prominence when he challenged the repression in the Soviet Union, particularly the use of the Gulag prison networks. Trimble said he had been reading Solzhenitsyn's work and was reminded that 'we should look for our brave men in prisons and for the fools amongst our politicians'.[16]

This was a direct attack on Paisley, who was often accused of whipping up loyalist sentiment on the streets which would lead to young people getting involved with paramilitaries and very often ending up in jail. Ever the performer, Paisley had a response ready to go. His remarks took everyone by surprise and threw proceedings at Stormont into chaos. The DUP leader had been well briefed, and he came out fighting. In boxing terms, he went for a knockout:

> There is a story going round Queen's University that a well-known member of Vanguard and a lecturer in law at Queen's University was toying with his personal side arm in a young lady's home.[17]

With the chamber listening to every word, Paisley then continued:

> After seemingly unloading it, he pulled the trigger and surprise, surprise, it went off and a bullet embedded itself in a wall behind the girl, missing her head by a mere inch. Our man from Vanguard very quickly filled in the bullet hole with Polyfilla. One wonders how good Polyfilla is for holes in the head. Mr Chairman, that might be an apocryphal story, but tonight the honourable gentleman was certainly toying with a situation with which he was not prepared to come clean out into the open.[18]

Paisley did not mention Trimble by name, but everyone listening knew exactly who he was referring to. The pointed and deeply personal remarks by the DUP leader prompted calls of 'withdraw' from many members in the chamber. It was a classic Paisley response, and although Trimble tried to get the DUP leader to give way during his comments, he refused to let him interrupt him.

Convention members were shocked by what they had heard, and even Trimble looked concerned by Paisley's remarks. If Trimble had tried to goad Paisley with his initial remarks, he had succeeded in getting a reaction from his fellow unionist. However, the Vanguard man was certainly not expecting the DUP leader to start telling the story that he did.

Daphne remembers being with David when a bullet was discharged. She was living in rented accommodation in Belfast, and David had taken out his personal protection weapon. It was a nine-millimetre automatic pistol, which was commonly carried by many public figures in Northern Ireland. Daphne recalls what happened next:

> He thought he had taken the round out but there was still a bullet left, and he did not realise that. He then pulled the trigger, and the gun went off and a bullet went into the wall. It sure as heck startled me and him. We were in

a state of shock. After that I did not want to have a gun around the house.[19]

Paisley was clearly well informed and was quite happy to portray Trimble as a reckless individual who had been hiding a secret. Following Vanguard's exit from the UUUC, there was no love lost between Trimble's party and the remaining unionists. In the battle for the hearts and minds of the unionist people, Paisley was determined to come out on top and paint Trimble as irresponsible and untrustworthy.

Trimble had clearly been careless in his handling of the weapon. He was embarrassed by what had happened, and he knew the consequences could have been fatal. Herb Wallace remembers Trimble talking to him about the gun incident:

> He did tell me about it very shortly after it had happened, and he was shaken by it. And there's no doubt about that but he was even more shaken, I believe, when Paisley spilled the beans. I don't know how Paisley knew about it, but Paisley spilled the beans.[20]

Wallace says Trimble often took out his personal protection weapon in company to impress people:

> We were in a friend's house, and he pulled the gun out and another of our group who was a QC now ran out of the room and said, 'I'm not going in there until he puts that thing away.' I mean there was a lot of drink taken, and he was showing off ... I think he was a bit childish about some things.[21]

Even though Trimble had handled a gun as a teenager in the ATC, he was never very comfortable having a personal protection weapon. He viewed the carrying of such a firearm as necessary, but the incident at

Daphne's house changed things. That evening with Daphne helped him come to a decision: he would soon give up carrying a gun.

By the summer of 1976, politics in Northern Ireland was once again on hold. The collapse of the Convention meant that Trimble spent more time at Queen's and less at Stormont. With little sign at this stage of a political breakthrough, he probably thought his days in public life were numbered.

The hard facts for Vanguard were brutal. Bill Craig had once been tipped to be the next leader of unionism. He'd had the measure of Paisley, and his party looked set to shape the agenda in Northern Ireland. Now, Craig's project was going nowhere politically. It was entering its final months as a functioning political party. The Convention, which was set up to establish common ground, had failed to come up with proposals that had cross-community support. Most unionists were still insisting on majority rule.

After Daphne graduated, she began her first steps in her legal career. She started a three-year apprenticeship on a salary of £15 a week with F.J. Orr and Co. solicitors in Upper Church Lane in Belfast. Daphne was not related to the founders of the practice but there was one familiar face in the office, and that was Sam Beattie, a friend of David's who had worked with him at Land Registry and, like David, had got a degree at Queen's. Beattie was a partner in the business, and thought highly of Daphne:

> Daphne was quietly spoken but she had her feet on the ground. And she was an asset to David. He might not have agreed to that statement, but I think she was. She was a calm girl, reflective, and shared his politics and so on. I think she was very good for David.[22]

Clearly, Daphne and David were a good match. Over time, David's friends and work colleagues got to socialise with the couple. Beattie's positive view of Daphne was shared by David's old Land Registry pal Herb Wallace, who was now working alongside him at Queen's:

Daphne made David, in many ways, you know, she made him what he was, just by being there and being supportive and tolerating some of his idiosyncrasies. I would have to say that she made him feel a lot better about himself.[23]

As Daphne settled into her job at F.J. Orr, David continued his work at Queen's with the realisation that, politically, Northern Ireland remained in the deep freeze. In September 1976, Roy Mason arrived as the new secretary of state and made it clear he was going to concentrate on a military approach rather than a political one. The chances of a new Assembly or any kind of fresh political initiative in the coming months were remote.

The new year saw little change, and by the spring of 1977, a coalition of loyalists and unionists started to talk about another strike like the one which had brought down the Sunningdale Agreement in 1974. Frustrated by Westminster's refusal to bring back majority rule, Ian Paisley and Ernest Baird set up a new body alongside paramilitary groups, including the UDA.

In May, the United Unionist Action Council called an indefinite strike. The group wanted the return of majority rule at Stormont and a more hard-line security policy from Westminster. Paisley and Baird thought they could repeat the success of May 1974 and bring Northern Ireland to a standstill.

It was a very optimistic objective, as unionism was divided over whether the stoppage should be happening in the first place. When the strike began on 3 May, roads were blocked and vehicles were hijacked. There was widespread intimidation, and many offices and shops were forced to close. Loyalist paramilitaries took to the streets, and in the days that followed they planted a bomb in a filling station and shot dead a bus driver. The violence appalled many, including some who had been initially sympathetic to the stoppage.

What was clear from the outset was that this strike was very different from the loyalist stoppage of 1974. This time the UK government seemed more determined to keep businesses and factories operational and defeat the strikers. After 10 days of disruption, the strike came to an end. Paisley and Baird had gambled and lost. Trimble and Craig watched the strike unfold largely as observers, unlike the role they had played some three years earlier, when they were involved in the stoppages surrounding Sunningdale. They sensed from the outset that this strike run by their unionist rivals would fail. They knew it did not have widespread support, and they felt its motives were questionable.

In May 1977, Trimble and Craig had other matters on their mind, as Vanguard candidates contested the local council elections. It would prove to be the party's swansong, and Trimble's last poll as deputy leader. Across Northern Ireland the organisation almost disappeared, picking up just 1.5 per cent of the vote, which translated into five seats. The party was over. Trimble knew it was time to find a new political home.

7

TO HAVE AND TO HOLD

*'Many people in the Ulster Unionist Party when
I joined in 1978 regarded me as a dangerous liberal
for a very simple reason.'*
David Trimble on joining the Ulster Unionist Party

In 1978, David Trimble did something he had done before. He took out his pen and carefully answered each question, neatly filling in an application form to become a member of the UUP. This time, unlike in his previous attempt, he was successful. On the last occasion, his paperwork had got mislaid somewhere in party headquarters, then in Belfast's Glengall Street. It meant that for several years the eventual party leader was lost to a rival unionist movement.

Now, in a much-expected move, Trimble was trying again. Like many former Vanguard activists, he felt the Ulster Unionists were a natural fit. He had thought long and hard about which party he should join. In the end, it was a straightforward decision. First and foremost, he was a unionist, so he would not consider a party outside the unionist family. He had always seen himself as a unionist, and his parents and grandparents had voted the same way. As he thought about his political future, he instantly knew where he did not want to go. He was not a Paisleyite. He did not like the DUP's brand of politics and was uncomfortable with its mix of religious fundamentalism and street politics – which at times Trimble found dangerous, opportunistic and short-sighted. The DUP had opposed Trimble over his support for a voluntary coalition with the SDLP – so that was a major barrier as well. Trimble was convinced the DUP was not interested in securing a political accommodation that had cross-party support, as they were wedded to the idea of majority rule – another Trimble red flag.

Finally, Trimble and Paisley did not get on, as illustrated by their very personal clash in the Convention. So, a move to the DUP was most definitely not on the cards. Trimble also had no interest in being an Independent. He wanted to be in a political party, where he could advance and be offered opportunities. He was ambitious and harboured desires to be a full-time politician, and that led him to the UUP – the largest unionist party.

In many ways, Trimble was a good catch for the UUP. He was articulate, a good thinker with a legal background. He was an experienced debater at Stormont and was considered an impressive media performer. But not everyone welcomed the Queen's lecturer with open arms, as Trimble recalled later: 'Many people in the Ulster Unionist Party when I joined in 1978 regarded me as a dangerous liberal for a very simple reason.'[1] That simple reason was Trimble's support for a voluntary coalition with the SDLP back in 1975, a position which resulted in Trimble being thrown out of the UUUC – a body that contained the Ulster Unionists – who were opposed to Trimble's coalition plan.

Some UUP members now wondered, if Trimble joined their party, would he continue to campaign for a voluntary coalition? While some questioned Trimble's 'dangerous liberal' ideas, some were uneasy with his membership for other reasons. They saw him as an opportunist and a careerist, and some who had fought against him during his Vanguard days were not prepared to set that to one side.

Michael McGimpsey, who was in the UUP, first encountered Trimble in North Down, when the young academic stood unsuccessfully as a Vanguard candidate:

> He had to apply to the North Down Association, and I remember there was quite a row about that. A lot of people were adamant that he shouldn't be allowed in after the way he behaved with us and our candidates as a Vanguard

Unionist. But Harry West by that stage was leader, and Harry said David had far too much talent to be left on the sidelines. We had to have him in, the party needed him, and he was brought in against the wishes of the association. I remember there were members of the association resigned because of it.[2]

McGimpsey recalls that he did not have a problem with Trimble seeking membership of the UUP. His view was that he had taken a 'wrong turning at first'. However, he felt that the UUP should take in people of talent: 'It strengthens the party, the more the merrier, you know.'[3]

Trimble's application to join the UUP was accepted, even though there were numerous objections from party members. While the party operation was different from Vanguard, there was much familiarity. He already knew many activists from his days at Stormont, and he was on first-name terms with North Down and South Belfast members – where he had campaigned under Vanguard colours.

Joining the UUP was a big decision, but it was not Trimble's most important event that year. He and Daphne got married at Warrenpoint Methodist Church on Thursday 31 August 1978. At the ceremony at Daphne's family church, her twin sisters Caroline and Judy were bridesmaids and David's brother Iain was best man. After the service, friends and family gathered at the Bannville Hotel in Banbridge for the reception. In the photographs taken in the hotel grounds, the smiling bride and groom are pictured looking very happy. Daphne is captured in a traditional white wedding dress with a veil, standing beside David. He looks smart in a three-piece suit with a flower buttonhole and his trademark glasses.

After the formalities, the happy couple celebrated with their guests, including Daphne's friends from work and David's colleagues from Queen's University. It was, as Daphne would recall, a 'very traditional Northern Irish wedding where most of the guests were invited by the parents.'[4] Although David was largely away from the public spotlight, there was some media interest in his marriage to Daphne, and a picture of their wedding appeared in the local press.

Life for the newlyweds was busy after the excitement of their summer wedding. Daphne enjoyed her legal work, and David was lecturing full time; in his spare time he was getting used to life as a UUP member. The new Mr and Mrs Trimble bought their first home, and that inevitably meant DIY jobs – which Daphne soon discovered was not David's forte:

> In our first house where he was putting up shelves, he had an electric drill. It was my father's electric drill because he [David] would not have had that many tools. And he drilled into an electric cable. There was a big flash and a bang. I don't think he ever used a drill after that. I was standing there watching it but I think we were just fortunate. He could have electrocuted himself.[5]

A major mishap was narrowly avoided and, according to Daphne, the end of her husband's DIY career probably could not have come soon enough.

If Trimble was a tad dangerous with power tools around the home, he was at least more than capable in the kitchen. He enjoyed cooking and, years later, when children arrived, making a family meal became a regular occurrence. Richard, the eldest of the four Trimble children, says his father loved being in the kitchen:

> Dad would do the cooking on a Saturday. Typically, what he loved to cook was carbonara. Spaghetti carbonara was one of his go-to dishes. And his other go-to dish for cooking would be roast lamb. And he was always a great believer in Bangor lamb. He said if you could find a butcher that would sell you Bangor lamb, it was going to be better. The Bangor lamb was always the best because the sheep were grazing apparently by the sea on the Ards Peninsula, so they were getting a saltier diet.[6]

Richard had been born in 1982 and his sister Vicky arrived in 1984. Nicholas (better known as Nicky), who would eventually follow his father into elected politics, was born in 1986, and six years later, in 1992, the youngest, Sarah, was born. Daphne and David had always wanted kids, but before the children arrived, they had already had some experience of what it was like to be parents, when they agreed to become the legal guardian of David's nephew – also called David.

The eight-year-old was the son of Iain, David's brother, and he was sent to board at Methodist College in Belfast while his dad was away serving with the RAF. Known simply as Methody, the grammar school was the largest in Northern Ireland and had a good academic reputation. It was David senior who recommended it to his brother, and in 1980, young David began boarding. Daphne and David effectively became his surrogate parents, and it gave the couple an introduction into what it was like having a child.

Young David saw his aunt and uncle at weekends, but on weekday nights, he was in the boarding school:

> Obviously, there was no Mum or Dad there to give you a hug or welcome you home from school. 'How did you get on?' and all that kind of stuff. So, I suppose in some ways David and Daphne were that to me.[7]

The Trimbles and young David quickly got into a routine. On Friday afternoons, either Daphne or David would pick him up from school, and he would then go and stay at the Trimble home for a couple of nights. He had his own room in their house, and on Saturday they might have a day out or simply play in the garden.

The next day, there would be a Sunday roast often cooked by David, and later young David would return to Methody. He recalls how his aunt and uncle lovingly looked after him in those early years:

> Daphne is a very affectionate person. I was asked about how I was doing, how was I getting on and what I was

getting up to. There were bits of advice they could give me as and when I needed it.⁸

Young David got on well with his uncle, who was emotionally different from Daphne and kept his feelings often under wraps:

> David was not, you know, overly touchy feely. I don't have memories of rolling around the floor playing rough and tumble and all that kind of stuff with David, but he was very humorous and obviously conversational.⁹

Daphne and David worked hard at fulfilling their official role of legal guardians. They wanted to give their young guest the best childhood they could, although young David remembers that, at times, they were not quite sure what to do:

> This was prior to Daphne and David having children themselves, so in some ways I think probably it was their first experience of a little child in their home. I think there was sometimes a little sense of 'What do we do with this little boy?' at some points, you know. And they introduced me to things. For example my first experience of classical music was through David and Daphne. David was a mad music lover, particularly classical music and opera. And he was a keen lover of a wide variety of music, particularly Elvis Presley, and I was introduced to Elvis by David.¹⁰

After joining the UUP in 1978, Trimble tried to seize opportunities that came his way. He was keen to resurrect his political career, and in 1979, a chance arose to run for Westminster. The party was looking for a candidate to stand in North Down, the constituency he grew up in and the seat where he had stood during the 1973 Assembly election. This was his home turf, but it would not be straightforward.

Jim Kilfedder had parted company from the Ulster Unionists, and was intending to run as an Independent. Well liked, with a strong support base, he was seen as the favourite. The Ulster Unionists needed a heavy hitter to take him on, and the party hierarchy knew this was a tall order. Trimble threw his hat in the ring, but he faced strong opposition from two other party members. Hazel Bradford, who lived locally and was well connected, put herself forward, as did Clifford Smyth, a former DUP member of the Convention who had switched to the UUP.

It was premature for Trimble to get selected. There was still some distrust of Vanguard members who had made the switch, and he had only been in the party for a year. Even though he knew the geography of the seat well and did have name recognition because of his Vanguard experience, he did not have enough support amongst members in the constituency. His support was not there, and he was pushed into third place during the selection process. Bradford came second, and Smyth won the nomination. On polling day, the UUP candidate was no match for the popular Kilfedder, who ended up with a stunning majority of 23,000 votes.

Trimble continued to apply for roles within the party. His ambition was no secret, but he kept suffering knockbacks. Chris McGimpsey, who would serve as a UUP officer and as a councillor on Belfast City Council, says Trimble started to get a reputation of being the 'nearly man' of the party:

> He always seemed to be looking to get on the officer team or get selected for Europe or selected for Westminster and he seemed to keep missing out. He was getting a reputation of being the fellow that never made it.[11]

There was further disappointment for Trimble in the 1979 general election. His friend and political mentor Bill Craig defended his Westminster seat in East Belfast but was beaten. It was one of the tightest electoral battles across Northern Ireland – a three-way fight between Craig, Peter Robinson (the DUP's full-time general secretary) and Oliver

Napier (the Alliance Party leader). They each polled just over 15,000 votes, with Robinson ultimately becoming the surprise winner by just 64 votes.

It was a spectacular coup for the DUP and meant the party ended up with three MPs – two gains from the UUP in Belfast, and Ian Paisley successfully defended North Antrim. The two losses to the DUP plus Kilfedder's victory in North Down saw the UUP dropping three seats. The result meant Harry West was living on borrowed time as party leader. If it was a disaster for the UUP leader, it was also heartbreaking for his party colleague, Craig. His political career was now over, in his own political heartland.

The election changed British politics forever with the arrival of Margaret Thatcher as prime minister. The first woman to hold the office, she arrived in Downing Street with a mandate to change the country and, for the next 11 years, she would dominate the UK's political landscape.

Even though he had failed to get on the ballot paper for the general election in 1979, Trimble had a front-row seat for the European election in June of that year. The UUP stood two candidates, West and John Taylor, the former home affairs minister. Taylor asked Trimble to be his election agent, and he embraced the job with much enthusiasm and vigour. He drew up a campaign plan and organised canvassing and leafletting teams. It was the first European election there had ever been in Northern Ireland, and there were three seats up for grabs. It was a massive operation, but by the time polling day arrived Taylor was relieved to have secured a seat.

Ian Paisley topped the poll, taking nearly 30 per cent of the vote, and the SDLP deputy leader, John Hume, was in second place. The UUP vote was split between West and Taylor, and after all the votes were counted and transfers had taken place, Taylor was well behind in third place. It was a triumph for the DUP and the SDLP, but it was another disappointing election for the UUP and represented more bad news for West.

It would be the last time West would run as UUP leader, and in July he resigned. West was replaced by Jim Molyneaux, who was MP for South Antrim and a member of the Royal Black Institution and the

Orange Order. Molyneaux had lobbied the Labour government for more Northern Ireland representation at Westminster and was an integrationist rather than a devolutionist.

Molyneaux was not a fan of power-sharing, believing that unionism was best served through the House of Commons. His arrival in the leader's office was bad news for Trimble. West had been a supporter of Trimble's, had recognised his ability and had encouraged him to apply for party positions. It soon became clear that Molyneaux's leadership was going to be very different from West's.

Trimble resigned himself to the fact that Molyneaux was not interested in arguing for greater authority for Stormont, nor would he campaign for power-sharing. Trimble set up the Devolution Group, which was formed to lobby within the party for an Assembly with devolved powers. He found several party members who agreed with his analysis, including David McNarry, who had joined the party as a teenager and had been a member of the Young Unionists:

> David came on the scene in his own style and in his own way. Which is probably what I liked about him most. He protected his shyness by only speaking when he actually had something to say and acknowledged that a lot of us were Young Unionists. We had all had the battles coming through. When he first began to speak – and to this day, I would fight for it – he talked about an identity, a devolution identity. Now, we are not going to have an identity through integration: we are only going to have our identity through devolution, through being Northern Irish. I'm not somebody who could say I am British and Irish; I could never say that. I am not too sure David could either; I never heard him. But I could always say I'm Northern Irish – and David launched that very quietly and sowed a seed in my head. And from then on, we went through as the Devolution Group; we were a thorn in Molyneaux's side.[12]

Another party colleague who shared Trimble's analysis about devolution was Edgar Graham, who, like Trimble, had qualified as a barrister and now taught law at Queen's. Graham and Trimble had offices close to each other at the Queen's campus, and as party members and law lecturers they had much in common. The two men would often spend time together in the staff room chatting about politics and what was in the news that day.

Ten years younger than Trimble, Graham was from Randalstown in County Antrim and had gone to Ballymena Academy. Regarded as an exceptional student, he studied at Queen's, then went to Oxford and finally back to Queen's, where he was now teaching. Articulate and hard-working with a forensic mind, he became chairman of the Young Unionists and was tipped as a future politician. Some even went further, suggesting he was a future party leader.

Called to the Northern Ireland Bar in 1980, Graham made legal submissions to the European Commission of Human Rights. He was interested in a political career and unsuccessfully sought nominations for Westminster but would eventually become an Assemblyman for South Belfast in 1982. With one of the sharpest legal minds in the UUP, he was an asset to the party and would often speak to the media about security issues. supported the use of the supergrass system in the courts and opposed demands from republican and loyalist prisoners for segregation in the Maze prison. This brought him to the attention of the paramilitaries and led to threats to his life.

In March 1980, a paper was presented to the UUC in the name of Bill Craig and others. It was entitled 'Towards the Better Government of Ulster'. It summed up the position of the Devolution Group and over nine pages argued that the party should endorse the introduction of 'a devolved parliament and government' for Northern Ireland.

The paper detailed how a new form of government could work at Stormont and examined minority participation. McNarry remembers that the document was presented in Craig's name, but had Trimble's fingerprints all over it:

> David wrote that paper and that was David putting down a stamp. He was using Bill Craig. And not in the sense of using anybody, but he needed a name, bigger than his. And the three of us put it together, but David wrote it. And that was it. And that really was him getting noticed in the Ulster Unionist Party.[13]

At this stage Trimble was quite the prolific writer and did not just concentrate on academic essays or internal documents for the UUP. For some time, using a pseudonym, he had been commenting on political events in the current affairs magazine *Fortnight*. The publication itself was an interesting choice for Trimble, and he enjoyed writing for it. A left-of-centre magazine which chronicled political developments in Northern Ireland, it began publishing in 1970. Contributors included journalists, academics, writers, poets, cartoonists and politicians.

Tom Hadden, who commissioned the articles, was one of Trimble's colleagues at the Law Department at Queen's. Another key figure in the department was Sylvia Paisley, no relation to the DUP leader, who had joined the university in 1978. She had finished her degree the previous year at Aberystwyth University and was considering doing a PhD at Cambridge University in European law when a vacancy arose in Queen's to be a law lecturer. She recalls her first encounter with Trimble, when she came to be interviewed for the job at Queen's. He was sitting on the interview panel and asked her if there were any subjects she was not prepared to teach:

> I said, 'Oh yes, equity and land law', and he immediately came back and asked why wouldn't I be prepared to teach equity and land law? And I said with complete boldness and honesty, 'Because they are so dull and so boring I would absolutely hate to have to teach those.' And little did I know that these were actually David Trimble's pet subjects, his favourite subjects, the ones that he taught were land law and equity. And instead of being offended

or giving me a scolding or arguing with me, he chuckled. When David was in really good form he enjoyed a joke. And he did have a good sense of humour, as it turned out. It was not exactly a guffaw, but his shoulders would actually shake, and he was really enjoying the moment. Of course, all the other people on the interview panel knew it was David Trimble, and they knew they were his subjects, and they joined in because he set the tone. It was laughter, it was relaxed. It was a wonderful response, and he didn't feel insulted, and I've always remembered that it was such a wonderful introduction to David Trimble.[14]

Sylvia Paisley's critical comments about land law and equity did her no harm at all. She was an impressive candidate and got the job and joined the Law Faculty. She would later marry the then RUC chief constable, Sir Jack Hermon, and as Lady Hermon would be best known for her role as MP for North Down. Her friendship with Trimble would last for decades and she became an important ally and friend during his time as leader and first minister.

In the early 1980s, Trimble's inability to land a role within the party continued, and he found party membership frustrating during Molyneaux's early years as leader. By 1981, Trimble was living in Lisburn and was interested in becoming a councillor. The Trimbles chose the area because it made geographical sense: Daphne was working in Banbridge and David was in Belfast, and Lisburn seemed the most central place to live.

Trimble hoped a successful election in Lisburn would be the first step in his political career with the UUP and an opportunity to begin to build a power base. He was ambitious and knew that an elected office would open doors for him. But his foray into the politics of local government was short-lived, and he failed to get elected. While Trimble struggled to make inroads with the party, Edgar Graham was seen as a rising star. He would move from the chairmanship of the Young Unionists to being an honorary secretary of the party and ultimately end up as a high-profile politician at Stormont.

In contrast, Trimble's political career was going nowhere. The council elections that saw him lose out on a seat were held in an atmosphere dominated by the IRA hunger strikes. The DUP saw its vote rise and the UUP vote went down. Sinn Féin was also making gains and Danny Morrison told the party's Ard Fheis, 'Who really believes we can win the war through the ballot box? But will anyone here object if, with a ballot paper in one hand and the Armalite in the other we take power in Ireland?'[15]

Violent events on the ground still dominated the political narrative, and in November 1981 an Ulster Unionist MP, the Reverend Robert Bradford, was shot dead at a community centre in Finaghy in Belfast. The politician was murdered alongside Kenneth Campbell, who was the caretaker of the complex where the MP was holding a constituency surgery. The killers, who were dressed in overalls, forced Campbell to his knees before opening fire. They then burst into an office and shot the MP. The murders were a brutal reminder that the IRA viewed political figures who challenged their viewpoint as 'legitimate targets'. It was also another painful warning to those in public life – that politics in Northern Ireland came with a huge personal cost, and soon Trimble would witness that at first hand.

8

MURDER IN THE MORNING

*'The person I saw coming towards me was Dermot,
who was saying Edgar had just been shot.'*
David Trimble on the murder of his friend Edgar Graham

On a December morning in 1983, Dermot Nesbitt was walking along the footpath close to Queen's University. A familiar face around the campus, he was on his way to the Accountancy Department, where he had been a lecturer since 1974. It was a cold, crisp winter's day, and the street was busy with students and staff making their way to and from classes.

Like David Trimble and Edgar Graham, Nesbitt was a member of the UUP. Viewed as a moderate, he was from South Down, where he had been Brian Faulkner's election agent. He shared his former leader's politics and had been a strong supporter of the 1974 power-sharing Executive. Unlike Trimble and Graham, Nesbitt was on the integrationist wing of the party and was not convinced by their arguments for devolution.

As Nesbitt walked along University Square, he spotted Graham. They were friends and would often stop for a chat or have a coffee together. They always had much to discuss. They were both elected representatives – Graham was in the Assembly and Nesbitt was a councillor – and they would talk about party business or just discuss what was in the news.

Graham had parked his car and been to the newsagents to pick up the newspapers and had gone to the postbox to post his Christmas cards. As he spotted his friend, he waved and then crossed the street. Nesbitt recalls what happened next:

> I remember my first words with Edgar, I was walking up from Botanic Avenue ... Edgar was coming down the other side to go to the Law Faculty and he crossed over to talk to me. And I said, 'You have crossed to my side', and he smiled because he knew what I meant. He was a devolutionist, and I was an integrationist.[1]

Graham set his briefcase down and the two men stood on the pavement and chatted. Graham told his colleague that he was about to go and see MPs from the Northern Ireland Affairs select committee. Nesbitt remarked that he was aware that John Biggs-Davidson, the Conservative chairman of the committee, happened to be an integrationist. Graham replied that Michael Mates, who was the vice-chairman, happened to be a devolutionist. Those were Edgar Graham's last words. At that moment, gunmen approached him from behind, opened fire and killed him.

To mark the 40th anniversary of the murder in December 2023, Dermot Nesbitt went back to the scene for the first time. On the spot where the shooting took place, he spoke to *Belfast Telegraph* journalist Sam McBride. He later gave this account of the moment of when the gunmen appeared:

> All of a sudden, I heard a shot, and he fell. I get covered in his blood which I learnt a little minute or two later. I naturally went back like that. And this person stood up on that wall with one foot on it, pumping the gun into him and I just – it was one of these things ... you know I can remember it like yesterday. And then I moved out to the road, and as I did that this fellow put his gun in what was a lever arch file with another colleague and ran off that way through where the music and the library was; it is not a library now. Probably, once he got round the corner they would have started to walk like students because they looked like students; they were dressed like students; they fitted in with the environment. But it just happened so quick, so quick.[2]

Law lecturer Judith Eve was teaching students in a room which looked out into the street. Four decades on, she can vividly recall what happened that December morning:

> I heard the gunshot, and I knew what it was. We all knew what gunshots were. I heard it. I heard the gunshot, and I ran to the window and looked out and I saw the gunman standing with the body on the ground. He had his arm still out and there was a body on the ground, and I said to the students, 'There's a guy out there with a gun', and I was afraid he might turn around and just fire off rounds.[3]

Herb Wallace was across the street in a ground-floor area where lecturers went most mornings to sit and have a tea break before or after tutorials and lectures. He was pouring a cup of coffee when the shooting began and initially thought the banging sounds indicated somebody was trying to get into his building:

> They were old Georgian houses. They had door knockers, and I thought this was somebody who was knocking on the door wanting in. And I was just wondering should I bother and go and see when David ran past me out into the street, and he said they've shot Edgar, and he was obviously distressed.[4]

Nesbitt could see students and university staff across the road looking out of the windows. He recalls how they were silhouetted against the lights, and he remembers how they reminded him of the matchstick figures that the English painter L.S. Lowry famously created. He then ran over to the Law Faculty and met Trimble.

> I remember vividly going across to the door and David Trimble opened the door. And I said it's Edgar. He said,

'He shouldn't have been here today'. Those were his very words: he shouldn't have been here today.[5]

Trimble remembered meeting Nesbitt:

> When I heard the shots and went to the door of the Faculty of Law, I came out and the person I saw coming towards me was Dermot, who was saying Edgar had just been shot. And Dermot had Edgar's blood on him and a short time later the police, when they arrived, asked me to … formally [identify] the body.[6]

Edgar Graham was not expected on campus that day. He had been due to give a lecture on European Economic Community law but had swapped duties with Sylvia Hermon, who was standing in for him. It was coming to the end of term, and she was addressing students in a first-floor lecture room across the road from where the shooting happened:

> I heard what sounded like nails being hammered into a tin roof. I immediately glanced out the window and I had a clear view of a man in a long brown coat falling down behind the car … I didn't recognise who this was immediately, but I stopped the lecture. I explained very quickly that I was a St John's Ambulance first-aider and if everyone would just keep their places, as someone had collapsed in the street. I felt duty bound to go as an ambulance first-aider and told them to please wait and I'll come back up. I ran down the stairs and across the street. It was immediately obvious that it was Edgar. It was immediately obvious that there was no first-aid that I could administer to Edgar that would have saved his life. It was very traumatic. It was absolutely ghastly and somehow, I don't even remember how, I managed to stagger back across the road. I do remember the students coming down very

upset, coming out of the building terribly, terribly distressed and upset and some putting their arms around me and trying to comfort me, but there was no comfort to be had. It was just horrible, a horrible experience, and it was a horrible day.[7]

Medical staff arrived at the university but there was nothing they could do. Graham died at the scene. The IRA issued a statement after the shooting saying that the killing should be 'a salutary lesson to those loyalists who stand foursquare behind the laws and forces of oppression of the nationalist people'.[8] Graham's killers were never caught, although two people were later convicted of withholding evidence from the police.

The planning and location of Graham's murder are worth examining. The IRA could have attacked him in a variety of locations – at home or en route to Belfast. They could have come to his house in the early morning or at night but chose to kill him at Queen's, where his attackers escaped easily and blended in with passing students. It was the easiest location for the killers to escape from.

The shooting sent shockwaves across the political establishment, and parallels were made with the murder of the Ulster Unionist MP Robert Bradford back in 1981. However, the killing was also a warning to other unionist-minded lecturers on campus, notably Nesbitt and Trimble. It is clear that Graham's death had a profound effect on both men. Staff at Queen's were angry and deeply shocked, and there was an understandable degree of fear. Trimble recalls coming into the university 24 hours after the murder:

> I remember the next day when I was coming in turning the corner into University Square and it was in University Square where Edgar was murdered. It really took an effort to get myself to walk around the corner and walk up the street. I was surprised actually at how much effort it took to walk in as though nothing had happened.[9]

Edgar Graham's funeral took place in Randalstown, and expressions of sympathy came to his family from all over the world. His death was raised in the House of Commons and there were numerous tributes to his legal and political work. Many saw the killing of an elected politician as an attack on democracy itself.

In time a memorial stone was erected at Stormont, where he had served as the representative for South Belfast. It simply stated 'In memory of Edgar Samuel David Graham. Assembly Member for Belfast South 1982–83. Shot by terrorists on 7 December 1983. Keep alive the light of justice.'

Judith Eve says that, in the aftermath of his murder, she and Trimble discussed the risks politicians in Northern Ireland took with their personal lives:

> We talked a bit about the dangers of it, but I mean I was quite amazed at him. I think I hadn't thought about the risk that politicians were taking until that particular event. And it being a colleague brought it home to us, it really did.[10]

Some within the Law Faculty genuinely feared for Trimble's safety and thought, after Graham's murder, he would be next. The killing of his friend and colleague gave him much to consider. Should he continue with his political activity, or was it now time to concentrate on his work at Queen's? Were the personal risks associated with being a public figure simply too much, and should he now step back from his UUP activities?

Trimble did not have the profile of Graham and was not elected, but his party membership was no secret, and neither was his past association with Vanguard. Unlike Graham's, Trimble's political career had stalled, and after five years of party membership and several attempts to get elected, he had failed to secure any office of note. All this was a consideration as he took stock of his life and career. He was also now a father, and he had family responsibilities. Politics was fun and interesting, but his family and his job came first:

> My political career between 1977 and 1980 was something that simply wasn't there. I sort of thought, 'I have had my go at that, and I have done something, it was worth it'. The business of settling down, married, starting a family, pursuing my career as a legal academic, those things were at the front of my mind at that stage, and my political activity at that time was very limited.[11]

Trimble did not turn his back completely on his party at this stage, but it is clear he was putting most of his time into family and work. His political roles were minimal, though he did get involved when opportunities presented themselves. In the summer of 1984, John Taylor asked him once again to be his election agent as he ran for the European Parliament. Trimble had managed Taylor's campaign at the previous poll in 1979, and this time, the result was no different, but there were some interesting trends. The DUP leader, Ian Paisley, topped the poll, was elected on the first count and secured a third of all the votes cast. It was an astonishing result for the DUP and reinforced the view that Paisley had appeal across Northern Ireland. The UUP wisely only ran one candidate – the previous time they ran two – and Taylor was elected on the second count. John Hume took the third and final seat.

For much of 1984, politics in Northern Ireland remained stagnant – and violence dominated the news agenda. The IRA bombed the Grand Hotel in Brighton during the Conservative Party conference in an attempt to kill members of the cabinet. Prime Minister Margaret Thatcher narrowly escaped. She had been in her bathroom minutes before it was wrecked by the blast, which killed five people and injured dozens. It was a dramatic and brutal attack by the IRA, who had come within seconds of killing the prime minister.

Thatcher had much to consider. Northern Ireland had been high on her agenda in recent months and was taking up much of her time. Behind the scenes her officials had been considering the conclusions of the New Ireland Forum – a body made up of Fianna Fáil, Fine Gael, the Irish Labour Party and the SDLP. The forum had come together to establish an agreed approach to Northern Ireland. Largely the brainchild of the SDLP's John Hume, the forum's first preference was a 32-county united Ireland, but the group did put forward other options.

In November 1984 the British and Irish governments came together for a summit in Chequers, the prime minister's country retreat. It was a chance for Taoiseach Garret FitzGerald and Prime Minister Margaret Thatcher to take stock of Anglo-Irish relations. It gave Thatcher the opportunity to respond to the conclusions of the forum's report, which had been published in May of that year. She was forthright and characteristically blunt:

> A united Ireland was one solution. That is out. A second solution was confederation of the two states. That is out. A third solution was joint authority. That is out. That is derogation from sovereignty.[12]

The remarks by the prime minister went down badly with Dublin. The taoiseach felt Thatcher had not given the New Ireland Forum's report the consideration it deserved and described her comments as 'gratuitously offensive'. On the face of it, it seemed Anglo-Irish relations had reached rock bottom but, in the months ahead, contacts between London and Dublin would develop well and would result in the Anglo-Irish Agreement of November 1985.

But that was a year away. The landscape of November 1984 seemed very different. The UUP leader, Jim Molyneaux, was clearly delighted with Thatcher's 'out, out, out' comments, believing that the unionist position was safe in her hands. Others in the party hierarchy seemed pleased that the prime minister had, in their view, rejected any change in Northern Ireland's status. They believed that the union was safe, and that Dublin had been told to back off.

Trimble, on the other hand, was sceptical and sensed that something was going on in the background. He felt that, behind the headlines, some kind of London–Dublin arrangement was going to emerge and that unionists needed to be prepared. He argued in party meetings that this was not the time for smug complacency.

In late 1984, Trimble became aware that the two governments were planning a raft of measures aimed at undermining the growth of Sinn Féin. One initiative would centre on the promotion of Irish culture in Northern Ireland. It would show that the British and Irish governments acknowledged that there were many people living in Northern Ireland who valued their Irish heritage and Irish identity. The nod towards recognising 'Irishness' was also an attempt to try to woo centre-ground nationalists who might be tempted to drift away from the SDLP and support Sinn Féin.

Trimble believed financial support would be made available to promote and encourage, amongst other things, the Irish language, Gaelic games and Irish traditional music. He saw a culture war as the next battleground, and he felt unionists needed to be prepared and organised. He set up the Ulster Society, which aimed to examine and promote a pro-British identity in Northern Ireland through talks and events and publications. Trimble wanted the society to give those of a unionist background a greater understanding of their sense of place.

The Ulster Society was launched at Brownlow House in Lurgan, which had been the headquarters of the 16th Battalion of the Royal Irish Rifles and the 10th Battalion Royal Irish Fusiliers during the First World War. Trimble became chairman of the society and Gordon Lucy, a young unionist from County Fermanagh, was secretary. Lucy was aware of Trimble from his television appearances and his previous role in Vanguard.

In fact, it was while Trimble was a representative with Vanguard that Lucy first met him. He visited Stormont back in 1975 and met up with his local Convention member Ernest Baird. While he was there, he encountered Trimble, and he remembers him 'speaking impressively'.[13] A graduate of Queen's, Lucy shared Trimble's analysis when it came to promoting and understanding the unionist viewpoint:

> The subtitle was to promote Ulster British heritage and culture. To some extent, even in the early 1980s, we felt

> that ... the Ulster British culture, the culture of that community as it were, was getting a raw deal. And the idea was to examine and promote it and produce publications about it.[14]

For Lucy it marked the start of his association and long friendship with Trimble. He was one of a number of young unionists who would help to play a key role when Trimble stood for the party leadership nearly a decade later. The Ulster Society gave Trimble the opportunity to indulge in one of his great loves, the study of history, and he wrote a number of historical pamphlets.

In 1991, Trimble published a booklet on the foundation of Northern Ireland in 1921, and the next year he published another on the Easter Rising of 1916, simply entitled *The Easter Rebellion of 1916*. In it he attempted to challenge some of the myths of the coup and argued that it had actually led to partition and the Irish Civil War of the 1920s. The 1991 publication that Trimble penned was closer to home and gave him an opportunity to focus on his political hero, Sir James Craig, the first prime minister of Northern Ireland. The short booklet, entitled *The Foundation of Northern Ireland*, mapped out how the six counties in the northeast corner of Ireland became modern-day Northern Ireland. Trimble presented his hero as a politician prepared to do business with his rivals – a unionist who, despite criticism from his side, was prepared to engage with nationalism. This was a situation Trimble would ultimately become very familiar with.

In his publication Trimble detailed how Craig had held talks first with the IRA leader Michael Collins and then with Éamon de Valera, who would become taoiseach. Trimble outlined the difficulties Craig encountered establishing Northern Ireland in the 1920s and showed that setting up a new administration was hard – as he would encounter in 1998, albeit under very different circumstances.

What Trimble tried to present was that Craig was a unionist worth celebrating and commemorating. He portrayed him as pragmatic and principled. There are obvious and rather uncanny parallels between the political lives of Craig and Trimble. They both walked a difficult path, faced similar dilemmas and had to make hard choices. Both men were leaders of unionism and became the leading minister in Northern Ireland. Both made peace with their political rivals and had to compromise.

Craig was the figure that Trimble would often refer to when he was making historical comparisons. In October 1998, six months after the Good Friday Agreement was negotiated, he was invited to speak at the Young Unionist conference. Trimble was first minister, and there was much still to be organised and agreed before power-sharing and the process of governing could begin. Decommissioning had not begun, and many sceptics and observers were concerned that the paramilitaries were not serious about destroying their weapons:

> The actions of James Craig were controversial at the time within the party just as current actions are also controversial within the party. James Craig knew that he had to respond to the events not in terms of what he'd like to see but in terms of what events actually were and the response that he brought did involve a genuine serious engagement with reality. We have taken some risks, but Craig took much more. He could do so because he had bags of confidence in himself and in the movement of which he was head. I would love to see a modern vigorous self-reliant self-confident unionism.[15]

Back in the summer of 1985, unionism was wracked with self-doubt as the rumour mill was suggesting that an Anglo-Irish Agreement was imminent, and it would anger and inflame unionists. All was revealed on Friday 15 November 1985, when Thatcher and FitzGerald finally declared the new Anglo-Irish Agreement at Hillsborough Castle in County Down.

The aims of the accord were to promote peace and political stability and create a new atmosphere that would defeat paramilitary violence. It set up a joint ministerial conference of Irish and British ministers backed by a permanent secretariat that would be based at Maryfield outside Belfast. This new unit would be home to Irish civil servants. For the first time, it gave an Irish administration a consultative role in the running of Northern Ireland. It was not joint authority, nor did it amount to the Republic having executive power, as some had predicted. What it would mean in practical terms was that grievances from the nationalist community relating to policing or discrimination could be raised quickly at government level. On the issue of Northern Ireland's constitutional future, the agreement stated that change would only come about with the consent of the majority of its people.

As ever, political reaction from the local parties was mixed and predictable. Nationalists generally welcomed the news, but unionists were very angry and hurt and felt deeply betrayed by London. Within days, they took to the streets.

9

THE WILDERNESS YEARS

*'There were some people who voted on the basis of
"anybody but Trimble".'*
Herb Wallace on Trimble's failure to be elected
dean of the Law Faculty at Queen's University

Belfast city centre came to a standstill as unionists in their thousands formed a gigantic ring around City Hall. On a crisp November day in 1985, the crowd jammed roads and pavements and shop doorways. It was a sight to behold. Some observers thought there were 100,000 protesters on the streets; others suggested the figure was twice that number. This was a slice of Northern Ireland's majority community, who were anxious, fired up and determined to be heard – a display of opposition across the unionist family. Farmers and factory workers stood shoulder to shoulder as uniformed bandsmen played loyalist tunes. Some carried homemade placards denouncing Margaret Thatcher; others held up banners or waved Union flags.

A number marched in their military fatigues with a scent of malice, yet all had come to register their anger. In front of them, on the makeshift stage, stood their leaders, who condemned the prime minister for what she had done. Ulster had, in their eyes, been sold to a foreign state. Standing alongside his UUP rival Jim Molyneaux, this was Ian Paisley's moment, and he stole the show. Wearing his 'Ulster Says No' badge, the DUP leader was ready to deliver the line of the day:

> Where do the terrorists return to for sanctuary? To
> the Irish Republic. And yet Mrs Thatcher tells us that

the Republic must have some say in our province. We say never, never, never, never.[1]

Unionism was in a state of flux. What should they do? How could they make Thatcher reconsider? As part of their protest, unionist MPs stood by their pledge to resign, and in January 1986 a series of by-elections was held across Northern Ireland. It did not go according to plan, and the UUP's Jim Nicholson lost his seat to the SDLP deputy leader, Seamus Mallon. The by-election tactic by unionists was an attempt to effectively hold a Northern Ireland-wide referendum on the London–Dublin deal.

Back in February 1974, after Sunningdale, there had been a general election that effectively became a poll on the deal. The results went the way of the UUUC – the coalition of unionists opposed to power-sharing. Trimble, like other unionists, thought history could repeat itself:

> The February 1974 elections had been a tremendous boost for the campaign against Sunningdale, and it was an attempt to reproduce that. Inside Northern Ireland, I think they were a success, because people in Northern Ireland thought of them as a referendum and looked at the votes. The effect in London I think was muted because people in London are not accustomed in terms of votes and percentages; they think in terms of seats and they say, 'Ah, you lost a seat'.[2]

From a unionist perspective the by-election strategy looked like a political and public relations disaster. The campaign then moved to the next stage and a 'Day of Action' was called. Jim Molyneaux and Ian Paisley both made it clear that the protests must be dignified and non-violent. Their calls were ignored, and the day of protest held on Monday 3 March was marred by violence, with looting and rioting. At one stage, the RUC was fired on by loyalist paramilitaries, and youths stoned shops and offices in Belfast city centre.

The stoppages and the disruption on the streets did little to change minds at Westminster. Politically, it failed to make an impact, and to many it seemed that the agreement was here to stay. The British government were digging in and Secretary of State Tom King sent extra troops into Northern Ireland as tensions continued. There were calls in some quarters of the unionist community for more strikes, but the violence on the streets was making some unionists very uneasy.

Molyneaux, the UUP leader, made it clear that after the disturbances in March he could not support future strike action. Trimble, no fan of Molyneaux's style of leadership, felt his leader was making a tactical mistake. He wanted his party to take a radical approach in opposing the agreement and was attracted to a new group that had been set up before the Anglo-Irish deal was signed.

The Ulster Clubs had originally been established to oppose the rerouting of Orange parades, but then they became better known for their opposition to the Anglo-Irish Agreement. Based loosely on the unionist clubs set up in 1912 at the time of the Home Rule Crisis, their objective was to attack the deal signed by the two governments back in November 1985. The group also aimed to promote and protect the union and to oppose nationalism. It was a broad-based coalition of unionists from different parties and its membership included loyalist paramilitaries.

Trimble felt at home with the new group and joined the Lisburn branch of the Ulster Clubs. Philip Black, who would go on to serve as the Ulster Clubs general secretary, remembers working with Trimble. He says he came across as aloof but highly intelligent, with political nous:

> Unionists are not always noted for that sort of thing, so he stood out even more. I got the impression that he was highly intelligent but perhaps a bit out of touch with the ordinary people because he was so intelligent. I mean I could imagine Paisley going into a cafe and sitting down and talking to everybody, but I could never imagine David Trimble doing that.[3]

As their membership included members of loyalist paramilitaries, the Ulster Clubs got a reputation for being militant and extreme. Even though paramilitaries were active in the group, those behind the organisation insisted it was a lawful body. Within months the group claimed to have nearly 50 branches across Northern Ireland and suggested that they had a membership of some 8,000. Ulster Clubs representatives routinely claimed that unionists had been discriminated against and that nationalist parties had been given political concessions.

The group called for civil disobedience, and its strong public statements about taking direct action cemented its reputation for being a body prepared to flout the law when necessary. Trimble believed radical measures were necessary and did not think parliamentary opposition was enough. The Ulster Clubs presented Trimble with a more radical vehicle with which to fight the Anglo-Irish Agreement. However, to some observers, the presence of Trimble, a Queen's University academic, in the Ulster Clubs seemed unusual. Was he giving this body an air of respectability? Why was a prominent law lecturer associating himself with a group that had loyalist paramilitaries in its ranks?

Denis Murray, who was a BBC journalist at the time, remembers a conversation with Trimble:

> I went up to interview David Trimble about this fairly arcane and dry matter and I went into his office up in the Law Department at Queen's. And I found him wearing an Ulster Clubs badge in his jacket lapel, which made me sort of go, 'What?' Why was a very respectable mainstream Ulster unionist, the party of restraint and smart suits, wearing this? This wasn't some mad loyalist type. So, we did the interview and at the end of it I said to him, 'What the hell are you doing wearing a loyalist clubs' badge?' And he said, 'Oh, you've got to get Valium into the situation.' And that sort of informed my opinion of him.[4]

So, what did Trimble mean about getting 'Valium into the situation'? Murray thinks the academic felt he could be a calming influence:

> I think he had this view of himself as somebody who could, not exactly ride the tide, but he was somebody who, if he was in a position of influence, could say, 'There's a smarter way to do this. And there's an easier, more peaceful way, if you think about it.'[5]

Was that how Trimble saw himself in the Ulster Clubs? Was he there as a voice of moderation? How did the prospect of violence and the role of paramilitaries in the anti-agreement campaign sit with him? He appears to accept that a certain level of violence was part of the package:

> Do you sit back and do nothing or move outside constitutional forms of protest? I don't think you can deal with the situation without the risk of an extra[-]parliamentary campaign. I would personally draw the line at terrorism and serious violence but if we were talking about a campaign that involves demonstrations and so on then a certain amount of violence may be inescapable.[6]

Trimble was categorically saying he did not support terrorist activities but insisted that violence might end up being attached to the protest campaign. He understood why violence might happen and was experienced enough to know that, if you bring hundreds of people out onto the streets, disorder can often follow. He had previous experience of being in the company of loyalist paramilitaries, notably during the Ulster Workers' Council strike of 1974. He disagreed with their methods, but he understood their political arguments.

As the campaign of opposition to the Anglo-Irish Agreement continued, Trimble remained keen on disrupting the machinery of government. He believed unionist politicians should support protests that were outside of the law, provided they were non-violent. He advocated the withholding of rates payments and in May 1986, with other protesters, he occupied a local rates office and encouraged householders to delay settling their bills.

By this point, his outside activities were well known to the university authorities, and many at Queen's were not enamoured with his behaviour. Judith Eve, his friend and colleague in the Law Faculty, was conscious that opinion was divided over Trimble's political stance:

> There was quite a bit of disquiet within the faculty. Everybody liked David as a person, but there were some colleagues who disagreed vehemently with his politics. And we had some people who'd be fairly republican in the faculty.[7]

In 1986, an opportunity arose on campus that looked like it would give Trimble an opportunity to advance his academic career. The position of dean of the Law Faculty became vacant. Normally the deanship moved in rotation but in an unusual move an election was to take place amongst staff to fill the post. At this stage, Trimble was a very experienced senior lecturer, and it initially looked like he would take the position. Then matters became complicated.

Eve was approached by senior figures at Queen's to put her name forward:

> Law was a very respected profession, a respected faculty, and had all these links into the Bar, into government and into the solicitor's profession. And they just thought it was the wrong image of the Law Faculty to have someone with such a political background.[8]

Eve considered the request carefully. She and David were good friends, and she liked him enormously. She was unsure about running against a pal and colleague and spent much time agonising over whether she should put her name forward. Then, in a surprise twist, she was visited by Trimble, who knew that she had been approached to run for the post. He told Eve that she must be a candidate for the position, as she recalled:

> He said the dean should have the support of colleagues, and ... he said, 'Why don't we both get nominated and we'll see what our colleagues think?' Because of the election there were people who said they didn't want David because of his allegiances. And there were other people whose view was that he was head of the department so he was next in turn, and he should be there. So, the only reason I let myself go forward was because David had encouraged me, which was a big step for him.[9]

Trimble's decision to encourage Eve to run for the post of dean is worth considering. Why did he encourage her to stand? It was a quite remarkable reaction and gives an insight into Trimble's character. Some of his colleagues may have expected him to discourage his friend from entering the race on the basis that he felt the position was his and that Eve was an unnecessary rival. He was more experienced than her, and, on paper, he was the leading candidate. He understood what was happening in the background and was supportive of his friend.

In other circumstances this conflict of career versus friendship could have ended a close relationship, but Trimble's encouragement strengthened their bond, and Eve viewed his actions as honourable. Trimble wanted his friend to run, and he also wanted his colleagues to have a choice. Without Trimble's intervention it is unlikely that she would have put her name her forward.

So, the campaign began in earnest and, unofficially, Herb Wallace set about organising Trimble's supporters:

> David had been around the faculty for a long time by that stage. He was a very competent head of department; he was my head of department. He was head of department

of property law. And I thought, and some people who were close to me thought, he was a shoo-in. There was no difficulty. I can't remember what the size of the electorate was at the time – around about 30 or something like that. And they were all people that we knew. We used to sit with pieces of paper and say, 'I think we can rely on him or her, but you know they'll never support you.'[10]

As the rather sedate and quiet campaign trundled along in the corridors at Queen's, Trimble continued with his visible protests against the Anglo-Irish Agreement with the Ulster Clubs – activities that did not go unnoticed in the staffroom as his colleagues in the Law Faculty considered how to vote.

Away from the campus, Trimble's double life continued. When loyalists decided to go to Hillsborough Castle, where the secretary of state lived, Trimble took a leading role. The event was billed as a 'suffragette'-style protest, and, looking smart in a suit and tie, Trimble joined other demonstrators and chained himself to the railings of the castle. The demonstration, attended by about 50 loyalists, was planned to coincide with the arrival of the Irish foreign minister, Peter Barry, at an event in Northern Ireland.

The press had been primed to be at the gates of Hillsborough Castle, and naturally the chaining at the railings caught the eye of the photographers. It was a stunt by Trimble and his loyalist friends. They all knew the media would love it and it would make headlines.

Sylvia Hermon remembers the incident well and recalls Herb Wallace coming to see her when the story appeared in the press:

> He said, 'Have you seen this, have you seen this?' He threw down a copy of the *News Letter* [a unionist-supporting newspaper] and on the front page ... was a photograph, as I recall, of David Trimble chained to the gates of Hillsborough Castle. And Herb was absolutely shocked. I mean he was very angry, very upset. And he said, 'Read

the caption, read the caption', so underneath it didn't say, 'Senior Lecturer Queen's University, Belfast'. Again, to the best of my recollection, it read 'David Trimble, Chairman of the Ulster Clubs Lisburn branch', and there he was.[11]

If some of Trimble's Queen's colleagues had been wavering in their support for him, the Hillsborough Castle photograph may well have pushed support in Judith Eve's direction. Certainly, Trimble's 'suffragette' stunt did not help his chances of winning. As the campaign for the dean of the Law Faculty entered its final days, it seemed that the staff were split roughly 50:50 on who to support. The feeling was that the vote between Trimble and Eve would be very close. Trimble knew he was in a fight to win the position and sensed that his former student had a good chance of beating him. He knew this could change his outlook and confided in Wallace that, if he was successful, he would 'give up politics and concentrate on academia'.[12]

The hierarchy at Queen's were keen that all those eligible to vote did so – so the result reflected the true feelings of staff. Hermon remembers the day of the vote. She had not voted and had left the university and gone home to County Tyrone because she was unwell with shingles. It was the days before mobile phones, and while she was resting, the house telephone rang and her father answered the call:

> He popped his head into the kitchen and said, 'This is for you, it's from Queen's.' Daddy tried to explain to the caller that in fact I wasn't at all well. But they were not having any of that. And I had to get back into the car. I had learned to drive by that stage, and I had to go back down to Belfast, and I had to cast a vote.[13]

After the voting closed, the candidates were called by the faculty secretary and came to see the ballot box being opened and watch as the votes were counted. Eve remembers standing beside Trimble as the box was emptied and the votes were put into three piles – her votes, David's and abstentions. As anticipated, the result was very close: with 35 members of staff voting, 18 backed Eve and 16 supported Trimble, with one person abstaining.

Eve remembers what happened next:

> I got it just by a whisker, which didn't make it any easier, I have to say, whenever I took over. But David, gracious as ever, said, 'Right, Judith, our colleagues have voted, you are elected. I'll give you my full support.' And he did. It got talked about a lot around the university, because there hadn't been a contested election before. I got criticised by people and I got applauded by people, but anyway David was totally objective and supportive about the whole thing.[14]

It was a big setback for Trimble, as it was a post he was well qualified for and had privately thought he would get. Wallace says there was a clear move to stop him getting the post: 'It was partly because there were some people who voted on the basis of anybody but Trimble.'[15] It was bitterly disappointing for him, but he felt there would be other opportunities at Queen's in the coming months. He was keen and ambitious but felt he was still young enough to progress up the academic ladder.

He was right to predict that there would be other opportunities, as some months afterwards another job appeared on the horizon which he was excited by. The Institute for Professional Legal Studies advertised for a director, and the position looked like a good fit for Trimble. The institute was part of the university but had links with the bodies that controlled the legal profession in Northern Ireland: the Law Society and the Honourable Society of the Inn of Court of Northern Ireland. It was set up to provide a one-year postgraduate course for trainee solicitors and trainee barristers.

On paper, Trimble had the perfect CV, and he applied in the hope that this time his luck would be in. He was currently acting director, so he hoped that would hold him in good stead. The post also attracted the interest of Mary McAleese, Trimble's former student, who was now a professor of criminal law at Trinity College in Dublin. McAleese had established a good reputation as a talented academic, and she, like Trimble, liked the sound of the job, so she applied.

Trimble and McAleese faced tough questions from a 10-strong panel made up of distinguished figures from Northern Ireland's legal fraternity. McAleese performed very well and got the job. For Trimble it was another setback, and it was particularly painful as once again he lost out to a former student.

McAleese was delighted to return to her alma mater and understood Trimble's disappointment:

> He was in post at that time as acting director. So clearly he was entitled to be very upset that a former pupil of his had got the job over and above him. And now I can understand that disappointment must have been dreadful. I never met him over that time. It was some time before I figured out what had happened.[16]

McAleese did not know during the recruitment process that Trimble was a rival candidate. She only became aware of his interest in the position after she had accepted the role. Trimble was devastated and began to think that his academic career had stalled, and that he was never going to get another better-paid position. Others were taken aback by his rejection, and some in the UUP felt that he had been poorly treated by the university.

The reality was that McAleese had been the best candidate in front of the interviewing panel, but that did not stop unionist politicians raising the issue. Questions were asked in the House of Commons by unionist MPs about the appointment, much to the annoyance of Queen's. The questions angered the university's hierarchy, and McAleese took legal action against a number of publications.

Eventually, the stories went away, and McAleese began to carry out her work in the institute and Trimble continued with his job, lecturing and organising tutorials. Trimble also threw himself back into political work and continued to attend protests against the Anglo-Irish Agreement. His activities had attracted the interest of the police, and he was charged with illegal parading and obstruction after an Ulster Clubs protest. He maintained a public profile, and the *News Letter* did a wide-ranging interview with him in November 1986. He talked about the unionist leadership, the tactics of the Ulster Clubs and the fears of the pro-union community. He criticised a number of serving unionist MPs, notably Enoch Powell and John Taylor.

The *News Letter* put Trimble's views beside their 'Morning View' editorial, and his comments appeared under the headline 'Loyalists will fight to the bitter end'. It was all pretty hard-line stuff from Trimble, who, for an unelected individual, had been given a large platform, and he was now cultivating quite a media profile. Trimble was becoming a much sought-after interviewee for journalists, primarily because he was articulate and was prepared to talk to reporters at short notice.

Journalist Mark Devenport, who would serve as the BBC's Ireland correspondent and BBC Northern Ireland's political editor, remembers his early contacts with Trimble. He was making a documentary for the BBC Northern Ireland *Spotlight* programme, and Ken Maginnis, the UUP MP, had recommended Trimble to Devenport as a potential interviewee:

> I obviously had never heard of him at this stage. And I remember at the time thinking, oh, you know, is he really that much of a big draw? And I went along to Queen's University, and I found him extremely helpful, knowledgeable of the topic, quite open to assisting me and giving me good quotes. And I was quite pleased when I did the interview. And certainly, in all of those early encounters that I had either at *Spotlight* or when I was correspondent for the network Radio 4 programme, I found him quite good to deal with, much more so than the older generation of the unionist leadership, like Jim Molyneaux. And to

that extent I think, you know, I had a reasonably decent working relationship with him.[17]

Other journalists had similar experiences and found Trimble very obliging when they asked him to give interviews, either for print or for broadcast. Ray Hayden (who would later go on to work with the UUP and be a special adviser at Stormont) first came across Trimble in the 1980s, when he worked for the BBC and produced the *Inside Politics* programme for Radio Ulster:

> He was immensely approachable, very down to earth, no airs or graces. He possessed the most incisive analytical brain I had come across. We used to record the programme on a Friday evening. At the end of recording once or twice he would come round to the BBC club for a small libation before heading home. I mean he was very comfortable in that space.[18]

The private Trimble was often very different from his public persona, as Hayden recalls. On television and on radio, Trimble came across as knowledgeable, but at times austere and hard-line. Yet, away from the microphone and with a glass of wine in his hand, he could be fun and good company. The problem was that few people saw that side to him. The journalist and writer Ruth Dudley Edwards was one of those who did. She was involved in the British–Irish Association, a group that brings together politicians, academics and reporters to talk about Anglo-Irish affairs.

Dudley Edwards was a keen student of Irish history, and her books included an account of the life of Pádraig Pearse, one of the leaders of the Easter Rising in 1916. Trimble enjoyed the British–Irish Association meetings, and he used the occasions to argue the unionist case. Dudley Edwards remembers meeting him for the first time at a conference. She decided to organise a party and, with the help of her friend Liam Hourican, drew up a guest list:

> So, I said let's just ask the interesting ones that will look like a bit of fun. But then I got an attack of being sorry for the completely silent person who never talked to anybody, who was a law lecturer for Queen's. And I said, 'Liam, let's invite him because he won't come anyway and it's a sort of gesture because he doesn't seem to know anybody.' Well, he [Trimble] duly came and stayed till 2 a.m. in the morning, and we sat beside each other. And we have slightly different recollections of it, but what I said to him was, 'The trouble with you is that you're permanently two pints under par.' Because he was rather good company once he has loosened up. So that was the beginning of it.[19]

From that moment on, Trimble and Dudley Edwards became friends. She was a Catholic writer from the Republic who had just written a book about Pearse, while Trimble was a Presbyterian, a unionist academic and a member of the Orange Order. Yet, their friendship would last over decades, and they would routinely see each other in Belfast and London.

Marion Smith, from Trimble's hometown of Bangor, got to know him through her work with the party. She says he was naturally guarded when he met people for the first time:

> David doesn't give friendship easily, and it takes a while to get through. There is almost a stare that he has. There is almost a blankness in the face until he gets to know you. And then, once he gets to know you, he's actually quite witty.[20]

By 1988, Trimble had made some headway with the UUP and was now on the party's ruling executive. He was also chairman of the Ulster Unionist constituency association in Lagan Valley, which was Jim Molyneaux's Westminster seat. The two men continued to have a difficult relationship. They were not friends, operated very differently and had contrasting personalities. Trimble had embedded himself in

Molyneaux's constituency, as that was where he lived, but he knew that political opportunities remained limited. Even though Molyneaux was in his mid-sixties there was no sign he was going to retire.

Then an opportunity unexpectedly opened up. John Taylor, the party's MEP, announced that he would be stepping down, and Trimble put his name forward to replace him. He faced opposition from Jim Nicholson, the former MP for Newry and Armagh, who had been ousted in the by-elections held in 1986. Nicholson was seen as the front-runner, and there was much goodwill for him in the party after he lost his Commons seat. Jeffrey Donaldson, one of the party's rising stars and a former Assemblyman, was also in the running, as was Nelson Wharton, a retired civil servant.

Trimble took the campaign to succeed Taylor seriously. He knew he would face criticism for his continued membership of the Ulster Clubs, so one of the first things he did was to resign his position. Over the next few weeks, Trimble held many conversations with party members. Phone calls were made, and pledges were offered to him. Through his Ulster Clubs work and his media profile he was well known, but he did not have the reach across the party that Nicholson had.

On 7 May 1988, when around 600 members of the 800-strong UUC gathered at the Europa Hotel in Belfast, 305 delegates supported Nicholson, with 137 backing Trimble. Wharton secured 92 votes and Donaldson was last, with 69 votes. It was a stunning victory for Nicholson. It was also another defeat for Trimble – whether at work in the Law Faculty or in the party, he was becoming used to being a serial runner-up.

As he tried to advance his political career, another opportunity for promotion arose at Queen's University. It would prove to be his last chance to climb the academic ladder. Two professorial appointments were going to be made, and Trimble was very hopeful that one might come his way. He felt he had the experience for the role and, having witnessed some of his contemporaries make the step up, believed he should be considered.

Not surprisingly, his desire for the title of professor was shared by Herb Wallace. So, the two old friends from Land Registry days, who were now university colleagues, found themselves in competition. Wallace remembers the time well:

> David and I both applied and I thought, 'He is going to get it.' I mean it seemed to me to be obvious that he was going to get it. I was confident enough to put in my application and so on. In the end I was appointed to the chair, and I think that was when David became completely disillusioned.[21]

Trimble's failure to be appointed a professor at Queen's was a watershed moment in his career. In his eyes he had reached the end of any prospect of advancement. This was the point when he realised that, under the university's current leadership, his opportunities would remain limited, and he was unlikely to ever be promoted. It marked a most frustrating time for him. Politically, within the UUP, he was a relatively minor figure, and his position as such meant he had limited influence and status at the university.

He had become the 'nearly man' both of the UUP and Queen's – one of life's runners-up. He reluctantly accepted that was the way it was. In contrast, his home life was happy, and he and Daphne were enjoying raising their growing family. With his love of books, music, foreign travel and history, there was much to enjoy and make his life content. A full-time career in politics remained a dream, a passion unfulfilled. Then, out of the blue, an opportunity arrived.

10

GOODBYE, QUEEN'S

'When I came to Westminster in 1990 there were a number of people who thought I was some sort of hard man.'
David Trimble on becoming an MP

Harold McCusker, the Ulster Unionist MP for Upper Bann, died from cancer on 12 February 1990. He was 50 years old, and his death shocked his colleagues and those who worked with him in the constituency. Although he had been ill for some time, many in the party thought his illness was under control and that he was in remission. McCusker was an able politician and, as deputy leader of the party, was seen by many in the media as the natural successor to Jim Molyneaux. His seat was a unionist stronghold, and at the 1987 general election he had secured a majority of just over 17,000 votes. An Orangeman, he was an enthusiastic Lambeg drummer, and he was a popular figure with grassroots unionists. McCusker had the common touch, and whoever considered replacing him knew he would be a hard act to follow.

In the days following his funeral, the talk within the UUP turned to who could be McCusker's replacement. A number of local party representatives were expected to put their names forward. McCusker's widow, Jennifer, who had run her husband's constituency office, was talked about as a possible replacement, and it soon became clear she was initially interested in putting her name forward.

To many local unionists, she was the perfect candidate. Well connected and knowledgeable about the business of being an MP, she was seen as a good fit by party members across the constituency. If she put her name forward, the feeling was that she would win the nomination. She was also seen as a breath of fresh air in the male-dominated world of unionist politics.

In late February 1990, David Trimble was having serious thoughts about applying for the Upper Bann seat. He knew his career opportunities at Queen's were limited, and he liked the idea of being an MP. As he considered adding his name to the growing list of candidates, he was approached by numerous party members who encouraged him to stand. Friends from the Ulster Society and former members of Vanguard also encouraged him, and, after talking to Daphne, he put his name forward.

In early March, he embarked on a series of meetings with party members in Upper Bann to win their support. He threw himself into the campaign and produced a leaflet outlining his ideas. Conscious that other candidates would play on their local connections, Trimble talked up his role with the Ulster Society, which was based in Lurgan, one of the major towns in the Upper Bann seat. He knew he faced a stiff fight to win the nomination, as it was a safe unionist seat and opportunities to stand for Westminster were rare.

For several weeks, Jennifer McCusker was seen as the favourite, and it seemed that once again Upper Bann would have a McCusker on the ballot paper. She had the support of a number of senior officers in the party and the backing of friends and family. However, in late March she had a change of heart and withdrew her application – a move that transformed the contest.

On 19 April 1990, just over 250 local party activists gathered at Brownlow House in Lurgan to choose their candidate, and members had quite the choice. The venue suited Trimble and he felt at home as this was where the Ulster Society met. All the would-be MPs presented themselves to the meeting – the majority were local – and a number, like Trimble, came from outside the constituency.

One of the strongest candidates was Sam Gardiner, a former mayor of Craigavon, who was a leading figure in the Orange Order and the Royal Black Institution. Understandably, he had support from members of the loyal orders and, as chairman of the Upper Bann Ulster Unionist

Association, had featured in the media in recent weeks. Trimble expected him to poll well.

Arnold Hatch was also in the running. Like Gardiner, Hatch was a former mayor of Craigavon and was well known to the majority of local members. Businessman Jim McCammick, the mayor of Craigavon at that time, was another who entered the race. They were joined by George Savage, a local farmer and councillor, and Samuel Walker, who was a councillor in Banbridge District Council. As expected, Jack Allen, a party official, also threw his hat in the ring, alongside William Ward from Lisburn. It was a crowded field. With Trimble in the line-up, it meant that a total of eight candidates were seeking the nomination.

Trimble was confident he could win but knew he was in a very competitive fight. He also received some positive publicity – north and south of the border. The Dublin-based newspaper *The Sunday Tribune* ran a story on 1 April 1990 saying he was the front-runner to succeed Harold McCusker. Closer to home, the *Lurgan Mail* also talked up Trimble's chances of winning the nomination.

At the selection meeting, each candidate spoke for around 10 minutes, followed by 5 minutes of questions from the floor. Trimble made a good speech and focused on the fact that the Upper Bann by-election would get much national media coverage. He encouraged members to select someone who could represent unionism on the national stage. He reminded activists that the Northern Ireland Conservatives would be fielding a candidate and that the UUP needed to select someone who was capable of challenging government ministers and had the ability to think on their feet in the House of Commons.

Trimble captured the mood of the gathering, and his address was well received. The organisers of the selection evening drafted in members of the Young Unionists to help with the logistics of the event. Peter Weir, who would later go on to become a UUP MLA, was invited down to help with counting the votes. He recalls that Trimble performed very well and was 'most impressive'. He also felt that he was 'ahead of the rest in terms of ability'.[1]

After the first round of voting, Sam Gardiner had secured 91 votes, with Trimble in second place with 68. George Savage was third with 37, Arnold Hatch got 18 votes, Jack Allen received 13 votes and Jim McCammick received the support of 12 activists. William Ward picked up 11 votes and Samuel Walker got 5.

Even though he had failed to top the poll, Trimble felt confident that he could catch Gardiner when the other candidates left the race. When the voting went to further rounds it became clear it was a two-horse race between Trimble and Gardiner, and activists then abandoned their first choice and switched to their next preferred candidate.

Gordon Lucy, who knew Trimble from their work together in the Ulster Society, says Trimble was clearly the second choice of many local activists:

> It was a fairly broad field, but I think what actually assisted David was that he was probably the second choice of a lot of the candidates without actually being their first choice. And I wouldn't go as far as to say that the other candidates all hated each other but they probably had their issues, as it were.[2]

The momentum was now with Trimble, and in the final round of voting he secured 136 votes and Gardiner received 114. Trimble's luck had finally turned. He had won the nomination, and he was no longer going to be the 'nearly man' of the UUP. He had been selected to run for Westminster, and it now looked likely that he would become Upper Bann's next MP.

In his acceptance speech, he told activists that they had a fight on their hands in the forthcoming by-election:

> Some people have said it is the selection that counts but I don't believe that is the case. I think we're going to have to treat this by-election campaign very seriously indeed. It is not a foregone conclusion. There are new candidates

in the field, new parties in the field for the first time, and we cannot discount the Ulster Tories. But I believe if we go out there, we will succeed and deal a crushing defeat to stop their bandwagon in its tracks.[3]

Trimble believed that the decision by the Conservatives to field a candidate helped him:

> I would not have been selected as a candidate but for that. In normal circumstances, with the death of the existing member, Harold McCusker, I think almost inevitably it would have been a local worthy who would have been selected. Some people from the constituency came to me and said, 'Why don't you come?' After a bit of hesitation, I decided, 'Well, I will give it a try.' What I think gained the selection for me was, at that stage – when by-elections were one of the BBC's great sports, of going and examining and reporting in great detail and all the rest of it, and because of the additional factor of the Conservatives putting up a candidate – the by-election circus would come to the constituency and the delegates of the constituency were thinking, 'We are going to need a chap who can cope with this.'[4]

Gary Kennedy was one of those party members who backed Trimble. He says local activists were looking for someone in the mould of their previous MP:

> We needed someone to go to the House of Commons as good as Harold McCusker. We needed someone who could think on their feet. As a lawyer, David could do that. I thought he was the most polished.[5]

The election date was set for 17 May, which was less than a month away, so Trimble moved quickly and appointed the Banbridge councillor

John Dobson as his election agent. A solicitor by trade, he was based in Banbridge and knew Daphne well and was happy to help. He would remain Trimble's agent throughout his parliamentary career.

In total, 11 parties nominated candidates, ranging from the traditional groupings to new parties hoping to break new ground. It was the largest number of candidates ever to stand in a Westminster election in a seat in Northern Ireland.

The DUP did not field a candidate – which was the same position they took at the general election in 1987. Bríd Rodgers, a local councillor, who had previously contested the seat, was nominated for the SDLP, and Sheena Campbell, a Queen's law student, who would later be murdered by loyalists, ran for Sinn Féin. The Reverend Hugh Ross was a candidate for the Ulster Independent Committee, and Tom French stood for the Workers' Party. Loyalist Gary McMichael, the son of John McMichael, the former UDA leader, entered the fray for the Ulster Democratic Party (UDP – seen as the political wing of the UDA). The Greens, Labour and the Social Democratic Party also put up candidates and, as Trimble had predicted, the Conservative Party selected Colette Jones, a local woman.

However, it would not be an easy ride for those flying Tory colours in Upper Bann. Trimble wanted to use the campaign as an opportunity to give the Conservative administration a bloody nose, and, in his press releases and interviews, the Tory candidate was often the target of his political attacks. The Conservatives were undeterred by the criticism and threw a lot into the Upper Bann constituency. Kenneth Baker, the then Tory party chairman, came to canvass, as did Secretary of State Peter Brooke and the environment secretary, Chris Patten.

The London- and Dublin-based newspapers sent correspondents to the constituency, and the major broadcasters all did pieces on the campaign trail. Trimble was the man in the spotlight, and even though he seemed like a shoo-in, according to most political commentators, he showed no signs of complacency.

As Trimble experienced his first election as a Westminster candidate, Daphne did her best to carry on with home life – organising school runs, meals and being around for family activities. She was thrilled he was a candidate and excited that he was in with a great chance of becoming an MP. She knew her life and those of her children were about to change.

Richard Trimble remembers being told that his dad could soon be off to Westminster:

> I remember my mum telling me that Dad was going to stand to be an MP. She told me in the garage downstairs just as she was taking the washing out. She said, 'By the way, your dad is going to stand for election to be a member of parliament and if he gets it things will change.' And so, I remember standing there thinking, 'Oh, this is interesting. I don't know what this will mean for us if he does get elected in terms of our lives changing.'[6]

With campaigning in full swing, the UUP leadership asked activists from across Northern Ireland to come to Upper Bann and help. Alex Kane, who would later go on to have a career as a writer and political columnist, spent time in the constituency:

> I do remember knocking a few doors for him [Trimble] at that stage. And again, I didn't find him terribly impressive. I was thinking, 'OK, he'll win the seat because it's a reasonably safe seat for the Ulster Unionist Party.' But again, I wasn't thinking that this was a man who was going to become a major player in Ulster unionism. Indeed, my fear was that he would just become like so many other Ulster Unionists of that generation who would just fall into line and do nothing to stir up the government or change unionism. Because at that stage in my life I was looking for someone who would lead unionism in a new direction, who would tell them, 'Listen, we need to take these challenges.'[7]

Party colleagues also got used to Trimble's manner and behaviour. Some found his shyness and awkwardness difficult, and others found him distant. Fellow UUP member Danny Kennedy, who was the brother of Gary Kennedy, says that, privately, Trimble could be great company. However, there were occasions when he was self-conscious and uncomfortable:

> He was obviously very able; he was also very serious, very serious-minded. You wouldn't have talked to David about last night's football match – you know what I mean? There was always a level that he was at; his intellect clearly brought him to a different level ... He [was] always very warm and enjoyed a joke. I recall that famous laugh and the shoulders would move and things like that. I found him relatively easy company. If anything, the accusation about David is that he was arrogant or whatever. I found him to be more shy than arrogant.[8]

During the Upper Bann by-election, Kane also observed how awkward Trimble seemed when he was out and about meeting the public:

> He had this weird way when he knocked on doors. He always looked terribly uncomfortable, as if somehow he shouldn't be there, that he was somehow disturbing them. He didn't do small talk. The one thing I've learnt over the years of electioneering and canvassing is you need to be able to do the small talk. 'Oh, it's a lovely evening.' 'How is the dog?' or 'How are the children?' He didn't do any of that. It was straight into 'I'm the candidate for the Ulster Unionist Party for this constituency and I hope I can rely on your vote.' It was that sort of approach. I suspect most people would either have closed the door thinking, 'Oh well, he's the Ulster Unionist, I'll just vote for him anyway.' Or they might just think, 'Oh, he's an odd one.'[9]

Gary Kennedy says Trimble canvassed at breakneck speed, power-walking from house to house, and that it was exhausting just to watch him:

> If you had an evening out canvassing with David, you were well exercised. He would quickly move on from house to house. The man never stood still. It was like an Olympic sport.[10]

The UUP turned the Upper Bann campaign into a mini referendum on the five-year-old Anglo-Irish Agreement. Voters were told this was their opportunity to send Thatcher a message. John Dobson, Trimble's election agent, remembers it very well.

> Nobody outside of unionist circles knew who David Trimble was. He wasn't well known in the constituency. However, it was remarked on frequently around the doors that he actually looked a bit like Harold McCusker. The similarity was often pointed out, and it didn't do us any harm.[11]

On polling day, Trimble triumphed. He secured 20,547 votes, which amounted to 58 per cent of the poll, and he secured a majority of 13,849 over Bríd Rodgers of the SDLP. Colette Jones of the Conservative Party finished in sixth place, polling just over a thousand votes, which was 3 per cent of the vote. The Ulster Unionists were delighted. The party had retained their seat with a sizeable majority and the Tories had been pegged back. It was a political victory for the UUP and a personal triumph for Trimble.

After years of knockbacks at Queen's and a number of rejections within the party, he felt his efforts and work had finally been rewarded. It meant his days as an academic were over, and he would be a full-time politician.

Jonathan Caine, who would advise numerous Northern Ireland secretaries of state, and later became Lord Caine, campaigned for the

Conservative candidate during the by-election. He remembers seeing Trimble for the first time:

> I was impressed by his clarity of thought and it did very much seem like he was a potential future leader. Even at that stage he was obviously quite an awkward individual, and difficult to get close to in any meaningful sense. He had his opinions, and, in those days, they were quite sort of trenchant opinions. Obviously, you must remember the context of all this. We were still in the shadow of the Anglo-Irish Agreement, and there was a unionist campaign to try and replace the agreement and to get rid of it. I can remember when he was elected, his speech in Banbridge was all about getting rid of the Anglo-Irish Agreement. I think even in those early days he was socially quite awkward and sometimes it was very difficult to get more than a cursory hello out of him.[12]

It soon became clear that Trimble's life, and that of his family, was about to change. Vicky Trimble was at primary school when her dad won the Upper Bann seat:

> I remember him becoming an MP. I would have been six. So, I would have been in P2 [primary school year 2]. I remember my teacher making a big deal about it. And I also remember thinking it was brilliant, and I was proud. 'My dad's an MP', you know. But I think I also hadn't quite internalised the fact that he would be away a lot becoming an MP. So, I think it took me a wee while. I think whenever Dad became an MP, I was expecting him to come home the first day, come home on the Monday from the House of Commons to tell us all what it was like.[13]

Trimble's children were going to see a lot less of him, and they would soon get used to watching him go to Westminster on a Monday and return home to Lisburn on a Thursday or Friday. Within days of winning the seat, Trimble was on a plane to London. Friends and family, including Daphne and his mother, Ivy, watched as he took his seat in the House of Commons. He got his chance to make his maiden speech on 23 May 1990, and, in typical Trimble style, he used the opportunity to criticise the Conservatives for running a candidate in Upper Bann.

Even though maiden speeches were traditionally meant to be uncontroversial, Trimble could not resist the chance to tell the government that his election had shown that Thatcher's administration had no mandate in Upper Bann. Quickly, he got to grips with the procedures of the Commons, and he began to share an office with John Taylor, the Strangford MP.

Taylor was a great help to Trimble in those early weeks. After all, he was a political veteran who had served the party in Stormont, Europe and Westminster. He was able to introduce Trimble to the key figures in the Commons and the Lords, and Trimble quickly picked up the way the Palace of Westminster operated. He and Taylor were a good match. One UUP insider recalls how the two men were viewed:

> They shared an office, but they were separate from the other MPs. David Trimble and John Taylor were the terrible twins. They felt they were not being kept in the picture. They did not trust Jim Molyneaux and felt that Jim was being duped by the British government.[14]

In Upper Bann, Trimble set up a constituency office in Lurgan, which was run by Daphne and Stephanie Roderick, who Trimble had met during his time with the Ulster Society. Roderick loved working for Trimble and says he was unlike other politicians she encountered:

> He would have been different. David was – initially, when he first became an MP – quite a shy man, until he got on

to the subject that he liked. He never really – at least in the early days, and I would have said in the latter days too … prepare a speech as such. He would have just got up and spoke on his subject.[15]

Trimble's ability to get up and speak without a prepared script impressed his colleagues. He quickly adopted the habit at Westminster of simply writing a few notes on the order paper and then outlining his thoughts when his time to speak came. When Lady Hermon became the MP for North Down, she adopted Trimble's technique:

> David didn't always have a prepared speech, but he used the order paper, and he would just scribble notes. And he would listen intently to what the prime minister had said and then the leader of the opposition. And so, the order paper would be covered in his handwriting. It is a lesson that I learned early: never to have a speech, just to have notes on the order paper. I followed his very good example.[16]

Trimble established a reputation in the House of Commons as an articulate and well-informed voice for unionism. He was viewed as diligent and hard-working, but some MPs from other parties found him distant and unfriendly. Kate Hoey, then the Labour MP for Vauxhall, who was born in Northern Ireland, understandably took an interest in the politics of her homeland. She says Trimble unfairly had a reputation for being very serious and dull:

> He wasn't desperately approachable. In the sense of other people walking around the Commons you wouldn't have gone up to him, because he was always striding along looking very purposeful and very dour. But people who then got to know him I think realised he was actually quite good fun. What his face said was not really like him. He could be very witty.[17]

Hoey's observation is very common amongst people who would become friends with Trimble. He understood he had a public reputation which was different from how he behaved in private with friends and colleagues he was comfortable with. He was also aware that his membership of the Orange Order, his association with Vanguard and Ulster Clubs and his strong opposition to the Anglo-Irish Agreement meant he was seen by the media and in some other parties as a disrupter. He told BBC interviewer John Humphrys that this reputation often went before him:

> One of the amusing things I had when I came to Westminster in 1990 was there were a number of people who thought I was some sort of hard man.[18]

David Blevins, who would later become Sky's Ireland correspondent, was a junior reporter at the *Banbridge Chronicle* at the time. After Trimble's election, he was tasked with writing a profile of him. He recalls meeting Trimble at the newspaper's office:

> Having stayed up late preparing for this deep and meaningful interview, I arrived at my desk early. The editor brought David into the office and introduced us. He proceeded to take his seat, hide his face behind the broadsheet newspaper he had brought to read, and he gave me one-word answers for the best part of an hour. Most politicians pontificate at length on their own greatness. 'Well, he's different.' I thought. Just how different we did not discover until Friday 10 April 1998.[19]

By 1991, Trimble's profile at Westminster and within the UUP was on the rise. As Legal Affairs spokesman, he was often in demand for media interviews, and when security in Northern Ireland was discussed in the Commons, he took the lead for the UUP. Molyneaux started to include Trimble in more party work, and he was at this point routinely invited to meetings with the government and other parties. In March 1991, the

Ulster Unionists, the DUP, the SDLP and the Alliance Party all agreed to take part in talks that were organised by Secretary of State Peter Brooke.

Trimble enjoyed his first 12 months as an MP:

> Within a year or so after the by-election, I had the sense that most people in London regarded me as a substantial figure. Within a year or so I think if you'd done a poll, you'd have found that people who had taken an interest in Northern Ireland in and around Westminster ... most of them would have told you the same thing, that they expected me to be the next leader of the party.
>
> I was not unconscious of that opinion and funnily enough I thought somehow that would actually have its own way of seeping back to people at home.[20]

With a love of history, Trimble liked the sense of ceremony and the trappings of the past that dominated the Palace of Westminster. He soon became knowledgeable about the multitude of statues and paintings which dominated the parliamentary estate. When constituents came to London, or relatives were in Westminster, he would often take them on an unofficial tour around the corridors, pointing out historical figures. He was in his element, talking about his two loves: history and politics. Away from the chamber he could also indulge in his passion for music and books by visiting record shops and bookshops, and he would often go to operas in London's theatres.

But he knew politics was a fickle business, and so rather than resign his post at Queen's University he applied for a leave of absence. He was being cautious and did not want to resign in case his tenure in Upper Bann was short-lived. He knew a general election would take place in the coming months and he wanted the leave of absence in place until he had successfully defended his seat. The hierarchy at Queen's granted a leave of absence, and Trimble was comforted by the fact that, if his political career stumbled, he had the safety net of returning to academia.

His working pattern meant that he was essentially in London during the week and at home in Lisburn at the weekend. His children initially loved seeing their dad on TV. Nicky recalls the first time he saw him on the news as an MP:

> I remember me and my older brother and sister – and Mum as well, because I think she was equally excited – we all crowded round the wee TV. And it was 'Oh, Dad is on TV.' And I remember some image of him on the green benches. I've no idea what it was about. It was a hugely exciting thing that Dad was on TV, this box that only important people go on. And I remember it having significance with everyone.[21]

Trimble's five days in London meant that the weekend was a really important time with the family. Richard remembers that this often revolved around mealtimes:

> Saturday lunchtime was just bread and cheese, that sort of thing, and then in the evening we would have something cooked as a meal on the Saturday night. And then on the Sundays we would go to church. We would enjoy church and then come back and have a late lunch. So, Dad would start cooking after church and we would eat around three or something like that. And we would eat together, and we would always sit together. I guess memories of family mealtimes are that Dad would tend to go into what I would call lecturer mode. So, there would be something to talk about and he would be at the head of the table and Mum would be at the other end of the table. The rest of us would be around either side. There would be something to discuss, and we would just really ask questions. And he would talk about various things that he was interested in at the time.[22]

Vicky recalls how she and her father often differed when they had political conversations. She says her dad was conservative-minded, whereas, when she was older, she had certain left-wing views:

> The really annoying thing about having political discussions with Dad was that he was so much more well informed. Hands down, he is the smartest person I have ever known. So even though I might not agree with everything he said it was very hard for me to counter what he was saying.[23]

What is clear is that David Trimble enjoyed debate and discussion, even in the family home. He tried to impress on his children that arguments needed to be backed up with facts. Nicky says his dad loved nothing more than reading about a subject and using research to illustrate his point. He says his dad was not a natural politician and was clearly more at ease being in academia:

> I fully believe and maintain that Dad at his heart was always an academic. He was an academic who ended up having to go into politics. I mean had Northern Ireland not had the Troubles, had he been born elsewhere, I don't think Dad would have gotten into politics. I think he was pulled into politics because of the situation here, and had it not been here I suspect he would have been an academic. I think that's where he was more comfortable.[24]

Martina Purdy observed Trimble close up when she was a political correspondent with the *Belfast Telegraph* and the BBC:

> I used to call him the accidental politician because he was not a natural politician. But I do think he was in politics for the right reasons. He was a very difficult person, I think, to really get a handle on, but he had a decent streak.

I came to admire his perseverance and his courage. I do think he had a vision, but he didn't have the sales skills, if you like, to deliver it and to articulate it, and to share it with the other people ... to give them a sense of confidence that this was correct.[25]

In the spring of 1992, nearly two years after he won the Upper Bann by-election, David Trimble prepared to defend his seat. It would be a crucial moment in his life and prove to be a very eventful year – eventful for all the family.

11

SNOWBALLS AND SECRET TALKS

'I've heard some people say I'm very rude. But I'm direct you know; I don't like beating around the bush.'
David Trimble on suggestions that he is difficult to deal with

John Major had a date with destiny. It was Thursday 9 April 1992. Would he return as prime minister? Were the Tories on course for a fourth consecutive election victory? Or was this the moment when 13 years of Conservative rule would end, and Neil Kinnock would get the keys to Downing Street?

If the opinion polls were correct, it could be a hung parliament or a narrow Labour victory. Daphne and David Trimble had their own date circled in red on their family calendar. Daphne was pregnant with Sarah, their fourth child, and her due date and the election day were perilously close. Daphne knew something had to give, so her baby daughter's arrival was brought forward:

> She was induced a month early and the timing was done to make sure that I would be able to go to the polling station to vote in person with David, because I would be out of hospital in time to go to vote. And there were nice photographs in the *Belfast Telegraph* and the local papers. And somebody said to David, 'You know you timed that well for the election.' And David did say, 'Wasn't it nice of John Major to give me the election date nine months in advance?'[1]

Trimble had much on his mind. As he enjoyed Sarah's safe arrival and being a father again, he had the small matter of knocking on thousands of doors in Upper Bann. He was defending a majority of nearly 14,000 votes, which he had secured in the by-election in 1990. When the result was announced, he was there with his new daughter, as Daphne recalls:

> Sarah's first ever outing was to the count in Banbridge. And thinking back, would you nowadays consider bringing a baby and a newborn to an election count? It just didn't seem to us to be the wrong thing to do. Back then it was a more relaxed atmosphere.[2]

When the votes were finally counted, Trimble's majority had risen to just over 16,000 votes. It was a great result, and meant he could officially say goodbye to academia and end his leave of absence from Queen's. The Ulster Unionists managed to retain all their MPs and were the largest party in Northern Ireland despite some challenges in certain constituencies from the DUP.

Winning all their seats was a UUP target, but an analysis of the voting strengths showed some worrying trends for Jim Molyneaux's party. The UUP vote had gone down, and the DUP vote had increased, and in certain seats the gap between the unionist candidates was quite narrow.

With the Conservatives back in power, Peter Brooke was replaced as Northern Ireland secretary by Sir Patrick Mayhew, and political discussions began under his watch. The talks took on the traditional three-stranded approach. Strand One looked at relationships in Northern Ireland, while Strand Two examined the links between Belfast and Dublin. Strand Three focused on Anglo-Irish relations.

During the Strand One discussions the SDLP suggested that Northern Ireland should be run by a six-person Executive Commission – three members would be directly elected and there would be one member from the British government, the Irish government and the European Community. It was a novel idea, the brainchild of John Hume, but it was rejected by the British government and the unionists, who felt it was impractical and undemocratic and undermined the union. The discussions amongst the parties continued in June and July, and the talks moved into Strand Two, but with no meeting of minds, talks were adjourned until September.

Behind the scenes, the two leaders of Northern nationalism, John Hume and Gerry Adams, continued to hold meetings and exchange documents. Hume crafted a document in 1991 that included statements on self-determination. He hoped this could become the joint position of the British and Irish governments. The SDLP leader believed his dialogue with Adams would lead to an IRA ceasefire and ultimately create the conditions for all-party talks involving Sinn Féin.

The final draft of the Hume–Adams document was completed in June 1993, and it was passed on to the British and Irish governments. However, the two governments did not react quickly to Hume's proposal and matters dragged on. Hume became frustrated at the slow pace, and he travelled to London to see John Major to try to move the process forward. Afterwards, speaking to reporters, Hume's frustration spilled out. He was pressed by Jim Dougal, then BBC Northern Ireland's political editor, about his ongoing dialogue with Adams, and the criticism that surrounded their talks:

> I don't give two balls of roasted snow, Jim, what advice anybody gives me about these talks. Because I will continue with them until they reach what I hope will be a positive conclusion.[3]

Hume's flowery language captured the headlines, and his frustration was now on public display. Adams and Hume then issued a joint statement saying their discussions had made 'considerable progress', and they confirmed that their document had been given to Dublin. What was not made clear was that a copy had also been given to London.

While the press focused on the Hume–Adams talks, officials in Dublin and London continued their own discussions in the hope of producing a joint declaration. In correspondence with this author, Sir

John Major outlined the difficulties he had with the work done by Hume and Adams:

> The political problem with the Hume–Adams initiative was its source which invariably ensured the suspicion of hard-line Northern Irish unionist opinion and thus in the House of Commons right of centre conservatives.
>
> Any initiative labelled Hume–Adams was seen instinctively by a majority of unionists as hostile. This was frustrating since the same proposal from a different source – the churches for example – would have had a greater chance of being accepted. This presented a problem for the British government as we sought to bring opposing sides together.[4]

Major was right: unionists were suspicious of the Hume–Adams initiative and doubted whether it could deliver the peace that Hume boasted it could deliver. Trimble was a strong critic of the Sinn Féin–SDLP discussions and told journalists that he had fundamental problems with the talks the two men were having. He also criticised Hume's 'roasted snow' comments to reporters after he met Major:

> His manner and demeanour outside Downing St indicated to me that he is a man who knows that what he is doing is not supported by other people in the political process. He is proceeding to box himself into a corner, and I hope he has the sense to get himself out of it because it is not helpful in the present situation.[5]

Trimble was not a fan of Hume's. The two men did not have a warm relationship, and there was little personal chemistry. Many unionists blamed Hume for the failure of the Mayhew talks and felt he had become preoccupied with Sinn Féin. Hume was hurt by the collapse of Sunningdale in 1974 and was well aware of Trimble's role in opposing it during his days in Vanguard.

For his part Trimble found Hume hard to deal with. He would later confide to a British minister that he found the SDLP leader 'duplicitous' and likened dealing with Hume to 'grappling with fog'. To be fair, Trimble and Hume could be difficult individuals – both could be moody, brusque and sometimes seem rude. Trimble's manner and the perception that he was difficult to deal with was put to him by the author and journalist Frank Millar. Trimble replied:

> I don't know what their problem is to be quite honest.
>
> I've heard some people say I'm very rude. But I'm direct you know; I don't like beating around the bush. I remember one senior Irish diplomat when I was making a point to him about something which wasn't exactly rocket science – and rather than engage with the argument he just pretended and said, 'Oh I've never heard anybody say that.' It was so transparently false that it really did make me very irritated. In fact, on that occasion, I had to put the conversation on hold and go and get some air. But the point is this: I'm not there to be easy for other people. And if some people find me difficult or say they find me difficult that gives me some reassurance.[6]

Back in 1993, while Adams and Hume were having their discussions, the British government were secretly in contact with the IRA. There were rumours at Westminster that talks were underway, but any time Major was challenged, he emphatically denied that such contacts were in place. And as the behind-the-scenes contacts continued, Northern Ireland witnessed the highest death toll of any month since 1976.

On Saturday 23 October, an IRA bomb went off without warning on Belfast's Shankill Road. It killed 10 people including the bomber, Thomas Begley. Two children were among the dead, and nearly 60 people were injured. The bomb was carried into Frizzell's fish shop by Begley and another IRA man, both dressed in fishmongers' white coats. They arrived at a time when the street was packed with Saturday afternoon shoppers.

The IRA would later say that its intended target was an office above the shop, where it claimed members of the West Belfast UDA were meeting.

The television pictures of people digging with their hands in the rubble on the Shankill Road to find bodies went round the world. The attack raised a whole series of questions about Sinn Féin's peace strategy. How could republicans talk about peace when at the same time the IRA was indiscriminately killing men, women and children? How was the Shankill Road attack part of a peace process? The killings put Adams once again in the media spotlight, and questions were raised about Hume's ongoing relationship with the Sinn Féin leader.

When MPs gathered in the House of Commons on Monday 25 October to discuss the bombing, Trimble used the opportunity to insist that loyalists should not be goaded into retaliation. He criticised Hume for being party to talks with Adams, and he called for the IRA to abandon violence for good:

> Does the Secretary of State appreciate that the best way of answering that initiative [Hume–Adams] is to end the uncertainty by making it clear that the government will not entertain or advance that initiative in any way whatsoever? And that the government's response to the IRA Sinn Féin will be similar to that which this country gave to Nazi Germany during the war that we are interested only in its unconditional surrender.[7]

Trimble was emphatic. Nothing less than an IRA surrender would do. In his view, the IRA needed to cease their operations for good on a permanent basis. As the Shankill Road victims were being buried, loyalist paramilitaries were planning revenge attacks. It did not take long for another community to witness horror and grief. On Saturday 30 October, UDA gunmen arrived at the Rising Sun pub in Greysteel, a village some nine miles east of Derry on the A2. As one of the gunmen entered the bar, he shouted, 'Trick or treat!' before opening fire with an automatic weapon. Eight people were killed in the attack, which the UDA said was a reprisal for the IRA bombing on the Shankill Road. It meant that in one week more than 20 people had been killed, as Northern Ireland experienced its worst violence for decades. Trimble's appeal in the House of Commons for no retaliation had fallen on deaf ears.

Like Trimble, Hume found the events of October 1993 mentally and physically exhausting, but that did not stop his efforts to try to move things along politically. Hours after he attended one of the Greysteel funerals, he travelled to Downing Street to see Prime Minister John Major. Hume was so convinced that the document he co-authored with Adams was workable that he boldly told reporters that his document could deliver peace 'within a week'. His optimism was shared by neither the unionists nor the British government.

Major had to play a careful game. His administration had a slender majority, and when it came to some crucial votes, he had relied on the support of nine Ulster Unionist MPs. He had a group of Eurosceptic MPs in his own party who would rebel, so the support of Jim Molyneaux's group was proving most helpful. Even though behind-the-scenes discussions had been ongoing for some time, Major kept up the pretence that there was no dialogue with the IRA. When pressed in the House of Commons, he made this declaration:

> I can only say to the honourable gentleman that it would turn my stomach over and most people in this House and we will not do it.[8]

Major would later tell BBC Northern Ireland why his government had been involved in secret conversations with the IRA:

> We were already engaged in private conversations and although one often despaired about where they would go it was important we did that if we were going to create peace. If we hadn't had the secret channel to the IRA [and] if we hadn't had those talks and kept them secret, there would be no peace process.[9]

Major's secret contacts with the IRA were about to go public. On 28 November 1993, the *Observer* revealed how the prime minister had established a secret communications link between the UK government and the IRA. The front-page report written by journalists Anthony Bevins, Mary Holland and Eamonn Mallie made dramatic reading. The reporters outlined how a back channel, run by unofficial intermediaries, had been in operation for some time and was so secret that it had not even been disclosed to Taoiseach Albert Reynolds.

It was a sensational development after months of denials and was a great scoop for the journalists involved. Predictably, unionists reacted with anger to the news. The DUP leader, Ian Paisley, was dramatically ordered out of the House of Commons for five days after he accused Northern Ireland Secretary Sir Patrick Mayhew of lying. Trimble wanted to know what unauthorised contact had been made with the IRA by MI6, the intelligence service. Mayhew confirmed that, over the past two or three years, there were possibly two instances of unauthorised contact.

The news that the British government had been in contact with the IRA understandably deepened unionist suspicions and added to feelings of hurt and betrayal. Even though the UUP was prepared to support Major's administration at Westminster during key votes, trust between the Conservatives and many of the Ulster Unionist MPs was now at rock bottom. The secret contacts also strained London–Dublin relations. The Irish government felt London were guilty of double-dealing by not informing them of their discussions with the IRA.

On 3 December, the two governments held talks in Dublin, and against the backdrop of the *Observer* story the atmosphere was understandably tense. The discussions had a poor start, but after a few hours the mood changed and both parties started to make progress. The aim was to create a joint declaration before Christmas. The Dublin talks ended on a high, and a week later the discussions recommenced. Finally, on 15 December, the Downing Street Declaration was unveiled by Major and Reynolds.

The agreement between the two governments addressed the issue of Irish self-determination, and this was clearly a move in the direction of Hume's thinking. There was also an acknowledgement from the British government that nationalists had the right to pursue Irish unity, but any constitutional change had to have the consent of a majority in Northern Ireland.

Hume saw the declaration as a positive move. He believed there was enough in the agreement to convince the IRA to call a permanent ceasefire. Major and Reynolds hoped there was enough in their document to get support from unionists, nationalists and republicans. The DUP and the UUP took very different approaches to the declaration. Paisley said, 'It is a sell-out. It envisages no alternative to Ulster's tragedy but a united Ireland.'[10]

For the UUP, Molyneaux's response was measured, and he said, 'Neither unionists nor nationalists have anything to fear from this document. It is recognition by both governments, jointly for the first time[,] that the will of the greater number of people in Northern Ireland must prevail in all circumstances.'[11]

Even though there were some within the UUP who were uneasy with the Downing Street Declaration, Molyneaux managed to keep the party together and present a united front. As UUP leader he had been consulted by Major, and many felt Molyneaux had at least helped to keep the text largely unionist-friendly. The declaration was aimed at bringing republicans in from the cold and ultimately securing an IRA ceasefire, but it also needed to keep mainstream unionism onside.

Before they would commit to a response to the document, Sinn Féin wanted clarification on a series of points raised by the two governments' declaration. It was essentially a stalling tactic to buy the republican movement some time.

While republicans demanded clarification, Molyneaux concluded that Sinn Féin had rejected the declaration and assumed it was now dead. In January 1994, Trimble followed up this argument and called on the British government to act rather than wait for Sinn Féin's response. He said the Conservative administration should get tough:

If the IRA refuses to accept the declaration the government must enact strong security measures putting pressure on Albert Reynolds to do likewise. And the government must move on by doing things instead of talking.[12]

To some in the UUP, Trimble was beginning to sound like a leader in waiting. He knew his tough stance with the IRA would play well with unionist grassroots.

As unionists pressed the Conservatives for action, so too did Sinn Féin. During the early months of 1994, they continued to ask for clarification, and in May the British government responded to a series of questions republicans had asked about December's joint declaration. In the early part of the summer, rumours persisted that the IRA was about to call a ceasefire.

However, the violence on both sides showed little sign of stopping. On Saturday 18 June, Ulster Volunteer Force (UVF) gunmen burst into a Catholic bar in Loughinisland in County Down as drinkers watched a World Cup soccer match and killed six people, injuring five others. The attack sent shockwaves across the UK and Ireland. Mayhew said those responsible had shown 'moral squalor' and Dick Spring, the tánaiste, said the attack was a 'night of savagery'.[13]

The violence was not confined to one paramilitary group. On 11 July, the IRA killed Ray Smallwoods, a member of the UDP, outside his home in Lisburn. He had also been a member of the UDA. On 31 July, the IRA struck again and killed Joe Bratty and Raymond Elder, both members of the UDA. The idea of an IRA ceasefire seemed fanciful and further away than ever, but behind the scenes republicans were discussing such a scenario. Then a move happened that would transform the peace process.

On 31 August, the IRA Army Council issued a statement which said, 'as of midnight 31 August there will be a complete cessation of military operations'.[14]

The announcement was greeted with scenes of jubilation in nationalist parts of Belfast and Derry. Sinn Féin President Gerry Adams welcomed the news and praised the IRA for its statement. Clutching flowers and a bottle of champagne, he addressed supporters outside Connolly House in Belfast, who cheered and waved placards and flags. John Hume, the SDLP leader, who met with Adams just hours before the announcement, was delighted. Hume had every reason to feel vindicated for the time he had spent with Adams trying to secure a ceasefire. He said the news was something everyone in Northern Ireland had been waiting for.

The UK government and unionists took a very different approach. Unionists sensed betrayal, and they were sceptical about the IRA's motives. The DUP leader, Ian Paisley, rejected the IRA's move and pointed out that there was 'no expression of regret'.[15] For the Ulster Unionists, Jim Molyneaux said there should be no move towards talks with Sinn Féin until the word 'permanent' appeared in an IRA ceasefire statement.

John Major now had to persuade his Westminster partners in the UUP that a secret deal had not been done with the IRA. He needed to keep Ulster Unionist MPs on side, and he was particularly interested in hearing the views of the MP for Upper Bann. He had watched and listened to Trimble speak in the House of Commons chamber and been impressed. It was now time to seek him out for a quiet conversation.

12

STALKING AND WALKING

*'We are delighted to be back down our traditional
route as we expect to be again.'*
David Trimble after Orange Order members
walk along Portadown's Garvaghy Road

The Highcliff Hotel on Bournemouth's beachfront offers guests a stunning view of the sea. The cliff-side location in the Dorset resort is hard to beat, and it is home to fine dining and top-of-the-range wines.

In October 1994, David Trimble walked through its doors, but he had not come to take in the scenery or relax with a glass of wine. John Major was in town for the Conservative Party conference, and he wanted to hear Trimble's view on current events. The two men chatted about political developments of recent weeks and naturally the IRA ceasefire dominated their conversation. Major listened intently to Trimble's analysis and was clearly impressed with the Upper Bann MP. It was their first real opportunity to spend time together, and Major was keen to hear how unionists viewed the IRA's decision and how the British government should now approach Sinn Féin. Trimble recalled the prime minister asked him for advice:

> What Major said to me was this: 'If you were in my shoes what would you do?' He wasn't asking me what a unionist should do but what he should do.
> And I knew that I had to give him a sensible answer, so I said it has to be something like this. We are proceeding

on the basis that this ceasefire is permanent with a hint that if there's any backsliding there will be hell to pay. But this is the basis on which we're talking and if you're talking to us then you're talking to us on this basis too.[1]

Major and Trimble would see a lot of each other during the Bournemouth conference and would share a drink together at the ITN party. Ken Reid, then UTV's political editor, invited Trimble to the event, and he observed how he and Major appeared at ease in each other's company:

> Major and Trimble seemed very friendly, which surprised me. Trimble introduced me to Major, which turned out to be a great contact in the time ahead. David went away to get a drink, and I remember Major saying to me, 'You know, David has considerable talent. I think we're going to hear a lot of him.' And that took me aback. I hadn't thought of it that way at all, but Major was to be proved right.[2]

It was clear that Major and officials in Downing Street viewed Trimble as a serious politician who was clever and articulate and could be a successor to Jim Molyneaux. By the autumn of 1994, the UUP leader had chalked up 15 years in charge. He was 74 years old and increasingly there was a body of opinion in the party that believed he was out of date in the modern political world. Trimble privately felt frustrated at the way Molyneaux dealt with the parliamentary party at Westminster. He felt his leader did not share enough information with his colleagues. Molyneaux was very much a lone operator and routinely held meetings with government ministers on his own. Trimble believed that the UUP parliamentary group was only getting half the story from its leader and information was being kept back from them. On one occasion, Molyneaux told his parliamentary colleagues that he had been in contact with the prime minister, and he was awaiting correspondence from Number 10.

Trimble was convinced Molyneaux was being too secretive and did not think he would share the full contents of the letter from Downing Street. One source remembers what happened next:

> Everyone was waiting for this letter from the prime minister, and it arrived at the party offices at Westminster. David Trimble came in early and told one of the secretaries he had permission to open Jim Molyneaux's letter from the prime minister. She was puzzled and surprised but reluctantly let David take the letter. Trimble took the letter away, read it and left it back into Jim Molyneaux's in-tray in the office. Jim found out about it and there was an almighty row about Trimble opening private correspondence.[3]

Trimble's behaviour is worth examining. He knew his decision to intercept Molyneaux's mail would cause a row, yet he clearly calculated that his need to discover the contents of the letter was more important than preserving good relations with his party leader. It was a highly unusual move by Trimble. He was generally seen as someone who observed the social norms and respected people's privacy – but on this occasion he felt compelled to act.

One close associate says Trimble would not have worried about the consequences of opening Molyneaux's mail and would have justified his behaviour by saying it was 'for the good of the party'. Relations between the leader and the Upper Bann MP were not great, and Trimble may well have thought that they could not get any worse.

Alex Kane, who would later work for the UUP as communications director, says Trimble did not have a high regard for Molyneaux:

> I don't think he rated him as an intellectual. I don't think he rated him as a political thinker. I don't think he rated him as a party leader in the sense of knowing the challenges that the party faced or how to deal with them. He thought he was the wrong person at the wrong time.[4]

The IRA ceasefire of August 1994 changed the political landscape, and in October the loyalist paramilitaries called their own cessation. The Combined Loyalist Military Command (CLMC), which was the umbrella body for the UFF, UVF and Red Hand Commando, held a press conference on 13 October. In front of assembled journalists, Gusty Spence, a UVF veteran, read out a statement announcing a ceasefire and declared that loyalist paramilitaries had 'abject and true remorse' for the killing of 'innocent victims'.

Northern Ireland was now entering a new era. The peace process was now more than just the Hume–Adams initiative or the work of mainstream parties in Dublin, London and Belfast. The CLMC statement meant loyalists and their political representatives were part of a much wider conversation about what should happen next. Trimble had some weeks earlier predicted that the loyalist paramilitaries would call a halt to their campaign of violence. In September, while he was visiting the United States, he declared:

> I think that, provided the government can reassure them there has been no sell-out, there will be a ceasefire.[5]

Trimble's political antenna was well tuned. He had good loyalist contacts and the information he had received in September turned out to be correct. The loyalist groups accepted assurances from the government that there had been no backroom deals. Major's administration was delighted by the loyalist move, and his civil servants, together with officials in Dublin, began working on a new Anglo-Irish initiative.

However, before the document was made public, the *Times* got hold of a copy of it and leaked its contents. The story made grim reading for unionists, as the newspaper reported that the forthcoming declaration, which would become known as the Framework Document, brought 'the prospect of a united Ireland closer than it had been since partition'. Understandably, the unionists were alarmed by the disclosures, and the UUP quickly demanded a meeting with Major to discuss the detail contained in the article.

Trimble, with his fellow MPs Willie Ross and the Reverend Martin Smyth, met the prime minister and made it clear that they could not support much of what had appeared in the press. In the meeting, which lasted nearly two hours, Trimble articulated numerous concerns. He was particularly worried about the North–South bodies that were being proposed. He felt the Irish government was getting too much of a say and that its executive powers were too strong. It was an area he was very familiar with – after all, he had campaigned against the Council of Ireland, which was part of the Sunningdale Agreement in 1974.

Despite the protestations of the UUP, Major went ahead with his move with the Irish government, and in February 1995 the joint initiative was unveiled. In the Framework Document, the headline proposals fell into two categories: there were proposals for internal devolved structures in Northern Ireland and, despite unionist concerns, there were plans for North–South bodies. The publication confirmed that the talks process would follow a template of three strands.

The document proposed the establishment of a 90-seat Assembly at Stormont, with elections conducted by proportional representation. There would be a new North–South body, and there were commitments from the Irish and British governments to amend legislation relating to Northern Ireland. The principle of consent was at the heart of the document, and it was based on getting the agreement of the local parties.

Trimble made his opposition to the Framework Document clear in speeches in the House of Commons and in endless interviews to the press and broadcast media. He described the proposals as 'ill-conceived' and said the North–South bodies were completely unacceptable. On the plans to create all-Ireland structures he was particularly forthright:

> The prime minister and the taoiseach cannot reasonably expect unionists to accept what is tantamount to Dublin rule – it isn't on. Our first priority is to see how serious the government is about this, given written assurances in the document and verbal assurances in the House that the majority will be listened to.[6]

The biggest loser in the fallout from the Framework Document was Jim Molyneaux. It became clear that his quiet leadership of the UUP and his personal relationship with John Major had not delivered for unionism. Party members were now beginning to question if he was the right man to lead the party. Some activists were suggesting that he had been too soft and too quiet in his approach to Downing Street. Many wondered if history had repeated itself. They argued that, twice in a decade, unionism, and in particular Molyneaux, had been betrayed by a Conservative prime minister. First, the UUP leader had placed his trust in Margaret Thatcher, and then she had delivered the Anglo-Irish Agreement in 1985. Now, some 10 years on, Molyneaux had trusted Major, and the Tory prime minister had produced the Framework Document – once again putting unionism on the back foot.

Alan McFarland began working for the Reverend Martin Smyth at Westminster in 1992. He says that, after the Framework Document was published, the view was that Molyneaux had been misled and had shown poor judgement:

> I think there was a feeling that Jim had been kept in the dark. Duped, you could argue, if we're using that sort of language, and that he was being fed lines. I remember at the time referring to it as negotiation by illusion. Things were alluded to by the government. They would assure Jim that all was well, and he had nothing to worry about. Then, suddenly, when the document came out, there was a whole load of information that sent unionism, you know, bananas. So, I think there was a large degree of distrust of the government. The view was they weren't looking after unionists' interests; they weren't consulting us properly. We were being kept in the dark, and in particular I think David Trimble felt like this – that the old guard weren't looking after unionists' interests in the way they should.[7]

In the days after the Framework Document was published, Molyneaux's critics turned their words into action and a plan was hatched to challenge his leadership. When the name of the contender was made public, most party members had never heard of him. Lee Reynolds was a 21-year-old student at Queen's University and a member of the UUP. He had concluded that his party had been let down again by the Conservative government and it was time Molyneaux should step aside. He remembers talking to a friend about it and recalls how the discussion went:

> We chatted about it, and I wondered is anybody going to challenge him [Molyneaux], and we concluded probably not. So, I said, 'If nobody challenges him, what needs to be done?' I remembered that there had been a stalking horse challenge against Thatcher by one of the backbenchers. So, I said, 'What we need is a stalking horse.' And then the question was, well, who's going to do it, and I then stated the immortal words: 'If nobody else will do it, I will.'[8]

What started as an informal chat amongst friends had turned into something rather serious. Reynolds decided to challenge Molyneaux for the party leadership, and it was agreed that he would organise a press conference to announce his candidacy. It was going to be the most unlikely contest. The contrast between the two candidates could not have been starker. Molyneaux, the 74-year-old party leader, who was a privy counsellor and a Second World War veteran, was being challenged by an inexperienced student in his twenties.

Before Reynolds could make his formal announcement, his candidacy was leaked to the unionist-supporting newspaper the *News Letter*. Reynolds had planned to tell his parents, but the story appeared in the press before he could reach them:

> My father discovered that basically when he went in to buy his *News Letter* – that I was going to be a stalking horse

challenger against James Molyneaux. I got a phone call at half nine in the morning from my dad. He said, 'I've just had my first whiskey at 9:30 in the morning for the first time in my life.' And I'm going, 'Why?' And he says, 'Because I've just read on the front of the *News Letter* you are going to challenge James Molyneaux.' He says, 'Is this true?' and I went, 'Yes.' So, we then had a bit of a discussion, and he agreed to come up the next day and buy me a suit.[9]

Suited and booted, Reynolds began his campaign for the party leadership. It was a surreal experience for the young party activist, as he knew he was never going to win. His aim was to raise question marks about Molyneaux's leadership and hopefully get members to realise that a change was necessary. Even though no one predicted Reynolds would win, there were some in the party who were beginning to think that Molyneaux's days as leader were numbered.

On Saturday 18 March 1995, just over 600 members of the UUP's ruling body, the UUC, gathered to vote in the leadership election. Molyneaux received 521 votes and Reynolds got 88 votes. Molyneaux had a large majority, as expected, but Reynolds's tally of 88 surprised many political observers. It meant the largely unknown candidate had polled 15 per cent of the electorate, which was quite a respectable figure for a rookie candidate. Molyneaux tried to dismiss the Reynolds vote by telling journalists that those who backed his rival were 'taking a kick at John Major through me'.[10]

Even though he had triumphed, it was not a good day for the re-elected UUP leader, and there was further trouble ahead. Two days later, the Independent Unionist MP Jim Kilfedder died. This meant there would be a by-election in his North Down constituency, and there was talk of Bob McCartney putting his name forward as a candidate.

McCartney was a well-known QC and lived in the constituency. Originally from the Shankill Road in Belfast, he was an articulate unionist who had previously been an Assembly member in North Down for the UUP. He was no longer in the party and was very sceptical about the developing peace process, believing the IRA ceasefire was merely tactical. He had contested the 1987 general election as a Real Unionist and had performed well, polling 14,467 votes. On that occasion he had been runner-up to Kilfedder, who had been returned to Westminster with a much-reduced majority of just under 4,000 votes. In 1995, McCartney entered the North Down race and stood under the banner of UK Unionist, and he knew he had good chance of taking the seat.

The Ulster Unionists held a selection meeting to choose their candidate, and it looked like a straight choice between Reg Empey, a former Belfast lord mayor, and Alan McFarland, an ex-British Army officer who was working for the UUP at Westminster. Empey was the favourite to win the nomination, but, by a slender majority of just two votes, activists in North Down chose McFarland.

McCartney was a tough opponent for the UUP. His appeal straddled the working-class and the middle-class parts of the constituency, and he was a good performer in the media and in public meetings. He was the best-known candidate in the race and, at a time when many unionist voters were looking for a strong voice, he fitted the bill. When the votes were counted, he took the seat, securing 10,124 votes, nearly 3,000 votes ahead of McFarland, who was backed by 7,232 voters.

The turnout was extremely low at 38.6 per cent – the lowest ever in a parliamentary by-election in Northern Ireland. Molyneaux had come to North Down to canvass for McFarland, and the result was another setback for the UUP leader. The party ran a poor campaign and, bizarrely, did not invite Bangor-educated Trimble to join their election effort. The turnout was particularly disappointing for the UUP. The seat was always going to be won by a unionist – of whatever hue – and the Ulster Unionist hierarchy genuinely thought they could win.

Molyneaux compounded his difficulties by saying that the low turnout was because the voters in North Down had 'suffered least from terrorist savagery and can afford to forget people in the frontier counties'.[11] It was a crass and ill-advised remark to make, and heaped more pressure on his battered and bruised leadership.

Newspaper columnists and political commentators now started to speculate that the 74-year-old would step down in the autumn of 1995. Some suggested that Molyneaux's impending 75th birthday in August would be the appropriate time to declare that he was stepping away from the party leadership.

If Trimble's profile was low during the North Down by-election campaign, the month of July would put him on people's television screens on a nightly basis. Events began on Sunday 9 July, when the Portadown Orangemen were prevented by the RUC from walking down the mainly nationalist Garvaghy Road. The police blocked their way, and a standoff began at Drumcree Parish Church, where the Orangemen had held their traditional service. Hundreds of Orange Order members then travelled to Portadown to offer support, and soon the atmosphere became tense. Within hours, violence broke out, and plastic bullets were fired after a rally was addressed by Trimble and Paisley.

As the local MP, Trimble found himself at the centre of things and was a key part of the discussions between the Orange Order and the RUC. At one stage, Trimble approached some RUC officers who were kitted out in riot gear. One officer recalled the exchange:

> David came over to me. He said, 'Put those shields away, you are only provoking the protesters.' At that moment, the biggest rock I have ever seen smashed into my shield. I said, 'David, I tell you what. You just stand where I am standing.' With that, Trimble just walked away.[12]

The story has an interesting postscript. The police officer concerned would later join Trimble's close protection team. In a bizarre twist, some years later, he ended up accompanying Trimble to Drumcree Parish Church, where his responsibility was to keep Trimble safe – from critical Orange Order members. Back in 1995, Drumcree began a rallying cry for Orange Order members and the dispute led to trouble in towns and villages and to key routes being blocked across Northern Ireland.

The atmosphere was extremely tense, and, with little sign of the dispute ending, there were genuine fears that the trouble and disruption would last for weeks. Finally, after much negotiation, a deal was agreed, and the Orangemen were allowed to walk from Drumcree Parish Church back into Portadown via the Garvaghy Road. On the morning of 11 July, members of the Portadown District Lodge walked in silence down the Garvaghy Road. There was no accompanying music, and the protesters turned their backs on the Orangemen as they walked by.

The detail of the deal is still contested today, as members of the Orange Order and the residents have different accounts of what was agreed back in July 1995. An agreement was reached with the help of a team of mediators, a deal that meant the Orangemen could walk down the Garvaghy Road silently with no bands, but the Order would not return along the route on the Twelfth – the main day for Orange Order parades.

Trimble was not a member of the local lodge and said he would not take part in the parade from Drumcree into the town centre. Instead, he waited at Carleton Street in Portadown, the location of the headquarters of the Portadown Orange Order. What happened next would capture headlines around the world and have serious political repercussions.

At Carleton Street, as supporters cheered the arriving Orangemen, Harold Gracey, Portadown's district master, took a position at the front, and the crowd then shouted for Trimble and Paisley. The DUP leader was slightly ahead of Trimble, who caught up with him and then grabbed his hand. The waiting television crews captured the moment perfectly. It was an image of Trimble and Paisley walking together with their hands aloft in triumph in front of cheering crowds.

The sight of two unionists from rival parties walking together sent the crowd into greater raptures. Trimble looked overjoyed, and, in a raised voice, he proudly declared:

> 'We are delighted to be back down our traditional route, as we expect to be again.' His remarks received cheers from the crowd, and someone shouted, 'No surrender.' Then a reporter asked Trimble, 'Are you happy with the

compromise?' He replied, 'There was no compromise by us, we have come down our traditional route in normal format with our flags flying.'[13]

However, not everyone saw the Trimble and Paisley 'dance' in a positive light. Nationalists thought the two MPs were being deliberately provocative and triumphalist. Alban Maginness, who was taught by Trimble at Queen's University and was by then chairperson of the SDLP, remembers watching the television pictures with horror:

> It was appalling. It was seen by Catholics and by nationalists as awful. And you didn't have to be a republican to see this. You saw this as a dreadful dance of sectarian solidarity. And it was wilful and very bitterly anti-nationalist, anti-Catholic. It was just a huge backward step and one of the lowest points, in my opinion.[14]

Republicans like Mitchel McLaughlin, who would go on to be speaker of the Assembly, shared Maginness's assessment. He also believes that Trimble's behaviour was all part of the intra-unionist battle with the DUP:

> I mean he [Trimble] did truly get up people's noses and annoy people. And Drumcree in particular was regarded as a calculated kind of insult. But on reflection, over a number of years you can actually see that he was also trying to deal with the presence and influence and posturing of Ian Paisley Senior. So, it was maybe there was an internal battle for the leadership of unionism going on. That is part of the story, at least, of what happened at Drumcree.[15]

McLaughlin's analysis of the inter-party rivalry between the DUP and UUP is borne out by Trimble's recollection of the events of 1995 in

Portadown. In a BBC radio interview, he recalled how the Orangemen arrived at Carleton Street from their walk from Drumcree Parish Church, and then they began to line up:

> A shout went up from them for their District Master, Harold Gracey, to walk down through the column – where they applauded him. Then Ian Paisley stepped forward to do the same. I am the member of parliament for the constituency. I'm not going to have him parading in front of me. So, I grabbed his hand, to hold him back. I grabbed his wrist – actually, he had his hand up ... He had his arm up to acknowledge the crowd. I held his wrist to make sure he could not get in front of me ... The appearance of a common front caused me enormous difficulty a few months later. When the incident happened, I did not twig how it was going to be portrayed, and it was portrayed as something not quite what had happened and portrayed in quite inflammatory terms. I was pretty excited at the time. It was a quite remarkable situation.[16]

The Trimble–Paisley double act in Portadown was endlessly played on television, and many who watched it now viewed the UUP MP as being as hard-line as the DUP leader. Numerous political commentators concluded that the former Vanguard man, who had been in the Ulster Clubs, was now the standard bearer of hard-line unionism within the UUP. His arm-in-arm walk with Paisley had managed to anger not only Garvaghy Road residents and nationalist and republican politicians but also the liberal wing of his own party.

In July 1995, David Trimble's profile had never been greater. The sash-wearing MP had appeared on television screens the world over. For days he was pictured on the front pages of British and Irish newspapers. And there was delight in the hierarchy of the Orange Order that their brethren in Portadown had made the return walk home. Drumcree would now have a place in Orange folklore and would be seen as a famous victory in their fight for their civil and religious liberty – a battle they believed they had won by adopting the age-old principle of 'No surrender'.

Trimble was seen in the eyes of grassroots Orangemen as a hero. Others, notably civil servants and advisers at the Northern Ireland Office, had a very different opinion of his behaviour at Drumcree. Officials privately took a very dim view of the MP's behaviour. In recently released documents, civil servants were highly critical of Trimble's stance and public comments. John Steele, then the senior security adviser of the Northern Ireland Office (NIO), wrote:

> The Portadown situation was very unpleasant but there was eventual agreement which the dreadful Trimble did his best to obstruct and spoil.[17]

Steele's scathing attack on the Upper Bann representative was mirrored in other civil service correspondence. J.M. Legge, another official at the NIO, gave this assessment:

> It is clear that the final compromise at Garvaghy Road was available at least 24 hours earlier, and had come unstitched by the disgraceful behaviour of Trimble et al.[18]

If July had been a mad month for Trimble, August was largely quiet until the final few days. On 28 August, the day after his 75th birthday, Jim Molyneaux announced that he would be stepping down as leader of the UUP. During the Drumcree dispute, he had been visited by a number of party officers and agreed to step aside. He agreed to stay in post until his successor was voted in by the UUC, the party's ruling council, which would convene on 8 September.

The media quickly turned its attention to who Molyneaux's successor could be. There was much focus on John Taylor, who was a former Stormont minister and the most experienced MP after Molyneaux. Trimble knew that his Westminster roommate would be in the running. Taylor was quickly made the favourite by journalists and bookmakers.

There was also speculation about Ken Maginnis, the Fermanagh and South Tyrone MP, who was the UUP's security spokesman. Maginnis was media-friendly and considered to be on the party's liberal wing, but the general feeling amongst activists was that he would not have enough support.

Willie Ross, the MP for East Londonderry, was another being mentioned in the press as a potential leader. Ross was seen as hardline and, even though Molyneaux was remaining neutral, some speculated that he might be the current leader's preferred choice. The South Belfast MP Reverend Martin Smyth was another name being linked to the top job.

On the day of Molyneaux's resignation, Trimble was in Lisburn and went into Eason's newsagents to buy newspapers. Daphne remembers that he bumped into a couple of party members, including a woman from Hillsborough, who had heard the news about Molyneaux's departure:

> She said to him, 'Oh, you must stand.' And ... that changed his mind about standing. But I knew he had to stand, and if that hadn't happened then I was sort of bracing myself to tell him, 'Look, you've got to put your name in the hat.'[19]

The meeting in Eason's clearly buoyed Trimble up. Naturally, he and Daphne discussed Molyneaux's departure, and he told Daphne that, if he did enter the race, he knew he would win. However, he clearly needed some thinking time, as Daphne recalls:

> It took him a long time to come to that point. He wasn't going to run to begin with because John Taylor was going to be the new leader, in his mind. He gave an interview – I think it was to the BBC. He didn't specifically say that he would stand for leader, but I think he said something to make it sound like he wasn't going to put his name in the hat.[20]

Trimble initially thought that Taylor was Molyneaux's natural successor. It was not a prospect that concerned him. He and Taylor got on well and shared similar outlooks. Trimble initially thought he might benefit if Taylor became leader:

> It seemed to me that John had a good chance of becoming leader. And I was fairly comfortable with that. I respected his judgement, and I also thought to myself that because I was able to get on with him, I could become his chief whip and that would put me in a nice position, because I would know what was going on without having the responsibility for it as leader.[21]

At this stage, Trimble was being a little coy about his true intentions. He was now at the centre of a guessing game – for political correspondents. He had only been an MP for five years and was the least experienced of the UUP's parliamentarians, but he now had a national profile. Outside of his supporters in Upper Bann, he knew he appealed to a wide range of party members.

He had impressed many rank-and-file activists with his performances in Westminster, his understanding of legislation and his ability to debate. On radio and television, he was regarded as a clever and articulate voice for unionism who could argue well, with clarity and vision. His stance at Drumcree had gone down well with members of the Orange Order and he was seen as a tough, uncompromising figure.

Trimble got some friends to canvass members of the UUC, and the feedback was positive. He knew he had a strong band of supporters if he decided to run. In the days after Molyneaux's resignation, he kept his counsel, but he knew he could not maintain such a silence for much longer. As August ended, he had a big decision to make.

13

FOLLOW THE LEADER

'Fuck, that is not what I expected to happen.'
David Trimble on becoming UUP leader

Vincent Kearney and Mark Simpson were a journalistic double act. They were both political correspondents at the *Belfast Telegraph* and often worked on stories together. Their interviews frequently ended up as exclusives on the front page.

Northern Ireland's media landscape was competitive in the 1990s, and press and broadcast journalists were always keen to break a story which could set the political agenda. Up until early 1995, unionist leadership stories were a rare commodity – and now reporters found themselves analysing two contests in six months. This time it was different. The initial move by Lee Reynolds in March 1995 was about wounding Jim Molyneaux and speeding up his departure. This contest in September was the real thing. It involved the party's big hitters and raised a series of questions.

Would the new UUP chief take his party into talks? If so, under what conditions? What were the UUP's red lines in negotiations? Could unionists work with Sinn Féin? How should the UUP change as a party? They were big questions for any new leader – the sort of areas both journalists and party members would be interested in talking about. In the *Belfast Telegraph* newsroom, Kearney and Simpson discussed the names of potential successors to Molyneaux, and, as they chatted, David Trimble's name inevitably came up.

Kearney wanted to know more about what the Upper Bann MP might do if he became UUP leader. After a series of phone calls to unionist sources, he concluded that he needed to meet and talk to Trimble. So, he rang him and asked if he would come to lunch. Trimble agreed and met Simpson and Kearney at Belfast's Europa Hotel – the city's most famous hotel, which was close to UUP headquarters.

Kearney recalls the encounter:

> I remember he came in and he was a few minutes late.
>
> We sat down, and I said, 'David, thank you very much for joining us.'
>
> I remember he said, 'No, thank you very much.'
>
> I said, 'Why are you thanking us?'
>
> He said, 'You are the only journalists who have taken me for lunch.'
>
> He then said, 'You appear to be the only journalists who think I will win.'
>
> At which point I said, 'Do you think you can win?'
>
> I will always remember what Trimble said, 'I wouldn't be in this race if I didn't think I was going to win.'[1]

Simpson clearly remembers meeting Trimble in the Europa Hotel:

> Somewhat embarrassingly, in hindsight, I was reluctant to go to that lunch in 1995, as I felt David Trimble had no chance of winning the UUP leadership. In those days he didn't look like a leader. Also, he was not part of the mainstream in the party. I knew he was very popular amongst the younger wing of the UUP, the so-called 'baby barristers', but I didn't think that would be enough to win the leadership contest. I underestimated him, and I wasn't alone. However, in fairness to my *Belfast Telegraph* colleague at the time, Vincent Kearney, he insisted we take him out to lunch, just as we did with the other potential candidates. So, we went to the Europa Hotel in Belfast. We sat at a table near the window which looked out over

Glengall Street, where the UUP headquarters were situated. We ordered lunch and I nearly spat my soup over the table when Trimble said, 'If I enter the leadership contest, I'll win it.'²

Kearney and Simpson were not the only journalists trying to work out who might succeed Molyneaux. In newsrooms across Belfast, reporters were making calls trying to assess the strengths of the different candidates and work out who might emerge victorious on 8 September.

At Broadcasting House in Belfast, Gareth Gordon, who would later become a BBC Northern Ireland political correspondent, recalls conversations with colleagues about the contest:

> There was some discussion in the BBC newsroom about whether he [Trimble] would run or not. I decided to call him from a studio, and he said something like, 'It is funny you should ask. I have a woman in my office right now begging me to stand' – though he refused to say if he would or not. I came off the call thinking, 'He just might, you know'. I went to the news desk and told some senior people what he had said. And a very senior journalist who will remain nameless said he'll not run, and he turned on his heel and left.³

Trimble at this point was having daily conversations with constituents, party members and friends, all urging him to put his name forward for the leadership. David McNarry was one of those in discussions with him:

> By the time he'd come into the Ulster Unionist Party I reckon David had understood that the establishment needed to be cracked. In fact, you had to become part of the establishment to get anything done. And the only way

to become part of it ... as far as David was concerned, was to take it over.⁴

Dermot Nesbitt was another party colleague who was keen to see Trimble enter the race. Nesbitt and Trimble had worked together at Queen's University, and he rated the Upper Bann MP highly:

> He was someone I respected at Queen's. He was intelligent and communicative, and therefore I thought he was the right person to be the leader, given his background.⁵

However, not everyone in the party took the same approach, and Trimble received a number of calls asking him to stay out of the contest. Peter Weir admired much about Trimble's early politics. He would later become a critic but in 1995 he was a natural ally of Trimble and shared much of his unionist thinking. Weir was part of a group of young unionists who were legal professionals and had been given the nickname the 'baby barristers'. This group discussed the contest, and some had concerns that, if Taylor and Trimble both ran, then Ken Maginnis, viewed as being on the 'liberal' wing, would be the beneficiary:

> Potentially it would mean that it would increase the chances of Ken Maginnis getting the job. And that's nothing hostile to Ken, but we didn't entirely gel with Ken's politics in that regard, and that really our advice was that he [Trimble] shouldn't be putting his name forward.⁶

Trimble listened to Weir's pitch to stay out of the race and to the argument that it might let other candidates in. He recalls how Trimble responded:

> David was polite – curt, maybe. He ... made it firmly clear that he did not agree with our analysis, and he was going to run.⁷

Trimble was now getting used to callers passing on their opinion about his leadership chances, and whether he should be a candidate. Danny Kennedy was another party colleague who reached for the phone in an attempt to stop Trimble from entering the contest:

> I sort of pleaded with him not to run. I knew he was close enough to John [Taylor], and I just took the view that time was on his side, and it would come to him if he was prepared to wait. He listened very politely, and he thanked me for the call. But he said he thought he was determined to run, and he thought he would do well. To be fair, he never ever held that against me, when he became leader and when he was in charge of the party. He didn't remember that I didn't back him, and I told him not to run.[8]

Trimble was also having conversations with a number of friends whose opinions he valued. John Dobson, who was his election agent, and a Banbridge councillor, remembers one particular discussion:

> He turned to me and said, 'Do you think I should run for leader?'
> I said, 'Yes, at some stage the UUP are going to have to talk to Sinn Féin, and you are the only man who can do that.'
> He was, in my view, head and shoulders above anyone else.

Gordon Lucy was another who had chats with Trimble. The two men had worked together in the Ulster Society, and Trimble was keen to get Lucy's analysis on the leadership contest and his view on Molyneaux's legacy. Lucy believed the outgoing leader had lost his focus:

> I think the Unionist Party needed serious modernisation. There was another thing that you could argue that

Molyneaux had let things slide. His attitude was 'Steady as we go', and perhaps we had missed opportunities and failed to take advantage of situations. Now, in terms of wanting him [Trimble] to become leader, he kept asking me, you know, 'Should I become leader?' And I said, 'No, that's a decision that you have to make with respect to your family.' And Daphne Trimble told me that was the wrong answer.[9]

Daphne was completely in favour of her husband running for the party leadership. She had witnessed the phone calls of support to the family home, and he had already confided in her his belief that he would win if he ran.

The approaches to Trimble continued by phone and in person. He was even encouraged to run for leader while he was attending church. The Trimble family were members of Harmony Hill Presbyterian Church in Lisburn, and a member of the congregation encouraged him to put his name forward. Trimble's daughter Vicky recalls the encounter:

> I remember before he went to run for leader, I have a very clear memory of someone in our church telling Dad … that he should run. And Dad saying there was no way that he was doing it. So, I don't know if that was just bluster. It was someone who approached Dad in the corridor and Dad laughed it off. And said, 'No, no, no.' But of course, he did run.[10]

Was this classic Trimble shyness? Or was he simply keeping his options open and waiting for the right time to announce that he was in the race? Or had he still not decided if he wanted to succeed Molyneaux? Ten days before the vote, Trimble had still not announced his candidacy, and the guessing game was in full flow in unionist circles.

On 31 August, Trimble told the *News Letter* that his 'original intention was not to run but I am now giving the matter active consideration'. It was a holding statement, and within hours of making that comment, he was a candidate. On Friday 1 September 1995, he announced his intention to run for the leadership. At a press conference in Belfast's Europa Hotel, he told journalists he was the right man to be party leader:

> I am confident I can win this one even though some commentators are saying at 50 I am too young. True, I am the youngest in the field, but I feel this is the ideal age to seek such a responsibility.[11]

Trimble's band of supporters swung into action. A small team secured the list of delegates to the UUC and, methodically, telephone calls were made to party members to see if they would support Trimble. The numbers were encouraging, and it seemed that Trimble's campaign had some momentum. All the leadership candidates were offered platform pieces in a number of newspapers, and Trimble set out his stall in the unionist-supporting *News Letter*:

> Unionism is not a narrow, insular creed but recognises the many ties, economic, social and cultural which bind us in the greater part of the British Isles together in a genuinely pluralist and tolerant state in which it is possible to be Irish and British or Ulster and British. Why then should any want to join a monocultural state founded solely in order to be Gaelic and Roman Catholic which could scarcely accommodate the social range that actually exists within northern nationalism? The Union is worth preserving and defending with all the vigour we can summon.[12]

It was a classic Trimble pitch – by appealing to modernisers he argued that unionists needed to preserve the union, but they could not be blind to change. His *News Letter* piece also included some old-style rhetoric, particularly his barbed reference to the Irish Republic and the claim it was a monoculture. That was aimed at the traditional wing of the UUP.

As the vote approached, Trimble remained convinced he would win. It was clear he had a strong support base, and even those who were backing other candidates were amenable to making him their second choice. The night before the poll, he took a call from his old friend from Queen's University, Herb Wallace:

> I phoned David before the vote and I said to him, 'I just wanted to wish you all the best'. And he said, 'Thank you very much.' I then said, 'I hope it goes well for you'. And he said, 'I'm going to win.' And I said, 'Are you sure?' And he said, 'Oh yes, I wouldn't have put my name forward unless I was sure I was going to win.' I thought at the time he was talking rubbish, but he was right. His figures were much better than when I was his campaign manager for the deanship.[13]

Trimble was consistent throughout the campaign in his conversations with friends and journalists. In every discussion, he was absolutely convinced he would triumph. It was a level of confidence that surprised some, who thought he was being arrogant. Was he right to be so convinced that the leadership was his? Trimble's confidence was based on the canvassing returns he had received from the unionist council, and the support he was being offered in person and on the phone. After Drumcree, his stock in the party had risen, and he now had a national profile as well.

On Friday 8 September, the day of the vote, the BBC's Ireland correspondent, Denis Murray, went down to the Ulster Hall, as he was going to be reporting on the story later that evening. He made the short journey from Broadcasting House to the venue on Belfast's Bedford Street and stepped inside. The building was being made ready for the event. Chairs and microphones were being put in place in readiness for the speeches from the candidates.

The hall was largely empty apart from some staff and a small group of senior officials from the UUP. Murray bumped into Josias Cunningham, who was president of the UUP, and asked him who would win the leadership. Cunningham, a party grandee who was steeped in unionist politics, was wise enough and experienced enough not to offer up a name but, according to Murray, he made this observation:

> I've been going to all these constituency meetings, and there was one where it was kicked around for about three hours. And at the end of it a guy stood up at the back and said, 'We have tried having a gentleman for the last 12 years, now it's time we got ourselves a bastard.' And the place rose to echo it. In other words, Jim Molyneaux was the gentleman, and whoever will succeed him would be a very tough guy with very thick political elbows and would take no nonsense.[14]

If that was the prevailing mood, what tough guy would succeed Molyneaux? John Taylor was the front-runner, and for the past 10 days he had been talked up by journalists as the heir apparent. Was he the hard man with sharp elbows who clearly some unionist grassroots wanted? Taylor was a no-nonsense politician and fitted the bill, as did Trimble, who had earned his political spurs at the police lines in Drumcree.

The venue for the leadership contest, the Ulster Hall, was appropriate, as it had been the venue for the UUC's first public meeting, in 1905, and it was where unionists gathered in 1912 when they took part in an Ulster Day rally. On the night of the election, the agenda was straightforward. There were speeches from the five candidates and then delegates voted over a series of rounds, until a winner emerged. Reg Empey, who would later sit in the House of Lords as Lord Empey, was a party officer and was on duty that night to help with the election:

> Taylor came into the room as favourite by a long shot. You had Willie Ross, Ken Maginnis, Martin Smyth, David Trimble and John Taylor. And I think most of them had set out in advance some literature … There was a ballot

taken for the order in which they spoke, and whenever Taylor came to the platform, his speech – I would have to say it was one of the worst speeches I had ever heard him make. He was taking his glasses on and off, and he didn't seem to be following the script. He was all over the place, and it was a very disappointing performance.[15]

Taylor's below-par address to party members shocked many in the hall. It was not the confident, coherent politician they were used to seeing at meetings and on television. Even his strongest supporters were taken aback by his presentation to members. David Burnside, who supported Taylor, says people in the hall were quite surprised:

Taylor made a very poor speech … for the leadership of the party. Trimble offered an alternative. I had the greatest respect for Jim Molyneaux. He was a holder, a consolidator; he held on to winning unionist seats, holding on to a position, not taking risks, not wanting any typical initiative. So, Jim was a man of his time where he held on to the electorate. David offered an alternative to drag us out of the Troubles.[16]

Daphne Trimble was also surprised at Taylor's speech. She wonders if the occasion got the better of him:

John struck me as terribly nervous [during] his speech. I can't even remember the details of it. It was not a good speech. I heard him make far better speeches in the past.[17]

In contrast, Trimble's speech went down well in the hall. He was keen to outline how he would be different from Molyneaux:

I gave them a political speech about the issues that we were going to be confronted with and the decisions we were going to have to make. And I also said the party was going to have to face the issue of inter-party talks and that would be one of the most difficult decisions we would have to take.

I also said that I would go anywhere to sell the Ulster Unionist Party. And I said that deliberately because I saw the way Molyneaux had got himself into a straitjacket by saying he wouldn't go to Dublin or do this or do that. And I just ... wanted to be free from all those constraints. So those were some of the factors. Drumcree was also there in the background but not necessarily as a good factor – because the bulk of the party doesn't like trouble, and the bulk of the party doesn't like working closely with Ian Paisley. But when I found the Drumcree issue on my lap I didn't run away from it.[18]

Trimble had appointed Mark Neale as one of the voting scrutineers. From Portadown, Neale would later go on to work for Trimble when he became first minister. After delegates had voted in the first round, Neale was able to give Trimble the good news privately that he was the lead candidate. The votes were then read out to the activists in the hall:

Martyn Smyth – 60 (7%)
Willie Ross – 116 (14%)
Ken Maginnis – 117 (15%)
John Taylor – 226 (28%)
David Trimble – 287 (36%)

Neale remembers how Trimble reacted when he gave him the news:

He was standing right against the pillar, and he then said something I never expected him to say. I rarely heard him use language like this, and he put his head on the pillar, and he said, 'Fuck, that is not what I expected to happen.' And I said to Daphne, 'You know, he's won.' And then I said, 'You know he's going to win it. Did he expect it?' And she said, 'Well, he wouldn't have gone in for it if he didn't expect to win.'[19]

Trimble was ahead of the pack, but he knew it was not a done deal, and there could be a twist in the race to be leader. He had experience from his Upper Bann selection to stand as a Westminster candidate, when Sam Gardiner was initially ahead in the first round and Trimble subsequently triumphed. A second round of voting then took place after Martin Smyth dropped out, and the results looked just as good for Trimble, who saw his vote tally rise and his percentage creep towards the 50 per cent mark. The second round looked like this:

Ross – 91 (11%)
Maginnis – 110 (13.5%)
Taylor – 255 (31.5%)
Trimble – 353 (44%)

It now seemed likely that Trimble would be the next leader of the UUP. Reg Empey remembers collecting the voting slips from delegates after the second round:

> I was going around collecting the ballots and there was a large number of people from Foyle and the Londonderry area at the front. And I could detect from them that they were switching to Trimble. And Ken Maginnis was the third to drop out. I think most of us assumed that that would help Taylor, but when it did, to a point it wasn't enough. So, it was obvious as the count went on: I could feel, going round the delegates, that they were moving towards Trimble.[20]

There was a third ballot after Willie Ross and Ken Maginnis bowed out. Then Jim Nicholson declared the result:

Taylor – 333 (42%)
Trimble – 466 (58%)

It was a remarkable result for the least experienced candidate in the race. The youngest contender, who had only become an MP in 1990, had outflanked his older, more seasoned rivals – a man who had previously found it difficult to get selected at party meetings and had failed to win a council seat. Trimble, the 'nearly man', as some in the party called him, had finally arrived. The grassroots wanted a 'bastard', as Josias Cunningham had predicted, and in some people's eyes Trimble fitted the bill. He was seen as tough and uncompromising. It seemed the days of having a 'gentleman' leader were over.

Trimble, who had served his political apprenticeship in Vanguard and then the Ulster Clubs, and was a hero in Drumcree, was now at the top of the unionist establishment. Jim Wilson, who was UUP's general secretary at the time, says the party grassroots wanted someone who could stand up and sell unionism, and Trimble fitted the bill:

> I think he had ambition. He was very good on the media, television and radio. I just thought the man was the right man for the job.[21]

Even close observers of unionist politics misread Trimble's ascent. Paul Bew, then a Queen's University academic who would go on to become one of Trimble's unofficial advisers, was surprised by his victory. Bew and Trimble knew each other well and shared a love of history and books. They would have had coffee together during Trimble's lecturing days. Bew would later sit in the House of Lords and would become an influential figure in Westminster as the chair of the Committee on Standards in Public Life.

Back in 1995, Bew had been convinced Taylor would be Molyneaux's successor:

> The signs of who would be the modernising leader of unionism were there. If you looked at what was being written and said at the time, Taylor was the more obvious choice, and this is so until David actually takes over. Taylor *is* the more obvious choice. It was a big surprise. I thought Taylor would win.[22]

Trimble was now in charge, and it soon became clear he was a leader in a hurry. The night of the leadership vote, the four Trimble children were being looked after by their regular babysitter. They were all conscious that it was a big night for their father – although naturally Sarah, who was just three years old, had little understanding of what was happening. Vicky Trimble remembers how she and her brothers tried to involve her in what was happening:

> We told her that Dad was in a race to become leader of the party. He won the race and was now leader of the party. We made it a bit of a game for her, and that is how we dealt with it. We dealt it with it by talking to my wee sister. I do remember I came into school my first day in school after he became leader. There was a guy in my class, and he just said, 'Does that make you rich now?'[23]

The Trimbles were not about to become wealthy, despite the perception of Vicky's classmate, but their lives were certainly about to change. With the added pressure of leadership on Trimble's shoulders, there would be more media scrutiny on his words and actions. He was now the biggest voice of Ulster unionism. What Trimble said mattered and would impact on Northern Ireland's political landscape.

In his first formal press conference as leader, he made it clear what needed to happen before inter-party talks could begin:

> I certainly can't see talks proceeding without progress on decommissioning. But really what I'm saying is the

decommissioning, handing up some weapons[,] may not be enough, because it may not establish a commitment to exclusively peaceful methods.[24]

John Hume, the SDLP leader, said his wish was that the discussions his party had previously had with Jim Molyneaux would continue under Trimble's leadership. Gerry Adams, the Sinn Féin president, said he hoped Trimble would reach out and have talks with political parties across the board:

> One could argue that you're better dealing with the hardliners. Someone softer could not deliver. And you know, one of the challenges of leadership is to lead – not to stay behind the barricades shouting the old 'no surrender' slogan but to actually lead the situation forward, and to lead his section of our people forward.[25]

Trimble's rivals for the leadership gave the new UUP chief their public support. It was difficult for the four losers, and particularly for John Taylor, who had been tipped to become Molyneaux's successor. Taylor, who would assume the role of deputy leader, pledged his loyalty and described Trimble's victory as 'magnificent'.

Ken Maginnis, who was pushed into third place, also pledged his support to Trimble, but not before offering the new leader some rather pointed advice:

> I think he has had a mantle cast around his shoulders now – a new mantle. And that new mantle will give him new thoughts. It will foster new ideas. It will bring a new sense of responsibility, one hopes.[26]

What Maginnis was saying was he hoped that David Trimble, as leader, would turn out to be different from David Trimble the so-called 'hero of Drumcree'. He hoped the burden of leadership would push

Trimble down the road of political accommodation rather than confrontation. Maginnis's comment had a jag attached, just as the remarks of Adams and Hume had underlying wishes attached.

Trimble's surprise victory was quite the story. It made many political commentators begin to examine the mood of the party and pose serious questions. Was this a lurch to the right? Was it simply the Drumcree factor that got Trimble elected? Would Trimble be as tough and uncompromising a leader as he was during his Vanguard and Ulster Clubs days? Did this put the peace process in jeopardy?

Many journalists had got their prediction wrong, although in fairness, so too did the bookmakers, who had made Taylor the favourite. Understandably, Trimble's success brought much comment on the airwaves and in print, and a large degree of it was hostile. The Dublin-based newspaper the *Sunday Tribune* declared:

> The political impact of the David Trimble victory is still being assessed. The result was a disappointment to nationalists and generally regarded as a contemptuous rejection of the peace process and the hopes that a unionist [F.W] De Klerk [the South African president who helped to end apartheid] might emerge on the scene.[27]

The *Derry Journal* reported that nationalists would have preferred either John Taylor or Ken Maginnis to triumph. It also stated:

> David Trimble has already shown himself an astute politician and by far the best communicator among the unionist politicians. If he can add pragmatism to his already formidable skills his election could turn out to be a decisive positive turning point in Northern Ireland.[28]

It was a bold hope from the *Derry Journal*, which clearly spotted something in Trimble that many in other parts of the media had not registered. Was there more to Trimble than this hard man image from

Drumcree? Was Trimble the street protester about to become Trimble the pragmatist?

On the weekend of Trimble's election as leader, many political activists, academics and journalists gathered for a meeting of the British–Irish Association in Cambridge. It was an annual get-together and was very much part of the political calendar for anyone interested in Anglo-Irish relations and the politics of Northern Ireland. As delegates arrived, there was a general expectation amongst those attending that Taylor was on track to succeed Molyneaux. There was real shock when news of Trimble's triumph filtered through.

UUP party member Michael McGimpsey attended the Ulster Hall vote and then travelled over to Cambridge:

> We got into the British–Irish Association on the Saturday morning, and everybody was suffering from a massive hangover. They could hardly move about because when they heard that David Trimble had been elected leader of the Ulster Unionist Party, they concluded that it was the end of the peace process.[29]

Michael's brother Chris also travelled over to Cambridge. The McGimpseys were seen to be on the liberal wing of the party and had both backed Ken Maginnis for leader. Chris remembers that there were real fears about what direction Trimble was about to take the party in:

> I thought he would provoke all sorts of violence. I thought he'd not got the diplomacy or the vision that Molyneaux had. And I thought this guy is going to be our version of Ian Paisley. Molyneaux always held Paisley back, you know. So, who is going to hold anybody back when you have somebody so far right?[30]

Trimble's friend Ruth Dudley Edwards was also at the British–Irish Association conference in Cambridge. She was genuinely taken aback at the negative reaction to Trimble's election, and thought delegates predicting 'doom and gloom' were exaggerating about what Trimble would do as leader:

> I couldn't believe what was going on, and the McGimpseys were as bad as anybody. This was the 'end of civilisation' as anybody knew it. 'The man was a monster.' It is a bit like Trump, except that there is less reason for it, you know? And I thought, 'Well, I don't think so, you know'. And I remember the following morning actually. All of this tirade. The awfulness of it. It was all terrible.[31]

John Alderdice of the Alliance Party, who would later become speaker of the Assembly, was also in Cambridge that weekend. He recalls how the news of Trimble's victory changed the mood of the conference:

> The announcement came through that David had been elected leader. And it was as though this great pool of gloom descended over the whole meeting. Because all that everybody really knew was that he'd been elected because of his role in Drumcree. That was the sense of things. How could this possibly be a positive thing for the kind of people who were there who basically wanted some kind of negotiated agreement? And it was bad enough if you had Ian Paisley, but with the leader of unionism also involved with Drumcree getting elected for that reason? Goodness me. So, I just remember this kind of sense of a great black cloud descending over the meeting at the time.[32]

Trimble's critics immediately suggested that the new leader would now try to outflank Paisley and take the UUP to the right, recalling the recent image of Paisley and Trimble walking together in Portadown – which they viewed as triumphalist.

Mark Durkan was also in Cambridge that weekend:

> The defining image that people had of David Trimble as a prospective leader of unionism was hand in hand with Paisley at Carleton Street, and there was a sense ... of defiance and triumphalism. So, people kind of thought, 'Is that what the standard of his leadership is going to be?' And very much the chat around the British–Irish Association then was 'That's a bit of a shock', but you know not everybody was completely rubbishing Trimble. Other people would have been saying, 'Well, you know, we have to work with whatever we have to work with', that sort of thing.[33]

In Dublin, Trimble's ascent to the UUP leadership was initially greeted with shock and some fear. Bertie Ahern, who would later develop a warm working relationship with Trimble, remembers how his opponents viewed him:

> They saw him, as I did too, as being a kind of an extremist, and we were going to have problems with him. I suppose I hadn't met him at that stage. I remember when he got the leadership, I was at one of those British–Irish debates ... and there was a lot of consternation when he got elected. People didn't expect that he was going to get elected at that time, as you recall. And when he was elected, we said, 'Oh God, how are we going to deal with this guy? How is this going to pan out? He is one of Paisley's allies and we're not going to get anywhere with him.'[34]

Ahern's shock and concern were echoed in the Irish civil service, particularly amongst staff who had responsibility for Northern Ireland. Dublin diplomat Tim O'Connor worked in the Anglo-Irish division and was one of a number of 'travellers' – the name given to civil servants who regularly visited Northern Ireland to meet political contacts. O'Connor's knowledge of Trimble was based on what he had read and observed:

We didn't quite know what to make of him. In politics, a big part of what you're doing is a judgement, an assessment about where somebody is coming from and how serious they are, and what's their likely direction of travel and so on. So, all of that was going on. He was a bit of an unknown quantity, so there was a bit of a rapid catch-up going on.[35]

In London, the general feeling in political and diplomatic circles regarding Trimble's success was one of surprise. One British government minister would later reveal that he almost spat out his breakfast cereal on the Saturday morning when he heard on the radio that Trimble had won. Ruth Dudley Edwards remembers the negative coverage surrounding Trimble's election and disagreed with a lot of the analysis:

I did write him a letter at the time, just a note. And I said, 'I don't think the things that are being said about you are fair.' And he just sent me a note back saying something like, 'It will all become clear in time.'[36]

Trimble was being coy with his friend. Would it all become clear? Was there a secret plan he had in mind? Was the serial protester who epitomised unionist intransigence about to walk the road of a statesman and a peacemaker? The Upper Bann MP now had a strong mandate from party members, and he had a plan of action – albeit a private one.

One of his first actions was to host Proinsias De Rossa, the leader of Democratic Left, at UUP headquarters in Glengall Street. De Rossa was a former vice president of Official Sinn Féin and had been in the IRA. It was a symbolic move by Trimble, an acknowledgement that he was prepared to talk to his rivals, and particularly those who embraced democratic politics. It was a signal that, as a unionist leader, he would be outward-looking.

His move to invite a politician from the Republic did not enamour him to the DUP. In the months to come, however, they would have much bigger differences with the Ulster Unionists' 12th leader.

14

NEW LABOUR, NEW IDEAS

*'There were times when you thought he could
start a fight in an empty room.'*
Tony Blair on David Trimble

David Kerr was experiencing the most unusual job interview of his life. In truth, the young graduate had not had that many, but this was the oddest and the one that would change his life. He was sitting in the passenger seat of David Trimble's car outside UUP headquarters in Belfast. It was a Saturday in February 1996, and Kerr, the son of Bertie, a Fermanagh unionist councillor, was keen to get a part-time position with the party.

Trimble, some five months into his leadership, needed someone to help with media inquiries and deal with correspondence. He naturally wanted somebody whose judgement he could trust and who shared his views on what position unionists needed to take in the months ahead. There was most likely going to be inter-party talks and the UUP needed to be prepared. Trimble wanted an ideas man, and Kerr had mapped out his thoughts in a newspaper article, which the Upper Bann MP had read.

For 30 minutes, the young student and the politician talked about what Kerr had done at university and what his views were. They chatted about what the UUP needed to do, and what was likely to happen in the coming months. As Kerr recalled:

> We seemed to get on very well. The whole thing was very polite. It kind of felt like a meeting with your university tutor, in the sense you are getting some kind of

academic review of your CV, and they are trying to find out a bit about you. But he knew my father. He had been in Vanguard with Dad many years ago. So, he knew the pedigree, the Ulster unionist pedigree in our family going back many years.[1]

David Kerr began working for Trimble in March 1996 from an office in party headquarters in Glengall Street. He quickly got used to the Trimble style of leadership, which was unpredictable:

It was organised, busy, strategic, energetic, sometimes bad-tempered but sometimes good-humoured. I think I've used various phrases over the years, but he could be abrasive most of the time.[2]

Kerr quickly got to know how to read Trimble's mood and style. He could sense when he was going to be relaxed and when he was most likely going to be angry about a particular political development. Kerr began his job at party headquarters at an exciting political time, although it perhaps did not always feel like it. His father, Bertie, had offered rather prophetic words of encouragement to him when he was appointed:

You never know what might happen in the next year or two. You never know, there might even be a deal.[3]

Bertie Kerr's prescient comment in March 1996 came to pass two years later in April 1998 on the afternoon of Good Friday. The seeds of that groundbreaking deal were planted in a series of discussions with the local parties and the two governments that happened in the months leading up to 1998.

In 1996, the bones of a deal were already being discussed. Any future settlement would involve a new Assembly, an Executive, North–South bodies and commitments over the principle of consent, paramilitary activity and decommissioning. The issue of policing would also have to be addressed. David Kerr was present at a series of meetings with other party leaders, and he particularly remembers an encounter with the SDLP. The two parties met at the Stormont Estate, and Kerr recalls how he found the encounter with John Hume positive and uplifting.

Kerr remembers what SDLP leader John Hume told the meeting:

> [Hume said,] 'We are all here to make an agreement. You want an Assembly. Basically, you know we want a North–South dimension to the agreement to recognise our Irish identity and to give some balance to the overall political equation here ...' And he [Hume] actually said, 'I don't care what it's called. If we can get agreement on how that works, and we can get a deal on power-sharing, then we will have a deal.' And Trimble said, in response to that, 'Look, if the North–South element is not a threat to unionism, then we are up for that. Basically, we are up for a deal.'[4]

Kerr, then a novice in the art of political negotiation, was blown away by the positivity of the meeting:

> When I got up from the meeting I thought, 'My God we will have this deal done in no time.'[5]

Kerr felt very positive about the way the UUP and the SDLP had interacted. In his eyes, it was a good sign and an indication of how the two leading parties could do business. However, he was warned by senior figures in the party that the political mood could change. While the chemistry on this occasion between Hume and Trimble had been good, it was made clear to Kerr by his colleagues that it was not always like that.

By this point, Senator George Mitchell had become an important figure in the political process, and he devised a set of principles on which inter-party negotiations should be based. In January 1996, he outlined a series of ground rules that would eventually underpin the Good Friday negotiations. Mitchell wanted the political parties to give guarantees that they would use democratic and exclusively peaceful means of resolving political issues. He suggested there must be the 'total disarmament of all paramilitary organisations', and for the parties to agree that 'disarmament must be verifiable to the satisfaction of an independent commission'. The parties also had to renounce violence and any threat to use force 'to influence the course of all-party negotiations'.[6]

These areas would become known as the 'Mitchell Principles'. Steeped in the politics of the Democratic Party, Mitchell was a highly experienced political operator. He served as a federal judge, was a former Senate majority leader and was a close friend of President Bill Clinton's. Of Irish descent, he was no stranger to Northern Ireland and was widely respected by the local parties.

For much of 1996, the issue of weapons and violence dominated the political conversation. On 9 February, just over two weeks after the Mitchell Report on Decommissioning was published, the IRA ended its ceasefire with a large bomb in the Docklands area of London. It would have devastating consequences for those caught up in the explosion and the political ramifications were far-reaching. The bombing threw the peace process into crisis, and Sinn Féin found themselves frozen out of meetings and talks.

Sceptics of the IRA's original ceasefire in August 1994 suggested that they were right to question the bona fides of republicans. Prime Minister John Major described the attack as 'an appalling outrage', while Taoiseach John Bruton immediately broke off ministerial contact with Sinn Féin. Trimble said republicans who had previously been lobbying for their inclusion in peace talks were clearly sending mixed messages:

> If there has been a resumption of violence, then it has clearly been done in order to try and prevent elections in Northern Ireland. It is incredible that people who, for the last 18 months, have been telling us they want to move into the democratic process should be resorting to violence.[7]

Gerry Adams, the Sinn Féin president, said that he was saddened by the Docklands bombing in London and that he regretted that an opportunity for peace had foundered because of the 'refusal of the British government and unionist leaders to enter into dialogue and substantive negotiations'.[8]

Discussions between Irish and British officials went on in March and April to find new ways to advance the political process. Then the two governments announced that talks would begin on 10 June, and that the parties would have to agree to the Mitchell Principles laid out by the former US senator. Proximity talks began in early March, with Sinn Féin being refused entry due to the collapse of the IRA ceasefire.

In late March, John Major announced that elections would be held in May to a new body called the Northern Ireland Forum for Political Dialogue, which would be made up of 110 delegates. The aim was to get widespread political involvement. The two governments were particularly keen to get loyalist representatives involved, in the knowledge that they could help deliver a peace deal in the months ahead.

For Trimble, the elections to the forum on 30 May marked his first electoral test as UUP leader, and he and his party performed well. The Ulster Unionists emerged as the largest party, with 30 seats on a vote share of 24.2 per cent. The DUP took 24 seats, the SDLP won 21, Sinn Féin took 17 and the Alliance secured 7. The result marked a good poll debut for Trimble. It kept the UUP as Northern Ireland's largest party, and the tally of 30 seats was a healthy return. The top-up system boosted the main parties, but also meant that the smaller parties had a say. The UK Unionists ended up with 3 seats. The loyalist groupings, the Progressive Unionist Party (PUP) and the UDP; the NI Women's Coalition; and the Labour Coalition – all got 2 seats. The results produced a representative spread of opinion, as officials in London and Dublin had hoped.

In June, talks began at Stormont, and Sinn Féin was still refused entry because of the collapsed IRA ceasefire. The discussions did not get off to a smooth beginning, and there were early arguments over the role of George Mitchell. Trimble made it abundantly clear he was not happy with the format.

In an interview for this book, Mitchell recalled how the talks began in 1996:

> Trimble did not support me at first, but he made it clear that he was not opposed to me personally. He was opposed to the British and Irish governments trying to establish the agenda and the process by which it would occur. So, he withheld support from me until the British and Irish governments agreed that it would be the parties that would decide how to proceed in the talks. So, it began with great difficulty in 1996. Sinn Féin was not then in the talks. And we proceeded with the nine political parties and the two governments ... It took us three months just to establish a set of rules ... [There was] a lot of hostility and a lot of negativism and criticism. No offence to the press ... but there was one gate, and right outside the gate reporters congregated, and of course all the delegates had to walk through. And every day they would be questioned, 'Well, look here, your opponent said this. You don't agree with that, do you?' And 'There is a rumour there might be an agreement on that. You would never do that, would you?' And so the delegates, as they entered and left the talks, were subjected to intense questioning, and it was very hard.[9]

Progress was painstakingly slow. In fact, to political observers, it was hard to point out what had been achieved, apart from the fact that people were talking and were in the same room. In the summer of 1996, the prospects of a breakthrough looked incredibly unlikely. As ever, the political agenda was driven by events on the ground, and in July the annual Orange Order parade at Drumcree raised tensions across the community.

The RUC prevented Orangemen from returning to Portadown via the Garvaghy Road after the service at Drumcree Parish Church, and the ban led to protests, roadblocks and violence. Michael McGoldrick, a Catholic taxi driver, was shot dead by loyalists, and the finger of blame was pointed in the direction of a breakaway group from the UVF controlled by leading Portadown loyalist Billy Wright.

At the talks at Stormont, the UUP, the DUP and the UK Unionist Party all pulled out. In the days that followed, towns and villages were blockaded, and RUC officers were severely stretched. The government sent in an extra 1,000 troops, and the news bulletins were filled with reports of rioting and intimidation. Then, on 11 July, the RUC chief constable overturned his original decision and allowed the Drumcree Orangemen to return to Portadown town centre down the Garvaghy Road. Nationalists and republicans were appalled by the decision and accused the police of giving in to threats of violence. Rioting broke out in nationalist areas across Northern Ireland, and within days the SDLP announced they were withdrawing from the forum.

The events in Drumcree, in Trimble's constituency, placed him once again firmly in the media spotlight. The BBC programme *Panorama* revealed Trimble had met Billy Wright, whose splinter group was being blamed for the killing of Michael McGoldrick. The SDLP said Trimble was guilty of having double standards by speaking to Wright but refusing to speak to the Garvaghy residents' group. Trimble justified his meeting with Wright, saying the circumstances were unusual and the loyalist ceasefire was 'under dire threat'.[10]

The explanation did little to impress those in the nationalist and republican community, who felt that Trimble, as the local MP, should engage with the Garvaghy Road residents. Others suggested he was also being hypocritical because he was prepared to criticise John Hume for having discussions with Gerry Adams, yet he was talking with a man associated with loyalist paramilitaries.

The SDLP claimed Trimble's meeting with Wright meant he had potentially breached the Mitchell Principles. As the summer ended, its relationship with the UUP was now becoming strained. It was light years away from the positive meeting between Hume and Trimble – an encounter which David Kerr had found most positive.

By September, Trimble had been UUP leader for a year and the forum reconvened for more discussions, but the SDLP stayed away. It was not a good look and was testament to the breakdown in inter-party relations over the summer. Within the UUP, Trimble had tried to put the party on a more professional footing during his first 12 months as leader. That included sharpening the media message.

On one occasion, Councillor Chris McGimpsey was to appear on the BBC *Newsnight* programme, but Trimble was initially unaware of it. When he found out, he rang McGimpsey's home, but his party colleague had left and was already at Broadcasting House in Belfast, as McGimpsey recalls:

> And I was just about to go on air when my wife came on in dreadful tears. She said, 'I've had that horrible man Trimble on the phone screaming and shouting and yelling at me because he wants you not to go on the TV.' I said, 'Well, just ignore him.' She said, 'I could not go through that again.' And she got me to promise to pull out of the programme, which was a mistake. And then I got this letter. It was clearly a letter dictated by him.[11]

The letter made it clear that all future media appearances needed to be approved by party headquarters. It was all part of Trimble's plan to control the way the UUP looked to the outside world.

In the autumn of 1996, as the party conference season approached in Britain, Trimble decided to reach out to the Labour Party, the official opposition at Westminster. Tony Blair, who had become leader in 1994, following the sudden death of John Smith, was now being widely tipped to be the next prime minister.

Trimble knew it was important for the UUP to have good relations with any future government, and he sanctioned the first official trip to the Labour Party's annual conference. He boarded a plane in Belfast, but his travel plans were thrown into chaos when thick fog meant the flight was first diverted to the Isle of Man and then rerouted to Liverpool.

Journalists Hugh Jordan and Henry McDonald were also on the plane and, like Trimble, were bound for the Winter Gardens conference centre in Blackpool. The reporters and the politician struck up a conversation and chatted about history, politics and music. Inevitably, the subject turned to one of Trimble's favourite composers, Richard Wagner, the German musician famed for his operas. Jordan recalls how the conversation went:

> So, I said to him, 'Wagner, he was a Nazi?' He said, 'No, he wasn't. He was anti-Semitic. There is a difference.' And that's quite an insight into Trimble's personality. He likes the minutiae of things, and there's a difference between Nazism and anti-Semitism, and he knew the difference. He wasn't going to allow old Wagner to be maligned by someone from Glasgow who'd never listened to him in his life.[12]

Jordan recalls that Trimble was relaxed and in good humour, and over the day he saw a different side to him. When they finally arrived at the airport in Liverpool, they met a PR man from Northern Ireland who was also going to the conference. He had hired a car and invited Trimble and the journalists to join him on the road trip to Blackpool. Jordan recalls that, as they were leaving the terminal, his phone beeped:

> So, my phone went in my pocket, and I took it out. And a voice said, 'You have a new voice message.' So, I hit the number, and the voice said, 'You are through to the Orange answering service.' I said, 'Mr Trimble, what kind of power have you got here, the Orange answering service.' Which we didn't have in Northern Ireland. But he knew all about it. And he loved it, and he burst out laughing at that.[13]

The silly phone gag set the tone for a relaxed, joke-laden few hours as the four men made their way to Blackpool. Jordan recalls at one stage their journey came to halt at Lytham St Annes, a seaside town south of Blackpool. A man leading a group of around 20 donkeys walked in front of the car, bringing traffic to a standstill. The donkeys were being taken to the beach for rides for children. It gave Jordan, who was sitting in the back seat, another opportunity to test his schoolboy humour on the UUP leader:

> I leant forward and said to Trimble, 'Do you know what those donkeys get for their lunch?' And, he said, 'I don't, as a matter of fact.' I said, 'They get about half an hour.' And he buckles in laughter, and he went into fits. It was as though no one else in the world had ever told a joke before. He just laughed and laughed and laughed and couldn't stop laughing. What that gave me in the future was, if I ever bumped into him or ever phoned him – and I didn't phone him very much – but it gave me access to him, that stupid joke. He always took my call. Or if he saw me somewhere he would come up and have a chat. All over that stupid joke.[14]

After his journey to Blackpool, Jordan was left with a different view of the unionist leader. He knew Trimble was often prickly with journalists and was short-tempered, but he had seen a different side to the man, and it was far removed from the pent-up, humourless politician that newspaper cartoonists were keen to portray.

Blackpool was a new experience for Trimble. Traditionally, he would have been more at home in Conservative gatherings, so his time at Labour's annual conference was an eye-opener. There was a sense of optimism in the air. Labour activists believed they were on course to finally unseat the Tories and get back into Downing Street after an 18-year absence.

Tony Blair and his advisers had rebranded the party as 'New Labour', and his leadership had struck a chord with the electorate. If the opinion polls were right, he would be the next prime minister. Trimble knew he and his party needed to make connections and be ready for a Labour administration.

At Blackpool, he met up with David Montgomery, a family friend from his Bangor days, who was now a senior executive with the Mirror

Group of Newspapers. As the *Daily Mirror* was a Labour-supporting newspaper, Montgomery was a key figure at the conference and very useful to Trimble in making contacts. Montgomery remembers how difficult it was to get Trimble to mix with Labour MPs:

> He was an object of great fascination to the Labour front bench, as you would expect, because he was the first unionist leader ever to turn up at a Labour conference. And therefore, many of the front bench, people like Alistair Darling, came up to David and said, 'You must have dinner with us', meaning him and a number of other shadow ministers. And David continually refused. And we all sat down and had dinner with some of the shadow ministers, and we all sat down together. I went off somewhere to make a call and I found him [Trimble] in this grand hotel room with big pillars. I found David sitting behind a pillar at a table for one with a book propped up against a pillar as he was eating his dinner in solitary isolation. Bookish is a good description of him, because he was among the party leadership that was likely to assume the Westminster government within a year or so, [and] there he was sitting by himself, with all these interesting people around him. But he preferred to immerse himself in a book.[15]

Trimble's inability to mix and network at social occasions frustrated his colleagues, who often felt he was wasting good opportunities to make contacts and develop personal relationships. Much of it rests with Trimble's personality. He was by nature introverted and was very content being on his own. There was an expectation, though, as party leader, that he would reach out to people at social functions.

Dennis Rogan, who would go on to sit in the House of Lords as Lord Rogan, was at many UUP gatherings with Trimble and remembers trying to get his party leader to go round the room and mix socially:

> We would go to functions and he and Daphne would be there. My wife and I would be at the function with all the party and David and Daphne would arrive. And what did he do? He came and he wanted to talk to me, and I'd say, 'David, for goodness' sake, I can see you tomorrow. Do what Jim Molyneaux would have done: work the room.' He found it very difficult to do that. I put it down to him being shy.[16]

Those days in Blackpool in October 1996 were an opportunity for Trimble to acquaint himself with a government in waiting. His relationship with Tony Blair would be a crucial one – particularly during the negotiations leading up to Good Friday 1998. One of the first moves Blair had made as the new Labour leader was to drop Kevin McNamara as shadow Northern Ireland Secretary. He was seen as 'too green' by unionists, and Blair replaced him with Mo Mowlam. Blair says this move was part of his fresh approach to a new Labour policy on Northern Ireland, and Trimble realised what he was trying to do.

In an interview for this book, Sir Tony Blair says he thought early on that he and Trimble would get on:

> I first came across David really when I became leader of the opposition. And I realised Northern Ireland is one of those issues we're going to have to deal with. I met him and I found him actually pretty easy to deal with. I found him quite insightful, actually. He recognised when I made the change and moved Kevin McNamara. He realised that I was prepared to be open to unionists' point of view, which was important.[17]

Blair says that, in those early conversations with Trimble, his intellect shone through:

> The thing I realised about David straight away was that he was highly intelligent. So, for me that was important,

because it meant that whatever his politics you could have a proper conversation with him. You were not going to be speaking to a brick wall.[18]

Even though the encounters were personable and thoughtful, Blair eventually experienced the famous Trimble temper – when his anger and frustration sometimes got the better of him:

There were times when you thought he could start a fight in an empty room. And you could never be sure what was going to trigger it, by the way. But it kind of came and went.[19]

Alastair Campbell was working for Tony Blair at this stage. He first came into contact with David Trimble when he was employed as a journalist with the *Daily Mirror*. He would contact the UUP leader when he was writing stories about Northern Ireland. Campbell would later go to work in Downing Street, after Labour's election victory in 1997, and he would become a key strategist with Blair. He says that, in the early days, he found Trimble hard to engage with:

If I had an overwhelming impression from those times, it is that he was quite difficult to talk to. He had a nice manner about him in some ways. Obviously working on the *Mirror*, you had to get on, you had to know everybody. And so those would have been my first encounters with him. Asking him, 'What is going on?' and 'What is happening?' I did find him quite difficult to talk to. I normally can usually bring people out quite well. I found him quite sober and quite straight and quite difficult to engage.[20]

Others found Trimble much easier to deal with. Eileen Bell of the Alliance Party, who became the first female Speaker of the Assembly, says he was supportive, courteous and kind:

> He always treated me in a way that he showed his respect for me, which wasn't the thing that always happened in my time in politics. He actually treated me as a woman who had ideas about politics and had opinions about politics, and he listened to them.[21]

After the Labour conference of 1996, Trimble and Blair continued to have discussions about Northern Ireland and how an incoming Labour administration should handle the political process. As the year ended, there was little progress to report. In March 1997, the multi-party talks were adjourned to allow the parties to contest the general election. By this point, the opinion polls continued to look healthy for Labour, and it seemed certain that John Major would be leaving Downing Street.

Blair remembers having discussions with David Trimble about what should happen in the early days of a Labour government:

> I would see him from time to time and he gave me the advice before the 1997 election, 'If you really want to have a go at this Northern Ireland thing, the first thing you should do is go and make a pitch to the unionist community.' And I think he was quite instrumental in deciding what, how and where I would do that.[22]

On 1 May 1997, the UK went to the polls and, as expected, returned a Labour government, with a massive majority of 147 seats. It was an astounding victory for Tony Blair and his 'New Labour' project, and he became the first Labour prime minister to occupy Downing Street in 18 years. Blair's dramatic success would change the British political landscape, and in turn his election would help to kick-start the peace process. The general election also proved successful for the UUP, and the party continued to have the lion's share of Westminster seats.

Trimble enjoyed his first general election as leader, and the party returned 10 MPs. The SDLP went back to the Commons with 3 MPs, the DUP 2, Sinn Féin 2 and Bob McCartney retained his seat in North Down. It was a good result for the UUP and for Trimble, and he retained his position as the leading voice of unionism.

It was all change as well in the NIO as Mo Mowlam, the MP for Redcar, became the first woman to become Northern Ireland secretary. She was a breath of fresh air compared to previous office holders and instantly became a hit with the public for her chatty, easy-going style.

There was a sense in London and in Belfast that things were going to be very different from the 18 years of Conservative rule. Blair kept his word to Trimble that Northern Ireland would be a political priority, and the UUP leader came to Downing Street for talks within days of Labour taking power. It was agreed that Blair would travel to Belfast and make a speech that was designed to reinvigorate the political process, reassure unionists and urge republicans to abandon violence and embrace the democratic path.

On Friday 16 May 1997, Blair visited the Balmoral Show in Belfast. It is an annual highlight for Northern Ireland's farming community, and traditionally the event attracts great crowds and garners much media interest. Before the prime minister left London, journalists were tipped off that there would be some important passages in his speech, and in political circles there was an expectation that Blair was about to make a major intervention.

In Belfast, Blair committed his new administration to fully supporting the Framework Document and to backing the Mitchell Principles, and he said how he valued Northern Ireland's place within the UK. He made it clear, as Trimble had suggested in their previous conversations, that he cherished the union between Northern Ireland and the rest of the UK. On political progress, Blair mapped out what had to happen, and he talked about the need for an IRA ceasefire and decommissioning.

This, according to Blair, was essential and had to happen, and he issued this warning to republicans:

> The settlement train is leaving. I want you on that train, but it is leaving anyway, and I will not allow it to wait for you. You cannot hold the process to ransom any longer. So, end the violence now. I want to hear Sinn Féin's answer.[23]

Blair recalls how Trimble influenced the contents of his Belfast speech:

> He said to me (and it did make an impression): ... 'You have got to show the unionist people that you actually value the union. If you can't show them that you value the union, then they'll never really accept anything else you say.' So that was really the purpose of that speech, even though it got slightly different publicity. But the fact that it was the first speech I made as prime minister, and it was to the unionist community, was in part because that was David's strong advice.[24]

Trimble was pleased with the Balmoral Show speech, and it was clear his personal relationship with Blair was already paying dividends. The Labour leader had only been in office a matter of days, but already his Belfast comments had set the agenda and the tone. He was a prime minister in a hurry and wanted the political process in Northern Ireland to step up a gear.

He was not the only new leader determined to make his mark. In June 1997, voters in the Republic of Ireland went to the polls, and a new coalition emerged made up of Fianna Fáil, the Progressive Democrats and a number of Independents. Bertie Ahern became the new taoiseach, and, like Blair, he was keen to see movement in Northern Ireland.

Ahern and Blair were similar leaders. In their mid-forties, articulate and likeable, they were deal makers with a refreshing lack of political baggage. The two premiers quickly established a warm working relationship. The peace process in Northern Ireland had shown little progress in recent months, but political changes in London and Dublin would give it a new impetus. Ahern and Blair were now central to making things happen.

15

THE FINAL COUNTDOWN

'Nerves of steel will be needed.'
David Trimble in the run-up to Good Friday 1998

On Wednesday 17 September 1997, David Trimble was standing in a car park at Castle Buildings on the Stormont Estate. His mobile phone rang, and he looked at the name on the screen. It was Tony Blair. The prime minister began with a very simple question: 'Where are we now?' The UUP leader told him where he was and said that he was about to enter the talks building. Blair was genuinely shocked, 'Oh. They told me you would never do it.'[1]

Blair believed Trimble was going to boycott this latest round of discussions. He had been expected to turn up the previous day. When he did not appear, officials in London assumed Trimble was going to stay away permanently. Instead of going to the talks, Trimble had gone to visit the scene of a bomb attack:

> There was a major bomb in Markethill, a bomb set off by dissident republicans. And it was timed for that [the start of talks] and clearly timed to bounce us out of the situation. Now Markethill wasn't in my constituency, it was just across the line from my constituency. And I just sort of said, 'Right, we are not going in today [to the talks]. I've got to go down to Markethill.' Which I did, and we will go in the next day. And I kept Blair waiting for a while, unclear as to what I was doing and why I was doing it.[2]

After the trip to Markethill, it was game on. Flanked by his party colleagues and representatives of the two loyalist parties, the UDP and the PUP, Trimble walked past the camera crews into the talks complex. It was David Kerr's idea for the UUP delegation to walk into the building with the loyalist groupings.

It was a defining moment in more ways than one. It showed that Trimble and the UUP were serious about negotiating a deal, and it indicated that he was prepared to be different from other unionists, notably the DUP and the UK Unionists, who had walked out in July. The photograph of Trimble and the loyalists walking in together became an iconic picture, appearing in news bulletins and on newspaper front pages.

The image prompted wisecracks from Belfast's watching press corps. One reporter suggested it resembled a famous walking scene from the iconic Quentin Tarantino movie *Reservoir Dogs*. Another journalist suggested Trimble's version should be called 'Reservoir Prods'. The picture showed a unity of purpose, but there were others in the UUP who were uneasy seeing their leader pictured with representatives of loyalist paramilitaries.

Dawn Purvis was one of those who walked into Castle Buildings that day with Trimble. A member of the PUP, she would later go on to become an MLA and lead her party. She found Trimble detached and distant:

> I always regarded him as a bit of a cold fish – very focused and very determined in terms of his views, his mind and the way he wanted things done. And he didn't like people to get in his way. He did not suffer fools easily. And I often thought that he regretted or resented the fact that he had to deal with loyalism, that he had to deal with the PUP and the UDP.[3]

The reality is that, in September 1997, the UUP and the smaller loyalist parties needed each other. It meant that a majority of unionists were in the talks process. David Adams, of the UDP, remembers the time very well. He had previously been a member of the loyalist paramilitary group,

David as a child. Here with his mother, Ivy, his sister, Rosemary, and his grandmother, Ida. The picture was taken close to the family home in Bangor. (Photo courtesy of the Trimble family.)

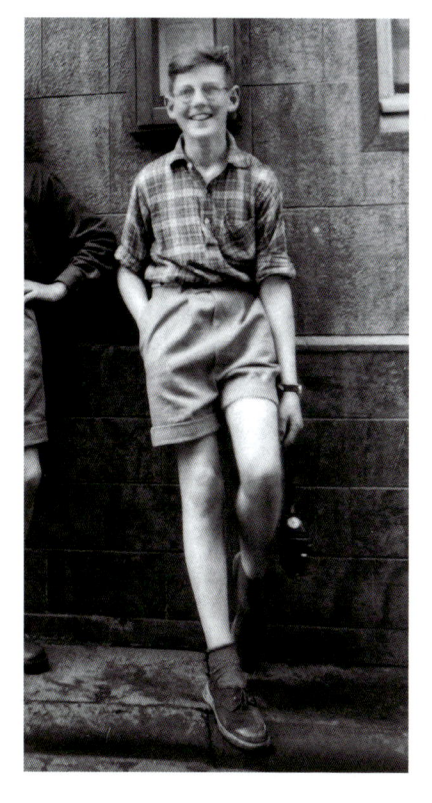

Trimble the teenager. David enjoying a school trip to Germany in the 1950s. (Photo courtesy of Terry Neill.)

[*Above*] As a schoolboy, Trimble (back row, far left) was in the Air Training Corps. He and Leslie Cree (back row, on the right) became good friends. The two also joined the Orange Order and the Ulster Unionist Party. Like Trimble, Cree would become a politician. (Photo courtesy of Leslie Cree.)

[*Right*] Trimble made front page news in 1968 after he was awarded a first-class honours in law at Queen's University. His hometown newspaper, the *County Down Spectator*, carried the story. (Photo courtesy of the *County Down Spectator*.)

Mr. DAVID TRIMBLE, who gained his LL.B. with first class honours

Many local students successful

AT this time of year it gives us pleasure—if also a headache, trying to follow the fortunes of the many local students at Queen's—to record academic successes as they become known.

In the Faculty of Law William David Trimble, 39 Clifton Road, Bangor, gained the Degree of Bachelor of Laws with first class honours, the only Queen's student to do so for the past three years.

David achieved this while studying part-time at Queen's and working in the Civil Service.

Another Bangor man, Patrick Coughlin, Ashley Drive, has gained his LL.B. with second class honours, first division.

Ian J. H. S. Moore, 53 Main Street, Groomsport, had notable success by gaining first class honours in Applied Science and Technology, completing the four year electrical engineering course in three years.

On the election trail. In 1975 Trimble and Raymond Jordan campaigned together in South Belfast. Trimble, a member of Vanguard, was elected but Jordan was unsuccessful. (Photo courtesy of the Linen Hall, Belfast.)

Trimble the politician. As a member of the Northern Ireland Convention, Trimble quickly established himself as an articulate speaker and an able debater. (Photo courtesy of the Trimble family.)

Mr Trimble goes to Westminster. David won the Upper Bann by-election in 1990. He would remain an MP until 2005. (© Pacemaker Press)

As the MP for Upper Bann, Trimble found himself at the heart of the Drumcree dispute involving the Orange Order and local residents.
(© PA Images/Alamy Stock Photo)

The slow walk to peace. As UUP leader, Trimble led his party into talks in 1997. He walked in with representatives from the loyalist parties.
(© PA Images/Alamy Stock Photo)

Daphne met David at Queen's University. Friends credit her with influencing him and say she helped him to see things differently.
(© PA Images/Alamy Stock Photo)

The appearance of John Hume and David Trimble with Bono during the Good Friday Agreement referendum campaign was a PR masterstroke. (© PA Images/Alamy Stock Photo)

Ulster says Yes. In May 1998, 71 per cent of voters in Northern Ireland backed the Good Friday Agreement referendum. For Trimble, it was confirmation that he was right to back the deal. (© Pacemaker Press)

In December 1998, David Trimble and John Hume travelled to Oslo. They were awarded the Nobel Peace Prize for their work in Northern Ireland.
(© NTB / Alamy Stock Photo)

David Trimble and Prime Minister Tony Blair worked well together in the early part of their relationship. However, Blair thought the UUP leader could 'start a fight in an empty room'.
(© Allstar Picture Library Ltd/Alamy Stock Photo)

The Rogan group. (Left to right) Jack Allen, David Campbell, Reg Empey, Denis Rogan, David Trimble, Ken Maginnis and James Cooper. This group advised Trimble during his time as UUP leader. (Photo courtesy of Lord Rogan.)

Trimble loved holidays with his family. (Left to right) David Trimble, Sarah, Vicky, Richard, Nicky. (Photo courtesy of the Trimble family.)

David Trimble as first minister. Behind him is Seamus Mallon who was deputy first minister. At the top of the picture is Mark Durkan, who would succeed Mallon as deputy first minister. (© *POOL/AFP via Getty Images*)

The odd couple. Trimble and Mallon worked well at times and clashed on other occasions. Pictured behind Mallon is Stormont press officer Colin Ross who found Trimble 'fascinating and mercurial'.
(© *PA Images/Alamy Stock Photo*)

The UUP talks team during a period of negotiations. (Left to right) Michael McGimpsey, James Cooper, David Trimble, Lady Hermon, David Campbell, Dermot Nesbitt. (Photo courtesy of Alan McFarland.)

David Trimble and President Clinton talked and met many times. Clinton famously phoned Trimble on Good Friday in 1998 and encouraged him to support the deal. (© Getty Images)

David backed Daphne when she was a candidate in Lagan Valley in 2010. (Left to right) Lady Trimble, Dominic Grieve, Lord Trimble, Stephen Walker (author). (Photo courtesy of the Trimble family.)

Like father, like son. Nicky Trimble became Mayor of Lisburn and Castlereagh City Council in 2020. (Photo courtesy of the Trimble family.)

Amongst his peers. David Trimble became Lord Trimble in April 2006. He loved the House of Lords. (© Getty Images)

Trimble joined the Conservative Party in 2007. There was speculation he would become a minister in a David Cameron-led government. However, when Cameron became prime minister in 2010 he was not offered a job. (© PA Images/Alamy Stock Photo)

Trimble loved exploring the waterways of England. Pictured here with his daughter Sarah and his granddaughter Georgia.
(Photo courtesy of the Trimble family.)

Trimble liked nothing more than spending time reading.
His friends said he was more at home being an academic than a politician.
(Photo courtesy of the Trimble family.)

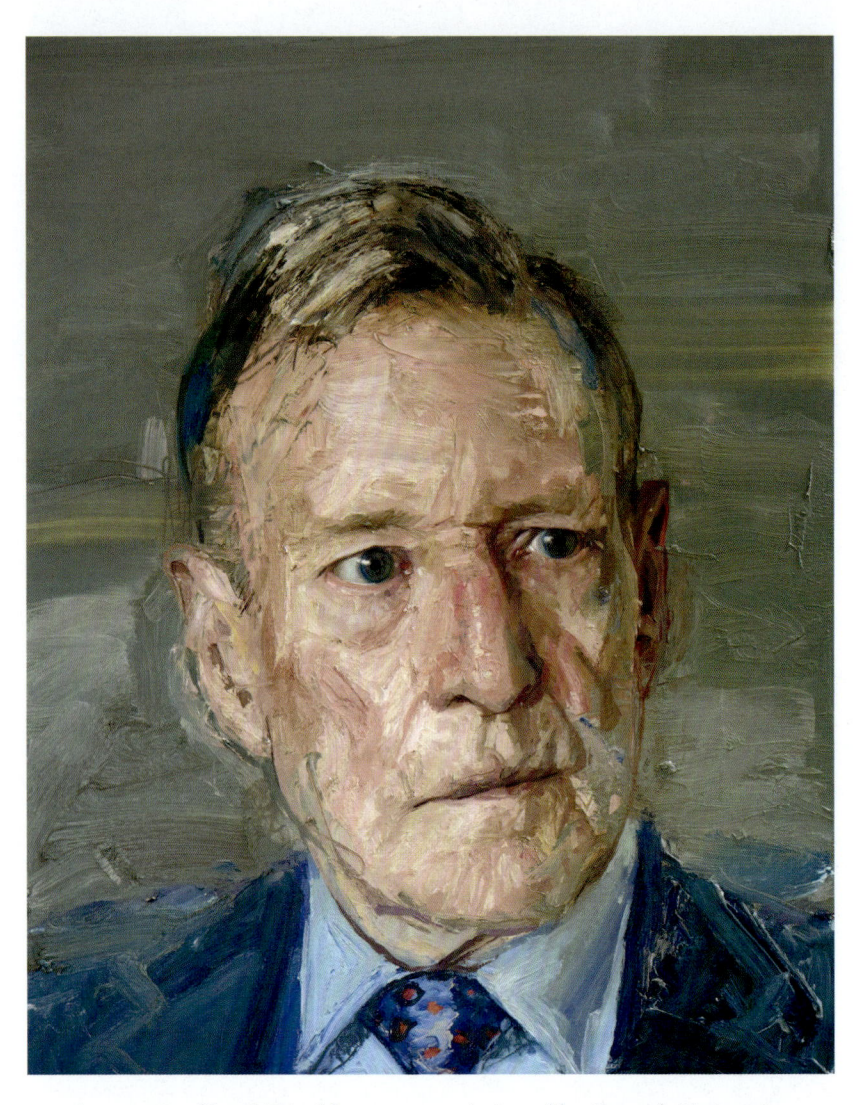

A portrait of Lord Trimble was commissioned by Queen's University, where it was unveiled in 2022. It was painted by the internationally renowned artist Colin Davidson. (Colin Davidson, oil on canvas, 2022. Courtesy of the Queen's University Belfast Art Collection.)

The advisors. (Left to right) Philip Robinson, Ray Hayden, David Kerr, Mark Neale, Lord Trimble and Lady Trimble at Queen's University in June 2022. (Photo courtesy of David Kerr.)

Lord Trimble and Bertie Ahern enjoyed a warm relationship. This was their last meeting at his portrait unveiling at Queen's University. (Photo courtesy of the Trimble family.)

Portrait of a peacemaker. Lord Trimble enjoying his garden at home.
This photograph was taken shortly before he died on 25 July 2022.
(Photo courtesy of the Trimble family.)

the UDA, and was convinced that dialogue was the way forward. Like Purvis, Adams was also at Castle Buildings with Trimble. He remembers that the unionist and loyalist delegations agreed to walk into the building together:

> What essentially it meant was to send a message that this is the majority of unionism going in, or the majority of unionist representation going in. But also, from Trimble and his party's point of view, it was this statement: these hard men are backing us, so it is worth pursuing if there is a chance of bringing the violence to an end.[4]

Adams enjoyed working with Trimble in those early days and believed the UUP leader was determined to make the process work:

> I found him to be a very decent and honourable man and, despite the caricatures of him, pretty easy to get on with. He was a straight talker, which I like. And I don't mean that in an ignorant type of way. He was like Seamus Mallon in that respect. If you asked a question, you got a straight answer.[5]

So why did Trimble take his party into talks? From Blair's Belfast speech in May 1997 to September 1997, much had changed, politically, to create the conditions for the UUP to attend. The biggest development came in July, when the IRA reinstated their ceasefire. This was a crucial turning point. Sinn Féin President Gerry Adams said he supported the move because there was a commitment from the two governments for 'inclusive peace talks'. The cessation of violence was welcomed by the British and Irish governments, but amongst unionists there was scepticism.

In August, both governments agreed to set up the Independent International Commission on Decommissioning, and as the month ended the British government said it would be inviting Sinn Féin to the multi-party talks in September. Trimble then began a consultation process to see if his party should attend the planned discussions. There were strong arguments in the party to follow the lead taken by Bob McCartney and Ian Paisley and stay away from the talks. Equally, there were party members who felt this was the right time to enter discussions.

When Sinn Féin signed up to the Mitchell Principles in September, just days before talks were due to begin, Blair urged Trimble to participate. This would be Trimble's biggest decision since becoming leader two years earlier.

James Cooper says he detected a change in Trimble's attitude over the summer months of 1997. Cooper, Trimble and other party figures had travelled to South Africa with delegations from other local parties. Unionists had only agreed to take part in the conference organised by Padraig O'Malley if they were kept apart from Sinn Féin. There were no plenary sessions, and there were no face-to-face negotiations, but some, like Cooper, saw Trimble's attendance in itself as positive:

> There was an element of breaking the ice. And I think David, after that, was certainly very much aware that we were going to have to do business with the other side. In a way ... up until then, the hallmark of his leadership actually was quite aggressive, you know marching and Drumcree, pretty overt unionism, and that clearly wasn't going to get us home and dry.[6]

When Trimble returned from South Africa, he still needed an endorsement from his party if he was going to participate in the multi-party discussions. In September 1997, as the talks were about to begin, he got his party's backing. George Mitchell says that decision gave Trimble the opportunity to come to the talks and speak up for unionism. He also says the absence of the DUP and Bob McCartney gave Trimble great freedom:

It was liberating for him. Because up until then the internal dynamic of internal unionist politics was the DUP against the UUP, which was very present during the talks. I describe it this way: the major plot was unionists against the nationalists; the subplot was the internal unionist contest, and sometimes the subplot overwhelmed the main plot. So, the departure of the DUP, Dr Paisley and his party, and Bob McCartney and his small party, was liberating in a sense for Trimble, because he could now concentrate on the main battle.[7]

The talks began in earnest, but the early weeks were slow. For the watching journalists there was little to report, and many veteran reporters wondered if this process was going to go the same way as previous attempts. The former US senator's patience was certainly being tested, and as 1997 ended, Mitchell remembers that he was very despondent:

I felt as discouraged as I'd ever been in my life – that this was impossible, that they cannot even agree on what the issues are to be resolved, let alone the solution to the issues. And so, I left to go home for Christmas 1997 very discouraged. And while I was at home on December 27 (I remember it like it was yesterday), I received a phone call informing me that Billy Wright, a prominent loyalist figure, had been killed in prison by a group of republican prisoners. And the fear was that it would spark off a round of violence, which it did.[8]

Mitchell's fears came to pass, and the early weeks of 1998 were dominated by violence. Members of the UDA and the UFF in the Maze prison withdrew their support for the talks process, which led Secretary of State Mo Mowlam to visit the prison to try to get them to change their minds. The Continuity IRA, a dissident republican group which opposed the peace process, carried out a series of bomb attacks and the breakaway Loyalist Volunteer Force and the UFF were responsible for a series of killings.

Northern Ireland was being drawn back into the dark days, and the ongoing violence dominated the political agenda. In an attempt to keep politicians focused on the talks, the two governments published a 'Heads of Agreement' paper that outlined what a potential deal could look like. It suggested that, amongst other moves, a multi-party deal could deliver a new Assembly, a fresh British–Irish agreement and a North–South Ministerial Council. It suggested changes to Articles 2 and 3 of the Irish Constitution and to the Government of Ireland Act at Westminster. It was a bold plan by Tony Blair and Bertie Ahern, made public against the backdrop of the loyalist and republican violence. The two premiers knew George Mitchell's political initiative was in big trouble, and they were trying to keep it alive.

In the first few weeks of 1998, more pressure was placed on the talks process.

By late January, the talks were moved to Lancaster House in London, in the hope that a change of venue might aid progress. The two governments expelled the UDP from the discussions. The loyalist paramilitary group the UFF, a cover name for the UDA, had been involved in the recent killing of three Catholics, which meant the UDP had breached the Mitchell Principles with the result that the UDP could no longer take part in talks.

February brought greater strains for the talks process after the RUC declared that the IRA had been involved in recent murders. That meant that this time it was Sinn Féin who were in breach of the Mitchell Principles. Consequently Gerry Adams and his negotiating team were barred from formal discussions.

Adams said the two governments were being unduly influenced by Trimble:

> It's going to be a kangaroo court in which the British government has already decided we have to walk. They are trying to put everybody else including the Irish

government into that loop with them all at the behest of David Trimble.[9]

Sinn Féin politicians were told they could return to the talks in March. Adams described the ban as 'disgraceful', while the Ulster Unionists said the exclusion, at just over two weeks, was too short.

As February ended, Mitchell had few grounds for optimism. Even though he was an experienced political operator who had been at the centre of many negotiations, he was concerned that his Belfast initiative was faltering. The decision to move the talks temporarily to London had not worked. Mitchell says he found the experience 'entirely negative'. He had also organised some functions between the parties in the hope of breaking down barriers. Sometimes they did not go as planned.

Kate Fearon of the Women's Coalition remembers being at one dinner with Trimble. She was discussing the differences in the unemployment rate between Protestants and Catholics when the UUP leader exploded:

> Trimble just blew up. I mean he started shouting at me across the table and he was, 'What do you mean? That is completely untrue.' So, I was kind of shocked. I think the others around the table were a little bit shocked as well. But, you know, he flared up. Because it was something. It was a fact that he didn't like, I guess. What it says to me, although I'm not sure I would have processed this at the time, was that he was really under pressure. I mean it's not really normal behaviour, I don't think. One could argue back and say, 'I don't think that's correct' or 'I have a different perspective.' But he had no control of himself in one sense.[10]

Trimble was feeling the strain. Away from the talks, the atmosphere across Northern Ireland was tense. February saw more violence on the streets, with car bombs in Moira and Portadown, and both attacks were blamed on the Continuity IRA. The month of March also brought an act of sectarian savagery that would have a huge political impact. Two friends, Philip Allen, a Protestant, and Damien Trainor, a Catholic, were shot dead at the Railway Bar in Poyntzpass in County Armagh.

Loyalist paramilitaries believed to be members of the Loyalist Volunteer Force entered the pub and shot the two men and injured others. Allen and Trainor had attended different schools and were from different religious backgrounds, but they were the best of pals and were often seen together. Allen, who was older, was about to be married and had asked Trainor to be his best man. It is thought they were discussing the wedding arrangements when the shooting occurred.

Such incidents were rare in this part of Northern Ireland, and it was the first time in decades that something like this had happened in the village – a place where community relations were described as excellent. To many, it was the friendship of the two men that was the true face of Northern Ireland – not the sectarian killers who ended their lives.

Understandably, there was widespread condemnation of the killing from right across the political spectrum. Seamus Mallon, the local SDLP MP, decided to visit the scene the next day, and although it was unplanned, David Trimble, who represented the adjoining constituency, joined him in the village. The two politicians spent time with relatives of the murdered men, and the sight of Trimble and Mallon walking together sent out a positive image of political unity.

It was a moment of hope amidst a time of real sadness and abject horror. The visit to Poyntzpass moved Trimble, and he made it clear he wanted to see the democratic process prevail:

> All they are doing is killing off the hope we are trying to engender. But despite this and mainly because of this we are going to try to continue to do our best to bring some political stability.[11]

Mallon, who knew the area intimately, was, like Trimble, very emotional when he spoke to the family and friends of the two men. He would later reveal that his visit to Poyntzpass had a profound impact on what happened during the political negotiations:

> We went to both funerals together. It was heartening and a heart-rending situation. I think that experience stayed with Trimble; it certainly stayed with me. And it helped as we moved towards the crunch stage in the final weeks of the negotiations. There was hope in the air then that I had not experienced since the days of Sunningdale. It was a terrible but seminal moment.[12]

Hundreds of miles away in Downing Street, Tony Blair was watching the television images of Mallon and Trimble walking together. He, like others, was appalled by the killings of Philip Allen and Damien Trainor. The issue of Northern Ireland had already taken up much of his premiership. Since he took office in May 1997, there had been a series of bombings and shootings, and he was determined to bring them to an end.

Mallon and Trimble's joint appearance in the County Armagh village would become a watershed moment in the peace process, during one of Northern Ireland's blackest times. Trimble got support from his party colleagues for his visit, and it meant a lot to those who lived nearby.

Aubrene Willis, a long-standing UUP member, ran a family hardware business in Markethill, a pretty village some seven miles away. Willis was no stranger to the Troubles. Her store had been damaged on numerous occasions by IRA bombs. She recalls how the visit affected local people:

> It was very moving, especially to us who knew the people and knew Seamus and David. That was a big step, because people are always angry on both sides. There was a stillness in Poyntzpass, and they were respected for doing it. I thought it was a big step, and that it was a very good Christian act from both.[13]

Like many, Mark Durkan of the SDLP, a confidant of John Hume's, was struck by the television pictures of the two men. He believed the rival politicians had shown great leadership, and their display of unity got him thinking. At that time, there were discussions about how a future Northern Ireland government might be run with an Executive made up of different ministers. With the Poyntzpass experience as inspiration, Durkan got the idea that there could be a joint first minister's office with a first minister and a deputy first minister.

> We didn't like the idea of a hierarchy of designations but ... we were faced with a number of criticisms of our proposals, and we hadn't worked out exactly how to appoint the first minister and whether there is a second minister. The pictures from Poyntzpass created this idea of a joint office.[14]

Durkan recalls that he went and spoke to library staff at Stormont to get some research done on the idea. He wanted to know if there were any examples where governments across the world had joint offices. The suggestion of a first and deputy first minister was then presented to the UUP leader:

> David Trimble had the idea put in front of him and it was only two weeks out from the Good Friday Agreement. He was very clear he was possibly on for the joint office. But it had to have different titles. So, the insistence was, one would be First and the other deputy First. But the substantive point was the powers would be joint and equal.[15]

Against the backdrop of the talks process, Trimble addressed party members at the AGM of the UUC on Saturday 21 March. He was in buoyant form and began by reminding his audience that the UUP had fought two recent elections and remained the largest party in Northern Ireland. Understandably, much of Trimble's address was about the ongoing discussions at Castle Buildings, and he told party members that, in the days ahead, 'nerves of steel will be needed'.

A copy of the UUP talks proposals had been left on each seat in the hall for delegates to read. Trimble also quoted the words of his friend Paul Bew, who was now an important figure in his inner circle of informal advisers. Bew, writing in the contemporary issue of *Parliamentary Brief*, stated that:

> The biggest mistake made by Sinn Féin has been its underestimate of Ulster Unionists. Their unexpected decision to stay in the talks process and actively seek a settlement has left them rudderless.[16]

Trimble's address at the AGM had one major objective. He needed to steady the ship. He was mindful that, in the absence of any detail emerging from the talks process, the political rumour mill was in full operation. He also promised party members that they would be kept informed and pledged: 'Nothing can be agreed without your consent.'

Reading between the lines of Trimble's speech, the impression emerges that he was ready to do a deal – if that deal was right. It would not have been a traditional Trimble speech without a nod to history, and he made reference to the Home Rule Crisis and Sunningdale. The actions of the last unionist politician to agree to a power-sharing deal may have been close to his thoughts. He was about to emulate Brian Faulkner and agree to enter a cross-party government.

History was slowly turning full circle, and Trimble was at the centre of it. As he ended his speech, he reminded his colleagues that he was personally ready for what lay ahead:

> Whatever may come out of the talks over the next few weeks, colleagues, we must be prepared. I did not lead this party into negotiations to shy away from difficult decisions.[17]

That line in the speech about 'difficult decisions' underscores what Trimble was thinking. He was preparing the grassroots for a deal – an agreement that might not secure everything for unionism but nonetheless would be worth backing. Two days after Trimble addressed the party faithful, Sinn Féin rejoined the talks at Stormont, after having been expelled in February. It marked a key moment but did not have the dramatic effect some predicted. At this stage, contacts between republicans and unionists were limited.

The UUP and Sinn Féin had not had any face-to-face meetings in the talks process, even though they were in the same building. There was one memorable occasion when Trimble and Adams did bump into each other in the gents' toilets. Trimble recalls that he was in no mood to chat to the Sinn Féin president:

> The funniest moment of the lot was when I was in the toilet and there was Gerry at the next urinal standing there talking to me. And I told him to 'grow up'. Because doing things like that wasn't helping. I was nearly tempted to tell him that it wouldn't do him a lot of good if I mentioned that he was going round propositioning people in the toilet.[18]

Inside the talks process the mood remained pessimistic, and there was no sense that a breakthrough was imminent. By that time, George Mitchell had been chairing the discussions for close to two years, and he was well aware of each party's position. He then decided that the discussions needed a timetable with an end point:

> I decided we had to come up with a way to bring this to a head, that the process was spiralling out of control. The violence was rising every day, there were retaliatory killings, and so I devised this scheme of having a fixed, unbreakable deadline and then [an] intense two-week period leading up to it, and [Canadian peace negotiator General John] de

Chastelain and [Finnish peace negotiator Harri] Holkeri agreed. We came back in March of 1998, and we spent a month persuading the two governments and the remaining eight parties to agree to this. This was, in my mind, one of the most decisive points in the talks, because I had no authority as chairman to impose a deadline.[19]

The idea of a timetable started to focus minds. Mitchell remembers discussing the idea with Trimble:

Trimble was his usual precise, well-organised self. He clearly ... wanted to go forward; all the others did too. But he had concerns, and I knew what his concerns were [given] that he expressed them publicly. There was no secret about it. The unionists wanted an agreement to end the violence, but they opposed any nationalist effort to create a substantial web of contacts between Northern Ireland and the Republic, which the unionists feared would be the precursor to a united Ireland.[20]

There was now an intensity to meetings which had not existed before, and Trimble and the prime minister were in constant contact. Tony Blair knew that the UUP leader was key to any deal, and he felt that the bones of an agreement were in place, as did Bertie Ahern. The question was: how much negotiating space did Trimble have? What would he accept?

Trimble visited Downing Street on Thursday 26 March for discussions and, three days later, on Sunday 29 March, he returned to England. This time he had talks at Chequers, the prime minister's weekend residence in Buckinghamshire, some 40 miles from London. On Wednesday 1 April, it was Ahern's turn to visit London, and he and Blair spent hours trying to reach a common position, but after lengthy talks the two men could not reach an agreement.

Two days later, they tried again and had further talks, in what amounted to their third meeting in three days. Once again, a breakthrough was proving elusive, but some progress had been made. To inject momentum into the process, the Alliance leader, John Alderdice, called on the two premiers to take personal control of the process. On Sunday 5 April, he rang Blair and made it clear that he needed to come to Belfast and see the parties personally.

For Ahern, the last few days had been draining. It had been an intensive time not just politically but personally. Julia Ahern, his 87-year-old mother, died, and Ahern knew he would have to stay in Dublin to organise funeral arrangements. George Mitchell was in Belfast preparing for what he expected to be the last full week of talks. On that Sunday evening, he finally received the British and Irish governments' paper on Strand Two – which looked at the North–South relationship.

This is what officials in Dublin and London had spent many hours preparing. The document contained a long list of North–South bodies. Mitchell read the paper thoroughly, and instantly knew it would not be acceptable to the UUP. He knew it would be rejected immediately:

> This was 11 o'clock on Sunday night. I knew it right away. So, I called David Andrews, who was the then Irish Foreign Minister, with whom I'd been meeting very regularly, along with Mo Mowlam and all of the British officials. I told him I wanted to meet with him early for breakfast the next morning, on Monday. So, we met, and I told him, 'I can guarantee you there's no possibility that the unionists are going to agree to this, so I ask you to ask Prime Minister Ahern please to reconsider.' It was a big decision for Ahern, because the agreement was favourable to the position he wanted … I knew what was coming, because about an hour later I got a call from Trimble: 'I need to see you'. So, I said, 'Come on up, I've been expecting you.' He came up. I'll never forget it. He had a big batch of papers in his hand; he slammed them down on the table and he said, 'This is a bad paper, it's unacceptable.' I said, 'I understand, I know it is.' He said, 'You do?' I said, 'Yes.' He said, 'Well, you've got to tell Bertie Ahern

that he's got to negotiate.' I said, 'I already have.' He said, 'You have?' I said, 'Yes, I've just met with David Andrews and told him.' Well, Trimble said, 'I think you should call Bertie Ahern.' And we discussed it. And he told me that it was unacceptable, which is exactly what I had expected. Because if you've been there, you would know what was going on. So later, I met with Tony Blair, and he said he thought it had to be negotiated, and he asked me to contact Bertie Ahern. And I said, well talk to David Andrews; he said the same thing to Trimble. So, I called Bertie. You will recall his mother had just died. He was organising his mother's funeral – the toughest time in the world to ask somebody questions like this. But it ended up late that night, Monday night, Bertie called me. It was 10:30 or so. He told me he was walking the streets of Dublin after his mother's removal, and he decided to agree to renegotiate. Which was a huge decision by Bertie, because if the talks had failed then it would have been a unionist/UK government split, of course. Now, Bertie was taking the pressure off them and putting it on himself.[21]

Ahern agreed to look again at the document, and both Blair and Mitchell explained to the taoiseach that the unionists were so angry the talks process could collapse. Ahern remembers their warnings:

Tony Blair said this to me and Mitchell said it to me, you know he's [Trimble] so upset, and his negotiating team were so upset, that if I don't come up and calm it down, they could walk altogether. So that's what led me to going up on the Wednesday morning, the morning of my mam's funeral. And going up and meeting them at eight in the morning or half eight in the morning. And having a meeting first of all with George Mitchell, a short meeting with him over breakfast. Then meeting Tony, then meeting David, explaining where I was prepared to go. Then meeting Sinn Féin and the SDLP to tell them what I was going to do. So, between about 7.30 a.m. and about 11.00 a.m. in the morning we sorted that out. And then I said, 'Well, listen, I'm off down to the funeral.'[22]

Around this time, Trimble bumped into John Hume at a stairwell in Castle Buildings, and the UUP leader made his frustration very clear. Mark Durkan was there too and recalls a 'very crimson Trimble' wagging his finger at Hume as he accused the Irish government of 'gross overreach'. Trimble told Hume, 'That is why Sunningdale failed – it was your overreach.'[23]

Ahern's decision to travel to Belfast the morning of his mother's funeral and meet the parties ultimately saved the talks process. His intervention introduced some calmness into the discussions. As he returned to Dublin on Wednesday 8 April, the deal was far from done and there was no guarantee of success. Ahern returned to Belfast on Wednesday evening and there were intensive discussions between the UUP and the Irish government over Strand Two and negotiation over the North–South element contained in the Mitchell document. It was agreed the proposed North–South Ministerial Council would not be able to take a decision without the consent of a unionist minister. By the early hours of Thursday morning, Trimble returned to the UUP talks room. David Kerr recalls how the UUP leader looked pleased:

> David said that the team had whittled down the original demands of the Irish government down to a mere six bodies. The new North–South Ministerial Council could not take a decision without the consent of a unionist minister. In that act Trimble felt he had banished the ghost of Sunningdale.[24]

By Thursday mid-morning the atmosphere had improved. The talks were no longer on the brink of collapse, but there was still work to be done. It was going to be a long day and an eventful night – and a very long Good Friday.

16

DEAL OR NO DEAL

'We are ready to do the business.'
David Trimble tells George Mitchell the UUP
will endorse the Good Friday Agreement

On Good Friday morning in 1998, David Trimble slipped away from the talks to get a few hours' sleep in the Stormont Hotel. The four-star establishment was the closest accommodation to Castle Buildings and just yards from the gates of the Stormont Estate. It provided some much-needed respite. The UUP leader was lucky to get a bed. Other politicians used sofas and chairs in the talks complex and grabbed some rest when they could. By mid-morning, the building was full of tired bodies, but there was an optimistic mood. Both governments thought there was a deal.

Much work had been done throughout the night. The SDLP and the UUP had reached agreement over Strand One – which examined how Northern Ireland should be run. There would be a cabinet-style government with ministers, and each would be held accountable by a committee of Assembly members. The silhouette image through the window of the SDLP's Bríd Rodgers hugging her colleague Seamus Mallon was captured by the television cameras – and to the watching world it was confirmation that a deal was coming.

Agreement had been reached over cross-border bodies, and the Irish government had also pledged to amend Articles 2 and 3 of the Irish Constitution, which stated that the natural territory of Ireland was the whole island including Northern Ireland. For Trimble and the UUP that change was a major victory. Unionists had long argued that both articles were hostile and unlawful and should be removed. There was also cross-party acceptance that a commission would be set up to reform the RUC.

The symbolism of Good Friday loomed large. A day of such importance in the Christian calendar looked like it was about to provide the ever-patient media with a jaw-dropping story of hope, a tale of peacemaking that would travel the world. Mitchell McLaughlin of Sinn Féin told reporters that it was a 'beautiful day', and David Andrews went even further by informing journalists that 'we are at this moment making history'.[1]

But behind the scenes all was not as it seemed. The final draft had been circulated to the parties, and it quickly became apparent that Trimble was having significant trouble selling the deal. There were big concerns over the prisoner-release scheme, and there were worries that Sinn Féin would be in government without the need for IRA decommissioning.

By this point, the UUP delegation was supported by many more ordinary party members, and Trimble put them to good use. He divided them into teams and got the groups to read through the different sections of the proposed agreement. Trimble's biggest critic was Jeffrey Donaldson, the UUP MP for Lagan Valley. He did not like parts of the document, particularly the sections on decommissioning and the release of paramilitary prisoners. Donaldson was not alone and was joined by a series of young unionists including Peter Weir and Arlene Foster.

All three would later defect to the DUP, with Weir becoming a Stormont minister and Foster and Donaldson both becoming DUP leaders at different stages. Foster would serve as DUP first minister between 2016 and 2017 and later between 2020 and 2021. In April 1998, she was at Castle Buildings not as a negotiator but as a party officer. Throughout the night, she had typed up the arguments for and against the deal. Ultimately, she would conclude, like her colleagues Weir and Donaldson, that she could not support the agreement, and she would leave the talks building. She subsequently explained that her main objections were the early release of prisoners and the changes to the RUC:

> I fundamentally believe that allowing people who have committed crimes out of prison is wrong. It is an amnesty, and that's why republicans and loyalists can argue today that they should get a full amnesty, which is wrong. It is against the rule of law, and as a lawyer I felt that was wrong.[2]

Foster was the daughter of an RUC officer, and her father had been shot and badly injured by the IRA at their Fermanagh home in 1979. She found the planned changes to the force unacceptable:

> The police were a worry for me obviously because I'm from a police family. The prisoner thing came out of the blue – the release of prisoners. So those were the things that really played on my mind.[3]

Deadlines were beginning to slip, and the early-morning optimism had evaporated. George Mitchell had originally hoped to bring the parties together at 1 p.m. and then that moved again to 3 p.m. Now the 3 p.m. start looked increasingly unlikely. Rumours persisted that the Ulster Unionists were going to walk out – suggestions fuelled by the knowledge that Donaldson, Weir and Foster were all against the deal.

Shortly after lunchtime, Trimble and his colleagues were all crammed in the empty office of Bob McCartney, a rival unionist politician who had boycotted the talks process. As leader, Trimble initiated the discussion in front of his negotiating team. This was his kitchen cabinet. If they did not support the deal, the agreement was off. John Taylor, a veteran of high political drama, so often the pulse of Ulster Unionist thinking, had much to say. He had an ability to colourfully sum up what the rank-and-file members thought. Days before, he had warned that he would not touch the 'Mitchell' draft deal with a 'forty-foot barge pole'.[4]

Taylor was by far the most experienced politician in the party. His career spanned the Troubles, and he had respect right across the membership. He had served as a minister in the old Stormont government back in the early 1970s and nearly died after he was shot and seriously wounded by the Official IRA. Trimble needed his support and listened as his deputy outlined his concerns. Taylor had the text of the deal in front of him, and with his pen he had marked up his worries. Many of his questions focused on policing, the release of prisoners and whether the conditions over paramilitary decommissioning were strong enough. He had around 20 questions about the deal, and, as he outlined them, Trimble listened in silence.

Donaldson had made his position clear, highlighting the areas of the document he found particularly unpalatable. Trimble did not know it at the time, but Donaldson was just minutes away from walking out in protest. Others sitting close to Trimble were more positive, including Reg Empey, who hours earlier had agreed a deal with the SDLP on how power-sharing would work.

Empey and Trimble were old allies and had previously been members of Vanguard, which had opposed the Sunningdale deal that ushered in power-sharing between unionists and nationalists back in 1974. Twenty-four years later, times had changed, and Empey now believed this agreement was better for unionism. He recalls the intensity of the discussions and how the atmosphere became quite heated:

> I think the most difficult bit was policing at that stage. And I think at the end of the day, when we were in our negotiating team and the officers had reached their positions in the room. And then George Mitchell sent down a message telling us that he wanted an answer. And we were debating and talking and having our various meetings. And there was one incident when John Alderdice [Alliance leader] came down the corridor and I think Jim Nicholson [UUP MEP] and a couple of others were outside. And he [Alderdice] started berating us for the time we were taking, and at one stage I think Jim Nicholson was ready to chin him.[5]

Nicholson remembers Alderdice approaching the unionist negotiating rooms and asking why they were taking so long to come to a decision:

> Well, he [Alderdice] came to the door and tried to talk to Trimble and was giving out to Trimble. Because the word had got out that Trimble wasn't going to sign. I assume the place was a rumour mill. And he came to the door and there was quite an exchange of views at the door. Let's put it that way.[6]

Alderdice recalls going to the Ulster Unionists' room in the hope of seeing Trimble to find out what was happening:

> It was clear the Ulster Unionists were just going on and on. There was some kind of argument going on inside their room. And they weren't telling any of us what was going on. And we were all hanging around. And we were getting pretty frustrated, because you know we were all tensed up. There was a lack of sleep, and we had all been working very hard. And everyone else had indicated they were agreed, and these guys were buggering about, basically, as far as we were concerned. And there was no word coming out from them, no indication that we're having problems or any statement like 'Give us more time'. So, everybody else had to wait for them, was the sense I got. So, I went storming up to the door and opened up to them. I can't remember the exact words I said, something pretty strong. I didn't use any bad language or anything like that, but something pretty strong about, 'Look, come on, the rest of us are all waiting', and 'What are you hanging about for?' Something of that kind.[7]

Alderdice's frustration was shared by many others in Castle Buildings, who were now becoming concerned at how long the UUP were taking.

All the other party negotiators and civil servants could do was wait for a decision. They did not know how long Trimble and his colleagues were going to take, or if the UUP were going to reject or accept the deal. Jack Allen, who was part of the Ulster Unionist team, remembers bumping into the SDLP leader, John Hume:

> Hume was in the corridor, and I said to Hume, 'John, go easy on Trimble.' And John Hume lit on me, and he said, 'Jackie, we need the decision now. We need the decision now.' And I said, 'Well, you might press him too hard, and you won't get a decision, do you see?' But Hume wouldn't. He was quite adamant that they get in and get the decision.[8]

All the other parties could do was wait and watch and wait some more.

It was now in Trimble's hands, and Mitchell's initiative would either fall or succeed depending on how the UUP would ultimately see things. Liz O'Donnell, minister of state at Foreign Affairs, was part of the Irish government delegation. She always felt Trimble would ultimately agree to a deal and remembers being in Castle Buildings and waiting for hours for the UUP decision. She recalls that it was never a straightforward process and remembers that, the night before, relations between the government and the UUP had become strained over the issue of cross-border bodies.

O'Donnell recalled how Trimble had become rather agitated:

> I was in the optimistic camp. But you see, the previous night we had a wobble because of the North–South bodies. There was a group in the taoiseach's office led by Wally Kirwan, who was a very distinguished civil servant. And he had been given the task of drawing up a list of possible North–South bodies, which, in the context of the overall agreement, were going to be one of the last things to be agreed. It became known as Wally's list. But it nearly caused a heart attack and an explosion from David

Trimble the night before. I think it was overly ambitious. The list, it was lengthy, I suppose. There were possible areas where you could have North–South bodies. But in fact, when David saw the list, he nearly went mad, and we had to fillet it down.[9]

By late afternoon on Good Friday, O'Donnell and the others in the Irish delegation had become observers – waiting for Northern Ireland's largest party to say yes or no. In the UUP talks team meeting, Ken Maginnis had his say. The Fermanagh and South Tyrone MP was seen by commentators as a moderate voice in the party, and Trimble was hoping for his backing. A former soldier in the UDR, who had been targeted by the IRA, Maginnis spoke for the party on security issues. He was bluff and direct and had been supportive of Trimble in the past. He began his contribution with a heavy sigh.

A veteran of various talks processes, Maginnis told his colleagues that he had seen different negotiations come and go and told the gathering that he had been trying to find a political deal for the past 30 years. He argued that every time inter-party discussions collapsed, a period of violence followed, and when unionists finally returned to the negotiating table the deal on offer was often worse.

As his colleagues listened, Maginnis insisted that this time his party had negotiated well, and Northern Ireland's place in the UK was safer than before. He said the planned amendment of Articles 2 and 3 of the Irish Constitution, which claimed jurisdiction over Northern Ireland, was a gain for unionism. He accepted there were parts of the deal he did not like, but he felt if an agreement was not reached, the British and Irish governments would most likely ignore the local parties and impose their own solution. For Maginnis, it was a straightforward choice. Ulster Unionists needed to say yes.

It was a powerful intervention from a politician who had witnessed much of Northern Ireland's bloody past, and the words struck a chord with the youngest person in the room. David Kerr was impressed with the strength of Maginnis's argument. They were words spoken from the heart, and they won Kerr over. He firmly believed Trimble had secured what he had set out to achieve and believed Northern Ireland's status within the UK was settled, and the consent principle was key. There would be a functioning cross-community government with devolved powers.

The contentious cross-border bodies, in Kerr's view, were not a threat to unionism, and Dublin had rowed back on their demands after unionist objections. For Trimble's young assistant and now director of communications, the contribution of Maginnis was the most impressive he had heard all day. He was now ready to back the deal.

Thomas Hennessey was another member of the UUP team who was listening intently to the arguments for and against the deal. In 1997, he was a research fellow at Queen's University, and Trimble had invited him onto the talks team as an adviser to look at Strand Two of the process. Hennessey recalls being in the meeting with John Taylor and Ken Maginnis when the deal was discussed. He was sceptical at first, but that he changed his mind:

> Trimble said, 'We've got everything we came into the talks for. We have got the Assembly back. We've got no executive power in the North–South Ministerial Council. It is essentially' – I don't know if he actually said this – 'it's a talking shop, a consultancy. We have got the British–Irish agreement. We've got the British–Irish Council. We've got the British link, which mirrors anything that was set up in the North–South.' And at that point I literally … just changed my view. I saw sense. And there was a conversation about what do we do next, and everyone agreed we had to get something on decommissioning.[10]

Trimble was winning hearts and minds around the table, but it was not enough. He knew the deal was weak over decommissioning, and he needed reassurance from the UK government. He told the meeting he would go back to Tony Blair on a single issue and asked his colleagues what that should be. They all agreed there must be a stronger link between the decommissioning of paramilitary weapons and Sinn Féin's participation in a power-sharing government.

Trimble left the unionist offices, and went to see Blair in his room in Castle Buildings. The prime minister was exhausted and, like so many in the building, had only managed a few hours' sleep. He had catnapped through the night, and while Trimble was fortunate to have found a bed in a nearby hotel, Blair had pushed two chairs together and dozed between meetings. By early afternoon, he was beginning to get rather exasperated with the UUP and wanted them to concentrate on what he saw as their gains in the deal: an Assembly, cross-border bodies they could live with, the amendment of Articles 2 and 3 and the end of the Belfast-based Maryfield Secretariat, which had housed officials from the Irish Government.

Blair impressed on Trimble that they were big wins for unionism. Northern Ireland remained part of the UK, and any change in its status would need the consent of the majority of its people. He urged the UUP leader to see the agreement in the round. In Blair's eyes, it was a good deal for unionism, and it helped to secure the union.

The prime minister then listened as Trimble outlined his party's difficulties over any plan that could put Sinn Féin in government with no guarantee of decommissioning. Trimble said his party was in revolt, and that, without a stronger commitment on decommissioning, the Ulster Unionists could not support the deal. Blair knew it was too late to rewrite the Mitchell deal, so he needed to think of something else.

Trimble left the meeting and returned to the UUP offices. Blair and his advisers, including Jonathan Powell, his chief of staff, had some thinking to do. He decided that he needed outside help, so he got Powell to ring David Montgomery, the newspaper executive from the Mirror Group, who was a long-standing friend of Trimble's. Powell asked Montgomery if he could influence his fellow Ulsterman.

Montgomery was in Gatwick Airport, about to fly to Italy, and remembers taking the call:

> Jonathan Powell phoned and said, 'We can't get there, we're stuck, you speak to David Trimble.'[11]

When Montgomery rang Trimble, John Taylor grabbed the phone. Montgomery told Taylor that, if the UUP walked out or rejected the deal, they would be criticised. He said such a move would reinforce the stereotype that unionists were stubborn and incapable of compromise. Montgomery warned Taylor:

> Look, the world is going to find this is just another example of obstinacy. The inability to have some flexibility. It will further entrench the reputation of Ulster Prods and unionism as being incapable of compromise, incapable of moving to a different future. You as a unionist will receive the criticism of the world.[12]

Montgomery then agreed to cancel his flight to Italy and said he would go off to make plans to fly to Belfast and come to Castle Buildings.

As Montgomery went off in search of a ticket desk at Gatwick Airport, Blair had another idea that he hoped might persuade Trimble to back the deal – an idea that actually rested in his own hands. He agreed that he would write a letter to Trimble to reassure him that he would support the exclusion of Sinn Féin from government if there had not been any decommissioning. This side letter to Trimble was designed to offer comfort to the UUP that action would be taken if there was no decommissioning.

Blair's chief of staff, Jonathan Powell, typed the letter on his laptop, printed it and then went in search of the Ulster Unionist leader:

> I snatched it off the printer and raced down to give it to Trimble. There was no time to lose because we feared he was about to walk out. But down on the unionist floor I was confronted by a locked door. They were debating whether or not to accept the agreement inside and I couldn't get in to give Trimble the letter. Finally, I attracted the attention of one of the young unionists near the door and he let me in. Trimble read the letter with John Taylor looking over his shoulder.[13]

Trimble was in a meeting when the letter arrived. Understandably, decommissioning, policing and the release of paramilitaries dominated the discussion. When Blair's letter arrived, the conversation was paused. The key parts to Blair's note read:

> I understand that your problem with paragraph 25 of Strand One is that it requires decisions on those who should be excluded or removed from office in the Northern Ireland Executive to be taken on a cross-community basis.
>
> This letter is to let you know that if during the course of the first six months of the shadow Assembly or the Assembly itself these provisions have been shown to be ineffective, we will support changes to these provisions to enable them to be made properly effective in preventing such people from holding office.
>
> Furthermore, I confirm that in our view the effect of the decommissioning section of the agreement with decommissioning schemes coming into effect in April is that the process of decommissioning should begin straight away.[14]

Trimble read the letter, as did Taylor, who was standing behind him. Taylor finished the note and declared that it was acceptable, as did Trimble. He had got the assurances he was looking for, and with Taylor's endorsement, he knew this would get the party over the line. Trimble and his colleagues discussed the side letter from Blair.

But although it was enough for Taylor, Donaldson could not be convinced. He was not going to shift, and he was not alone. David Brewster and Jim Rodgers – both honorary secretaries of the party – were against the deal and made their opposition clear. Brewster, a solicitor from Limavady, would become quite a critic of Trimble's and would later join the DUP.

It was a big call for Rodgers, though. He had known Trimble for decades. They were contemporaries and had been in Vanguard together and had campaigned against the 1974 power-sharing executive. Now, he and Trimble were on opposite sides. Rodgers was against the plans to release paramilitary prisoners, and he opposed the suggested changes to policing:

> I thought we were giving up too much, and that wasn't going to bring the ordinary man and the woman in the street with us. They just felt it was a sell-out coming, and that was my view too. I was worried about that, even though I'm a flexible individual and want to work with people and I'm prepared to give up a little. But I'm not prepared to sell Northern Ireland.[15]

Around 4 p.m., as the UUP activists continued their deliberations, Trimble's phone rang. It was a transatlantic call and another of Blair's ideas. He had asked Bill Clinton to help, and the US president rang the UUP leader and urged him to endorse the agreement. He told Trimble what a difference the deal would make to Northern Ireland's future. The call did little to influence things, except Trimble asked Clinton to ring Ahern and Hume and ask them not to criticise Blair's side letter.

Trimble was in no rush to declare his hand. As the other parties and the two governments waited inside the building and the media waited outside, the UUP kept them guessing. There was still some important business to be done. With the support of Taylor, Empey and Maginnis, Trimble knew he was on solid ground. He concluded the meeting by telling the party officers that he was going to back the agreement. He walked to the office, lifted the phone and called George Mitchell.

Mitchell recalls how tired he was when the phone rang:

> I sat at my desk, and I think I kind of dozed off. Then the phone rang, and it was maybe 4.45, ten to five, and it was Trimble. I remember the words exactly: 'How are you, David?' And he said, 'We are ready to do the business.' Those were his words. I said, 'That's great, thank

you, I'm so pleased. That's great, thank you.' And I said to him, 'I want to vote right away.' Because I was fearful that something would intervene. This was such a great accomplishment, and I was afraid something might intervene. So, it was about 4.50 p.m., and I said I'd like a meeting at 5 p.m.[16]

After calling Mitchell, Trimble made his way into one of the nearby rooms, where activists and party workers had gathered. It was jam-packed and noisy, and Trimble stood at the front with a copy of the agreement in his hand. He only had a few minutes to tell his colleagues what was happening. Many already knew; some had no idea what he was about to say.

As he began to speak there was a hush. Reg Empey remembers it well:

> David came into the room, and he either stood on a chair or a table. I can't quite remember which. And there was about 40 to 50 people in the room. It was really hectic; they'd been there all night. There was no food in the place, there was no heating, it was just a horrible atmosphere. And he said he had a message from George [Mitchell], and he had consultations with the party and his intention was to go up, and … anybody of those who felt very happy were very welcome to join him. That's what I thought was an example of a real leadership, and that was how it happened that day.[17]

Danny Kennedy, who would go on to become an MLA and a minister at Stormont, was also in the room. He had been in Castle Buildings for many hours and says those words from Trimble, in the late afternoon of Good Friday, were inspiring. He was bowled over by his leader's short address:

> It was one of those moments where the hair literally stood on the back of your neck, and you thought, well, whatever about it, you've got guts. You know what I mean, it was real leadership in that sense, in that he was stepping out, beyond stretching out, and stretching others.[18]

Trimble was aware of the dissent in party ranks. He knew Arlene Foster, Peter Weir, Jim Rodgers, David Brewster and Jeffrey Donaldson did not support the deal. Conversations had taken place with them all, but they were not for turning. The SDLP's Mark Durkan recalls bumping into Donaldson in one of the corridors:

> I said, 'Is there anything that any of the rest of us can be saying that could help the people with problems?' And Jeffrey was more or less saying, 'Let me stop you there. I'm one of the people with the problems.'[19]

Unhappy with what was about to happen, Donaldson left Castle Buildings, and his departure was picked up by the television cameras and by others in the complex. They could only guess why the Lagan Valley MP was making an early exit.

Civil servant Ray Bassett, who was with the Irish government delegation, recalls seeing Donaldson walking towards his car:

> I remember looking out the window and saw Donaldson leaving. And at that stage that was the first hint we had that the Ulster Unionists were going to say yes. Because we knew there was probably a split on the way. I mean, people said he was going to a family function, but nobody believed that for a second. So, when Donaldson left, the chances were that the Ulster Unionists were going for it.[20]

While Trimble knew party members were perfectly entitled to oppose the deal, he was particularly exercised by Donaldson's decision. The two men had worked closely together in the months leading up to Good Friday. Trimble felt let down when Donaldson rejected the agreement and left the talks building.

UTV journalist Ken Reid said Trimble regarded Donaldson as a very capable politician:

> He rated Jeffrey Donaldson. I think he probably saw Jeffrey Donaldson as his successor. And you know when the tension arose, particularly in the week before the Good Friday Agreement, and Donaldson was pulling away from him, that hurt David. Because he felt Donaldson had ability, he had pedigree.[21]

After 5 p.m. Trimble led his talks team upstairs to the plenary session, which was in a large room full to capacity with Mitchell and his staff, the two premiers, the other party negotiators and officials. Trimble sat at the front with Taylor, Maginnis and Empey. Mitchell asked each party leader in turn if they accepted the agreement. Trimble declared, 'Yes', when he was asked.

When the session ended, Trimble went out to face the media, who had been waiting patiently for days for something to report. Most journalists knew what the final deal might look like. BBC Northern Ireland's political editor, Stephen Grimason, had actually managed to get hold of a copy of the agreement and revealed it to BBC viewers. The deal would be dubbed the Good Friday Agreement, although others would refer to it as the Belfast Agreement.

As anticipated, there would be an Assembly at Stormont with 108 seats elected using proportional representation. The Assembly would elect an Executive, and these ministers would run the departments, such as Education, Health and Finance. These posts would be divided up in line with the different party strengths. There would be a first minister and a deputy first minister, and there would be a North–South Ministerial Council. Articles 2 and 3 of the Irish Constitution would be changed, and there would be a commission which would look at new policing arrangements. Controversially, paramilitary prisoners would be released, and the deal would be put to a vote in referenda on both sides of the border on the same day. There was much to take in, and inevitably, the media had a multitude of questions.

As Trimble stood in front of reporters, it started to snow. David Kerr thought the weather was highly appropriate:

> It snowed and rained. And goodness me, I thought, if that isn't a metaphor for what is ahead of me, I don't know what is.[22]

He was right. There were political storms ahead. Unionism was bitterly divided over the contents of the Good Friday Agreement. Trimble was embarking on a new political journey. There were many internal battles on the horizon, and Trimble knew there was a referendum to win, if the deal was to come into effect.

As the rain and the sleet swirled above his head, Trimble apologised to the media for keeping them waiting when he spoke to them outside Castle Buildings. He said the delay was because the UUP had raised serious concerns about parties being in government if there had not been decommissioning. He said his party had received assurances from the prime minister which had alleviated those concerns. On the issue of Northern Ireland's place in the UK, he said that the agreement strengthened the union between Great Britain and Northern Ireland:

> We rise from this table knowing that the union is stronger than it was when we sat down. We know that the fundamental Act of Union is there intact.[23]

To Trimble, the agreement marked a win for unionism. In the question-and-answer session with reporters he was asked about the position of Jeffrey Donaldson. Journalists had seen him leave early and knew the Lagan Valley MP was opposed to the deal. Trimble played down his unexpected exit from Castle Buildings, saying his colleague had left because of family commitments. It was not a lie – but it was not the full story. Donaldson's opposition to the agreement would be well documented in the days ahead, and he would take on the unofficial role of chief critic within the party. Donaldson was not the only colleague of Trimble's to oppose what had been negotiated during those days in April 1998. John Hunter, who had helped Trimble in his leadership campaign, was another who thought the agreement was a bad deal:

> After reading the agreement I came to the conclusion very quickly this was disaster for unionism. There was nothing in it to force the Provos to decommission.[24]

Despite the opposition and the decision of some party members to desert him, Good Friday was a day of triumph for Trimble. He had stayed the course when others had predicted he would walk out. He had secured concessions and got the best deal he believed was on offer. It was not perfect – there was pain attached to it, and much detail still had to be worked out – but he felt there was a lot in the deal unionists could be pleased with.

Even Trimble's political rivals acknowledged the UUP leader's courage in endorsing the deal. The SDLP's Seamus Mallon, who would become deputy first minister and work with Trimble as first minister, believed his unionist partner deserved much credit:

> If John Hume or Gerry Adams had faced the degree of division in their parties that Trimble had they would not even have been at the negotiating table. Almost all his MPs were against him as were half his Assembly members and a large proportion of his local councillors.[25]

George Mitchell also acknowledged Trimble's staying power.

> Each day of the nearly two years of negotiations was for him a struggle to avoid being thrown off balance. Attacked

daily by some unionists for selling out the union, criticised often by some nationalists for recalcitrance, he threaded his way through a minefield of problems, guided by his intelligence, his sure grasp of the political situation and his determination to reach agreement.[26]

For John Hume, the events of Good Friday marked a high point in his career. He had every right to feel vindicated after the years of personal abuse he had suffered for talking to Gerry Adams. His fingerprints were all over the agreement, and it was littered with his language and his ideas. The negotiating skills of Seamus Mallon and Mark Durkan and others in the SDLP delegation had helped turn some of those ideas into reality.

Hume knew the peace process was far from over, though. There were other major battles to come, and he and those who backed power-sharing had to win the referendum campaign, the vote for which was scheduled for 22 May 1998. It had always been one of Hume's big regrets that the Sunningdale Agreement was not put to a vote in a referendum. Now, there was an opportunity to try again – albeit nearly 25 years later.

On the evening of Good Friday 1998, Trimble headed for his Lisburn home. He was shattered physically and mentally. Daphne Trimble had followed the day's events on the radio and on television. Her husband had not told her in detail how the day had gone, nor had they discussed the contents of the final agreement. They had a lot to catch up on. She jokingly recalls that her husband's first question that night at home was not political but practical: what were they going to have for dinner?

17

JUST SAY YES

*'We are not going to get simple majority rule.
We will have to take nationalists with us.'*
David Trimble campaigning in the referendum
for the Good Friday Agreement

There was little chance of David Trimble getting much rest after a frenetic few weeks. After the deal was agreed by the parties, he had to sell it: first to the UUP rank and file, and then to the electorate. On Saturday 11 April 1998, the party's executive met at headquarters in Belfast's Glengall Street. This was the meeting that had been adjourned the night before Good Friday. Trimble was confident he had the numbers, and he did. A motion supporting the deal was supported by 55 votes to 23. It was a handsome victory, vindicating Trimble's decision and setting the tone for days ahead. The Glengall Street meeting was simply the first stage in getting the party to formally support the deal.

A week later, members who made up the UUC gathered in Belfast's city centre to debate the agreement and vote on it. The council – an unwieldy body that included MPs, councillors, constituency representatives and members of the Orange Order – was at the centre of the party's decision-making process. Without the backing of this body, Trimble's plans would be in ruins, but he had done his homework and was confident of a good margin of victory.

Nearly 900 delegates came to the Europa Hotel – which had been a particular target of the IRA during the Troubles – giving it the unfortunate reputation of being the most bombed hotel in Europe. During a five-hour debate, the pros and cons of the agreement were discussed, and when it came to a vote, Trimble triumphed: 540 delegates backed the Good Friday deal and 210 opposed it. This meant that, despite the opposition, 72 per cent supported the agreement. It was a decisive victory and buoyed up Trimble, who now had the senior leadership of his party and a large proportion of the grassroots behind him.

However, there was still a major battle to be won. The opposition to the agreement came from a number of fronts. Trimble's opponents included a majority of UUP MPs, the Orange Order and a large band of up-and-coming members like Peter Weir, Arlene Foster and David Brewster – who had all made their concerns clear at Castle Buildings. Trimble was also worried about the position of his predecessor, Jim Molyneaux. Would he keep his powder dry, or would he join the anti-agreement unionists and campaign against the deal?

Outside of his critics in the UUP, Trimble faced opposition from Ian Paisley's DUP and Bob McCartney of the UK Unionist Party. Paisley and McCartney were formidable opponents, and Trimble knew he had a battle on his hands. Both were articulate leaders and seasoned campaigners whose message very often struck a chord with large swathes of the pro-union electorate. In the referendum vote, the result would rest on whose vision won the hearts and minds of the majority community.

Within days, a United Unionist campaign was formed, aimed at highlighting what they saw as the perils of the deal from a unionist perspective. The No campaign started to put together an effective critique of the agreement and started to organise public meetings and rallies. The group also produced an eye-catching pin badge with a Union Jack heart and the slogan 'A Heart for Ulster'.

There was much emotion attached to the No campaign. The thrust of their argument was that those who supported terrorism were the big winners and democrats were the big losers. They centred on Trimble's weakest areas – the release of prisoners, the reform of policing and the commitments over decommissioning – which No campaigners argued were too weak and would allow Sinn Féin into government without arms being destroyed or surrendered.

The early days of the campaign were set by the anti-agreement camp, and it seemed that they were winning many converts to their cause. Trimble and his pro-agreement colleagues knew that things had to change, and they had to campaign in a more sophisticated way. They needed help, so the UUP hierarchy turned to a familiar face.

The former television journalist Ray Hayden was approached to see if he could assist with communications and improve the way pro-agreement unionists were promoting the Good Friday deal. He would join David Kerr in running the UUP referendum campaign.

Hayden had his own consultancy business and had previously organised media training for the party. He remembers beginning to work at party headquarters in Glengall Street:

> I thought, this will not be easy. We will see lots of blood on the carpet as we go through this campaign. So, within a short space of time, Jack Allen had obtained some computers. I had a band of three or four volunteers. And basically, it was down to a news management operation where you attended meetings at 8.30. You decided what the line was for that day. We were holding press conferences, don't forget, virtually every day. It was 14/15/16-hour days throughout the campaign. It was very hot and heavy.[1]

Part of Trimble's strategy to secure a Yes vote was to try to persuade traditional non-voters to turn up and cast their ballot. He was well aware that there were many unionists who stayed at home at election time. Politics seemed irrelevant to them, and they tarred politicians with the same brush.

Trimble and his team needed to persuade this sizeable section of the community that this referendum was extremely important and had the potential to change their lives. He needed to convince them that, if they wanted things to change, they needed to support a Yes vote. It was about showing them that the Good Friday deal presented a new Northern Ireland – very different from the past 30 years.

Opinion polls showed that unionists had valid concerns, and surveys also registered that there was a high proportion of undecided voters. Behind the scenes, there was much number crunching going on, in both the anti-agreement and pro-agreement camps. Surveys and focus groups were commissioned and polling data was forensically studied. Trimble knew that the referendum needed to get majority support in both the unionist and nationalist communities. The Good Friday deal needed to be backed by around 70 per cent, a target set by the pro-agreement lobby, so it was crucial that traditional non-voters were encouraged to come out and vote.

Trimble's campaign had been doing reasonably well by the first week of May. The appointment of Hayden had given the press operation structure, and Trimble was getting good coverage. However, it was by and large a limited operation, and, at this stage, there was very little cross-party work. Although pro-agreement unionists were privately talking to supporters of the Good Friday deal in the SDLP and the Alliance Party, no major joint campaign events were planned.

Trimble sounded confident and assured in his media interviews – rather like the assuredness he showed when he was running for UUP leader in 1995. He repeatedly talked up the benefits of the Good Friday deal: how it enhanced the union and put the power in the hands of local politicians. He also maintained that there would be a high turnout on 22 May, and he predicted, as you would expect, that the Yes camp would win.

Then disaster struck, and the No camp received a propaganda boost – though not of their making. Leading IRA prisoners had been given temporary leave by the Irish government to attend the Sinn Féin Ard Fheis at the RDS in Dublin. Those given weekend leave included members of the Balcombe Street Gang. This group had carried out a bombing campaign in England in the 1970s and had a ruthless reputation. They were given a tumultuous welcome at the conference centre, greeted with a standing ovation and hailed by Gerry Adams.

Other IRA prisoners who were serving time in the Maze prison in Northern Ireland were also allowed out to go to the conference. The logic of Secretary of State Mo Mowlam was that the prisoners could be instrumental in persuading republicans to back the agreement. It was a gamble. What occurred in front of the watching media were moments of triumphalism, and the television pictures of the cheering crowds dominated the news bulletins. To anti-agreement unionists, it proved their point.

When Trimble heard what had happened, he was furious:

> We were nearly sunk right at the beginning with that incredibly stupid action by Mo Mowlam allowing a number of IRA prisoners ... out for a Sinn Féin rally in Dublin on Saturday night, which played out again and again and again on television screens on the Sunday. The Shinners [Sinn Féin] played it for all it was worth with the 'These are our Nelson Mandelas' and all that crap. I hadn't seen it on TV but when I arrived in Armagh on the Monday to go out canvassing my workers and local association members were shell-shocked, completely demoralised and saying that 'we can't go out there because we will be annihilated.' And, in essence, we had to restart our campaign after that.[2]

It was a massive moment in the referendum campaign. It floored the pro-agreement lobby and buoyed up the anti-agreement camp. Trimble and his team were crushed by what they had witnessed. They were convinced the scenes from Dublin would push thousands of wavering unionists to now vote No.

The move also did nothing to improve Trimble's relationship with Mowlam, which was already at rock bottom. The two did not get on. He did not like her manner and thought she was too close to nationalists and republicans. She found him arrogant and rude, and very often he bypassed her and went straight to Tony Blair if he had a problem.

The images of the IRA men being lauded by Adams in Dublin also angered the Irish government – even though IRA men had been released by the Irish authorities. Liz O'Donnell, who was a minister of state in Foreign Affairs, remembers seeing the television pictures:

> I mean, that was a disaster. I ran out of my kitchen when I saw that on television. I said, 'What the hell, what a stupid thing to do', to have them at a Sinn Féin meeting and to have a kind of triumphalist welcoming home ... for the bombers. It was just a disastrous thing to do, so close to the referendum.³

Trimble and his colleagues had to rethink their strategy and reset the campaign. The whole operation needed fresh thinking, new ideas and, above all, momentum. More needed to be done to convince unionists that they should back the agreement. It was about reassurance.

Tony Blair arrived on 14 May for a visit and delivered a keynote speech at the Balmoral Show grounds in Belfast – almost a year since he had spoken there in the wake of his general election victory. He said a Yes vote was a vote for hope, peace and stability, and he claimed that voting No would be to 'turn your back on the future'.

If the Blair visit was about reassuring wavering unionists and offering reassurance, within 24 hours Trimble and his team suffered another setback. The UDP, the political wing of the UDA, held a rally in favour of the Yes campaign. Michael Stone, a loyalist prisoner serving a sentence for killing three people, had been given special permission to attend. He was lauded by supporters – just as the Balcombe Street Gang had been cheered by republicans days earlier in Dublin. His appearance and reception appalled many and again raised the whole issue of prisoner releases.

With time running out, Trimble and his team needed to keep the campaign going. It was tricky. Half his parliamentary team was against the deal and appeared at anti-agreement events. The No camp was running a very effective campaign compared with the Yes campaign. Such was the antagonism and vitriol directed towards Trimble that he often needed security at public meetings. At one in an Orange Hall in County Tyrone, he was told by one anti-agreement unionist that he was not prepared to 'sit down with a Sinn Féin man today, tomorrow or 30 years hence'.

The questioner was applauded; it was clear he had support in the room. Trimble had been heckled and jeered by flag-waving protesters when he arrived at the hall, and as he walked in, he was accompanied by members of the RUC. The UUP leader cooly listened to the question, then stood up and delivered his response:

> We are at a very important point in our history. It is not a time for windy rhetoric. It is not a time for false prospects or false hopes. Anybody who thinks that in 1998 the unionist people can impose their will on all the people of Northern Ireland, the British government and world opinion is deluded.

Trimble was later pressed about how power-sharing would work, and he made his view very clear:

> We are not going to get simple majority rule. We will have to take nationalists with us. But again, who thought we were going to do things otherwise?[4]

Days before the referendum vote, a cross-party visit was organised by Trimble's team involving Viscount Cranborne, the leader of the Conservatives in the House of Lords, and Kate Hoey, the Ulster-born Labour MP for Vauxhall. It was intended to show that pro-union politicians like Hoey and Cranborne backed the agreement, and it was an attempt to reassure unionist grassroots that the union was secure.

They travelled to Portstewart, a popular seaside resort on the north coast, and Hoey recalls how difficult it was to get Trimble to engage with the public:

> Any time I was meeting somebody I would sort of say, 'Hello, would you like to meet David Trimble?' And of course, most people did. But David was not good at making them feel at ease. He wasn't good at it. So, I got a bit frustrated.[5]

After their stop at the seaside, Hoey, Cranborne and Trimble made their way around the coast for a photo shoot at Derry's walls, and the pictures were carried in the newspapers the next day. It was all very pleasant and straightforward, but with referendum day fast approaching, it was clear the Yes campaign needed some momentum. Events were being organised at grassroots level, but nothing had the wow factor.

For some time, activists in the SDLP had been trying to come up with an event that could bring pro-agreement unionism and nationalism together. Tim Attwood of the SDLP was becoming concerned that the numbers were drifting away from the Yes camp, and he started to think about which celebrities he could use to endorse a pro-agreement message.

He remembered John Hume's friendship with Bono and wondered if the U2 lead singer would help them out. So, Attwood rang the musician and asked him to help:

> I said, 'Trimble is in trouble, so we have to change the dynamic.' He said, 'Put it this way, I'll do whatever John [Hume] wants me to do.'[6]

The idea of a concert was then discussed, with the suggestion that Trimble and Hume would make a guest appearance at an event in Belfast. Attwood then contacted Eamonn McCann, the music promoter, who offered to help, and the local band Ash was also approached, and they agreed to perform. Now, Attwood had to get Trimble and his team to agree to participate, so he contacted David Kerr, and a meeting was organised at Belfast's Europa Hotel.

Kerr was a U2 fan and instantly got the idea of the two political leaders appearing with Bono in front of a crowd of young people. He liked the imagery and the message such an event would send. He thought it had the potential to show 'the centre ground of unionism and nationalism coming together, locking hands to say we will forge a new political future together'.[7]

David Kerr also felt the Bono event with Trimble and Hume could be a game changer:

> I knew instantly it was the opportunity to get the image the campaign desperately needed. We were in trouble. Something had to happen. It was obvious to me we needed to engage with people who did not normally vote, especially young people.[8]

The idea was then put to Trimble, who agreed. He knew he was in the fight of his life, and anything that could help to push undecided voters over the line was worth considering. The Waterfront Hall was booked, and free tickets were distributed to teenagers and students across Northern Ireland.

After Hume and Trimble arrived at the venue, there was a discussion backstage about how the two men should be introduced. It was agreed they would come on stage together and would be pictured alongside Bono, but there would be no speeches. Trimble was nervous, which was understandable, as he was out of his comfort zone. Kerr recalls that Hume helped to 'calm David more than the other way round',[9] though the two politicians were both out of their comfort zones. Hoey knew this was unnatural territory for Trimble and says it was the first time she had seen him 'genuinely frightened'.[10]

The band Ash played for around 40 minutes, and they got the crowd of around 2,000 into a party mood. U2 then followed, and when the moment came, Bono called Trimble and Hume onto the stage. Political consultant Mark Fullbrook, who had been helping the UUP, was in the crowd when the two politicians emerged:

> I was sitting next to Daphne, and it was massively powerful, massively emotional. I remember saying to David, who was originally going on wearing his suit, and I told him to take his jacket off and roll up his sleeves, and he said, 'I don't do that, Mark.' And I said, 'No, you sort of really have to.'[11]

After a discussion involving a number of staff in both parties, Trimble and Hume appeared without their jackets, in shirts and ties. The crowd cheered as the two leaders appeared on opposite sides of Bono as he raised their arms into the air.

That was the moment the photographers and the television crews had come to capture: a sign of togetherness, unionism and nationalism united, an image of a new Northern Ireland. For both the Trimble and Hume teams it was mission complete. The Yes campaign had secured a wow moment, which was badly needed.

In the hours that followed, the footage of the three men on the Waterfront Hall stage dominated the news bulletins. It was played and played again, and the photograph of Bono and the two politicians dominated the next day's newspapers. Kerr believes that image changed the narrative of the referendum debate:

> That, for me, was the defining moment of the campaign. And despite everything else that had happened, all the negative stuff, all the emotive stuff with that campaign, when you saw the two of them standing there, you knew they embodied the centre ground of Northern Ireland politics, the moderate unionists and the moderate nationalists, and they spoke for that.[12]

Kerr believes that the Waterfront Hall image was worth 'more than 100,000 votes' for the Yes campaign in the referendum. It is hard to establish the precise figure, but the photograph certainly helped to convince waverers that they should vote for the agreement.

Daphne also believes that the photo of her husband and Hume at the U2 concert mattered:

> That's the picture that everyone still remembers, of Bono with Hume on one arm and David on the other. It was kind of iconic. I honestly believe that without it the referendum might have gone the other way.[13]

On 22 May, in what was one of the highest turnouts in local electoral history, 71.1 per cent backed the Good Friday Agreement, with 28.9 per cent voting against. In the Republic, the margin of success was even greater, with 94 per cent voting Yes and 6 per cent voting No. For the Yes campaigners it was a convincing result, and for Trimble it marked a moment of great personal triumph. He had faced strong opposition, the campaign had been difficult and his party had been divided, but he had achieved a great result. He had set a target of 70 per cent, so the result of just over 71 per cent was particularly pleasing.

As the result was being broadcast, David and Daphne Trimble celebrated at the King's Hall in Belfast, while their teenage son Richard was at home in Lisburn watching the coverage. He remembers the phone ringing:

> We didn't often get many phone calls to the house, but I remember having to answer the phone to someone who basically said they wanted to kill Dad. That was a bit unpleasant, because my parents were out, and I was at home, so I ... had to answer the phone. This guy was ringing from – I can't remember, I think it was Enniskillen he said he was ringing from. He didn't tell me his name, funny enough. He said that basically he was making veiled threats. He said, 'If your dad is out in the street, something will happen to him.'[14]

Richard did not tell his parents about the threatening call. In the excitement of the referendum campaign, the phone conversation and its disturbing contents were forgotten. However, in 1998, the menacing message was a stark reminder of the pressure and dangers that came with public life in Northern Ireland. Daphne often worried about David's safety, and after he became first minister, security precautions were put in place in the house. But he continued to live in the family home.

Both Daphne and David always tried to shield their children from anything which would cause them distress. They wanted them to have as normal a childhood as possible. Daphne says they tried to keep home life and David's work separate, as best they could:

> We tried to keep the house as a sort of family zone. So, we rarely would have had meetings or people coming to the house on political matters. Occasionally, but not all that often. I think we guarded our privacy, is the best way of putting it, so that the children were not exposed to things.[15]

Sarah, the youngest Trimble child, says when she was very young much of the political activity passed her by. She recalls her father helping with the school run and being self-conscious that she was the daughter of a high-profile politician:

> I always remember being a little embarrassed of the police car. If Dad did the school run, he'd be in the police car. Or the police car would be behind. If he drove our car, they would be following behind. And I always remember being a little embarrassed of that.[16]

Nicky Trimble remembers people coming to their street to protest:

> There were occasions where we had groups outside the house protesting with placards. 'Trimble the traitor' was painted in rather large letters on the railway line bridge. It was in big letters where Dad would see it. Later, there was a letter bomb to the office. Apparently, the device that was posted to Dad's office was not sophisticated, and Mum had it in her hands. She noticed there was powder coming out of it, so she quickly put it down and ran to the back, and the police were informed. But again, that sort of stuff was normalised.[17]

Trimble's home address was well known, and although he was encouraged on security grounds by the NIO to move house, he and

Daphne decided to stay put. There were concerns that Trimble was vulnerable to attacks from both republicans and loyalists. It was later reported that loyalists who had access to weapons and who were anti-Trimble had planned to attack his car one morning, but the move was abandoned at the last minute.

As she got older, Sarah Trimble became conscious that not everyone shared her father's politics, and that others were strongly opposed to him. She knew she had to exercise caution:

> I was definitely aware there were people that did not like Dad. And I was aware enough, especially as a child, that maybe to be careful. But like, if I said, 'I am David Trimble's daughter', you know you might get a different reaction. But I think I was quite oblivious to those things.[18]

With the referendum vote secured, Trimble and his team now had to focus on the Assembly election campaign. The battle for Stormont was like a rematch, particularly for the unionist parties, as the arguments over the Good Friday Agreement continued in TV studios and in the press. If the UUP ended up as the largest party on 25 June, Trimble would become first minister. His colleagues knew that, in the coming weeks, he had to project an image as Northern Ireland's leader in waiting.

Ken Maginnis felt that Trimble needed to smarten himself up, so he got a message to Jane Wells to see if she could assist. Wells started life as a French teacher and then crafted a successful career in public relations. She began working for John Laird, who had launched his own PR business in the 1970s. Her link to the UUP was initiated when she was called in by the party to help with Jim Nicholson's European election campaign. When she was later approached by Maginnis, in May 1998, she agreed to return and offer some advice.

However, before Wells did anything, she told Maginnis that she had to speak to Daphne Trimble:

> I said, I don't want to step on Daphne's toes – Mrs Trimble, as I called her then. Because if someone was buying clothes for my husband, I'd go bananas. So, I said, 'Listen, you need to give me Daphne's phone number.'[19]

The two women had a warm and positive phone call, and Daphne was very relaxed about the plans to smarten up her husband. Her only stipulation surrounded the purchase of shirts. She was insistent that they had to be a certain kind: 'Would you please make sure they are non-iron shirts, because I have not got the time to do a lot of ironing.'

Armed with David Trimble's measurements and with the green light from Daphne, Wells was able to spring into action. She arranged to meet him at party headquarters and initially was a bit worried about how the conversation might go:

> I had never met David Trimble. Obviously, I knew Maginnis and Rogan and Empey, but I had never actually met Trimble. I always thought he was a bit of a scary person, a bit intimidating.[20]

Wells went to UUP headquarters in Glengall Street, introduced herself to Trimble and somewhat nervously explained what she had been asked to do:

> Look, I've been given this job to buy you a few suits and buy you a few ties and get you smartened up a wee bit. And he was kind of bemused, but it was very strange. Although he was sort of bemused, he was accepting, you know.[21]

The meeting dispelled her initial views, and Wells soon enjoyed working with the UUP leader. With his blessing, she went and purchased suits, ties and shirts. She also bought shoes and organised regular haircuts. The leader of unionism was now suited and booted, ready for the fray of an election campaign.

Improving Trimble's image was one thing – getting the UUP's message right was another. Ray Hayden had been retained after the referendum campaign and was now helping with the media side of things:

> You know, we were building on success ... the key message here was 'Now give us the tools to finish the job. You voted in your tens of thousands in favour of the Good Friday Agreement, but the job is not done yet. And we need your support.'[22]

The party decided to bar MPs from running as candidates in the Assembly election, but Trimble and John Taylor were given a dispensation as leader and deputy leader, respectively. That meant that Trimble's chief critic, Jeffrey Donaldson, MP for Lagan Valley, would not be a candidate. Even though Donaldson was not on the ballot paper, other anti-agreement UUP members were selected to run, including Peter Weir in North Down and John Hunter in South Antrim.

Even Trimble's home patch of Upper Bann was not immune from the divisions within unionism. Denis Watson, who was county grand master of Armagh, was running as an independent on an anti-agreement ticket. Trimble was now fighting a series of battles. He was hoping to get as many pro-agreement candidates as possible selected in winnable UUP seats, and he was having to fend off the constant attacks from the anti-agreement unionists in the DUP and in the UK Unionists.

The main issues on the doorsteps were the same ones that were raised during the referendum campaign. Unionist voters were exercised about the release of paramilitary prisoners, the reform of the RUC and whether Sinn Féin should be allowed into government without decommissioning. The atmosphere on the campaign trail was often hostile, and sometimes that descended into violence, with Trimble's Lurgan office being attacked.

Opinion polls suggested that support for the UUP was falling, and there was confidence amongst anti-agreement unionists. Trimble was hoping to secure more than 30 seats. On a good day, some observers predicted 32 seats could be won, while party strategists knew anything under 30 would be tricky to manage.

When the results came in, it was seen as a setback for Trimble. In the end he had managed to win 28 seats, two short of his 30 minimum. His main unionist rival, the DUP, took 20, Sinn Féin won 18 and the Alliance got 6. Bob McCartney's UK Unionist Party won 5 seats, and 3 independent unionists won places, while the Women's Coalition and the PUP both secured 2 seats. The figures meant there was a narrow majority in unionist ranks of pro-agreement supporters.

The vagaries of the proportional representation voting system also meant that, even though the SDLP secured the highest number of votes, they only won 24 seats and were behind the UUP in terms of actual seats. John Hume's party topped the poll with 177,963 first preferences on 22 per cent. The UUP came in next at 172,225 votes, which represented just over 21 per cent of the total vote. The UUP vote tally was down on the forum election results of 1996, when the party polled 24 per cent.

When the outcome of the Assembly election became clear, Ray Hayden remembers discussing the results with Trimble:

> I remember saying to David the day of the count, towards the closing stages, we were in the boardroom in Glengall Street [and] I said to him, 'That was good, 28 seats.' He said, 'Yes, it's a pity it wasn't 32, that would have given an additional seat in the Executive.' And I thought, that's the guy[,] you know, he's always pushing. He wanted more, politically. He wanted more. Because I think he realised he could only really properly secure his objectives, his political objectives, by coming at it from a position of strength.[23]

Trimble could now begin preparations for the first sitting of the Assembly and the Executive. He would obviously become first minister, and if John Hume wanted to be deputy first minister, the job was his.

However, the SDLP leader had no desire to take the job, and at a party meeting in a Belfast hotel he took Seamus Mallon aside and told him that he would not be in the new Stormont Executive.

Hume had been a power-sharing minister in 1974, but history was not going to repeat itself. He did not want the job, and he wanted Seamus to step in. Mallon recalled how the conversation with Hume went: 'This deputy first minister thing, you're going to have to do it, because the doctors have told me I shouldn't.'[24]

Hume simply had no desire for the post, and he was worried about his health at this stage, so it seemed sensible to scale down his work rather than increase it.

But there were other factors at play as well. Hume was not a fan of Stormont. Of all the places where he had worked as a politician, it was his least favourite. He was a committed European and preferred being in the confines of the European Parliament. The job of deputy first minster was simply not for him, and even many of Hume's colleagues believed Mallon would potentially be a better fit for the job. Interestingly, many unionists preferred to deal with Mallon rather than Hume, as they found him more direct and better at day-to-day detail.

On 1 July 1998, David Trimble became first minister designate and Seamus Mallon became deputy first minister designate. They were elected jointly at a sitting of the Assembly in Castle Buildings, as the chamber in Parliament Buildings was still being renovated. Trimble used his acceptance speech to talk about his friend and university colleague Edgar Graham, who had been killed by the IRA in December 1983. He also talked about other acts of violence:

> A number of members who are here today have done terrible things; I do not need to elaborate. Though I should say that those concerned are not all in one corner of the chamber. Many awful things have happened.[25]

Seamus Mallon had warm words for his new political partner:

> I look forward to working with Mr David Trimble. I have known him for a long time. We have not always agreed, and there will still be times when we disagree, but the disagreements will be sorted out face to face, for I am sure that his back is sore enough at the moment.[26]

Mallon's reference to the level of backstabbing was accurate. He was well aware of Trimble's difficulties inside and outside of the UUP. The two men were in position, but the formation of the rest of the Executive would have to wait. For those who were pro-agreement, the election of Trimble and Mallon was seen as a fresh start and required different thinking.

Ray Hayden remembers being with Trimble and party stalwart May Steele at an event at Stormont. The mood was celebratory, as the party had secured the most Assembly seats:

> May Steele and David glided into our conversation. And she turned to him and said, 'David, isn't it wonderful? We're back. We're back.' And he said, 'Yes, May, and now we have to learn to share it.' And that's an insight into the man and into the mindset of a unionist leader who, in my opinion ... was the best we've ever seen in the history of the Ulster Unionist Party. This was a guy who had courage for breakfast, courage for lunch, courage for dinner.[27]

Trimble's courage would be severely tested in the summer of 1998.

18

FROM OMAGH TO OSLO

'Ulster Unionists, fearful of being isolated on the island, built a solid house, but it was a cold house for Catholics.'
David Trimble, speaking at the Nobel Peace Prize ceremony in Oslo

On Saturday 15 August 1998, the Trimbles were taking in the last few hours of a family holiday in the Moselle Valley. It had been a much-needed break after a tumultuous year of personal and political change. They had initially spent a fortnight in England on a narrowboat, which David and Daphne and their children enjoyed.

Nicky Trimble says he and his siblings found the canal holidays lots of fun:

> I mean we all loved it, because when you're young, you are enthusiastic. All of us would run ahead and open up the lock. Then we go for the next one, so there was lots of activity. And of course, the canals in England are all peppered with pubs all along them. So, there's plenty of places to stop. And I think all of us enjoyed those holidays.[1]

The Trimbles had added the additional break in Germany in case the boating holiday had not been a success with their children. As a family they were all due to return to the UK the next day, and by the Saturday night their car was, as normal, packed with luggage but also with a healthy supply of local wine. They had managed to switch off while they were abroad, and during their time away Trimble was not contacted about matters from home.

As they got ready for bed, there was a knock on their apartment door. It was the owner, who said there was an urgent call from David Campbell, a friend of Trimble's and his chief of staff, having been appointed over the summer. Back home in Northern Ireland, friends and colleagues had all been desperately trying to contact Trimble, and Campbell was the only party official or civil servant who knew where he was in Germany.

Campbell's news was shocking and heartbreaking to David and Daphne. The Real IRA, a dissident group that had split from the Provisional IRA, had planted a car bomb in Omagh that afternoon. The explosion killed 31 men, women and children. Amongst the dead was a woman pregnant with twins, and the blast had also injured hundreds of people and destroyed property. The bomb went off in the heart of the town while it was packed with shoppers.

It was the biggest loss of life in a single incident in the Troubles. Daphne remembers that David was initially quiet and devastated by the news: 'It was absolutely horrendous. It was the horror; we were hearing the full horror of it.'[2]

Trimble knew he had to get home to Northern Ireland as soon as possible, and after Campbell's conversation there was a flurry of calls about getting him back to Belfast with great speed. The Trimbles then explained to their children that they were having to go home earlier than planned because of the bombing.

Vicky Trimble remembers the conversation:

> My parents just came in and said there had been a bomb in Omagh – 'We have to go.' And because it was so soon after the Good Friday Agreement my first reaction was 'That was supposed to have stopped'. But that was it. We packed our bags and went straight home.[3]

Daphne recalls that they finished their packing as discussions continued about getting David back to Northern Ireland. She recalls how the process to get him home became complicated:

> The civil servants didn't seem capable of getting him back home from Germany. What would have been sensible was to have got him on a flight from an airport close by, but they didn't seem able to do that. So, we started to drive to the channel port, just the way that we would normally have done. And as we were driving across Belgium, the phone was going. They were looking for an airfield, looking for somewhere to get him home. It didn't happen. So, what actually happened in the end was they got him flown back from England.[4]

The Trimbles drove to Calais and crossed to Dover, and from there David left his family and went to a nearby airfield, where he was flown back to Northern Ireland. Daphne ended up driving the children back home, stopping first at David's London flat before travelling via ferry back to Northern Ireland. Once he was back home, Trimble made his way to Hillsborough Castle, where he met Tony Blair, who had arrived from London.

Blair had been to the Royal Victoria Hospital in Belfast, where he had spent time with some of the injured from Omagh. He was deeply saddened and upset by what he had seen, and he and Trimble discussed what the security response should be. Trimble needed to visit Omagh and wanted to get there as quickly as possible. So on Monday 17 August he travelled down to County Tyrone, where he met up with the local UUP MP, William Thompson. As first minister he visited the Tyrone County Hospital and spent time with some of the injured. As with Blair's visit to the hospital in Belfast, for Trimble it brought home the abject horror of the bombing.

Within days, funerals were being arranged, and Trimble was determined as first minster that he would attend as many services as he could.

He and Dennis Rogan, the UUP chairman, went to a funeral Mass at St Mary's Church in Buncrana in County Donegal for three boys who died in the bombing. Trimble's presence at the church took on much symbolism. First, it was over the border in the Irish Republic, and secondly, it was a Catholic church service. As Orangemen, both Trimble and Rogan knew that membership of the Orange Order forbad members from being present at a Catholic Mass.

Trimble and Rogan were made very welcome at the Mass for eight-year-old Oran Doherty and for James Barker and Sean McLoughlin, who were both aged 12. The Bishop of Derry, Dr Séamus Hegarty, who addressed the congregation, made it clear that there was genuine warmth directed towards the visitors from Belfast:

> We want to assure you that you are among friends. Among people who are looking to you and your colleagues to give us the type of climate in Northern Ireland which will be conducive to the building of a genuine and lasting just peace.[5]

Trimble was not the only high-profile mourner there that day. Sinn Féin President Gerry Adams also attended, as did Trimble's former colleague from Queen's University, Mary McAleese. After a successful career in academia, McAleese had been elected president of Ireland in 1997. She was sitting in front of Trimble, and at the beginning of the church service she turned around to greet him:

> I was there and David was there, and he was sitting behind me in the seat. Now, you know we hadn't ever been really bosom pals, let's face it. I would always have regarded Daphne very highly, and he was sitting behind me and I turned initially just to welcome him and was going to shake his hand, and the two of us just stood up and hugged, and both of us were very tearful. But that was a moment, I think, when a lot of things just fell away, a lot

of old baggage. A lot of old stuff just fell away. I saw in him the man he had become – the quite extraordinary person he had become. Now, he hadn't abandoned unionism, and he hadn't abandoned his beliefs, and he hadn't abandoned those principles. Still, of course, there would be times, you know, when he would be quite scathing about the Republic. But that was a different David Trimble. That was a man who had been on the hot-red forge of life.[6]

Was McAleese right? Was the David Trimble she embraced in Buncrana very different from the man she had encountered as an undergraduate? Trimble was on a political journey, and he was in County Donegal speaking for everyone in Northern Ireland as its first minister. As she observed, his politics had not fundamentally changed, but his outlook had. The coming together of McAleese and Trimble that day in St Mary's Church was a powerful image, a moment when two leaders from different parts of the island were united in sorrow and grief.

Their encounter was not just political; it was also personal – an acknowledgement that whatever had happened in the past was over, and that working together was the way forward. Trimble's decision to travel to Catholic funeral Masses did attract some criticism from Orange Order members. Some even suggested that the UUP leader and party chairman, Dennis Rogan, should be disciplined.

The Orange Order made it clear that any disciplinary proceedings would have to come from the two men's lodges – in Trimble's case that was Bangor Abbey, and in Rogan's case it was a lodge in Belfast. Irrespective of the rules and the calls for them to be disciplined, both Rogan and Trimble insisted that their presence in Buncrana was the right thing to do. Lord Rogan told journalists that 'David Trimble and I did a Christian act'.[7]

Prior to the Omagh bombing, the Orange Order had dominated much of Trimble's first few weeks as first minister. In July, the standoff at Drumcree had continued, as members of the Order were prevented from marching along Portadown's Garvaghy Road. Once again police and protesters had clashed, and the dispute led to a series of disturbances across Northern Ireland. It was the first big test for Mallon and Trimble's leadership, and the two men worked together to try to find a solution. On 12 July, three Catholic boys were killed in Ballymoney when their house was petrol bombed by the UVF. Their deaths caused shock and outrage throughout Northern Ireland and stretched the fragile political process. However, the Reverend William Bingham, an Orange Order chaplain, made it clear that 'no road is worth a life', and the protests ended.[8]

Understandably, in the aftermath of the Omagh bombing the issue of security topped the political agenda. Trimble and the UUP were still concerned about the whole issue of the decommissioning of paramilitary weapons. The debate went round and round in circles. Republicans made it clear that decommissioning looked like surrender and said it was never a prerequisite to being part of government.

However, what became clear was that Trimble's strategy now depended on the IRA acting, and therefore he was effectively placing his future in the hands of republican strategists. He argued that people could not be in government if they had a private army. Soon, there were developments, and on 2 September Sinn Féin announced that Martin McGuinness would work with the International Decommissioning Commission. That was followed by Gerry Adams telling the *Irish Times* that 'the violence we have seen must be for all of us now a thing of the past, over, done with and gone'.[9]

As republicans made these moves, President Clinton arrived in Northern Ireland, and he was joined by Prime Minister Tony Blair. Clinton, Blair, Trimble and Mallon all addressed a crowd at the Waterfront Hall in Belfast. Clinton said that the local politicians had a chance to change history, and that they should build on what was achieved at the talks earlier in the year:

> Do not let it slip away. It will not come again in our lifetimes.[10]

In the audience were senior republicans, including Adams and McGuinness. Trimble had worked hard at his address. It had been written by David Kerr and there had been some limited input from Downing Street. He used the occasion to make a direct plea to Sinn Féin:

> Each part of the agreement, including decommissioning, must be implemented. But if you take the road of peace and do so in genuine good faith you will find me a willing leader in the journey.[11]

Trimble's remarks made the headlines, and some days later, on the BBC's *Breakfast with Frost* programme, he declared that McGuinness's engagement with the decommissioning body meant that the IRA was on a 'conveyor belt' to actual decommissioning. He was also asked about whether he would shake Adams's hand in the coming days in a planned UUP–Sinn Féin meeting. Trimble most likely guessed the question was coming and had probably thought about his answer in advance. He remarked:

> There is a point about hands being held out open to show they are not containing any weapons, but Mr Adams cannot do that.[12]

Trimble's potential meeting with the Sinn Féin president had been talked about for weeks, and he had the backing of the UUP Executive to meet him. There was no mass party revolt, but Trimble knew the encounter had to be handled well and, ideally, he wanted to play the significance down. The media had other ideas, and there was natural fascination with the two leaders coming together – unionism and republicanism – like the meeting of Sir James Craig and Michael Collins in 1922. This was a bit of history, which Trimble was well aware of.

On Thursday 10 September 1998, it took place. The agreement was that the two men would be alone. Adams recalls what happened:

I said to him, 'Will we shake hands, or will we just get on with the business?' And he said, 'Let's just get on with the business.'[13]

It was a start. There was no handshake, but Trimble had already made that clear to the media. He was not going to do that. As agreed, the two leaders were the only individuals in the room, and there was no notetaker or observer. Trimble put forward his thoughts on decommissioning and what he felt were the obligations of republicans. He believed the Good Friday Agreement would last, but he was cynical about the motives of republicans. Adams detailed what steps he thought had to take place in the coming weeks. He told Trimble that decommissioning was 'not within our gift but we will do our very best'.[14]

The meeting was cordial and businesslike, and both Adams and Trimble gave positive accounts to the media. It was a start to their relationship, but both men knew their dealings were probably always going to be tense and awkward. Trimble did not like Adams and made no secret of that both privately and publicly.

Lord Bew, who became a confidant of Trimble's, said the UUP leader preferred to deal with Martin McGuinness:

> Adams is always double talk; you can't pin him down. If Martin [McGuinness] tells you something's going to happen, it will happen. That was the widespread view among unionists and British government officials.
>
> [Stephen Walker:] Trimble didn't like Adams, did he?
>
> [Lord Bew:] No, not one bit. Whereas there was a sneaky regard for Martin.
>
> [Stephen Walker:] Why didn't he like Adams?

[Lord Bew:] I don't know, he just – why would you? I mean, there's a kind of, you know, his lugubrious sentimentality. You know, he would just be off-putting. His whole style would be off-putting immediately.[15]

Adams found Trimble curt in their dealings but says he learned to accept that that was part of his make-up:

Whatever about my personal view about the handshakes or personal view about this or that, we had a job to do, and we just had to do it. And you know, you have to deal with the objective reality of it, of when it was writ. So, it is true to say that David didn't just have a bad day, as you and I might have a bad day or be cranky or grumpy. David had an abrasive personality … it was part of his make-up … it was just part of who he was. So, you've got to learn, that … it wasn't maybe all the time intended the way it sounded … even if he was having a good day, he would still say the wrong thing or he would be dismissive. You would just have to accept that's who he was, and what he was, and that worked for him in doing what he did within unionism.[16]

The dealings between the UUP and Sinn Féin would become central to the future of the peace process and would be tied to Trimble's chances of success – or indeed failure – as first minister. It was not the only key relationship in the process, and Trimble had many to juggle. He did some successfully, while others broke down. He worked well with Bertie Ahern, for example, despite their obvious political differences.

Dr Graham Gudgin, who advised Trimble, would later recall observing the relationship with Ahern at first hand:

I was often in his office when he was on the phone to Bertie Ahern, and so I couldn't hear Bertie Ahern's part of the conversation, but David's side of the conversation was friendly and warm, and I thought he was taking advice from Bertie. I think he trusted Bertie Ahern.[17]

Trimble initially warmed to Tony Blair, and they got on very well (although matters changed later). But his relationship with Mo Mowlam was not good. It had started well, and it was businesslike and cordial, but Trimble had by this point lost faith in her. He felt her judgement was flawed and that she had made too many mistakes. She found him rude and claimed he often ignored her.

They were very different characters. Mowlam was outgoing and amusing, and used swear words liberally and often dispensed with formality, whereas Trimble was more strait-laced and conventional and was personally awkward and shy. In many ways it was a classic personality clash, but it was making the political process strained behind the scenes.

Alastair Campbell, one of Blair's key advisers, remembers being in a meeting with Mowlam and Trimble. He recalls Trimble repeatedly whispering something in the prime minister's ear, and Campbell knew something was not right:

> Mo was sort of sitting there just looking like thunder. And I got up and said to her, 'Mo, what the fuck is going on?' And she said, 'What is going on is he [Trimble] doesn't want me here, so he's just talking to Tony.' And [Trimble] was whispering to Tony. And there was something about Mo. Mo was a fantastic character, but if you had to design somebody who was not going to be somebody that David Trimble would warm to, it was Mo, taking the wig off, belching from time to time, feet up on the table. And David was always very proper with Tony, you know, 'Prime minister this, prime minister that'. And we were very much 'Tony' and Mo was very much 'Tony'. And she would swear, so I do remember that, and him [Trimble] whispering.[18]

The media executive David Montgomery, who knew Trimble from his Bangor days, was very familiar with the strained relationship. He had observed it on occasion and was aware of how Trimble bypassed Mowlam as Northern Ireland secretary and preferred to deal directly with Downing Street. He says in simple terms that they could not make it work, as they 'rubbed each other the wrong way'.[19]

Lord Empey is another who watched the personal difficulties develop. He says the cracks in the Mowlam–Trimble relationship can be traced to her decision to allow prisoners out on temporary leave during the 1998 Good Friday referendum campaign:

> He [Trimble] never got on with Mo and that was a source of tension. And of course, her activities in the middle of the referendum just stumped us, which wasn't very charitable. I have to say, none of us probably realised how ill she was at the time, but she did a lot of damage.[20]

Mowlam had been diagnosed with a brain tumour in 1997 and had received radiotherapy while continuing with her parliamentary duties. She was determined to carry on with life as best she could. After her hair loss, she took to wearing a wig, which, as Campbell described earlier, she often removed in private meetings – a move that sometimes shocked onlookers. She kept her illness private, but when it became public, she received much public affection. She was particularly popular with community and women's groups in Northern Ireland and was accommodating with the media.

In September 1998, at the Labour Party Conference, she got a standing ovation for her work in Northern Ireland. It was an unprecedented display of gratitude, as it actually happened during Blair's speech. Like many involved in the Good Friday talks, Mowlam showed much bravery during the peace process and was prepared to be innovative when trying to solve problems – her visit to loyalist prisoners in the Maze prison in January 1998 is an example of that. She remained an MP until 2001 and died in August 2005 aged 55.

But there is a nice postscript to the Mowlam–Trimble story. Some years after their relationship had been at its worst, David Montgomery invited them both to his house:

> That was the first time they had spoken to each other since the fallout, and frankly they got on like a house on fire. You know I think it was a testimony to both of them that they didn't bear grudges. I think they saw the whole of the development of Northern Ireland as something they had participated in, and it would have been imperfect in many respects, but they got a result. And, you know, I didn't force the issue. They they ended up talking to each other, having a drink together and I think they felt better for that.[21]

By the autumn of 1998 there were still large parts of the Good Friday Agreement to be implemented. There was still no Executive in place, the North–South bodies were not up and running and neither was the British–Irish Council, though the Assembly was operational, and Trimble and Mallon now had staff in place to help them function as first and deputy first ministers. Trimble's team was designed in a similar way to the structure that Blair had in place in Downing Street.

Maura Quinn was appointed as Trimble's private secretary. An experienced civil servant, Quinn had previously worked in the Political Affairs Division of the NIO. She found local politics fascinating and had originally applied to work for either Trimble or Mallon. Her job with Trimble meant she had to run his office, manage his time, organise his diary and make sure correspondence was dealt with. She had gone for the job working for the first minister but did not think that she, a Catholic from Coalisland, would be appointed:

> I didn't know him particularly well ... and he was in the media still seen at that stage as a bit of a hardliner. So, I suppose maybe in the back of my head I sort of assumed

someone who would have been more familiar with the unionist tradition may have been considered a better fit, if I can put it that way.[22]

But Quinn had impressed Trimble at the interview, and once appointed she got to work with three of Trimble's close advisers: David Kerr, Graham Gudgin and David Campbell. Kerr had obviously been with Trimble early on in his leadership days and knew him well. Campbell was an old friend and was now operating as his chief of staff. Gudgin had been an economist at Cambridge University and then went to work for the Northern Ireland Economic Research Centre.

It was while working for the centre that Gudgin came to Trimble's attention, and he was brought in to advise the first minister on economic matters:

> I used to joke to people that the only problem with being an economic adviser to David Trimble was that, firstly, he had no interest in economics. And secondly, he didn't take advice from anyone on anything.[23]

The reality is that Trimble did take Gudgin's advice. Although he says at first his role seemed unclear, he was essentially there to offer assistance on financial matters:

> David said he'd like me to go up and work for him, but he didn't give any real guidance. It was only later that I really worked out what he wanted was an economist to watch his back with the civil service, and to help him with the economics of public spending.[24]

As Trimble began to organise his staff, so too did Seamus Mallon. He appointed Hugh Logue as his head of office. Logue had been a civil rights activist alongside John Hume. He had previously represented the SDLP in the Assembly and had also stood unsuccessfully for Westminster.

He was particularly remembered for a speech he gave at the time of the Sunningdale Executive in 1974, when he talked about the Council of Ireland. He said that the council was 'the vehicle that will trundle through to deliver a united Ireland. The speed of that vehicle will depend on the unionist population.'

Logue remembers his first day in his new role. He was being shown around by Colin Ross, a Stormont press officer, when they encountered Trimble. Logue recalls what happened next:

> In walked David Trimble with papers in his hand. And Colin says, 'Mr Trimble', and he is about to introduce me, 'This is —' And Trimble said, 'I know very well who he is, and I have no wish to be introduced.' And he turned on his heel and walked out.[25]

Trimble's behaviour in front of Logue was quite typical. I experienced the Trimble brush-off in Westminster when I waited to introduce myself to him as BBC Northern Ireland's newly appointed London correspondent. After chatting to the ever-helpful Barry White, who worked in the UUP offices, we came up with a plan to engineer a short introductory meeting. It was suggested I wait outside the studio where Trimble was doing an interview and then afterwards we could have an impromptu 'meet and greet'.

When Trimble emerged and walked towards me, I introduced myself and proffered a hand. I said, 'Mr Trimble, I am Stephen Walker, BBC Northern Ireland's new London correspondent. I just wanted to say hello.' To which Trimble uttered three words: 'Hello and goodbye.' He then walked off, and that was it. Things did get better, and our relationship improved. However, as a journalist you were never sure what version of the UUP leader you were going to get.

Trimble's reputation for being brusque was well known, although sometimes he could surprise people and challenge their assumptions. Felicity Huston was on the House of Lords Appointment Commission, and remembers being worried about meeting Trimble:

> I can clearly remember sitting in our living room before the meeting and saying to my husband [that] I really didn't want to go because I really didn't know what I [would] be facing. So, I went off in great trepidation because I thought, 'This is going to be ghastly.' A completely different David Trimble met me. He was the life and soul of the party and in tremendous form. You really would have thought it was his nice twin that I had met. He was completely different from the man you hear about. I came home and said to my husband, 'Goodness me, all those stories are not true, because I've just met this lovely man.'[26]

However, Huston did experience the other side of Trimble and recalls encounters with the first minister when he was uncommunicative and appeared distant.

As deputy first minister, Seamus Mallon got to see Trimble daily, and he too experienced his different moods. I recall him joking that there were seven versions of his political partner – 'one for every day of the week'.[27]

In the autumn of 1998, Mallon and Trimble were starting to find their feet in their new roles – although it was an odd position to be in without fellow members of the Executive. The two men went off to the United States on a promotional tour aimed at attracting investment for Northern Ireland.

While they were there, newspapers back home were full of speculation over who might be awarded that year's Nobel Peace Prize. There was talk that Trimble and Hume might share the honour. Another suggestion was that Gerry Adams would also be nominated. For Trimble and others in the UUP, the suggestion that Adams might be awarded the honour alongside their man caused problems, as David Kerr recalled:

> The big fear was, what if Gerry Adams gets it as well? Are they stupid or crazy enough to give it to all three of them? Because if they do, we're always going to have to pull out of it.[28]

The time difference between Europe and America meant that announcement of the Nobel Peace Prize was due in the middle of the night, when Trimble would be sleeping in his hotel room in Denver, Colorado. He had given Maura Quinn instructions that he was not to be woken. For the first minister, sleep was more important at this stage.

When it emerged back in Northern Ireland that Trimble and Hume had jointly got the award, Mallon decided that the news simply could not wait. He had been phoned and told that Trimble and Hume were being honoured and he immediately wanted to tell his political partner the news. In his pyjamas, the deputy first minster set off to find Trimble's room, and when he found it he knocked on the door.

The response was initially unwelcoming, with Trimble declaring, 'Too late, too late.' But Mallon persevered: 'Open up. I've got a piece of news for you that you would probably like to hear.' A sleepy Trimble opened the door to face Mallon and was told that he was sharing the prestigious honour with Hume. He went red with embarrassment and turned to Mallon and said, 'Thank, thank you. Leave it with me.'[29]

With that, the first minister and Nobel laureate in waiting went back to sleep. By early morning there would be other callers to Trimble's room to share the good news. Quinn decided she needed to go and tell her boss that he was getting the Nobel Peace Prize:

> So, I decided I would go early but not too early ... I think it was about 6 a.m. I rapped on his door and said, 'Listen, I know you told me not to disturb you until 7, but yes, you've been awarded the Nobel Peace Prize along with John Hume.' And his response was, 'The nightmare hasn't happened.' I remember him saying that.[30]

For Trimble, the nightmare scenario was an award being given to Gerry Adams as well. The UUP leader could relax now and enjoy the moment. David Kerr says he was delighted, and that, when he heard about the award, he thought back to the Waterfront Hall concert with Bono earlier in the year:

> When it was just John and David it was perfect, because it vindicated both men. And again, for me it goes back to that image on the stage: it's about the two of them.[31]

In December 1998, Trimble and Hume and their families and friends all travelled out to Oslo for the ceremony. The world's media were decamped there, and the two political leaders were in constant demand for interviews. This was a global story – how two men from very different political and religious traditions had helped to end decades of conflict and bring peace to Northern Ireland. Hume and Trimble were now joining a long and esteemed list that included Nelson Mandela, F.W. de Klerk, Mikhail Gorbachev and the Dalai Lama.

However, young Sarah Trimble had other matters on her mind when she was told of the trip to Norway. Unfortunately for her it meant she would not be starring in her school's nativity play:

> I remember being very upset in the weeks beforehand because I wasn't allowed to be in the school nativity. I would be missing the day that the play was on. So that was my big memory going into that. I wouldn't be in the school nativity, obviously having no idea or understanding about what was about to happen.[32]

Sarah made the trip with her siblings and her parents. For Daphne Trimble, their time in Oslo was very exciting and full of surprises. She was taken aback by the magnitude of the events that surrounded the Peace Prize:

> It was just great. It was amazing. They closed the roads for us, so we were driven in from the airport to the centre of Oslo and it was all closed off for the whole occasion. And all the schoolchildren came down to the Grand Hotel, and David and John stayed out on the balcony and were serenaded by all these schoolchildren with their little candles, and it was just super.[33]

Before Hume and Trimble received their awards, there was a rehearsal of events, as is tradition. Both leaders met King Harald and Queen Sonja at the royal palace. The ceremony itself was a star-studded affair, with diplomats, politicians, celebrities and leading figures from around the world. In his acceptance speech, Hume talked about reconciliation and partnership, and he referred to a better future. It was a traditional Hume address, full of his familiar themes, and he ended it with the familiar words 'We shall overcome', a phrase that he and thousands of others sang back in the 1960s during civil rights marches.

Trimble's speech was very different. He had been assisted by Eoghan Harris, the broadcaster and journalist who wrote for the *Sunday Times*. Harris and Trimble had a good relationship, and Harris would often send Trimble ideas or give him suggested lines. Trimble did not always use them or agree with them, but he liked the intellectual challenge of sometimes looking at issues from different angles. The speech contained a raft of academic references, from Edmund Burke to Amos Oz, from Plato to Samuel Beckett.

Trimble talked about 'acts of good authority', which was one of the themes Harris was keen to promote. As Harris recalled:

> When I talked to David, he was very taken with the notion of good authority. Which is basically that rather than upbraid the other tribe you should reprimand your own first. I compared it regularly in *The Sunday Times* to parents who hear a row going on the road, comes to the door and see their children involved in a fight with other kids. Good authority means calling in your own child and reprimanding your own child publicly in front of the others, rather than abusing the parents of the other child.[34]

Trimble used this idea to talk about the actions of unionists that had hurt the Catholic community in Northern Ireland over the past decades. In his Oslo address he declared:

> Ulster Unionists, fearful of being isolated on the island, built a solid house, but it was a cold house for Catholics. And northern nationalists, although they had a roof over their heads, seemed to us as if they meant to burn the house down.[35]

While his lecture was at times quite academic, Trimble did address the current difficulties in Northern Ireland:

> There are hills in Northern Ireland and there are mountains. The hills are decommissioning and policing. But the mountain, if we could but see it clearly, is not in front of us but behind us, in history. The dark shadow we seem to see in the distance is not really a mountain ahead but the shadow of the mountain behind – a shadow from the past thrown forward into our future. It is a dark sludge of historical sectarianism. We can leave it behind us if we wish.[36]

Trimble ended his speech by referring to the deal that had been agreed at Castle Buildings on Good Friday earlier in the year:

> That agreement showed that the people of Northern Ireland are no petty people. They did good work that day. And tomorrow is now another day.[37]

Trimble's use of the phrase 'petty people' was pointed and deliberate. It was a reference to a comment John Hume made at a party conference in 1983, when he said unionists had become a 'petty people'.

Hume and Trimble were now statesmen of international standing. Their prize also came with a large financial award, and Hume donated his to charity. Trimble used some of the money for a holiday and set aside much of it for the future. He later donated money to assist a legal case brought by the Omagh bomb families. The Trimbles had travelled over to Oslo with many people who had helped David in his career, and, like Hume, he had brought over a number of family friends.

The Hume party included John's wife, Pat, and their grown-up children, colleagues from the SDLP and friends such as Bishop Edward Daly. The musician and composer Phil Coulter was also there. After the official ceremony both parties were able to relax away from the cameras. An impromptu party took place with Coulter on the piano and Hume joining him in a rendition of the Derry anthem 'The Town I Loved So Well'.

The UUP MEP Jim Nicholson later entertained the party with his version of 'The Boys of County Armagh'. To the amusement of some, Hume sang 'The Sash', and at one stage he was joined by the BBC journalist Noel Thompson. Even though Trimble had a wide knowledge of music, he did not sing; instead, the UUP leader let others take centre stage while he sat and chatted. It was all convivial and relaxed – a moment of joy after years of turmoil and sorrow.

It was a defining moment in the history of Northern Ireland. For Hume and Trimble, this marked the pinnacle of their careers. They had achieved what many observers said was impossible. They had secured a cross-community deal in Northern Ireland that had majority support. It was a political and personal triumph.

Hume and Trimble were MPs, party chiefs and leaders of nationalism and unionism, respectively. As 1998 ended, they could add one more title to this list. They were both Nobel laureates.

19

GUNS AND GOVERNMENT

'Mr Adams, it's over to you. We've jumped. You follow.'
David Trimble agrees to go into government
in advance of decommissioning

In mid-December 1998, Trimble and Hume returned to Northern Ireland after the Oslo trip. They came back to a political climate very different from the one they had just experienced. The British government, Irish government, SDLP and UUP were discussing the number and remit of the cross-border bodies, but, despite hours of talks, there was no agreement. The standoff was over how many bodies there should be and what their remit was.

The dispute put more strains on the SDLP–UUP relationship and did not help the atmosphere between Seamus Mallon and Trimble. At times the two men could be tetchy with each other, but, as Hugh Logue recalls, there were other big moments when the partnership worked:

> When it was good it was very good; when it was bad it was awful. So, they got on well abroad: they got on well in Brussels, they got on well in Paris. And Trimble could be quite open-minded. I mean I was allowed to do the negotiations for the North–South bodies. And Trimble just sort of said to me, 'No surprises. We think we have the architecture right.'[1]

After hours of negotiations on Friday 18 December, a week before Christmas, a deal was finally agreed over cross-border bodies. The plan was backed by the two governments and the SDLP and UUP negotiating teams. The six North–South bodies would cover inland waterways; agriculture; food safety; European Union funding; the Irish and Ulster Scots languages; and trade and business development. Trimble had to get party backing for this move and was confident he would get the support.

The next day in Belfast, the UUP Executive overwhelmingly endorsed the plan, but again there were strong calls for the decommissioning of paramilitary weapons. Blair and Ahern both hoped that the deal over cross-border bodies would mean that other elements of the Good Friday Agreement could fall into place quickly. The two premiers wanted to see a full Executive in place by the spring of 1999.

Trimble had the same objective, but there needed to be decommissioning, and as 1999 got underway it was, not surprisingly, the number one subject on the political agenda. The early signs on whether there would be a move by the IRA were not promising, as they issued a New Year message saying that the Good Friday Agreement was being undermined by unionist preconditions. Republicans also urged the UK government to face down unionists.

On Monday 18 January, the Assembly debated the arrangements for the North–South institutions. Peter Weir, then a UUP MLA and member of the pressure group Union First, voted against his party position, which meant he had the whip removed. Matters got worse when John Taylor, to date a strong supporter of Trimble, stated that he thought the Good Friday Agreement only had a 50 per cent chance of survival. The cracks in the UUP were now on public display.

At this stage, Weir thought Trimble should have reached out more to his internal critics:

> I think David probably took a view, and maybe John Taylor and others as well, which was 'Right, the referendum has happened and there has been ultimately broad acceptance.' Everybody was simply just falling into line and saying this is all wonderful, and I don't think there was a great deal of reaching out. Now I think at the broader level there were

people around the agreement necessarily wanting to be reached out to.²

Alex Kane, who worked for the UUP as a director of communications and later became a political commentator, says Weir had a point. He says Trimble should have worked harder with his critics in the party:

> [Alex Kane:] If Trimble had put his arm around these people and said, 'Look, these are difficulties, I know these are difficulties. I need you to stay on board with me. I need you to stay in this because if this goes down the government is not going to reopen these negotiations again. The government is not going to say, "Let's go back to the drawing board."'
>
> [Stephen Walker:] And why didn't he do that?
>
> [Alex Kane:] Because it wasn't in his nature. It wasn't in his nature personally.³

Kane's analysis is correct. It was not in Trimble's personality to metaphorically or physically put his arm around his critics and try to convince them of his analysis. His approach was that decisions had been made for the right reasons and the party needed to move on and make the best of the situation. It was a literal approach rather than a managerial approach. In other words, he tackled issues more like a lawyer than a politician who needed to bring people with him. Arlene Foster, now Baroness Foster, says Trimble's lack of personal touch did not help:

> I think he always wanted to do what was right. I think sometimes he looked at it from a very academic, intellectual point of view. He didn't get the soft stuff that was around, which other people did.⁴

Foster was part of an active band of critics which included Peter Weir, Jeffrey Donaldson and David Brewster. Trimble was used to being challenged at meetings, and occasionally at public events he faced protests and heckling. Joan Carson, who was a UUP MLA, and a supporter of Trimble's, thinks he should have been tougher on his critics:

> [Joan Carson:] I have still got a drop of the teacher in me, and you know if the boss says something you like it or lump it. You obey him and get on with it. And if they weren't willing to take the lead from the leader ... that was very disappointing right from the very beginning.
>
> [Stephen Walker:] So, what should David have done?
>
> [Joan Carson:] I think he should have been firmer with them and not given Jeffrey Donaldson so much leeway.[5]

James Cooper, who became UUP chairman in 2000, says party meetings were particularly difficult:

> Every party executive that I chaired ended – I wouldn't say in disarray, but we often had to ask people to leave the meeting. We had people like Jeffrey [Donaldson], you know, shouting in the background and being told he'd have to sit down. We had constant unhappiness in the party, and whether we were in a position or strong enough I don't think we were to suddenly expel these people, which ultimately is what happens.[6]

Sinn Féin watched the internal UUP wrangling from the sidelines. They were conscious that Trimble had big difficulties with certain party members. So, should the UUP leader have taken them on and simply expelled those who rebelled? Would a purge have caused a greater split in the party?

Mitchel McLaughlin, who was Sinn Féin's national chairperson at the time, agrees:

> I don't think [Trimble] would have felt that would have been to his advantage. It might have just started an internal war in the party and at the end of the day made it impossible. He kept them in, and he was compromising them by keeping them in because he wanted to know what was going on.[7]

In February 1999, plans for the structures of government were backed by the Assembly. This allowed for the creation of new government departments and the North–South bodies. The date of 10 March was set as the deadline to establish the Executive. No one knew at the time, but the setting of deadlines would be become quite common in 1999; a number would be set and broken – like the 10 March deadline.

In the weeks that followed there was little sign that the IRA was going to surrender or destroy its weapons. The political impasse was eroding support for the Good Friday Agreement amongst unionists. An opinion poll conducted by PricewaterhouseCoopers for the BBC indicated that only 41 per cent of unionists now supported the deal negotiated in April 1998.

Trimble was made well aware of unionist anxiety at his party's AGM in March. In that month, talks involving the parties continued at Hillsborough Castle to try to find a breakthrough, and a joint communiqué was issued by the Irish and British governments on 1 April. The date was not lost on the DUP leader. Ian Paisley branded the document the 'April Fool's Day Charter'.

The initiative by Bertie Ahern and Tony Blair laid out a timetable to set up an Executive. The plan would see a date, proposed by the Independent International Commission on Decommissioning, when a collective act of reconciliation would take place, which would see arms put beyond use in a verified way. The UUP reserved its judgement on the idea, but on Easter Sunday veteran IRA leader Brian Keenan told a rally that the IRA would not be forced into a 'surrender'. Discussions continued in the background, but it was clear republicans were not interested or willing to decommission.

On 13 April, when talks resumed, Sinn Féin officially rejected the Hillsborough proposals. The 1 April plan was now a dead duck. Ahern and Blair were determined to come up with a formula that would break the 'no guns, no government' logjam. They held talks in London aimed at coming up with proposals that would win cross-party support.

As the political crisis continued, Trimble had an important date to fulfil in the Vatican. As a Nobel Peace Prize winner, he had been invited to meet His Holiness the Pope. His audience with Pope John Paul II was historic, and he became the first unionist leader to meet a pontiff. Maura Quinn, Trimble's private secretary, accompanied him on the trip. She had not expected to be included in the actual meeting with the pope:

> There was a lot of commentary at the time about whether or not he [Trimble] should be doing that. But he decided he would, and I was there to accompany him on that trip. There wasn't anyone from the party with him, and he made a point of insisting that I was to accompany him when he met the pope, even though I hadn't asked him to do that. And it caused a bit of a flurry, because the plan was for each Nobel laureate as an individual just to meet with the pope. But they agreed to it, and when I asked him afterwards, 'Why did you make an issue of that?' he just sort of quietly said, 'Oh, I thought it might be nice for your mother.' And I've heard stories where others have talked about Trimble's thoughtfulness. Something people didn't always get to see.[8]

The visit to the pope drew some critical remarks from Orange Order figures. Trimble was well used to it by now, though, and it followed the criticism he got when he and Lord Rogan had attended the Catholic funerals of three of the Omagh bomb victims.

When he returned to Northern Ireland the political crisis he left was still in full swing and more talks were planned aimed at resolving the decommissioning issue.

On Friday 14 May 1999, Blair and Ahern hosted representatives from the UUP, the SDLP and Sinn Féin in Downing Street. It was another attempt to push the political process forward and reach some kind of cross-party agreement over devolution and decommissioning.

During the discussions, Blair clearly put pressure on Trimble to soften his position of 'no guns, no government'. The prime minister was trying to come up with a sequenced deal where devolution and decommissioning could take place in tandem. As the talks continued, journalists were tipped off by Downing Street sources that a deal could be done, and they should stand by to report a major breakthrough.

The plan was that General de Chastelain would hold talks with the parties on the issue of decommissioning and report back before 30 June – and the aim was to devolve power by that date. All the parties would also agree with the objective of decommissioning in line with the time frame set out in the Good Friday Agreement. In tandem, ministers in the new Executive would take their positions on or before 30 June. Number 10 was convinced Trimble would back this deal, and in one-to-one discussions with Blair, he did discuss it in detail.

However, the suggestions of an agreement proved to be premature. When Trimble returned to Northern Ireland and discussed it with his Assembly team at Stormont it was roundly rejected. The UUP MLAs had a series of questions. Where was the actual decommissioning? What happened to the 'no guns, no government' policy? Why was Blair prepared to let Sinn Féin into government without the destruction or surrender of arms? Why was Number 10 suggesting that this was a deal the UUP could accept?

David Kerr remembers the meeting Trimble had with his MLAs and he recalls telling Trimble that Blair's plan was a non-starter:

I was genuinely concerned that David was prepared to take the party down a route that I knew was unacceptable to the membership.⁹

The 14 May summit was odd in many ways – and clearly Downing Street thought they had a deal with Trimble's blessing. However, he insisted that he had not agreed to the sequencing laid out by Blair. Had Trimble given Blair the idea that the deal was possible? Had he also mistakenly seen the prime minister on a one-to-one basis? Had Trimble been dazzled by Blair's words?

Barry White, who worked for the UUP in Westminster, observed Trimble at close quarters in London. He recalls that he used to tease the UUP leader not to be taken in by Blair's charisma:

> He would quite often go and see him in Downing Street without any colleagues. He would go on his own, and if Blair wasn't available, he'd see Jonathan Powell. But I used to say to him, and it became a bit of a running joke, 'He is not your friend. He is not your friend. He has got a job to do. Don't be taken in.' Because, you know, he was starstruck, but he wasn't the only one, because Blair had that star quality about him. But he was also somebody who had a job to do. And I just wanted to make sure that David understood, and it became a bit of a standing joke.¹⁰

So, did the UUP leader trust Blair too much? Trimble's critics inside the UUP clearly thought so. They suggested that he was taking too much guidance from Downing Street and claimed that he was being influenced in a way that was not always in unionism's best interest.

The UTV journalist Ken Reid said that Trimble and Blair initially had a good relationship, and that the Upper Bann MP had a great respect for the office of prime minister:

David was also in awe of authority. You know, he was a different person when he went into Downing Street.[11]

Esmond Birnie, who served as a UUP MLA, says Trimble was not the only unionist who put a lot of faith in Blair. He says many in the party probably trusted the prime minister too much:

> I could see a bit of the perceived Blair magic, but over time it began to wear more and more thin. And I suppose if you were to criticise Trimble himself for being too trusting of Blair, I would admit probably a lot of the rest of us were similarly. So, we really did believe him and took him at his word.[12]

After the failure of the 14 May talks, discussions continued behind the scenes in Dublin and London in an attempt to make progress. Trimble made it clear that the UUP would not change its position and continued to call for decommissioning. The party wanted to see a 'creditable and verifiable start to the process of decommissioning before Sinn Féin can participate in government'.

Trimble was also reluctant to take political risks, as the UUP was fighting to retain their MEP seat in June's European Parliament elections. He knew the DUP would make much of the decommissioning issue, and it was paramount that Jim Nicholson, the UUP candidate, was re-elected. In June's poll, that is exactly what happened, and Nicholson joined the DUP leader, Ian Paisley, who topped the poll, and the SDLP leader, John Hume, who came in second.

Trimble was greatly relieved Nicholson was re-elected, but a fall in the UUP share of the vote was worrying. Before the election, Nicholson had been the subject of press stories because of an extramarital affair, and some in the UUP had suggested he should be deselected. Nicholson had been one of Trimble's strongest supporters at the time of the Good Friday Agreement, and, despite the criticism, Trimble stood by him and insisted he would run as the UUP candidate.

With the election out of the way, both Dublin and London intensified their efforts to get devolution up and running. Blair came to Belfast on 15 June and in a keynote speech at Stranmillis College said the two governments would have to look at an alternative way forward if the 30 June deadline was missed. Intensive discussions followed with the parties, but on 30 June, Blair's 'absolute deadline' came and went without a deal.

On 2 July, the British and Irish governments tried again and produced a plan entitled 'The Way Forward'. It called for the establishment of a devolved government, with ministers being nominated on 15 July, and in the meantime the decommissioning body would have urgent discussions with the paramilitary groups. Crucially, if commitments were not met regarding decommissioning, the governments would support the suspension of the Stormont institutions – notably the Executive. There would also be progress reports on decommissioning in the autumn of 1999 and in May 2000.

Blair's new deadline was 15 July, when the D'Hondt method would be used to nominate ministers, and then devolution would take effect three days later, on 18 July. (The D'Hondt method for allocating seats or ministerial positions was named after the Belgian lawyer Victor D'Hondt, who came up with a formula for allocating government positions based on electoral strength.) It was a big gamble by London and Dublin, but clearly Ahern and Blair felt it could work. The parties then took their time to consider what was on the table. Trimble promised Downing Street that the UUP would consider the plan.

On 9 July, the party executive met and rejected the Blair–Ahern proposals. The meeting was adjourned and members agreed to meet again on 14 July. In the meantime, legislation was presented in the House of Commons which Blair said was a failsafe measure if the paramilitaries defaulted on their obligations. The legislation would also map out what would happen if any of the parties failed to honour their commitments and how the Executive and Assembly could be suspended. Despite the legislation, the UUP stuck with their original decision and on 14 July stated that they could not sign up to 'The Way Forward'.

What happened next turned into political farce. Secretary of State Mo Mowlam triggered the D'Hondt system for nominating ministers to the Executive. Without a deal on decommissioning, Trimble and the UUP were not in a position to nominate ministers, and the UUP leader made it clear to Downing Street that his party would not participate in the process. Trimble and his colleagues would adopt a well-worn republican tactic: they became abstentionists. So, despite the UUP's boycott, the government decided to go ahead – which was an odd decision. The bizarre proceedings began in Stormont on 15 July, with the largest party absent from the chamber. When Speaker Lord Alderdice called for nominations from the UUP, he was met by silence and confronted by empty seats.

The SDLP and Sinn Féin went ahead and nominated their minsters. A full list of ministers was completed – all nationalists and republicans nominated by their respective leaders, John Hume and Gerry Adams. The DUP leader, Ian Paisley, told Lord Alderdice his party would not be nominating any minsters. This meant that the new SDLP–Sinn Féin Executive did not have cross-community support, so under the rules it could not be formed. It was a sorry sight. Northern Ireland's first cross-party administration in a quarter of a century lasted a matter of minutes – in what seemed like a parallel universe.

To outsiders it must have looked bizarre, as the world of Northern Irish politics was turned on its head. Nationalists and republicans were in government – albeit only on paper – and unionists were staying away in protest.

But there was more drama to come. After the farce came the fury, as Seamus Mallon got up to speak. The SDLP deputy leader was angry, and his frustration was obvious to everyone watching in the chamber and on television. He attacked unionists, saying they were trying to 'bleed this very process dry' by continuing to look for changes and concessions.[13]

He said their behaviour was against the principles of the Good Friday Agreement. He called for a fundamental review of the agreement and its outworkings, where all parties were treated as equals. Then, in a direct swipe at Trimble, he said he could not enter such a review 'from the privileged position as first minister of the Assembly'. Critical of the UUP leader's absence and tactics, he said, 'I do not treat this Assembly with contempt.' With that, Mallon resigned as deputy first minister. He felt he had no choice: 'I was very reluctant to do it, but I felt the deadlocked process needed a kick and resignation was the only way of kicking it.'[14]

The Good Friday Agreement was now in real trouble, and the political process was in freefall. Mallon's resignation shocked many people in the other parties and in the press, even though there had been rumours he was planning to stand down. This marked the low point in Mallon's relationship with Trimble; before his resignation, matters had been strained, but this took things to a different level.

The lack of a functioning Executive meant the British government had to act, so the process of devolving power was put on hold and Mowlam announced a review of the Good Friday Agreement, which would be conducted by George Mitchell. The secretary of state was also the subject of much press interest, as there were suggestions that she was going to be moved from her Northern Ireland brief.

Mowlam was well aware that one of her big critics was Trimble:

> The final frequent criticism was that I was disliked by the unionists and David Trimble wanted rid of me. It is true we had periods of not getting on. But quite simply put he did not like all that I was trying to achieve. And the easiest way not to move forward was to say I was unworkable with. I wasn't. And outside of the meetings many of the more mainstream unionists and I passed the time quite amicably.[15]

Mitchell was reluctant to get involved in Northern Ireland again, but he agreed to carry out a review, and he began his work in September 1999. He made it clear that his mission was to try to break the impasse over decommissioning and see devolution return to Stormont as soon as possible.

As Mitchell got to work on trying to design a political road map, the long-awaited Patten review into policing was made public. The

Independent Commission on Policing in Northern Ireland, as it was formally called, recommended wholesale change. The report examined the ethos of policing, the training and structures, and called for a new policing board and an oversight commissioner. The recommendations included reducing the size of the force, creating new symbols and scrapping the name RUC and replacing it with the title Northern Ireland Police Service. It would later become the Police Service of Northern Ireland.

Trimble was not at all impressed with the report and knew how much it would anger policing families and those who had lost officers during the Troubles. He felt that Chris Patten, a former Conservative MP and ex-Hong Kong governor, had done a poor job and said the report was the 'most shoddy piece of work I have ever seen in my entire life.'[16]

The Patten report was bad news for Trimble, and he felt it keenly. He knew those unionists who opposed the Good Friday Agreement would use it as a stick to beat the UUP. As the details of the Patten report started to sink in, there was much for Trimble and the UUP to consider in September 1999.

Mark Neale, who was a UUP councillor and came from an RUC family, was angered by plans to change the name. He would later become one of Trimble's advisers and remembers he rang Trimble and urged him to quit as first minister:

> I remember saying to him, 'Look, this is your moment. You've got to resign, you cannot continue with this.' And he said to me, 'No, Mark, you can only resign once like this, and this is not the time.' So, we disagreed on that. And afterwards, maybe five or six years later, he said to me, 'Look, maybe you were right. I didn't just appreciate the heat and anger that the name change caused.'[17]

Changes to policing was just one major item in Trimble's in-tray – the twin issues of decommissioning and devolution had not gone away. The party was committed to the Mitchell review, and soon cross-party meetings got underway at Castle Buildings on the Stormont Estate. They were long, repetitive affairs and progress was slow. Trimble then approached Mitchell with an idea which he thought might help the discussions.

Mitchell remembers the conversation with Trimble:

> We had many meetings during that time, and we were not making much progress. And then David came to me [and] said, 'Look, we have to go through this press gauntlet every day. It's very, very difficult. We get asked these provocative questions and it's just difficult to make progress.' He said, 'Is there some way we could move the meetings to a private location?' And Gerry Adams said – I don't know whether they talked about it themselves or not – Gerry came to me with the same request, so I said, 'I'll look into it.' And they both wanted me to move the meetings to the United States.[18]

The meetings were not switched to America but briefly moved to Winfield House in London, which was the US ambassador's residence. Mitchell hoped the change of scenery might improve the atmosphere between the parties, and he also insisted that at night they dine together and talk. However, Mitchell insisted that there was to be no politics discussed at the table; instead, the politicians should talk about their families and their hobbies:

> So, with dinner the first night it was a little bit strained, but it was mixed. And I was sitting on one side of the table and David [Trimble] was to my right and ... I can't remember who was to my left, I think it was [Martin] McGuinness. So, somebody yells out to Trimble, 'David' – one of the nationalist guys – 'I understand you like opera. What's the last opera you saw?' And David answered, 'Well, I haven't been to the opera recently, but last night I listened

to an opera.' And that was it, and I can't remember what he said but he described it and so forth. Then one of the guys yelled out to me, 'Senator Mitchell, do you ever go to the opera?' And I said, 'Well, yes, in fact, every time I leave the United States to come here to meet you guys, I go to the opera the night before.' And they all said, 'Well, why?' I said, 'Because when I go to the opera, I know in advance every word that's going to be spoken.' I said, 'I've seen the opera *La bohème* 12 times, and the lead guy, Rodolfo, sings exactly the same words every time.' I said, 'And that puts me in a frame of mind to come and meet with you guys.'[19]

Mitchell's opera joke had a jag. He had heard his guests' political arguments dozens of times. He knew their views off by heart, and he desperately wanted to change the narrative. What is apparent is that his decision to switch venues and get politicians to socialise was successful. The move to Winfield House created informality, improved cross-party relations and built up trust. It was what many involved in the process felt it needed, and to watching political observers it looked like a deal to restore the twin issues of devolution and decommissioning was now possible.

As the parties continued with their discussions, a new player arrived on the scene. After much speculation, Mo Mowlam was moved from her post as Northern Ireland Secretary and replaced by Peter Mandelson. He was Trimble's candidate of choice, so the UUP leader was pleased when Blair made the switch. Mowlam's departure heartened Trimble, as did the new atmosphere that had been generated by the Winfield House talks.

Rodney McCune, who worked for the UUP at Westminster at the time, immediately noticed a change in relations between the NIO and Trimble:

> When he [Mandelson] was secretary of state he would just come into the office and go and see David. And you could

see there was a respect there as well. And Mandelson was
seriously interesting and obviously again in terms of intellect and maybe political acumen he was on a pretty high
level. You could see that he also admired David.[20]

Lord Bew also noticed that there was good chemistry between Mandelson and Trimble:

The relationship with Trimble could not have been warmer
or more respectful. Mandelson in particular could not
have been more respectful.[21]

Trimble knew that the fine detail of any new devolution and decommissioning deal had to be right, and he was well aware he would be in for a big battle to sell it to the party faithful. The deal would involve a series of linked events; in political terms, it was now referred to as 'sequencing'. After more discussions involving Mitchell, Sinn Féin and the UUP, the sequencing was agreed.

It was a key moment for Trimble, and it marked a move away from the rigid 'no guns, no government' policy. He believed this deal would put the pressure on republicans to decommission which he hoped would follow once the Executive was in place. It was a leap of faith on Trimble's part.

Under the November 1999 deal, the IRA agreed to appoint an interlocutor who would meet with the decommissioning body after devolution had been restored and ministers were in place. That would then be followed by the first meeting of the North–South Ministerial Council and the British–Irish Council. There would also be a report on 31 January 2000 from General de Chastelain on the progress of decommissioning. Trimble hoped this sequencing deal could answer the guns and government issue for good.

Provided the UUP rank and file backed the deal, the nomination of ministers was now expected in late November. A meeting of the party's 860-strong council was called for the Waterfront Hall in Belfast. Trimble was confident that the deal would be backed, but he knew that there would be strong opposition to the idea of going into government before decommissioning had occurred. He faced criticism not just from his colleagues at the Assembly but also from MPs at Westminster, including colleagues like Willie Ross and Jeffrey Donaldson.

The meeting of the UUC was set for Saturday 27 November, which was five days before devolution was expected to begin. Trimble used the days before the meeting to try to convince his critics that his plan could work. He talked to party colleagues at Stormont, and he met activists from different constituencies. He also visited members of the Orange Order in Upper Bann with Peter Mandelson – and was greeted with much opposition.

When the Waterfront Hall debate took place there was high emotion on both sides. As the debate unfolded, the divisions across the party were pretty clear. Trimble told the audience that he believed the deal on offer was the best way of resolving the current political crisis. He then confirmed that he had already written a letter of resignation that would take effect if there was no actual decommissioning. Trimble said he had written the letter some days earlier, and he had already given it to party president, Josias Cunningham.

It was a smart move by Trimble. He was mapping out what might happen if the IRA did not decommission. He was trying to reassure his critics that he had a plan if no guns were produced by February 2000. If there was no decommissioning by then, Trimble was making it clear, he would resign as first minister.

But the move did not silence his critics completely. When he was addressing the gathering, he spoke of two unionist politicians murdered in the Troubles. They were his friends Edgar Graham and Robert Bradford. As he did, John Hunter, a former friend but now a critic, shouted at Trimble, 'And you have let them down'. The intervention shocked the hall into silence.

It was a poignant moment, but Trimble did not falter and talked of his friend and former colleague: 'I know if Edgar had not been murdered, he would probably be standing here speaking to you today, not me, and

I am fairly certain he would be saying what I am saying.' Trimble continued, talking about Robert Bradford, who had also been murdered by the IRA. Inside his jacket pocket he had a letter. He reached for it and read it out. It was from Nora Bradford, Robert's widow, and had been hand-delivered to the Trimble home the day before. Trimble read the short note: 'Dear David, Hang in there. Be strong and courageous. God Bless. Nora Bradford'.[22]

The audience was still and silent. Trimble was delivering one of the best speeches of his life and was winning over sceptics. The motion that the UUP should go into the Executive in advance of decommissioning was then put to the vote. When the result came, it was clear Trimble's gamble had paid off. The move was backed by 480 votes to 349, which meant the UUP leader had secured 58 per cent and his opponents got 42 per cent.

Northern Ireland was now days away from a cross-party government. History was turning full circle. Afterwards, looking relieved and relaxed, Trimble, with Daphne at his side, gave a press conference. He issued this challenge to Sinn Féin, and in particular to their party president:

> We have done our bit. Mr Adams, it's over to you. We've jumped, you follow.[23]

Trimble had won his party over, and many political commentators suggested he was now setting the political agenda. He had taken an enormous risk and emerged victorious. He and Daphne had talked about the Waterfront Hall vote in the days leading up to the debate. She knew what failure meant. If he had lost the vote he would have had to resign.

Daphne recalls that the philosophy was straightforward. First, win the votes at party meetings, and then just keep going:

> Paul Bew coined the term the 'Daphne Principle'. That was where we would talk about things together at each stage. If we just got enough support to make it worthwhile going on to the next stage, and if you just got enough support,

then you had to do it. It was always so difficult, but what was the point of doing it if you were not going to take it to fruition?[24]

The result at the UUP meeting did not stop the war of words – both inside or outside of the party. As delegates left the Waterfront Hall, they were either cheered or jeered. The UUP's main rival, the DUP, was watching events with great interest and took little time to criticise the decision of Trimble and his supporters. DUP leader Ian Paisley told his party's conference:

> Every vote cast today [for Trimble] is a vote of shame, a vote for darkness, a vote that tramples on the graves of innocent victims and a vote that not only tramples on them but dances upon their graves.[25]

It was vintage Paisley and straight out of his well-worn textbook for criticising rival unionist leaders. With the UUP vote secured, plans could go ahead at pace for the end of direct rule from Westminster and the introduction of devolution. At midnight on 1 December 1999, the changeover took place, and the next day the new Executive held its first meeting. The UUP had three ministers, the SDLP had three as well, Sinn Féin had two and the DUP had two, but because the DUP would not sit with Sinn Féin ministers, they pledged to stay away from Executive meetings. Reg Empey became Minster of Enterprise, Trade and Investment, and Michael McGimpsey was given the Culture, Arts and Leisure portfolio. Sam Foster, MLA for Fermanagh and South Tyrone, was an unexpected choice as Environment Minister, but clearly Trimble felt it was important that the party had ministerial representation west of the Bann.

For the SDLP, Bríd Rodgers became Agriculture Minister, Mark Durkan took Finance and Sean Farren became Minister for Higher and Further Education and Training. The big surprise came when Martin McGuinness was nominated to be Education Minister. There were cries of 'Shame!' from the public gallery and genuine shock in the chamber as the Derry republican accepted the nomination. Some unionists had expected Sinn Féin to give Bairbre de Brún the Education portfolio, but instead she became Minister for Health.

After the minsters were selected, the parties chose their nominees to head the various Assembly committees. Slowly, the machinery of devolution was being put in place, with David Trimble as first minister and Seamus Mallon installed as deputy first minister – now that his resignation had been reversed.

Northern Ireland was experiencing a new world. The IRA then responded to events at Stormont, saying they would now appoint a representative to the decommissioning body as agreed. However, in their statement they expressed concern about the Ulster Unionist demand for a three-month deadline for the start of decommissioning.

Those words worried many in the UUP; as 1999 ended, the party's hierarchy grew concerned that the issue of guns and government had perhaps not been settled after all.

20

STOP START STORMONT

*'As far as democracy is concerned,
these folk ain't house trained yet.'*
David Trimble speaking about Sinn Féin

As 1999 ended, the Trimble family were in London taking part in celebrations to mark the new millennium. David, Daphne and the children were invited to a series of events, including the New Year's Eve gala in Greenwich at the Millennium Dome with a host of dignitaries including Her Majesty the Queen, Prince Philip and Prime Minister Tony Blair.

For Trimble, just days after devolution had begun, it was a chance to relax and forget about the strains of political life in Northern Ireland. For the Trimble children, it was a great opportunity to have a bit of fun, experience new surroundings and meet famous people.

Vicky Trimble's memories are a little hazy. As an inquisitive 15-year-old, she had experimented a little too much with the free champagne, and as the night wore on, she was starting to feel the effects. She recalls that her introduction to Blair did not go as planned:

> I was making a beeline for the toilets and Dad saw me coming towards him and he was talking to Tony Blair. He was trying to introduce me to Tony Blair and I kind of shoved him out of the way because I needed the toilet, so I just had my priorities right. I had to push past the prime minister to get to the loo. I'm not sure I was even aware

it was Tony Blair, because to be honest, I was extremely drunk. I think Dad thought it was a bit funny.[1]

The incident became a family joke. For years Trimble teased his daughter that she had 'beaten up' the prime minister at the Millennium Dome on New Year's Eve. It was only later that he told her the full story.

The Trimble children got used to meeting famous faces, but sometimes they were blissfully unaware of who they were talking to. Richard Trimble remembers being in Oslo with his parents for the Nobel Peace Prize:

> I remember chatting with this man in a suit, and he came over and said, 'You must be very proud of your dad.' He was about the 50th person who said that to me that day, and I said, 'Yes, I am very proud of my dad.' I had a little chat with him. Dad snuck up to me afterwards and said, 'Do you know who you were talking to?' and I said, 'No clue.' And he said, 'That was the king of Norway.'[2]

David Trimble's children saw their father at home every day during his early days as first minister, and they got to witness the strains and stresses. They could see at first hand what the demands of the job were, and they could experience the pressure that he was under. He now had five jobs: husband, father, first minister, MP and party leader. It was a relentless schedule, as Nicky Trimble observes:

> There were always 101 fires that needed to be put out. And I think Dad actually was far calmer and far more reserved than I would be if I was in that situation. I just think about the sheer amount of pressure that he was under. He did not have a short fuse, certainly, at home. I mean, if you categorise someone who has anger management problems or a short fuse, you would think they would probably explode in the house. But Dad very rarely did.[3]

As January 2000 wore on, it became clear that the decommissioning issue was not going to be sorted soon. Much would depend on General de Chastelain's report that would come at the end of the month. Trimble hoped it would signify a start to decommissioning, but republicans continued to stress that no arms would be surrendered or destroyed by the end of the month. Just as the new ministers were finding their feet and devolution was kicking in, it seemed that Stormont was once again heading for a political showdown.

Trimble's problems were not just confined to endless discussions about decommissioning. The issue of policing dominated the headlines. The UK government endorsed the Patten recommendations with changes to the badge and the name.

The timing did not help Trimble, who needed some good news to silence his opponents. He also knew that, without any movement on weapons, his post-dated resignation letter would take effect and devolution would end in February. Much now rested on de Chastelain's report.

When it finally arrived it was a major setback for Trimble and his supporters. It declared:

> Our sole task is decommissioning and to date we have received no information from the IRA as to when decommissioning will start.[4]

Trimble's resignation now seemed inevitable, and with it the suspension of devolution and the reintroduction of direct rule. The UUC was due to meet on 12 February, when Trimble would make it clear that his time as first minister was over.

Both the British and Irish governments felt they had some time to rescue the situation, and over the next few days there were endless discussions involving officials from London, Dublin and Washington.

The day before the UUP key meeting, Dublin officials and Sinn Féin representatives met in a last-minute attempt to stop Stormont being suspended. To unionists, enough was enough, and Trimble needed action, not words, from the IRA. With the clock ticking towards Trimble's resignation, Martin McGuinness visited the first minister at Stormont. It was a cordial encounter, but Trimble heard nothing in the conversation to make him change his mind. He also had a phone call with the Sinn Féin president, Gerry Adams, but like the earlier discussion with McGuinness, their discussion did not change anything.

Just after 5 p.m. on Friday 11 February, Peter Mandelson signed an order at Castle Buildings to end devolution. Power-sharing had come to a crashing halt after only 72 days. After direct rule was introduced, the inevitable blame game took centre stage as the parties took to the airwaves to explain their positions.

There was much focus on a second report that was compiled by General de Chastelain. It stated that the IRA was prepared to put weapons beyond use once the Good Friday Agreement was fully implemented and after the causes of conflict had been addressed. There was some positive language in the second report, but ultimately the political die was cast.

On Saturday 12 February, members of the UUC once again made their way to the Waterfront Hall in Belfast, where they had previously agreed to go into government with Sinn Féin – but this time they were preparing to leave. Trimble told activists that unionists had forced the hand of the British government, and, without his post-dated resignation letter, suspension of devolution would not have happened. He said if there was another attempt to resurrect Stormont any proposal would be brought back to the UUC for consideration. That motion got the overwhelming backing of activists, and with that the matter was put to bed. The meeting was at times heated, but it did not have the level of acrimony of the November gathering. Trimble felt vindicated – but republicans had a very different response.

On 15 February, the IRA declared that they were withdrawing their interlocutor from the decommissioning body. The move was not entirely surprising, but it was seen as a setback, because it distanced republicans from the decommissioning process. For the next few weeks, the war of words about the suspension continued on the airwaves and in newspaper columns, and decommissioning – or the lack of it – remained the main topic of political conversation.

The debate was somewhat circular and did not seem to be going anywhere until Trimble changed the dynamic when he was in the United States for the annual St Patrick's Day celebrations. As he crossed the Atlantic, he had time to think about what ideas and thoughts he should convey to American officials and the media. He knew President Clinton would try to pressurise him, and he suspected that Sinn Féin would also use their meetings in the US to blame unionism for the collapse of devolution – so how could he change the agenda? What could he say that could alter the narrative and suggest that power-sharing could come back? How could he present it in a way that would keep his party intact?

At the National Press Club in Washington, Trimble stood in front of camera crews and journalists, including a number of correspondents who had travelled out from the Republic and Northern Ireland. He knew what he was about to say. He also knew within minutes that it would make headlines at home:

> I have made it clear that we are prepared to be involved in a fresh sequence which probably will not involve arms up front. But it has to involve the issue being dealt with and the matter working. The only people who can answer that is the republican movement.[5]

Trimble was ready to try again. Just as he had jumped before and asked Sinn Féin to follow, he was saying he was prepared to do that again. His remarks shocked his colleagues back in Northern Ireland, who had not been tipped off. UUP MLA Esmond Birnie says this was characteristic of Trimble but understandable given the fact he had critics inside and outside the party:

> Some of us at some time might have wished he shared the grand strategy a bit more widely. But given the context, as I say, of a deeply divided Assembly group and obviously the DUP sniping from the outside, I suppose I can understand.[6]

As expected, Trimble's Washington remarks made the news bulletins and the front pages, and his comments caught many by surprise. It wrong-footed Sinn Féin in America, and it meant the UUP leader had seized the news agenda at home and abroad. There were consequences, however.

Two days before the party's AGM, the Reverend Martin Smyth, the UUP chief whip at Westminster, announced that he would be challenging Trimble for the leadership. At nearly 70 years of age, Smyth stood for old-style unionism and was a former grand master of the Orange Order. He was hoping Trimble's critics in the party would coalesce behind his candidacy.

Ultimately, Smyth polled well, and, out of a potential pool of around 800 votes, he secured a creditable 348 votes, which amounted to 43 per cent of the vote. Trimble received 457 votes, which put him at 57 per cent. The challenger had lost, but the message was clear. Trimble should have polled much better against Smyth – a candidate who represented much of what the current leader wasn't.

Trimble knew he had a majority for now, but he was also brutally aware that there were hundreds of party members who did not like his leadership. He was damaged, his critics were real and organised, and he knew he could be toppled at some stage in the future.

Trimble's victory and his Washington speech helped to change the political atmosphere, and behind the scenes, officials in Dublin, London and Belfast began working on plans to get devolution back. The objective was well known and well rehearsed: come up with a plan that the UUP and Sinn Féin could buy into that addressed the thorny issues of guns and government. The next planned UUC meeting was expected to be Saturday 20 May, so the working assumption was that any potential deal had to be ready by that date.

By early May, the details of the new deal were put to Trimble and his colleagues by the UK government. The IRA had agreed to re-engage with General de Chastelain, weapon dumps would be opened and inspected by a third party who would report to de Chastelain, and the dumps could be regularly inspected to ensure nothing had been removed or added. It marked a major move by the IRA, and both governments believed it was a dramatic shift from republicans and hoped it would be enough to convince the UUP to re-enter government. The UUC meeting planned for 20 May was put back a week until 27 May and, in the days before it, there was much debate on the airwaves of the merits of the new IRA offer.

On that final Saturday in May, party members took the well-trodden path back to the Waterfront Hall in Belfast. That night Verdi's *Aida* was to be performed, and publicity for that event adorned the walls. In the hall where the UUP were meeting, the stage was set for the performance and, bizarrely, numerous party members made their speeches against a backdrop of Egyptian mummies. The scene provided colourful copy for journalists and rich pickings for headline writers – apart from the fact that the meeting was private and reporters were not allowed into the room to observe proceedings.

Students of Verdi in the press pack were quick to point out that the opera examined the themes of 'love, betrayal and loyalty' – which, in the circumstances, seemed rather appropriate for David Trimble's party. The coming together of Verdi and the UUP was not lost on the party's opera-loving leader.

His main rival, Jeffrey Donaldson, tried to convince delegates that there should be decommissioning before the Executive was reinstated. He argued that No voters must continue to be heard within the party.

In the end, Trimble triumphed again, and the margins were very familiar. His motion to take the UUP back into government was backed by 459 votes to 403 – representing 53 per cent to 47 per cent. The margin of victory was tight, but, as ever, the UUP leader knew it was enough.

Trimble was delighted, but his post-vote press conference was remembered for rather different reasons. Asked about Sinn Féin, he surprised journalists when he said: 'As far as democracy is concerned, these folk ain't house trained yet.' He added:

> It may take some time before they do become house trained and I think we need to see the Assembly up and running. So that the checks and balances that are there

eventually bring them to heel. We are dealing with a party that has not got accustomed to democratic procedures.⁷

Not surprisingly, Trimble's 'house trained' remarks caused a political outcry, with Sinn Féin's Martin McGuinness saying that he found the remarks 'highly offensive'. He said Trimble's comment was 'quite racist and highly sectarian and it has no place in the world of conflict resolution'.⁸

The Trimble remarks did not overshadow the bigger news story, which was the fact that power-sharing was back. Northern Ireland Secretary Peter Mandelson moved fast, signing the necessary paperwork to get the machinery of devolution back in place. The ministerial cars were refuelled, and on Tuesday 30 May the UK restored powers to Northern Ireland's politicians, and the cross-party Executive was back in business.

Trimble was returned to the office of first minister, with Seamus Mallon as deputy first minister. There was much Executive and Assembly business to consider, but away from the daily meetings and speeches, Trimble knew the findings of two international statesmen would have a bearing on his political future.

Cyril Ramaphosa, the former ANC leader, and Martti Ahtisaari, the ex-president of Finland, had been appointed arms inspectors for the Independent International Commission on Decommissioning to observe IRA arms dumps, and their report would have huge political implications. Devolution now depended on what these former politicians witnessed and could report on. In June they confirmed they had been taken to a number of IRA arms dumps and ensured that the weapons and explosives could not be used without detection.

Aside from his duties at Stormont and at Westminster, Trimble also had a major party-political matter to consider. Clifford Forsythe, the UUP MP for South Antrim, had died in April 2000, and the party had selected David Burnside to fight the by-election, which was set for September. Trimble had hoped his friend and colleague David Campbell would get the nomination, but at the selection meeting Burnside beat Jim Wilson in a two-person run-off.

Forsythe had secured a majority of over 16,000 at the last general election, and Trimble was pretty confident that Burnside would retain the seat for the party. It was a safe UUP seat, and Burnside was viewed as a good candidate, and so Trimble was hopeful of victory. His optimism and confidence were badly misplaced, however, as the DUP's Willie McCrea dramatically outpolled Burnside by some 800-odd votes, 11,601 to 10,779.

In the press the post-mortem began immediately. Why had the UUP lost such a safe seat? Was this evidence that Trimble's pro-agreement vision of unionism was in trouble? Some commentators even drew parallels to 1970, when the firebrand unionist Ian Paisley took the seat of Bannside off the Ulster Unionists. The South Antrim result and the closeness of the recent leadership battle were clear indicators that Trimble's continued leadership of the party could not be taken for granted.

Even though he was facing pressure from many fronts, there was never any sense from Trimble that he would step down. Civil servant Colin Ross, who worked for Trimble as his principal press officer, was often intrigued by how he coped with the abuse and scrutiny and was amazed at his staying power. He enjoyed working with him and found the first minister 'fascinating and mercurial and you could almost apply the word nerdy'. He once asked him if he had ever considered resigning for a quieter life:

> 'Why have you stayed here, when you could have had a completely different life, and, to use the biblical phrase, "shaken the dust off your feet"?' And he looked at me and said, 'I know, I can understand why you would ask that.' But he said, 'I believe if you stand for election to improve the lives of the people who may vote for you and then who do vote for you, it is your duty to remain doing that job for as long as you feasibly can.' And he said, 'That's what I set out to do, and that's what I will finish doing.'[9]

Trimble wanted the role of first minister to work, and even though the margins of victory at UUC meetings were perilously thin at times, he was determined to stay as UUP leader. At the party's annual gathering in October 2000, the internal divisions were on display again. Portions of the crowd gave him a standing ovation, while others showed their displeasure by jeering and booing.

Trimble was now used to the opposition, and days later he faced his critics again. At the end of the month, Jeffrey Donaldson tried to get the party to change tack. He wanted the UUP to leave the Executive if the IRA failed to decommission. Trimble offered an alternative proposal, which committed him to preventing Sinn Féin ministers from attending the cross-border bodies until the IRA had fully engaged with the Independent International Commission on Decommissioning. Trimble's motion was backed by 445 votes to 374.

In December, Ireland played host to a visit by President Clinton, and he and the First Lady travelled to Dublin, Dundalk and Belfast. The trip would be Clinton's third and final trip as president to Northern Ireland, and understandably it was high-profile and gathered international attention.

Trimble was pleased the event was happening, but it caused a diary clash. He had agreed to travel to a conference in Sicily hosted by the mayor of Palermo, and it meant he would have to leave the stage at the Odyssey Arena in Belfast to catch a flight to London and then on to Italy. When Trimble told Tony Blair that he would have to leave, the prime minister was genuinely shocked and declared, 'You must be joking'. Trimble was serious, as he wanted to make the flight, and that meant he had to leave the stage in front of the audience and speaker. It was not a good look, as he walked out in front of the US president. Trimble's early exit was filmed and interpreted by some journalists as a snub to Clinton, and when he read and heard the reports the UUP leader was genuinely taken aback by the criticism. The Italian trip ended Trimble's engagements for the year, and over Christmas he spent time with his family.

The year 2001 was barely a week old when his leadership suffered a setback. Ken Maginnis, the UUP MP for Fermanagh and South Tyrone, announced that he would step down from Westminster at the next general election. Maginnis was a strong supporter of Trimble's and had played a decisive role in 1998 on Good Friday, convincing some doubters of the need to agree to a power-sharing deal.

His seat was always finely balanced in a fight between unionism and nationalism and had once been held by the IRA hunger striker Bobby Sands. Trimble knew the departure of Maginnis could let Sinn Féin in. The party had polled well in the 1998 Assembly election, and he was concerned that, with the departure of a big UUP name, the seat could now be lost. A general election was coming, and it was expected in June. Trimble knew he would face big competition from the DUP, and he was keen not to experience further losses like South Antrim.

As the UUP leader contemplated losing Maginnis, Tony Blair faced a similar problem with Peter Mandelson. The secretary of state had resigned over his alleged role in a passport application from an Indian billionaire. Mandelson insisted he had done nothing wrong and said he wanted to distance himself from the 'countless stories and controversies'.

Mandelson was replaced by John Reid, a canny Scottish Labour MP, who became the 13th person to have had the role of secretary of state for Northern Ireland, and the media made much of the fact that he was the first Catholic to hold the post. Reid inherited a fragile political process, with police reform and decommissioning still threatening to destabilise power-sharing at Stormont. The new man at the NIO had little time to find his feet.

In February 2001, Trimble warned that there would have to be a review of the Good Friday Agreement because of a lack of progress over decommissioning. Seamus Mallon was even more pessimistic and warned that there was a real risk that agreement could collapse within days.

As the talking continued, so did the violence. The Real IRA planted a number of bombs, including one outside BBC Television Centre in London, which injured one man and caused extensive damage. Loyalists were active as well, and there were shootings and a series of pipe bomb attacks across Northern Ireland.

With a general election imminent, there was an acceptance in Dublin and London that the chances of political progress were slight, and any breakthrough would have to wait until after polling day. By early May, Trimble knew that the absence of IRA decommissioning would dominate the election campaign, and the DUP would make much of the lack of progress. He needed to look strong and tough to the unionist electorate. On 8 May he said that, if the IRA did not begin to decommission its weapons by 1 July, he would resign as first minister. It was a bold move.

He had asked republicans to move before, and he hoped this time it would prompt them into action. It was a trump card to play with voters during the campaign. However, the threat to resign did little to stem the tide of unionists switching their allegiances from the UUP to the DUP. Unfortunately for Trimble, June's general election heralded much success for Sinn Féin and the DUP.

Sinn Féin ended up with four seats and their tally included Fermanagh and South Tyrone, with the slimmest of majorities of 53.

Despite James Cooper's best efforts he failed to replace Ken Maginnis, and the UUP lost the seat. Across Northern Ireland the UUP got six seats. Trimble was re-elected in Upper Bann, Martin Smyth retained his seat in South Belfast, as did Roy Beggs Senior in East Antrim, and Jeffrey Donaldson once again won Lagan Valley. Sylvia Hermon, Trimble's former Queen's University colleague, triumphed in North Down, defeating Bob McCartney, and David Burnside managed to win back South Antrim from the DUP.

But there were losses in Strangford after John Taylor announced his retirement and was beaten by the DUP's Iris Robinson, and her colleague Nigel Dodds managed to oust the UUP's Cecil Walker in North Belfast. The headlines from the results were clear. Sinn Féin had outpolled the SDLP, and the DUP were on the march and breathing down the necks of the UUP.

For David and Daphne Trimble, the aftermath of the count in Banbridge turned into a horrible experience. As they left the building a large crowd gathered, and they faced much physical and verbal abuse from anti-agreement protesters. Daphne remembers being attacked as they made their way to their car:

> I was so scared that I would fall and be trampled underfoot. I just got kicked in the shins but there was a policewoman, I think, who got quite seriously injured. And David was cross with the police, because he felt they had lined up on the wrong side of the car. We were being jostled in the crowds on the way out once we got near the car. And we were then driven out. I was this close to being in tears. And it was only the sight of the television camera pointing at the car that put a bit of backbone into me. There have been nasty experiences, but that was one of the worst.[10]

The SDLP's Dolores Kelly was inside the count centre, where a crowd had also gathered, and remembers feeling frightened:

> It was symptomatic of what David Trimble had to face, in terms of being a champion, a supporter, of bringing forward the Good Friday Agreement. I think it brought home to me just how much he had sacrificed and how brave he was.[11]

Shaken and bruised, David and Daphne were then driven to Belfast, where Trimble was going to do an interview as part of BBC Northern Ireland's election coverage. Before he went on air, UUP press officer Philip Robinson had a brief chat with him:

> As a press officer, what you would often do is make sure someone's tie was straight, and they looked presentable. I saw this dirt on his coat, and I just tapped the shoulder to wipe away the dirt. And he said, 'Don't do that.' And he looked at me and he said, 'Philip, this is what they threw at me.' And he said, 'People need to see that.'[12]

Denis Murray, then the BBC's Ireland correspondent, remembers seeing Trimble's car arrive at Broadcasting House:

The car came in through the back gates at the BBC. And I was in the backyard and there was a boot print on the side at the top of the back passenger door that had just missed somebody's head as they were going in. I mean they hadn't stopped to clean it up on the motorway. I'm sure Trimble felt like resigning, but he wanted to see it through as far as he possibly could.[13]

After the dust had settled from the general election campaign, Trimble and the UUP hierarchy had a chance to assess how the party had fared. There were two seat losses which particularly annoyed Trimble: the DUP's capture of Strangford and Sinn Féin's victory in Fermanagh and South Tyrone. He had hoped that Cooper could have replaced Maginnis at Westminster, and he was also disappointed to lose Strangford following Taylor's retirement.

Asked by Alex Kane in 2015 about these seats, Trimble admitted he should have tried harder to keep both as MPs:

Yes, I did make mistakes. I should not have been so ready to let John Taylor and Ken Maginnis retire. I should have kept them in to fight that election. They would have held their seats and that would have made a very different situation afterwards.[14]

With the election out of the way, political talks began to try to find a way forward, but Trimble's promise to resign on 1 July still hung over proceedings. There was some media speculation that Trimble had fought his last election campaign as leader and even suggestions that he might be challenged in the days ahead. There were rumours that party activists wanted a 'dream ticket' of Jeffrey Donaldson and Reg Empey as new leaders, but when the rescheduled AGM took place in June 2001 there were no challengers to Trimble's leadership.

On Saturday 23 June he was re-elected unopposed as party leader by members of the UUC, and the expectation was that he would resign as first minster in the coming days if there was no decommissioning.

Six days later, as Trimble talked tactics with his colleagues at Stormont, the American rock band the Eagles had arrived at Parliament Buildings to play an open-air concert. As the politicians talked inside, the band began to tune up outside. Ray Hayden remembers that one of the Eagles' best-known songs suddenly became audible through the window:

> I said to David, 'Stop, we've got to stop.' He said, 'Why?' And, you know, he had that sort of bemused, bewildered look on his face. I said, 'They are playing your song.' He said, 'What do you mean, they are playing my song?' I said, 'They are playing "Take it to the limit one more time".' To which Michael McGimpsey turned and said, 'Well, David, at least they're not playing "Lying Eyes".' And the place just descended into uproar.[15]

It was moment of light relief at a time of great political angst.

Trimble found the Eagles reference funny. However, there were other musical experiences which did not go so well. Party Chairman James Cooper remembers flying into a military base in England for a series of inter-party talks. When Trimble came out of the plane, the welcoming party got their national anthems mixed up:

> Trimble went down the stairs and there was a band there and the Irish tricolour was flying, and they started playing the Irish national anthem. And he turned on the steps of the plane and charged up it again. Because they actually mixed our plane up with the one that was bringing Bertie Ahern in. So, he certainly took fright at that.[16]

In late June 2001 Trimble was on French soil, where it was expected he would carry out his threat to resign as first minister if republicans had not begun to decommission. The UUP leader had travelled to mark the commemorations for the Battle of the Somme. Secretary of State John Reid had made the journey too, as had many journalists from Northern Ireland tasked with reporting the latest twist to the peace process.

David Blevins, the Ireland correspondent for Sky, remembers Trimble resigning in France:

> Earlier in the evening, we had gone for dinner in Amiens only to find David Trimble in the same restaurant. When the doors opened, and the Northern Ireland secretary, John Reid, arrived, our eyes turned towards him. Had he come to find Trimble because the IRA had moved? 'Have you brought news, Secretary of State?' I asked. Trimble replied with that rare twinkle in his eye, 'It is in his pocket.' Reid pulled out a page and set it on my table: a blank page.[17]

Reid's joke had some substance. There was nothing on the table that could stop Trimble's resignation, and at midnight the UUP leader stepped down as first minister. What followed was a series of moves designed to keep the political institutions alive. After he stepped down Trimble nominated Reg Empey to become the stand-in first minister, which meant that the business of governing could continue.

The British and Irish governments then held talks and came up with a plan to try to rescue the situation. The parties were invited to talks at Weston Park in England, on the borders of Staffordshire and Shropshire. The DUP was not invited and stated publicly that the initiative would not succeed. Policing, decommissioning and the issue of demilitarisation dominated the discussions, and they took place against a backdrop of street violence back home. Ultimately, there would be no breakthrough, but the British and Irish governments agreed to come back with a fresh set of proposals for the parties to consider.

When the plans arrived in August, they included a pledge to revise the legislation on policing by October 2002 and the promise to hold inquiries into the murders of the human rights lawyers Pat Finucane and Rosemary Nelson by loyalist paramilitaries; of Robert Hamill, a Catholic beaten to death by loyalists in Portadown; of Billy Wright, shot in prison by republican prisoners; and of the senior RUC officers Harry Breen and Bob Buchanan, killed in an IRA ambush.

Much to the concern of unionists, there was limited comment on decommissioning. While the parties considered the document, Reid bought the political process more time by using a tactical device that allowed him to suspend Stormont and then reintroduce devolution 24 hours later. This created a window of six weeks, during which there would have to be another election of first and deputy first minister. It meant the new target for power-sharing would be 21 September – the latest in a long line of deadlines which had become the hallmark of politics in Northern Ireland.

Before the parties would reach that date, the world would change. An act of unbelievable terror in America would have repercussions right across the globe.

21

HEARTS AND MINDS

'I was ready to punch him on the nose.'
David Trimble on being questioned by
BBC *Hearts and Minds* presenter Noel Thompson

The shocking images of two planes crashing into the Twin Towers in New York on 11 September 2001, were difficult to comprehend. To the millions watching around the world on television, this seemed like a disaster movie – except this footage was real, and the devastation would change families for ever. The attack on the World Trade Center by Al-Qaeda created sheer, unadulterated terror on a scale never witnessed before in real time. After two other planes crashed at the Pentagon and in Pennsylvania, the death toll stood at nearly 3,000. They marked the deadliest attacks on US soil since the Japanese attack on Pearl Harbor in 1941.

Osama bin Laden's act of war put much of the United States into lockdown, as the country was now fearful of further attacks. Hundreds of messages of sympathy were sent to President George W. Bush from around the world, and the UK government pledged to stand with the US administration in the fight against terrorism. There was now a new world order, and life would never be the same.

By chance, President Bush's adviser Richard Haass happened to be in Belfast at the time of the attacks. He was meeting Sinn Féin and had come to deliver quite a blunt warning to republicans. Three Irishmen had recently been detained in Colombia on false passports, and the allegation was that they were there to assist FARC guerillas – a revolutionary group which the US administration opposed. The men denied any wrongdoing, but Haass wanted to use the meeting with Sinn Féin to tell them he did not believe them and that the incident had angered the US administration.

When news of the New York attacks came through, Haass had another reason to criticise Sinn Féin's position – and this time it was about the lack of decommissioning. He felt 9/11 had changed everything. The IRA simply could not hold on to its arsenal and had to move. In his eyes, the world was now a different place, and Sinn Féin needed to recognise that. Haass had a number of strong cards to play. Sinn Féin needed the support of the US administration, and Irish-Americans were important sources of fundraising. There was also the matter of visas for Sinn Féin politicians in America, which could be withdrawn if the US administration felt Irish republicans were not being cooperative.

Behind the scenes in London, Dublin and Belfast, the discussions continued, and speculation intensified that republicans would make a move in the weeks ahead. As Trimble was considering his next move, his fellow Nobel laureate had come to a big decision. John Hume called time on his leadership of the SDLP and announced that he was stepping down as party chief for health reasons. Hume said he had been thinking about resigning for a while and felt that the time was now right.

It was the end of a political era, and Hume's announcement briefly took the headlines away from decommissioning. The attention then switched to Seamus Mallon, who was the party's deputy leader and seen by many activists as the next leader. Mallon called a press conference and made it clear he was not a candidate for the party leadership. His wife, Gertrude, was ill, and he said she must be his priority. He also said he would be resigning as deputy leader as he felt it was a time for fresh leadership for the party. Mark Durkan would later be elected as party leader and ultimately would succeed Hume as Foyle MP.

By early October there was still no movement on decommissioning, and although the IRA had issued a statement in September it was viewed by the UUP as not enough. The waiting game continued. Trimble found all this intensely frustrating and knew that the longer this issue dragged on the longer it would damage his leadership and his party's credibility – which was already being questioned by parts of the electorate.

On 8 October, the DUP and the UUP tried to exclude Sinn Féin from the Executive. Not surprisingly, their attempts failed due to a lack of cross-community support, but afterwards Trimble came up with another tactic. He announced that UUP ministers would be leaving the Executive, and 10 days later that threat was carried out.

Reg Empey, Sam Foster and Michael McGimpsey all declared they had given resignation letters in to the Speaker's Office. The DUP then made the same move, and it became clear that, if the unionist places were not filled, the Executive would collapse. Once again, an air of crisis hung over Stormont, and it seemed power-sharing was going to be put into the political deep freeze, again.

Then the mood changed when there were strong indications that the IRA was about to decommission. On Monday 22 October, Gerry Adams confirmed that he had called on the IRA to 'make a groundbreaking move on the arms issue'. The Sinn Féin leader said this would 'save the peace process from collapse and transform the situation'. The next day, the IRA issued a statement that many thought they would never see, confirming that they had decommissioned weapons in order to 'save the peace process'.

The Independent International Decommissioning Commission later announced:

> We have now witnessed an event which we regard as significant – in which the IRA has put a quantity of arms completely beyond use. The material in question includes arms, ammunition and explosives.[1]

The statements from the IRA and the decommissioning body changed the political atmosphere. Trimble reappointed the three UUP ministers who had resigned, which stopped the Executive from falling, and their reinstatement set up the process for electing a first and deputy first minster. The Assembly met at Stormont to do that on Friday 2

November, but Trimble ran into trouble. He simply did not have the numbers, as rebel UUP MLAs Peter Weir and Pauline Armitage made it clear that they would not support him.

Under the rules, Trimble needed a majority of unionists to support him, and the lack of support from Weir and Armitage meant he fell short. However, in a spirit of generosity Women's Coalition members agreed to redesignate to help Trimble's numbers. Monica McWilliams redesignated as a nationalist and Jane Morrice switched her designation to unionist.

Morrice remembers going to tell Trimble what they were planning to do:

> We decided we would let Trimble know on the day of the vote that we were going to do this. And I went to the door to say, you know, 'I want to make sure you are aware we're going to do this for you', and 'What do you think?' It wasn't a negotiation. I was telling him we were doing it. So, we went into Trimble's office to let him know. We were a bit surprised, as it wasn't welcomed with open arms. But then I sort of slightly understood that he didn't want to be saved by the women. It was a fascinating moment.[2]

In the end the Women's Coalition redesignation did not help get Trimble elected. He won the vote across the whole Assembly by 72 votes to 30, but he lost the vote within designated unionists by 30 to 29. He failed to be elected. It was messy and embarrassing, and it frustrated Trimble. John Reid could have suspended the political institutions after the voting failure but soon another plan emerged to save Stormont and get Trimble elected. If members of the Alliance Party redesignated, that would get the UUP leader over the line.

Alliance leader, David Ford, got the backing of his party, and on Tuesday 6 November they tried again. Three Alliance members redesignated as unionists and Trimble got 31 unionist votes compared with 29 opposing him. The Assembly voted 70 to 29 in his favour. Trimble was elected first minister and Mark Durkan replaced Seamus Mallon as deputy first minister. With a bit of political chicanery, power-sharing was saved.

Ford says the move by his party shows how desperate the situation was:

> [David Ford:] David Trimble only got re-elected as first minister along with Mark Durkan in November 2001 because Seán Neeson and Eileen Bell and I pretended to be unionists for 22 minutes, which is an illustration of the problems with the system.
>
> [Stephen Walker:] And you were happy to do that?
>
> [David Ford:] No. Did I do it because I thought it had a chance of providing stability for my children to grow up in? Yes. Was I happy doing it? No.
>
> [Stephen Walker:] In a sense was he [Trimble] living on borrowed time when you had to do something like that?
>
> [David Ford:] He was living on borrowed time. Whether it would have been better if it had been Empey and Durkan rather than Trimble and Durkan at that stage? I wonder. It might have given a better restart.[3]

Trimble was back as first minister with the majority of MLAs supporting him. But the figures also revealed that he was in power as a minority unionist leader at Stormont, and that did not bode well. He had a new partner to work with in the Office of the First and Deputy First Minister. Mark Durkan had previously been Finance Minister and had established a reputation for being hard-working and good on detail. Before he entered elected politics Durkan had been a student leader and went to work for Hume in 1983. Hume was his mentor, and he was a confidant of the Nobel laureate. A Derryman like Hume, Durkan had been one of the SDLP negotiators at the time of the Good Friday Agreement, and he had an encyclopaedic knowledge of its clauses and sections.

As Durkan and Trimble began their political journey together, their new relationship hit the headlines for reasons no one could have predicted. As the two men left the Assembly chamber, they moved to the Great Hall at Stormont to conduct a press conference. As Trimble spoke to the media, he was surrounded by DUP members, and soon the heckling began. Trimble's credibility as first minister was questioned by anti-agreement MLAs, and soon the shouting turned into pushing and shoving, and scuffles ensued.

It was all very unseemly, and Stormont security staff had to move in to calm the atmosphere. It was captured on television and was quickly dubbed by journalists 'The Brawl in the Hall'. Most commentators suggested it was a most unfortunate start to a new era. It illustrated the point, if anyone needed reminding, that there were sharp and emotional divisions within unionism, and Trimble was operating as a first minister almost under siege.

Up until that point, Durkan's experience of dealing with Trimble had been in Executive meetings and before that during talks negotiations. Now he got to see Trimble close up:

> He could be quite skittish at times. And it's odd, because he could go from being grumpy to giddy and he could go from being giddy to grumpy in odd ways or whatever. He had a sense of humour, you know. You might be in the middle of some briefing from civil servants about something and they would be talking about something or whatever and then he would have a chuckle.[4]

Over time, Durkan got used to the way Trimble operated. He soon realised the UUP leader was interested in taking a long-term view of things, and he believed he genuinely wanted to create a better Northern Ireland:

> Those of us who were dealing with him probably underestimated him for all of the circumstantial reasons that we know. We had not been dealing with him long enough over a range of different things. And then in the circumstances of the process people were reacting to different events and different requirements. But he ended up being more in the business of enabling things and he was [more] open to a longer-term view of things than the immediate political plans allowed him to be talking about.[5]

November saw Durkan and Trimble work together to try to solve the long-running Holy Cross dispute. The Catholic primary school in north Belfast was close to the peace line and had become the centre of a protest by loyalists. As ever with Northern Ireland the origin of the dispute was contested. Loyalists claimed their homes had been attacked by nationalists and also said Protestants were being denied access to local facilities. There were reports that loyalists putting up paramilitary flags had been attacked. Catholic residents said that their homes were under constant attack and that they faced ongoing abuse and intimidation from loyalists. During the protests by loyalists, riot police had to form a cordon for children and their parents as they walked to school. They faced a barrage of abuse and stones, and on one occasion a blast bomb was thrown. The dispute seemed intractable and the story was reported across the world.

At that time, Mary Madden, who was once taught by Trimble at Queen's University, worked at the NIO. She remembers being in a meeting with Trimble and Northern Ireland Minister Jane Kennedy, who had responsibility for security. They were discussing a suggestion put forward by Trimble to install gates on the road close to the Holy Cross school in an attempt to control the movement of traffic and people. When Madden was asked for her opinion she expressed her concerns about Trimble's idea – which the first minister clearly did not like:

> The meeting had been on for about half an hour or more. He just exploded and got very upset and angry about it

and directed his annoyance and anger at me because I was the one who had spoken. So, they called the meeting to a halt and he left in high dudgeon and temper. And Jane Kennedy just sort of commented, 'You have not earned your stripes unless you have had one of those from David.' So, he was a man who could get very animated and agitated and cross when things were not quite the way he wanted them. But I think that is the pressure you have as a leader.[6]

A common criticism of Trimble's time as first minister and MP was that he was spending too much time in London on Westminster duties – which his critics suggested limited his ability to fully embrace his important role back at Stormont. Durkan says that many of those who questioned Trimble's double jobbing did not realise that he had to be in London to try to manage his MPs, who were mostly critical of his leadership:

All that time it wasn't occurring to us that, rather than going off to the opera and rather than having some nice, pleasant chat with a chap at the Cabinet Office or whatever, he maybe was just trying to keep the lid on things, party-wise or whatever, by thinking he had to do it with the MPs at Westminster.[7]

Dissent within the party remained an ongoing problem for Trimble. The lack of support from the two rebel MLAs, Peter Weir and Pauline Armitage, had obviously delayed his re-election as first minister and meant he had to rely on other parties redesignating. Weir was expelled for voting against the re-election of Trimble, and Armitage was suspended. The moves against the rebel MLAs did little to quieten Trimble's opponents, and anti-agreement party activists secured a meeting of the UUC for Saturday 1 December in an attempt to influence strategy.

A motion called for UUP ministers to leave the Executive by the end of February 2002 if there was no further decommissioning by the IRA. Trimble and his supporters argued against the move and won by 409 votes to 320 – 56 per cent to 44 per cent – which was a slight improvement on previous margins.

Trimble ended 2001 in a good place. On the positive side, there were lots of things which had gone his way. Devolution had been restored, and there had been a significant act of IRA decommissioning. He continued to win crucial votes at important meetings, and he was back as first minister. He was hopeful his new relationship with Durkan would work well.

The New Year marked a second chance for Trimble as first minister and provided another opportunity for the UUP to build a relationship with the SDLP. The party's dealings with Seamus Mallon had been fraught at times, and the UUP hierarchy hoped that the new pairing of Durkan and Trimble would provide a more stable and positive relationship.

The early days of 2002 were dominated by a series of attacks by loyalist paramilitaries, and on 9 January there was violence outside the Holy Cross Primary School in North Belfast. In January and February, Trimble and Durkan were busy with the business of joint government, and there was much to do. In February they travelled to the World Economic Forum in New York, and on their return, they announced a comprehensive review of public administration in Northern Ireland. That month also marked a big moment for David Kerr, who left his position after working with Trimble for six years.

Party matters took centre stage for Trimble on Saturday 9 March, when he addressed the AGM of the UUP. Sometimes such occasions could pass off without controversy, but Trimble's speech was seen as inflammatory when he described the Republic of Ireland as a 'pathetic, sectarian, mono-ethnic, monocultural state'.[8]

Many found his remarks deeply insulting, and they did little to help North–South relations or improve his dealings with Sinn Féin and the SDLP. Sinn Féin's Martin McGuinness said Trimble's behaviour was not what you would expect from a Nobel Peace Prize winner, and he described the first minister as a 'twit'.[9] Taoiseach Bertie Ahern, who had maintained a good relationship with Trimble, said no one would refer to the Republic of Ireland as a sectarian state, as it did not have places like Drumcree and the Garvaghy Road – two places in the first minister's constituency.

By the time Durkan and Trimble arrived in the United States for the annual St Patrick's celebrations, the controversial speech was still being reported – but not for long. As ever with the politics of Northern Ireland, unpredictable events change the news agenda. On the evening of 17 March, back in Belfast there was a dramatic break-in at the PSNI Special Branch headquarters in Castlereagh. The raid by the IRA would go down as one of the most embarrassing security breaches of the Troubles. The IRA managed to steal sensitive documents including a list of Special Branch officers, details of their paramilitary agents and their handlers, and other contact details.

The brazen theft at what was meant to be a secure unit sent shockwaves through the PSNI, as it meant that the security of dozens of police officers had been compromised. Many members of staff and police officers had to leave their homes and quickly find alternative accommodation. The events of St Patrick's evening alarmed Trimble greatly, and he knew his internal critics in the party would use the break-in as another example of why the IRA could not be trusted.

Trimble looked at the robbery with the 'gravest concern' and at Westminster during parliamentary exchanges said the incident created 'ramifications not just for national security but for the integrity of policing operations in Northern Ireland'. It now fell to the UK government to consider what to do next. Trimble wanted Tony Blair to sanction Sinn Féin. John Reid, the Northern Ireland secretary, warned the IRA that the government would exclude Sinn Féin from the Executive if there were more breaches of the IRA ceasefire – but to some he was playing for time, and his statement was viewed by many unionists as not strong enough.

The fallout from Castlereagh had understandably put more political focus on republicans and the IRA. After the Special Branch break-in in East Belfast and allegations surrounding FARC in Colombia, the IRA's commitment to the peace process was being questioned, even though

Sinn Féin insisted that the IRA were not behind Castlereagh and also claimed they had not done anything wrong in Colombia.

The questions persisted about the IRA, and by early April there were strong rumours that there was going to be another act of decommissioning. On 8 April, that speculation turned into substance when the IRA announced it had put more arms beyond use. In a statement it said the action was intended to 'stabilise, sustain and strengthen' the peace process.

The decommissioning body described the IRA move as 'substantial'. It failed to win over anti-agreement unionists, however, who believed this second act was a stunt. Despite the IRA move, Trimble felt the IRA had breached its ceasefire, and both the UUP and the DUP brought motions to the Assembly to have Sinn Féin excluded, but without cross-community support they had no effect.

Even though relations were strained, Adams and Trimble did meet and have discussions, although there was no meeting of minds, and republicans continued to insist that they had no involvement in Castlereagh. The discussions were cordial affairs with a degree of humour. Adams recalls one difficult encounter with the UUP:

> It was a really tense meeting and at one point David [Trimble] or somebody with papers flung them down on the table. And it was getting very uptight about whatever was going on. And I stood up and I said: 'I think it is time for a group hug!' And Martin McGuinness said: 'Count me out!'[10]

On another occasion Adams and Trimble were to meet in Trimble's office, but as they sat down window cleaners appeared outside on a ladder. They moved to another room and the same thing happened.

Looking urgently for some privacy, they finally settled on a smaller room belonging to Mark Neale, who was now working as one of Trimble's advisers. Neale recalls that, on entering the room, Adams saw Neale's bookcase, which was full of books relating to Northern Ireland politics and history:

And they closed the blinds and they're having this private meeting and apparently Adams went to the bookcase and looked at the books and said, 'I see he has none of my books.' To which Trimble replied, 'No, Mark doesn't read fiction.'[11]

Neale says Trimble was pleased with his witty retort to Adams and often repeated it – proof again that, despite Trimble's press image, he did have a sense of humour. The two politicians may have joked but their discussions were serious, and as they met, they knew the peace process was in deep trouble. The Executive was teetering on the brink of collapse, and it was the intentions and actions of the IRA which could bring it down.

Mindful of unionist concerns, John Reid told the House of Commons that an IRA ceasefire was 'not enough'. Trimble's critics in the party demanded a withdrawal of UUP ministers by 1 July, but that motion was comfortably defeated. However, the suggestion that Trimble might quit as first minister raised its head again. He had resigned on 1 July in France a year previously, and there were rumours that he would use that tactic again if the government would not exclude Sinn Féin. Trimble was under pressure, and it started to show publicly.

As the summer began, the omens for the peace process did not look good. The early optimism created by the new Trimble–Durkan relationship and the positivity that surrounded the initial round of IRA decommissioning had gone. The unexplained events in Castlereagh and Colombia had changed the atmosphere. Trimble was once again fighting fires on different fronts, and the pressure was on.

On 27 June, he appeared on BBC Northern Ireland's political programme *Hearts and Minds*. Mary Kelly, who was producing that edition, remembers Trimble turning up at Broadcasting House in Belfast for the interview, which had been arranged to be recorded at 11 a.m. She recalls that Trimble was half an hour early, and the background set for the interview was not ready, which meant filming could not begin immediately:

> As soon as he arrived, I said, 'Oh, Mr Trimble, you're early, but don't worry, we'll have you in the studio pretty soon.' I went straight in, and I said, 'For God's sake, quick as you can, Trimble's in and he's not in good form.' I just knew by his face. So, then I came back and said, 'Don't worry, we won't be long, can I get you a cup of coffee in the meantime?' And he replied, 'I will not be mollified.' And I thought, bloody hell, what is wrong with this man?[12]

Kelly then bumped into one of Trimble's protection officers, who was standing close to the studio:

> He had clearly been with him [Trimble] all morning and said, 'Someone should tell him to fuck off.' And I went, 'Away you go.' And the next thing David came out and he was on the phone, and he was shouting at somebody on the phone, really angry. And the next thing we brought him into [the presenter] Noel [Thompson], and they exchanged a few pleasantries.[13]

About halfway through the interview, Thompson began to challenge Trimble over the decommissioning issue. The interview got quite heated, and at times Trimble raised his voice and looked agitated and very angry. This extract gives a flavour of the exchange:

> [Noel Thompson:] Nowhere in the Good Friday legislation does it say that Sinn Féin have to get rid of IRA weapons. They have to use their best offices. That is what it says.
>
> [David Trimble:] That is quite wrong. You are quite, quite wrong about that, and you must not peddle these myths. Because it is no more than a myth. The Good Friday Agreement commits all the parties to achieve, to achieve disarmament.

[Noel Thompson:] By whatever offices they can use. Sinn Féin will say they are doing that.

[David Trimble:] Of course it does. Of course it does.

[Noel Thompson:] Sinn Féin will say they are doing that.

[David Trimble:] No. You are distorting the situation, Mr Thompson, entirely. Let me say this. Don't interrupt.

[Noel Thompson:] You may say that, Mr Trimble. Sinn Féin say that they are using their best offices. That is not me, that is Sinn Féin saying that. There is no point shouting at me.

[David Trimble:] Now, are you going to be quiet for a moment?

[Noel Thompson:] I will certainly look forward to your answer.[14]

It was quite the television moment. Thompson recalls being surprised by the way Trimble reacted.

> I had no idea what kind of mood he was in, but I knew he was always under pressure. And so, the interview started, and we finally eventually got on to decommissioning. And as I recall it (but I haven't seen the thing for ages), he was implying or saying that Sinn Féin had to bring about decommissioning. And I remember quoting from the Good Friday Agreement saying, no, the agreement says they have to use their best offices to secure decommissioning. And that's when he flew off the handle and, you know, accused me of totally misrepresenting the situation. And

I was very much ready for anything in those interviews, but I was slightly taken aback, I have to say.[15]

Mary Kelly vividly remembers Trimble leaving the studio after the interview:

> When he came out into make-up again to have his make-up taken off, he was as nice as pie. It was as if none of this had happened. And he said, 'I was ready to punch him on the nose.' And at the time I thought, 'God, do you know, I wish you had.' Noel said of course that wasn't very kind of me. But I remember thinking what brilliant TV that would be.[16]

Trimble's television encounter with Thompson clearly illustrated that the first minister was a man under extreme pressure, but it also showed that he had remarkable staying power and resilience. He wanted devolution to work, and he wanted decommissioning to be achieved. He needed the Good Friday Agreement to succeed and to be durable, but he was frustrated at the delays and diversions.

Since April 1998, Trimble's judgement and leadership had been questioned relentlessly by critics inside and outside of the party, but despite such attacks, he made it clear that he was intending to stay on as UUP leader. The parliamentary recess bought some time, and after Trimble came back from his summer holidays the crisis seemed to have lessened a little. He was quoted in the press saying that devolution was here to stay – intended as an obvious indication that things were stable and there was no impending crisis.

However, all was not well in the hearts and minds of UUP members, who felt their party had taken too many risks for not enough reward. At this stage, questions were being asked within the party about Trimble's continued leadership. A number of senior figures had conversations with him about him stepping down – but he was determined to stay on.

David Kerr, who had stopped working for Trimble in the spring of 2002, formed a view that it was now time for the UUP to have a new leader:

> [David Kerr:] I thought he should have stood down as leader in September 2002. That was my view, because it was where we had got with the unionist electorate. Peter Robinson and the DUP had done such a good job at poisoning David's name with the unionist electorate.
>
> [Stephen Walker:] Why specifically at that time in September 2002?
>
> [David Kerr:] Because we had so many complaints from voters during the 2001 election campaign. On the doorsteps all we were getting was: 'Look, we support you. We want this project to succeed and everything else, but you're going to have to do something about David Trimble.' I also knew we needed to heal the divisions in the party, because if we did not, people like Arlene Foster and Jeffrey Donaldson would go to the DUP.[17]

The mood within the party was changing. On 21 September, members of the UUC met to decide how the UUP should approach power-sharing with republicans in the months ahead. For Trimble it meant another showdown with his long-running adversary Donaldson and, sensing that some of his supporters were turning against him, Trimble felt he had to act.

The numbers were going to go against him, and he was worried he might lose a vote. There was some suggestion the party was split 50–50, and so Trimble felt he had to move towards the anti-agreement lobby in his own party. He needed to take on his critics but keep the majority of party members on his side. He therefore surprised Donaldson and agreed that, if there was no movement from republicans, he would resign as first minister and other UUP ministers would withdraw from the power-sharing Executive in January 2003. In the meantime, it was agreed that the party should step away from the North–South institutions. Trimble insisted that republicans had to show they had stepped away from violence for good.

It was a bold move, but as leader Trimble felt it was the only way to keep the party together. The new deadline for the IRA to act was 18 January 2003. Mark Durkan criticised the UUP threat to walk away and said its action had thrown the political process into crisis. The institutions that both the SDLP and the UUP had helped to create were now on life support.

The clock was ticking. However, within days, fresh revelations would push the process to breaking point – and speed up the collapse of power-sharing.

22

SPIES, SPLITS AND SUSPENSIONS

*'He could be very blunt, very irascible.
And sometimes, he could be difficult and even offensive.'*
Northern Ireland Secretary Paul Murphy on David Trimble

The first Friday in October 2002 turned Northern Ireland politics on its head. David Trimble was in Upper Bann, away from the first minister's office. He was spending the day like most other MLAs, in his constituency holding surgeries and dealing with the administration that comes with political life.

With no debates or committee meetings, Friday was normally the quietest day of the working week on the Stormont Estate. It was when the corridors and the canteen could feel a little soulless and empty – but not on this occasion. The PSNI had dramatically arrived at the Prince of Wales Avenue in a convoy of battleship-grey Land Rovers, which were now lined up outside the main Stormont building. In an unprecedented move, police officers began raiding the offices of Sinn Féin. Documents and computer disks were removed amidst strong protests from Sinn Féin MLAs Gerry Kelly and Bairbre de Brún. It was like a scene out of a Hollywood movie.

The UUP minister Dermot Nesbitt watched on rather bemused as the TV cameras focused on police officers wearing baseball caps moving hurriedly around the building. It would become clear that the PSNI were investigating spying allegations. They were searching for evidence that the IRA had been using Parliament Buildings for intelligence gathering.

The raid quickly became known as 'Stormontgate', and it moved the ailing political process from critical to fatal. Trimble compared the allegations of spying to events in Washington in 1972, when supporters of President Nixon broke into the Democratic National Committee headquarters at the Watergate complex. However, the UUP leader thought the affair was 'ten times worse than Watergate'.[1]

Three men were arrested as a result of the police raids, and they insisted they were innocent. Charges against all three men would be dropped in December 2005, but back in October 2002, the fallout from the events at Stormont was dramatic. The UUP leader told the media that it was 'no longer sustainable' to be in a power-sharing Executive with republicans after the allegations.[2]

Blair had a really big decision to make. Should he exclude Sinn Féin and try to keep devolution going? Or should he go for suspension? Over the next few days, Downing Street had a series of discussions, including contacts with Mark Durkan. Republicans did not accept the allegations of a spy ring at Stormont and suggested the PSNI move was politically orchestrated.

On 14 October, John Reid announced the suspension of devolution, and, with that, direct rule was introduced from London. The Executive collapsed, and David Trimble was no longer first minister. It was all over. It had optimistically started on Good Friday in 1998 with talk of peace. Now, four years later, it had dramatically ended on another Friday with allegations of spying. The parallels with the last cross-community government were uncanny.

The Irish and British governments were desperate to find a way forward. Blair came to Belfast and told local political leaders that Northern Ireland was at a critical point. The prime minister warned: 'We cannot carry on with the IRA half in, half out of this process. Another inch-by-inch negotiation won't work.'[3]

Days after Stormont fell, there was a new player for the local parties to deal with. However, he was a familiar face. Reid left Northern Ireland to become health secretary, and he was replaced by Paul Murphy, who had previous experience working as minister of state in the NIO.

Murphy says he and Trimble got on well and had a common love of music and history. They never had a cross word, but Murphy says Trimble could rub people up the wrong way:

> He was difficult for a reason. That is to say he was standing up for his community as he saw it, Northern Ireland as well. He was always highly intelligent in his approach to things. Almost laser-like in his acknowledgement of detail, his dealing with detail. And we were dealing with lots of detail, and he would be hugely impressive on that. But he could be very blunt, very irascible. And sometimes, he could be difficult and even offensive.[4]

Murphy had a different approach from his predecessors. The softly spoken Welshman had a likeable manner and was seen as thoughtful and considered, and he quickly built up the trust of local politicians. In the early weeks of 2003, he embarked on a series of discussions to gauge what common ground existed between the party leaders.

In February, the discussions between the two governments continued, and in March, Bertie Ahern and Tony Blair met the parties at Hillsborough. The hope was that republicans could categorically state that 'the war is over' and then make a major move on the issue of decommissioning. If their words and actions were enough to convince the UUP, the institutions could be re-established. Various texts and different permutations were discussed, and the issue of sequencing was again mooted as the way forward.

But in the background there was a major issue that was a factor in the discussions. An Assembly election was due to take place in May, and it was felt by the talks participants that any campaign would interfere with negotiations and would not be helpful. There was also the hope from both governments that if an Executive could be restored before the election, it might enhance the electoral chances of the pro-agreement parties.

Blair faced accusations that he was running a 'Save Dave' campaign by trying to orchestrate the return of Trimble as first minister before any election. By April 2003, the IRA outlined their position to officials in Dublin and London, but their words were not enough for the two governments. Blair insisted that a deal was 'frustratingly close' but made it clear that he had three questions for the IRA: Does the IRA intend to end all activities including targeting? Will the IRA put all its weapons beyond use? Does the IRA's position mean a final closure of the conflict?

On 1 May, Blair postponed the Assembly elections, saying that if the poll took place, it would make progress in the peace process 'less likely'. He blamed the IRA and said the elections would take place in the autumn. Ahern opposed the move and told reporters that he thought the postponement would cause 'more problems for the process than it solves'.[5] However, the two governments did agree on a way forward on other matters and published a joint declaration that included a plan to devolve policing and justice and create a monitoring body that would investigate paramilitary activity.

The summer months marked a defining period for Trimble's leadership, and over a number of weeks he faced a series of challenges within the party. In June, Jeffrey Donaldson tried again to get Trimble to change tack by tabling a motion that would have seen the party reject the proposals put forward by London and Dublin. Donaldson wanted a timetable for decommissioning and was concerned that a scaling down of security in Northern Ireland would leave Protestant communities vulnerable. He was also against the Irish government getting to choose a member of a new monitoring body.

The UUC met, and Trimble triumphed by 440 votes to 369, which represented a 54 per cent to 46 per cent split. It resulted in Donaldson declaring that he and his like-minded colleagues who disagreed with Trimble's leadership had to 'decide if this party now represents what we believe in'.

Matters then took a dramatic turn. David Burnside, the Reverend Martin Smyth and Donaldson resigned the UUP whip at Westminster. It meant that half the Ulster Unionist parliamentary party were not officially UUP. The party hierarchy met to consider what to do with them, and the three MPs were referred to a disciplinary committee and then suspended until 17 July.

The UUP 'civil war' had just taken another turn. The Westminster rebels then began legal proceedings to overturn their suspension, and on 7 July Mr Justice Girvan ruled that the moves against Burnside, Smyth and Donaldson had been unlawful. Trimble's troubles were continuing almost on a daily basis. The next day he faced a motion of no confidence in his Upper Bann constituency, which he won by 184 votes to 69. It had become a summer of discontent for the UUP leader. He was politically battered but determined to carry on.

Donaldson warned that the UUP would be punished by the electorate if it continued to follow Trimble's advice and guidance. From an Orange Order platform on 12 July, Donaldson declared:

> There is a real danger that, unless David Trimble revises his position and draws back from the brink ... the Ulster Unionist Party will implode and lose its position as the majority voice in unionism.[6]

For the rest of July and August, the divisions and the rancour in the party continued. There was an attempt to mend fences between the Trimble wing and the Donaldson faction, but that initiative failed. Another UUC was called for 6 September, which would consider how to deal with the three rebel MPs.

This would be the 13th time the party had gathered in such circumstances since the Good Friday Agreement. It would prove to be lucky for Trimble, and his good fortune continued. The party faithful were asked to back the continued suspension of Burnside, Donaldson and Smyth, and they supported Trimble by 443 votes to 359, which meant the leader had secured 55 per cent of the vote compared with 45 per cent who opposed the move.

It marked a good day for Trimble and effectively meant Donaldson was running out of road. Political journalists now wondered how many times the Lagan Valley MP could come and challenge Trimble at the UUC. They also started to speculate how long he could realistically remain in the party. There was a feeling that he was now moving towards an exit from the UUP, and that the DUP would most likely be his next political home.

Trimble's victory at the UUC buoyed him up, and, if the IRA would move substantially on the issue of weapons, he was hopeful that a deal could see the Executive back in place before the rescheduled Assembly elections. Much rested now on what republicans would do. Trimble for his part remained hopeful that there would be a major act of decommissioning and used his annual address to party conference on 18 October to appeal to the IRA:

> We are waiting to see if these acts of completion will be done. The issue is simple. Republicans know what has to be done. It has been absolutely clear since April. They need to make up their mind.[7]

Trimble did not have to wait long. British and Irish officials had been in discussions with Sinn Féin for days, and the UUP had also been in talks with republicans. The return of the Executive was dependent on the detail contained in General de Chastelain's report on decommissioning, and it was agreed that his assessment would be part of a sequence of events which would include the announcement of an election date. The deal to return devolution was being carefully choreographed – or that was the plan at least.

There would be statements from Sinn Féin, the UUP and the two governments, and the key announcement would be from de Chastelain. Both Blair and Ahern were heading to Northern Ireland, and the hope was that they would be able to jointly declare there had been a major act of decommissioning, and that devolution could return.

On the morning of Tuesday 21 October, it was announced that the postponed Assembly election would now take place on Wednesday 26 November. That was the start of the sequence, even though the two governments did not know exactly what moves the IRA had made. It was understood that de Chastelain had been away with IRA figures and visited arms dumps some hours before, but beyond that, the detail was limited.

The two premiers spoke on the telephone before they travelled to Belfast, and it is clear they were both unsure if their plan would work. Despite their reservations, they decided to go ahead with the trip. Ahern had serious doubts, and even before he boarded the short flight from Dublin he was questioning the wisdom of travelling north. He was right to be worried.

When de Chastelain started talking to the media, Trimble watched with horror. The Canadian told journalists that his report was short and confirmed that decommissioning had taken place, and that included the destruction of automatic weapons, explosives and ammunition. He would not say how much had been destroyed. Detail was limited, and it was all a little unclear.

For Trimble it was simply not enough. He needed clarity, detail and a sense of what had been destroyed, but he got none of those things. This would not bring Ulster Unionist ministers back into the Executive. Any deal about restoring devolution was off. Trimble and Blair spoke on the phone and the UUP leader made it clear that, as far as he was concerned, the process was still on pause.

Trimble let his frustration be known in a press conference and made it clear that any deal over choreographed statements was now off:

> We probably now have less confidence in the process than we had an hour ago because of that. I regret that I'm not in a position to make those statements. We are in effect now putting the sequence on hold.[8]

Ahern recalls that the situation was a mess. He says that his gut feeling was right when he sensed that the de Chastelain announcement would not work:

> When de Chastelain was off all night with the IRA and then came back to that press conference and was not able to give a substantive and authoritative answer ... that was the end of David, and that shouldn't have happened. And I knew that was going to happen. I said to Brian Cowen [Irish foreign affairs minister] at Dublin Airport, 'I really don't want to go back up here, it is tactically wrong. We're

walking in to have a meeting that is going to be a failure.'

It was a failure. It was a bloody disaster.⁹

The Irish and British governments had gambled that de Chastelain's presentational skills at the press conference would have been enough to sell the decommissioning move, but the situation was now, in effect, back to square one. Within minutes, efforts were made to get more information put into the public domain about the IRA's actions, but it was to no avail.

Trimble said he was putting the sequence 'on hold', but the reality was that the moment had passed and any plans to get devolution up and running were gone. Trimble blamed republicans and the UK government for the situation:

> Adams and McGuinness knew how important it was to build public confidence, and they deliberately decided not to create it. And I don't really blame John de Chastelain for the debacle. The debacle occurred because Adams and McGuinness wanted a debacle to occur. And unfortunately, the government gave them that opportunity.[10]

Trimble and his colleagues now had to face the electorate for the delayed Assembly election, and there were big worries within the party that this would be the DUP's moment. Once again, they were up against a confident and well-organised DUP, keen to exploit what they saw as UUP failings and party divisions.

Trimble found himself going into the election with a deeply split party. He was well aware of the old political maxim that divided parties don't win elections. Despite the very public splits and suspensions, he hoped he could stay ahead of Paisley's party. It was a short campaign, which suited the UUP, and much of it was routine and predictable – up until Tuesday 18 November.

On that morning, the DUP parked its battle bus outside Cunningham House in East Belfast, which was the headquarters of the UUP. It was a cheeky photo opportunity, as the DUP unveiled a mobile billboard which was meant to garner some press interest. The move was quickly spotted by Trimble and his staff, and he and a number of his colleagues left their offices to go outside to confront the DUP delegation on the pavement.

In front of watching reporters, Trimble became involved in a row with a number of DUP leading lights, including deputy leader, Peter Robinson; Iris Robinson; and Willie McCrea. Trimble challenged Ian Paisley to a TV debate and accused the DUP leader of being scared and said he was 'hiding away'. In turn, Peter Robinson said Trimble was 'yesterday's man' and Iris Robinson claimed that the UUP leader was so unpopular that he could not even 'walk in his own constituency'.[11]

The confrontation involved a lot of shouting and finger-pointing and lasted around 10 minutes. It made for good television and starkly illustrated the tensions that existed in the unionist community. For the watching press pack, it enlivened a lacklustre campaign, and they dubbed the encounter 'the Fuss on the Bus'.

Trimble would later regret going out to engage with his DUP rivals:

> That was a mistake. Even going out there was a mistake. The only way one could have, in retrospect, handled the situation effectively was to go out, as you say, with a smile on your face and invite them in for a cup of tea, which is what I should have done.[12]

Reflecting on the incident some years later, he admitted that his actions did not help the party:

> It was political theatre that worked very well for them, and I should not have gone out there and actually played into their hands, which is what it did.[13]

When election day came, it was clear that the unionist community now favoured Paisley's brand of politics, and the DUP triumphed with 30 seats compared with the UUP's 27. Sinn Féin won the nationalist battle, taking 24 seats compared with the SDLP's tally of 18. It was a major moment for Paisley, winning his first Assembly election, as the DUP gained 10 seats and he saw his party in pole position. It proved to be a defining shift in Northern Ireland politics and would signal a dramatic change in the direction of the peace process.

Trimble was re-elected in Upper Bann, and there was no repeat of the nastiness of the 2001 Westminster count, when he and Daphne had been jostled and kicked.

Bearing in mind the circumstances – the concerns over decommissioning, Stormontgate and party disunity – the UUP performance was better than some had expected. The party only lost one seat, and there was not the dramatic meltdown some commentators had predicted. However, the figures were still hard for party loyalists to accept, and it prompted much discussion about a change in leadership.

Talks began behind the scenes, and a series of ideas were talked about. There were rumours that Donaldson was about to quit the party and join the DUP. Some of his supporters saw him as a natural successor to Trimble and wanted him to stay in the UUP. Others viewed Reg Empey as the man to succeed Trimble.

There was also talk of a joint leadership ticket, with Empey as leader and Donaldson as his deputy. That idea of course rested on Donaldson staying in the party. David Burnside felt the UUP needed to radically change tack, and he hosted discussions with a series of senior figures:

> [David Burnside:] There was a meeting in my office between Reg, Jim Molyneaux and Jeffrey, where he [Donaldson] promised he wouldn't go and then decided to go. So, I think that would have been a compromise. I think we were looking at alternatives.
>
> [Stephen Walker:] Would you have been happy if David [Trimble] had gone, and Reg had been leader and Jeffrey would have been deputy?

[David Burnside:] I think it would have stabilised things.

[Stephen Walker:] And improved electoral fortunes?

[David Burnside:] Yeah. It would have stabilised things. David did a good job in very difficult circumstances.[14]

There were a number who supported Burnside's view that a change was necessary, and they were not all from the anti-agreement camp. Some were long-serving Trimble supporters such as Danny Kennedy, who had backed the Good Friday Agreement. Kennedy now felt it was time that Trimble stepped down:

> At the time I did think that a new leader would give us a better chance, because I think, electorally, we were really struggling, and because the DUP were able to land every punch on Trimble as being Trimble's fault, even though it wasn't ... He had lost the grassroots, and I think that was the difficulty. Now, would a new leader have made a significant difference at the time? Perhaps, perhaps not. But that was certainly my view at the time, that it would have given us a better chance.[15]

Empey was being talked about as Trimble's successor, but he concluded that a leadership contest was the last thing the party needed:

> Following bad election results in 2001 and all the pressures building following the 1998 agreement, the on-off operation of the Assembly and the absence of decommissioning, some in the party felt a change of leadership was likely to occur soon. I quickly came to the conclusion that the party could not sustain a divisive challenge to David. And it made sense to wait until a vacancy arose.[16]

The discussions behind closed doors about the party leadership amounted to nothing, and Trimble remained in charge. The British and Irish governments now accepted that the centre ground had gone, and they had to focus on the parties they had once considered 'extreme'. The facts were clear: the electorate had voted for change. The majority voice of unionism in Northern Ireland was now Ian Paisley, and the leading advocate for nationalism was the Sinn Féin leader, Gerry Adams. There had been a changing of the guard, and the parties who had helped negotiate the Good Friday Agreement were no longer in charge.

The SDLP had been outpolled by Sinn Féin for a variety of reasons. Mallon and Hume were no longer the dominant figures, and the party did not have politicians of the same stature to replace them. On the ground, Sinn Féin was seen by nationalist voters as sharper, more capable and better organised.

Similarly, Paisley's party – who portrayed the UUP as 'pushover unionists' – were seen as confident, with a clear message and, perhaps critically, they appeared to speak with one voice. As Lord Bew recalls, the DUP were presenting themselves as the future and Trimble as the past:

> The thing that the DUP had to do was to let the other parties know you don't have to put up with this irascible red-haired guy anymore, because there's an answer. You don't have to go out endlessly thinking about his problems of managing this one or that one. There's another answer.[17]

As 2003 came to a close and the election post-mortem continued, there was more bad news to come for Trimble. Donaldson, Foster and Norah Beare all announced they were leaving the party. The resignations meant that the majority of unionist Assembly members were now anti-agreement. The party had begun disciplinary proceedings against Donaldson, and he wanted to resign before he was expelled. The MP left with his constituency colleague Beare, a newly elected MLA for Lagan Valley.

Foster, who had just been elected in Fermanagh and South Tyrone as an Ulster Unionist MLA, also resigned. She remembers that the atmosphere at party meetings had become unbearable:

> [Arlene Foster:] When the election happened, and we were elected, the nastiness continued. Instead of healing, the nastiness continued, and I think there was going to be a point where there had to be a break unless something at the top changed.
>
> [Stephen Walker:] Did you think that was coming even when you were running for election in 2003?
>
> [Arlene Foster:] I didn't actually know what was going to happen in the election in 2003, because, as I say, there was so much angst going on within the party at the time.[18]

The UUP civil war had now reached a critical moment, with the three resignations and the DUP becoming the largest unionist party. Trimble's leadership was continuing to be questioned, and he did consider stepping down. The North Down MP Lady Hermon remembers ringing Trimble the day of the Assembly election results in 2003 and pleading with him to stay on as leader:

> [Lady Hermon:] I said, 'You cannot resign. You cannot leave us now. You cannot abandon us now. You have to lead us through this.' I pleaded with him. He was an inspirational leader.
>
> [Stephen Walker:] And was he seriously thinking of resigning?
>
> [Lady Hermon:] Yes, at that point. Yes, he was very disappointed with the Assembly election.[19]

Reflecting on this time some years later in a BBC interview, Trimble admitted that he should have stepped down after the Assembly elections in 2003:

> The mistake I made is to have stayed on. I think, in retrospect now, that I should have stood down after losing the Assembly election, because there was probably just enough time between the Assembly election and the Westminster election for a new leader to have shifted, possibly have shifted. Mind you, there was no sign of anyone volunteering.[20]

In the first week of 2004, Donaldson, Foster and Beare were welcomed into the DUP. It was a massive coup for Paisley's party and meant the DUP had 33 MLAs and 6 MPs, making it the largest Northern Ireland party at Westminster. After her move, Foster said the DUP was now 'the mainstream unionist party in Northern Ireland'.[21]

The defections to the DUP were no great surprise and underlined the new political dispensation – Paisley's party was the new unionist establishment. With Stormont suspended, the British government's efforts to restore devolution were now centred on the DUP and Sinn Féin. In February, a review of the Good Friday Agreement began, involving all parties, with the hope of finding ways of kick-starting the political institutions. Decommissioning once again remained the main issue, and it was now the DUP's turn to put pressure on republicans.

With a European Parliament election planned for June 2004, both governments knew that there was little prospect of movement before the summer. When the poll came, the retiring DUP MEP Ian Paisley was replaced by Jim Allister; sitting UUP MEP Jim Nicholson retained his seat; and Sinn Féin's Bairbre de Brún took John Hume's place. It was more bad news for the SDLP, and after the 2003 Assembly election result, the European result underlined Sinn Féin's electoral superiority.

Nicholson's victory was a relief for Trimble, and with the election out of the way political talks reconvened, beginning first at Stormont and then moving to the picturesque setting of Leeds Castle in Kent. All the focus was on whether there was enough common ground between the DUP and Sinn Féin, and whether the IRA would declare their war to be over and complete decommissioning.

Republicans faced further questions when, on 20 December 2004, a large gang took part in a dramatic £26 million robbery of the Northern Bank in Belfast. The IRA was blamed for the raid, which at the time was the biggest bank robbery in British and Irish history. In January 2005, the IRA was again in the spotlight when republicans were blamed for attempting to block an investigation into the murder of Belfast man Robert McCartney. It all furthered suspicion that the IRA was still active and had no intention of disappearing.

In April, Gerry Adams entered the debate, when he called on the IRA to 'fully embrace and accept' democratic means. His appeal was made as Sinn Féin and the other parties began campaigning for the general election called for 5 May 2005. For Trimble, this would be another crucial test of his leadership, and he knew that his future as both an MP and party chief was on the line.

In Trimble's Upper Bann constituency, David Simpson of the DUP had been chipping away at his majority over previous elections, and this time Trimble knew he was in the fight of his life. He was also concerned that a series of other UUP seats were at risk from a confident DUP. To help his own party, Trimble had floated the idea of the Alliance Party stepping aside in certain constituencies, as they had done in the 2001 general election.

He met the Alliance Party leader, David Ford, privately, and it was then that he made a surprising offer. Trimble offered Ford a peerage if Alliance withdrew candidates in certain constituencies. Ford says he told the UUP leader that he had no interest in going to the House of Lords, and that his party would not be withdrawing candidates:

> [David Ford:] We had made it absolutely clear that we had done it four years earlier. It hadn't worked, and we weren't doing it again.

[Stephen Walker:] But was he [Trimble] serious?

[David Ford:] It appeared to me at the time he was serious, whether he had got it agreed with Blair ... or that is something that would be offered if that happened, I don't know. But can you imagine what it would have done to the Alliance Party to find that we withdrew for the Ulster Unionists in certain places and the party leader ends up with a peerage the next week?[22]

The Alliance candidates remained in place, and Trimble and his team began campaigning hard to hold on to their five seats. On 20 April, the party unveiled its manifesto at the Stormont Hotel in Belfast, with their 18 candidates arriving on a Routemaster bus complete with a destination sign which read 'Westminster'.

The party used the slogan 'Decent People – Vote Ulster Unionist', but the words sparked controversy after the UUP was accused of insulting other voters, particularly those who opted for the DUP. Even some UUP members objected to the wording. It was not a great start to the campaign.

Away from the row about campaign slogans, Trimble was publicly optimistic about retaining his Westminster team. He told journalists he was sure the party would return with 'more than five members'.[23] His upbeat assessment was not shared by the bookmakers. One bookie predicted that the UUP would lose four of the five seats they held and suggested that the casualties would include the party leader: David Trimble.

Alex Benjamin, the UUP's director of communications, says there was a sense of foreboding amongst the staff working behind the scenes:

> Nobody wanted to take ownership of the campaign. And it felt that it was something that was kind of cobbled together without a central figurehead, that the party officers were sort of just going through the motions and nobody really wanted to say, 'I'm going to drive this forward.'[24]

The party put on a brave face, and Trimble canvassed far and wide, even using a helicopter on the campaign trail. Privately, he knew what was about to happen. On 6 May, the results started to come in, and the magnitude of the party's defeat was all too clear.

By lunchtime, it was obvious that the sitting MP Roy Beggs had lost in East Antrim to the DUP's Sammy Wilson. In South Belfast, it seemed that Michael McGimpsey was in third place, and the UUP would not retain the seat. In the Strangford and East Londonderry seats which were held by the DUP, the UUP were trailing.

By late afternoon, the bad news continued for Trimble, as it became apparent that David Burnside had lost in South Antrim to the DUP's Willie McCrea. It was a UUP wipeout. The only note of optimism for the party hierarchy was Lady Hermon's vote in North Down. Returns showed that she had polled well and looked on course to retain her seat.

The big worry was in Upper Bann and the political future of David Trimble. For the UUP, the news was catastrophic.

23

A GOOD INNINGS

'I think I had a good innings in terms of what we managed to do. I am proud of what we did.'
David Trimble after resigning as leader of the UUP

Standing at two microphones with the candidates behind her, the deputy returning officer for Upper Bann read the result slowly. Amanda Mason knew her figures would be scrutinised like for no other seat in Northern Ireland. Referring to her notes, she declared that David Simpson of the DUP had polled 16,679 votes, and William David Trimble had secured 11,381 votes. She paused and then calmly announced that David Simpson had been duly elected MP for the constituency.

Cheers went up around the hall. The DUP had secured their main prize and achieved their number one objective of the campaign. The party had toppled Trimble and sensationally ended his political career.

The dramatic announcement was broadcast live, and Noel Thompson, who was anchoring BBC Northern Ireland's election programme, summed it up: 'Well, that has to be the story of this election. David Trimble, the Ulster Unionist leader, has lost his seat to David Simpson of the Democratic Unionists.'[1]

To the many viewers across Northern Ireland, Thompson's words seemed unreal. The architect of the Good Friday Agreement, a Nobel laureate and a seemingly permanent fixture of Northern Ireland politics, had been dramatically ousted. Trimble's day as an elected politician was over. Simpson, the smiling winner, made his acceptance speech first, and he declared that 'pushover unionism has gone for ever'. Trimble stood behind him ashen-faced, and when Simpson finished, he stepped forward to speak to the crowd:

> I believe that the situation in Northern Ireland is now a much better one as a result of what we have done. I'm proud of our record. Today of course has been a considerable success for the Democratic Unionist Party, and that cannot be gainsaid. But they will know that with that success comes responsibility. I believe that they have inherited from Ulster unionism a very strong position for unionism, and I hope that they manage to safeguard that position over the course of the months to come.[2]

With that, David Trimble walked away. It was the defining image of the general election in Northern Ireland. In the BBC studio in Belfast, Thompson turned to one of his guests, Lord Kilclooney, who, as John Taylor MP, had been at Trimble's side for many of the key political events of the previous 15 years. The peer praised both David and Daphne for their commitment, and said they had worked 'morning, noon and night' for Northern Ireland and the UUP. He added that 'democracy is a cruel thing, and the people of Upper Bann had spoken'. Kilclooney tried to avoid Thompson's questions about whether Trimble should now step down. The presenter tried a final time, 'If you were the leader today would you resign?' Kilclooney replied, 'Personally, I would, yes.'[3]

At Cunningham House, the UUP headquarters, there was stunned silence. Party officers and campaign staff could not take in what they were witnessing. Other voices were now appearing on the airwaves suggesting the UUP leader would step down shortly. David McNarry, who had worked closely with Trimble as first minister, said that the party was preparing for a resignation statement:

> I would expect that certainly in 48 hours David will have made his decision. I expect David Trimble regrettably to

resign his position as party leader, and then the party will set about dealing with all of that.⁴

Lady Hermon spent the day in Newtownards at her own election count. Understandably, her attention was on the North Down seat, but she got snippets of news about the other constituencies. She had spoken to Trimble at lunchtime on the phone, and although it was early in the counting process he had sounded optimistic. He told her that he was 'holding his own'. Hermon was pleased and hopeful that her party leader would see off the challenge of the DUP.

Hermon then heard nothing until she got a text from a party colleague around teatime simply saying, 'Trimble has gone'. She immediately rang the texter:

> I said, 'What are you talking about?' And he said, 'He's gone.' And I said, 'What do you mean he's gone?' And he said, 'He's lost his seat.' And I could feel my chest was heaving just with the shock of it. I had come out of the count, and I had to stand there and give a speech knowing that my party leader had gone and I was going back to Westminster on my own, and I also reckoned that it wouldn't be long before David would resign as leader of the party.⁵

The loss of the Upper Bann seat and the collapse of the UUP vote were not complete surprises to the Trimble family. Nicky remembers chatting about the election in the house with his dad:

> I remember talking to Dad and he was very despondent. And he said, 'Well, it looks like the DUP are going to railroad us', or something like that. It must have been the evening before, because I remember it was before we knew the outcome. And I remember him saying, 'It looks like we're going to get railroaded.'⁶

Daphne Trimble says the entire family felt David's pain when he lost the Upper Bann seat: 'I certainly found it difficult whenever we lost. When I say "we", I felt it was us rather than just him.'[7]

On Saturday 7 May, David Trimble had a private meeting with Lord Rogan, the UUP president, and James Cooper, the party chairman. There was only ever one thing the former MP was going to do. After 10 years at the helm of the UUP, he was going to resign. He knew that, after overseeing the party's worst-ever Westminster election and the loss of his own seat, it was the only course he could take.

Alex Benjamin, the UUP director of communications, was called in to Cunningham House and remembers meeting Trimble in the office:

> He sort of announced matter of fact to me that he wanted to issue his resignation statement. So, he wrote what he wanted to write, handed it to me and I put it up on a standard format for press releases. I put it into the format that it was supposed to go into, and I topped and tailed it. And I remember sitting looking at this thing thinking, 'The moment that I send this', (rather selfishly), 'not only is my weekend over, but this is probably the most significant statement that I'll probably have to write.' And I went into him and said, 'Are you ready?' And he was very calm, and he said, 'I just need a couple of minutes.' So, I went back to my office (in those days I was able to smoke in the office), I lit up a couple of cigarettes and then he said, 'OK, send it.' And I sent it.[8]

On Monday 9 May, Trimble appeared at Cunningham House before the media and explained why he had decided to stand down. He said he had no regrets about how he had conducted himself in the Good Friday Agreement negotiations and said the UK government and republicans were at fault for not implementing the agreement fully.

Surrounded by colleagues and party staff, he looked emotional at times as he reflected on his decade as party leader and his 15 years at Westminster:

> I think I had a good innings in terms of what we managed to do. I am proud of what we did. I am proud of the progress which we achieved. If I think back to Northern Ireland 10 years ago and look at Northern Ireland today, I could say there's a darn good balance sheet there.[9]

As well as Trimble's resignation, political journalists had much to report that day as the results from the local elections started to come in. It was more bad news for the UUP, which polled around 18 per cent and saw them in third place behind Sinn Féin and the DUP. The poll, which was held on the same day as the Westminster election, once again confirmed Ian Paisley's party as the leading voice of unionism.

For Trimble, losing his seat was painful. His son Richard can recall the aftermath of the result:

> It was like a bereavement, I suppose, for him. People get made unemployed all the time, but for Dad in particular that had been his life. I think the loss of being able to go to Westminster and being part of that environment, that was a heavy one for him.[10]

On Saturday 14 May, the party executive met at UUP headquarters and Lord Rogan read out a letter from Trimble formally tendering his resignation as leader. Trimble then addressed the gathering and said that he no longer had the credibility to continue, and the party faced a massive rebuilding job. He thanked all those who had helped him over the previous 10 years and said he would still be involved in the party. He was given a standing ovation.

Terry Wright, a member of the committee, then spoke and paid tribute to Trimble's leadership. After the meeting, as Wright made his way out of the building, he bumped into Trimble:

> When I came down the stairs he was sitting at the switchboard. We had a very brief conversation. He didn't look

at me, as he was on his phone – as he was frequently during meetings. And I went up and said, 'David, you didn't deserve that.' I said, 'Tony Blair hung you out to dry.' And he said, 'You'll never know the half of it.' And I wished him well.[11]

As the UUP began the search for a new leader, Trimble began to adjust to being unemployed for the first time in his life. He had done three full-time jobs in his working life – civil servant, university lecturer and politician – and now he was not sure what came next. He was 60 years of age and believed he still had a contribution to make to public life.

There was much speculation in the press that he was going to be offered a peerage, and the expectation was that such an appointment would be made in the months ahead. As Trimble got used to his new life away from the party, in June 2005, Reg Empey, his colleague from their days together in Vanguard, became UUP leader. He inherited many of the issues Trimble had to deal with, and the political climate remained unchanged. The two D words still dominated the news agenda – decommissioning and devolution – and by midsummer rumours had spread that the IRA was on the verge of a major move.

In July, the IRA formally announced an end to their so-called 'armed campaign', and all IRA units were ordered to dump arms. The war was over: the very words that Trimble desperately wanted to hear during his time as first minister and UUP leader. And there was another development in September 2005, when the Independent International Commission on Decommissioning reported that the IRA had 'put all its arms beyond use'.[12]

Watching as an interested observer, Trimble found it all very familiar. He was still waiting to hear if his next stop was the House of Lords. For the next eight months, his wait continued. Then, finally, in April 2006, it was announced that he would become a member of Westminster's upper house.

Daphne Trimble says the delay to the appointment frustrated her husband:

That was really difficult. He had had a year at home. Blair had promised him, after he lost his seat, the House of Lords. And it didn't happen. He kept going back to Blair, who said, 'Yes, it's coming.' But it was well over a year before it actually happened. And he had the most awful year at home, just sitting with nothing to do.[13]

In front of friends and family in June 2006, Trimble took his seat in the House of Lords as Lord Trimble of Lisnagarvey, a townland in Lisburn. He loved life in the House of Lords and took to his new surroundings with ease. Paul Murphy, the former Northern Ireland secretary, joined Trimble in the Lords when he became Lord Murphy. He says Trimble was ideally suited to his new role:

> He enjoyed himself in the Lords. It was a place where he could contribute and where he could study as well. He was still, in his heart, I think, an academic, and so it suited him well.[14]

In December 2006, Trimble announced that he would not be contesting the next Assembly election and would be concentrating on life in Westminster. In the Lords he often spoke about the politics of Northern Ireland, but his speeches and interventions were not exclusively confined to Northern Irish-related matters. He had an interest in foreign affairs and spoke on the Middle East, the European Union, Zimbabwe, Bangladesh and Colombia. He was also keen to contribute to other debates about different parts of the UK.

Richard Trimble says his father loved being able to challenge ministers and influence policies:

> He was absolutely in his element in terms of lawmaking. He wanted to see good laws being established. So, there were lots of places where he could make a contribution in that way. So definitely when he did get into the Lords, he was like a duck to water.[15]

For many members of the House of Lords, Trimble got a reputation as someone worth listening to – even if they did not always agree with his politics. Lord Donoughue, the Labour peer, often stayed in the chamber to hear him speak:

> His academic background was helpful in organising his speeches and presenting them there. You know they were good to listen to. I always felt he had something to say. And even on Brexit, I mean, he made a better case for Brexit than most of the Tory Brexiteers.[16]

Even before the issue of Brexit became central to the political debate in the UK, Trimble had expressed disquiet over the European Union. He was a Eurosceptic and was concerned that Europe could become a superstate and try to rival the United States. He had openly criticised the EU as first minister in 2001, claiming that it had 'excessive bureaucratic structures'. He also argued that it had an inability to 'take decisions quickly'.[17]

Politically, he was now ready to make a move – a switch he had been thinking about for some time. He saw himself as a Conservative, and he had an ambition to join the Conservative Party. After some discussion with David Cameron, the Tory leader, he applied to join the Conservatives. Former Tory leader Iain Duncan Smith, an admirer of Trimble's, remembers being asked for his opinion on the application:

> I think it was Cameron's office that told me to see if I had any concerns or objections. And, of course, I immediately said no. I said, 'If that's what he wants then we should welcome him with open arms.' I must say, I was a little surprised at that point – not in a negative way. I was just a little surprised. And I think it brought home to me again the nature of the choice he made at the time of the settlement, which was that he must have understood that he and

Northern Ireland would politically part company not of his own desire, but he would become the fall guy for that.[18]

However, before the move was made public, Trimble wanted to tell a number of his close friends. One Friday afternoon, when he was back in Northern Ireland, he rang Lady Hermon and told her that he wanted to see her, but he did not say why. Hermon, who was a staunch critic of the Conservatives, wondered why he wanted to see her. She recalled their conversation when he arrived at her home in County Down:

> I said to him in the porch, 'David, are you all right?' And he sort of laughed, 'Yes, yes.' And I said, 'And Daphne and the family?' He said, 'Yes, yes.' And I said, 'Right, the only reason that you have come here is to tell me that you have joined the blank blank Tories.' And to say that he guffawed, [it] wasn't just a little laugh or a titter or whatever, he was chuckling. That was in the porch before I actually opened the door into the hallway. He knew how I would explode, but he wanted to tell me. So, we came in. I put the kettle on. And I was so pleased for him because I thought, by that stage, he hadn't been given the recognition. He was in the House of Lords, but I thought he hadn't been given the recognition that he so richly deserved.[19]

In April 2007, Trimble became a Conservative Party member and confirmed he would sit in the House of Lords as a Tory peer:

> It's something that's been on my mind many times over the years. Now that Northern Ireland is settled, I'm free to follow what's been an ambition for many years.[20]

A press conference was organised, and Trimble was pictured at College Green in Westminster with the Conservative leader, David Cameron. The move was seen by many observers as a coup for the Tory party. Trimble was, after all, a former first minister and a Nobel laureate, so he was seen as a talented addition to Conservative ranks. There was understandably speculation that Trimble might be offered a shadow cabinet job, but Trimble played down such talk:

> Actually, I said to David [Cameron], 'I don't want to be rushing into things. I don't want to be heading in that direction. I think the first thing I should do is get accustomed to their own way of doing things.'[21]

As Trimble settled into his new party, Northern Ireland experienced fundamental and historic change. After months of talks, the DUP and Sinn Féin agreed to share power, and on 8 May 2007 devolution was restored at Stormont. The sight of Martin McGuinness, a former IRA commander, and Ian Paisley, the DUP leader, laughing together provided one of the most surreal and jaw-dropping moments in the history of Northern Ireland.

As the DUP and Sinn Féin enjoyed their moment, it was very different for the parties which had secured the Good Friday Agreement. At this stage, the SDLP and Trimble's former party were facing difficulties. Under Sir Reg Empey's leadership, the UUP were hurting again, having lost nine seats at the Assembly election in March.

Empey's bid to reinvigorate the UUP had failed its first major electoral test, and the gap between the Ulster Unionists and the DUP had increased. For just over 12 months, Paisley was first minister. It was an amazing turn of events for a man who spent most of his life as the 'Dr No' of Northern Ireland politics. Such was his warm relationship with McGuinness that the two men were dubbed 'the Chuckle Brothers'. In 2008, Paisley stood down as first minister and DUP leader, and he was replaced by his long-serving deputy, Peter Robinson.

As the DUP changed its leader the UUP began to consider how they could best restore their electoral fortunes. The party needed fresh ideas and a new direction. After much discussion, Cameron and Empey agreed to work together and formed an electoral alliance named UCUNF

– which stood for Ulster Conservatives and Unionists New Force. The aim of this joint enterprise to integrate Northern Ireland into mainstream UK politics. The first outing under this new banner was in 2009, when Jim Nicholson was re-elected as MEP. The next battleground would be the general election.

Trimble supported the move, and at Westminster his focus was to help his colleagues in the Conservative Party return to power after a long absence. Even though he continued to play down suggestions that he would be part of the next government, he was still talked about in the press as a future minister should Cameron win the election.

Privately, the Conservative Party hierarchy was told by Trimble's friends that he would be interested in a government position should one arise. However, when the results of the 2010 general election became clear, Trimble's chance of a ministry disappeared. Voters delivered a hung parliament, and, after intensive discussions, the Conservatives entered a coalition government with the Liberal Democrats. It meant that, as prime minister, Cameron had a smaller number of ministries to allocate, and with a limited choice, Trimble's opportunity had disappeared.

Barry White, who worked for the UUP in Westminster, shared Trimble's frustration:

> I was very upset that he wasn't treated better. I mean, whenever he was unveiled as a Conservative peer he and David Cameron walked up and down College Green and did interviews. And then he was cast adrift. I was told subsequently that, had it not been for the coalition and the lack of jobs available, he would have gone to the Foreign Office.[22]

Empey shared White's view, and felt a place in government should have been offered to Lord Trimble:

> I am still quite angry about that. I think they could easily have done something for him, and I don't think the government gave him the recognition that he deserved.[23]

Daphne Trimble says her husband enjoyed being in the House of Lords and did admit in later years that he was disappointed a ministerial role was never offered by the Conservatives:

> He just loved the Lords. I mean he loved the Commons too. But, in the Lords, he didn't have to worry about his constituency. He didn't have constituency work to do, and he didn't have the pressure, and he wasn't party leader anymore. He joined the Conservative Party and towards the end of his life he did say he slightly regretted having joined the Conservative Party, because he felt they didn't make as much of him as they could have done.[24]

Back in Northern Ireland, the link-up between the Conservatives and the Ulster Unionists did not prove fruitful, and in the 2010 general election the alliance did not deliver a single MP. Empey stood down and would soon join Trimble in the Lords. Once again, after a poor election the Ulster Unionists began looking for a new leader, and in September 2010 Tom Elliott took charge.

In the Lords, Trimble was kept busy and continued to make a series of speeches and interventions on a host of subjects. He spoke in debates about Turkey, North Africa, Libya and often on the European Union, which was increasingly dominating the news agenda.

When legislation relating to Northern Ireland was raised, he made a point of attending and contributing. He was invited to be part of the Turkel Commission, which was an inquiry set up by the Israeli government to investigate a raid on a flotilla of aid ships trying to reach Gaza. Nine Turkish activists were killed during the raid, and the Israeli actions attracted criticism across the world. Trimble and his fellow panel members concluded that the behaviour of the Israeli navy had been legal under international law, but their conclusions were controversial. A separate UN inquiry said the navy had shown an 'unacceptable level of brutality' and Turkish politicians questioned the inquiry's credibility.

Life for Trimble in Westminster was varied and enjoyable, and although he did not have the trappings of office, he felt he was making a contribution to political life. He regularly offered support to the Omagh bomb victims' families, who were pursuing damages in a groundbreaking civil action against a number of men. That brought him into contact with their lawyer, Jason McCue, who says Trimble was invaluable in encouraging him to work on the Omagh case:

> He gave me the confidence. He didn't have a clue about my section of law, it wasn't his law, but he understood the bigger concepts. And he gave me the confidence and the time to sit through and go, 'That is clever, you've got to do it.' And that gives a young man the confidence to go, 'Yes, I'm doing this right.'[25]

The novelty of the Conservative and Liberal Democrat coalition government meant it was an exciting and fascinating time for Trimble to be at Westminster. The issue of Europe continued to dominate the news agenda, and in January 2013 David Cameron promised that there would be a referendum on EU membership if the Conservatives won the next election. The prime minister insisted that the people of the UK should 'have their say', and his move was welcomed by Eurosceptics. Trimble was pleased and welcomed the prospect of a vote.

It was not the only poll Cameron agreed to support. He had already agreed to hold a referendum on Scottish independence in the autumn of 2014 after he struck a deal with the Scottish National Party (SNP) first minister, Alex Salmond. As a committed unionist, Trimble understandably opposed the idea of Scotland leaving the UK, and he routinely spoke out against the prospect of Scottish independence.

As the Scottish independence debate gathered pace, parallels were drawn to the politics of Northern Ireland and the possibilities of a border poll. In May 2014, Trimble warned that a vote for Scottish independence could cause division in Northern Ireland, which he said was now enjoying a period of stability.

Cameron knew there were strong feelings in Scotland for independence, as the opinion polls had suggested, but he believed that ultimately voters would back the status quo. His gut feeling was right, but it was closer than some expected. In September 2014 the result showed that 55 per cent voted No to independence and 45 per cent voted Yes. Cameron was relieved that the campaign for independence had failed, and he declared that it would have 'broken his heart to see our United Kingdom come to an end'.[26]

He said the UK could have tried to block a referendum, but that would not have been democratic, and he added, 'we could have put it off, but just as with other big issues, it was right to take – not duck – the big decision'.[27] Cameron knew there was another 'big decision' waiting.

Eurosceptics looked at the Scottish poll and hoped that a vote on EU membership would be next on Cameron's agenda. He had pledged to hold a vote, but that was dependent on getting back into Downing Street with a majority after the next election.

When the Conservatives were back in power with a 12-seat majority, a referendum on the UK's membership in the EU was finally called, for 23 June 2016, and a new word entered the day-to-day conversation: Brexit. It had first been coined in 2012, but by 2016 it was everywhere and officially became the word of the year, as it summed up Britain's potential departure from the EU.

Trimble was passionately in favour of leaving, and as the referendum date approached, he argued that it was in the UK's interest to go it alone. In Northern Ireland, the majority of parties backed the UK staying in the EU, but the DUP swung in behind the campaign to leave. Trimble's old party, the UUP, believed that 'on balance', Northern Ireland was better remaining in the EU but understood that some individual members might vote to leave.

Weeks before the poll, former prime ministers Sir John Major and Tony Blair visited Northern Ireland and argued that a vote to leave would 'jeopardise the unity' of the UK and potentially put Northern Ireland's 'future at risk'.[28] Trimble and a number of former UUP MPs criticised their invention. A statement signed by Trimble, Lord Kilclooney, Lord

Maginnis, David Burnside and Roy Beggs rejected the suggestion that a vote to leave would undermine peace in Northern Ireland. They accused some in the Remain camp of 'dishonest scaremongering'.[29]

Theresa May, the home secretary who supported staying in the EU, also made a brief visit to Northern Ireland before polling day. Her intervention received limited coverage and across the UK there was scant attention on what Brexit might mean for Northern Ireland and its border with the Republic.

When the result finally came, the pollsters and the media were in shock, as 52 per cent of the electorate voted Leave, while 48 per cent supported Remain.

It was a truly historic moment, and within hours David Cameron resigned as prime minister. He became the first political casualty of Brexit – but he would not be the last. Britain's uneasy relationship with Europe was now entering uncharted territory, and the shockwaves from the result would be felt across the EU and beyond.

However, the outworkings of the result would prove to be far from straightforward. Over the next few years, Brexit would become mired in delays and extensions, and more prime ministerial resignations. The issue would go to court, and Trimble would find himself at the heart of the legal campaign to make Brexit happen.

The question on the referendum ballot paper had been simple – Yes or No – a binary choice. But in the months that followed, the move away from the EU evolved into a tortuous divorce. It became a complicated, unpredictable and incredibly slow process, one which featured political brinkmanship and broken deadlines, but as a veteran of Northern Ireland politics, Trimble was well used to that.

24

THE FINAL DAYS

"'I have a bit of an issue.' I said, "What is that?"
And he said, "I have dementia.""
David Trimble talking to his brother Iain

On Sunday 12 March 2017, David Trimble sat down and wrote a letter to Martin McGuinness. It was no ordinary note but a heartfelt acknowledgement of what he believed the republican had contributed to the peace process.

McGuinness was dying, and in a few days' time thousands of people would gather in his native Derry to mourn him. The Sinn Féin politician had resigned as deputy first minister the previous January, and as a result Northern Ireland's power-sharing government had collapsed. Looking gaunt in front of the cameras, he told journalists he was standing down in protest at the DUP's handling of a botched energy scheme called the Renewable Heat Incentive. He had previously called for Arlene Foster, the then first minster, to stand aside while an investigation took place. She refused to step down, so McGuinness decided that Sinn Féin could not stay in government. He accused the DUP of arrogance and said he had to resign – a move that plunged Stormont into another crisis.

Looking on from Westminster, Trimble, like many other observers, was deeply shocked at the turn of events and taken aback by the change in McGuinness's physical appearance. During his time as UUP leader, Trimble had observed him at close quarters, both in talks negotiations and later in Executive meetings. He now felt he needed to mark what McGuinness had done to secure peace. He wrote:

Like many I was surprised to learn of your illness and of its seriousness.

Then, on reflection, I thought it behoves me, as the first minister when we first achieved devolution to the Assembly created by the Good Friday Agreement some eighteen years ago, to say how much we appreciated all that you did to make that happen. In doing that you reached out to the Unionist community in a way some of them were reluctant to reach out to you.

Without knowing the detail of how the republican movement moved to that point, I and my colleagues believe that you were indispensable.

I will never forget the truly historic first meeting of the Executive and how we approached that seriously and in good humour, marred only by the absence of two ministers. I think that even tempered manner was characteristic of all your time in office, and we knew that it was never at the expense of your principles.

Perhaps the best expression of your approach was your meeting with Queen Elizabeth.[1]

Trimble's letter was warm and direct. It was an acknowledgement that the former IRA commander had genuinely worked for peace and stretched himself politically. There was much reflection on the Derry republican's contribution to peace when his funeral took place at St Columba's Church in his native city on 23 March. It was a large affair, and mourners included the former US president Bill Clinton and Irish president, Michael D. Higgins. When the DUP leader, Arlene Foster, entered the church, she was applauded.

The tone of Trimble's letter was a reminder of how far he had travelled as a politician and a person. It is hard to imagine the David Trimble of Vanguard writing such a note. Yet here he was praising the virtues of a man who for decades had fought to make Northern Ireland ungovernable.

McGuinness's resignation as deputy first minister triggered a snap Assembly election, and the results provided a watershed moment. For the first time in the history of Northern Ireland, unionists no longer held the majority at Stormont. Just 1,600 votes separated the DUP from Sinn Féin, which translated into Foster's party losing 10 seats.

Trimble's old party also fared badly, losing 6 seats and reducing their Stormont tally to 10. The election did little to improve relations between the DUP and Sinn Féin, and devolution remained on hold. Brexit continued to dominate the political agenda at Westminster, and the UK government formally triggered Article 50, which began the two-year countdown to the UK leaving the EU.

Prime Minister Theresa May hoped the process would be smooth, but the issue proved to be difficult and polarising, and it would ultimately end her premiership. However, in April 2017 she was feeling optimistic, and with opinion polls showing the Tories had a good lead over Labour, she called a surprise general election for June.

The gamble did not pay off, as the Conservatives lost their majority in the House of Commons. The political arithmetic meant that May needed help, so a 'confidence and supply' arrangement was agreed with the DUP. Under the agreement, the DUP would support the government on key votes such as the budget, national security and, of course, Brexit. The deal put the DUP's 10 MPs at the top table of British politics and gave them an influence at Westminster beyond their wildest dreams. In return for backing May, an additional £1 billion of public spending was promised for Northern Ireland.

With Brexit on course – or so it seemed – Northern Ireland was an important part of the debate. In December 2017, May said the UK government was committed to 'maintain the common travel area with Ireland, to uphold the Belfast Agreement in full; to avoid a hard border between Northern Ireland and Ireland, while upholding the constitutional and economic integrity of the whole United Kingdom'.[2]

Key questions remained unanswered. Should Northern Ireland have special EU status? Would there be new trading arrangements between Northern Ireland and the rest of the UK? What implications would any deal have on the Good Friday Agreement? Northern Ireland had become the most controversial part of the negotiations.

In February 2018, the EU published a draft withdrawal agreement suggesting that, if no other solutions were found, Northern Ireland would remain part of the EU customs territory. The news was greeted with opposition from Brexit-supporting MPs, and even May said that no UK prime minister could agree to such a move.

In April 2018, Trimble used the 20th anniversary of the Good Friday deal to talk about his concerns:

> What is happening now is that people are talking up the issue of Brexit and the border for the benefit of a different agenda from the agreement. The one thing that would provoke loyalist paramilitaries is the present Irish government saying silly things about the border and the constitutional issue. If it looks as though the constitutional arrangements of the agreement, based on the principle of consent, are going to be superseded by so-called 'special EU status' then that is going to weaken the union and undermine the very agreement that Dublin once said it wants to uphold.[3]

Understandably, Trimble's remarks were rejected by the Irish government. The SDLP leader, Colum Eastwood, went further and accused the former first minister of scaremongering, saying that 'he should know better'. Brexit continued to divide the local parties in Northern Ireland, and in particular it meant relations between Sinn Féin and the DUP remained poor, which did little to improve the chances of devolution being restored.

However, in November 2018, it seemed a way forward had been found in the EU–UK discussions. Both parties agreed that keeping the border open was essential, as was protecting what had been agreed on Good Friday 1998. After intensive talks, Theresa May accepted a withdrawal agreement with the EU which included a 'backstop' plan.

The backstop was aimed at making sure Northern Ireland's border remained open after Brexit. It was designed to stop a 'hard border', if no trade deal had been agreed by the end of the transition period. It would also mean that the UK would remain in the EU Customs Union and Northern Ireland would be in the Single Market until a replacement trade agreement could be reached. This would lead to Northern Ireland having different regulations from the rest of the UK. For unionists and for many in the Conservative Party, that part of the deal was completely unacceptable.

When it came to the House of Commons in January 2019, MPs resoundingly rejected May's plan, by 432 votes to 202. The result went into the record books as the biggest government defeat in British parliamentary history. May's troubles continued in March, when her EU withdrawal deal was rejected by MPs for a second time. Later in the month, she tried again, but it was not third time lucky, as MPs rejected her way forward. She was now running out of time and running out of support.

From the House of Lords, Trimble watched events with growing concern. He believed the backstop violated the principle of consent that was contained in the Good Friday Agreement and said he would mount a legal challenge to fight it. By the summer the issues remained the same, but the personalities had changed. Unable to secure an EU deal that garnered enough support, May resigned, becoming the second prime minister to step down over Europe. Brexit had claimed another scalp.

Her successor would be Boris Johnson, the controversial former foreign secretary, who promised to 'deliver Brexit, unite the country and defeat Jeremy Corbyn'. Johnson, who had coveted the role for years, entered Downing Street, and Trimble had high hopes that the new Tory leader would finally deliver a Brexit deal he could support.

Trimble continued to voice his concerns from the benches of the Lords, and he also wrote about them in a pamphlet published by the think tank Policy Exchange:

> The protocol is not capable of upholding the Good Friday Agreement – it has run a coach and horses through it; it has driven it into the ditch.

> In 1998 we were able to engage with the governments and explain our problems and they listened. The Irish government listened. We worked to create something that would work – and we succeeded: it is just gone 21 years since we agreed it. In contrast, the Protocol emerges out of a closed negotiation, apparently set in stone, with no participation from the communities most affected.[4]

Trimble's thoughts on the protocol appeared in July 2019 – the same month he made headlines for very different reasons, far removed from the debate about Brexit. He rose to speak in the House of Lords in a debate about legalising same-sex marriage in Northern Ireland. The former MP's position was well known, as he had voted against civil partnerships back in 2003 and previously in the UUP had opposed same-sex marriage.

But when he started to talk to his colleagues in the chamber, his comments caught people by surprise, and it soon became clear he was speaking from the heart:

> I have found myself taking a particular position with regard to same-sex marriage which was forced upon me when my elder daughter got married to her girlfriend. Now, I can't change that. And I can't go round saying I'm opposed to that because I acquiesced in it. There you are.[5]

Trimble was talking about his daughter Vicky, who had told her parents back in 2013 that she was gay. She remembers how they responded: 'My dad's reaction was to put his head in his hands.' However, she says her mum, Daphne, did not seem that surprised.[6]

Vicky met photographer Rosalind Stephens in London, and the pair were married at Achnagairn Castle in the Scottish Highlands in November 2017. It was a family occasion and Lord Trimble had given his daughter away. Vicky recalled that having her dad with her made the day particularly special:

> To have my dad support me and to walk up the aisle with him, our wedding was amazing and absolutely the best day of my life. I think if it had been a situation where he wasn't there or he wasn't supportive, that would have been upsetting and marred the day.[7]

Trimble's speech in the House of Lords revealed a very personal insight – something rarely glimpsed when he was UUP leader. It was a moment when his political and private life clashed. His fellow peer Baroness O'Loan, the former police ombudsman for Northern Ireland, remembers the speech well:

> He stood up and made this very simple, very powerful, not terribly long speech in which he declared that he would not oppose the legislation but would support it. And he talked of his daughter, the love he had for his daughter, and I just thought it was one of those rare moments in the House of Lords. People always listened to him very quietly. You know, sometimes when people speak, they mutter a bit. But people always listened to David with great courtesy and interest. On this occasion there was something else there, because he was talking so personally. Because David was not one who wore his heart on his sleeve, and yet that day, it seemed to me, he did.[8]

Baroness O'Loan was not the only peer to have been impressed with his speech. Lord Murphy, the former Northern Ireland secretary, said Trimble's remarks indicated how much the former first minister had changed:

> I thought that was another example of two things. One, to be able to speak out on something which was very personal, and that was unusual for David, because he wouldn't normally talk very much about his personal life

and situation. And, secondly, I think that he was actually willing to do all that publicly, it meant that things have changed. Probably that he'd been wrong and that he'd now accepted what his daughter wanted to do in life.[9]

Vicky Trimble did not know her father was going to talk about her in Westminster. She was tipped off about it in a phone call from her mother:

> I read it before I heard it. And reading it [he] seemed more reticent [than] when you hear it. Also, I was just, 'Wow, Dad has just talked about me in the Lords.' And I think I gave an interview saying he could have said a bit more. But whatever you think about an Ulster Protestant of a certain age, what else is he going to say?[10]

The speech by Trimble received a lot of media coverage, and that was understandable. It was a very surprising development and because of Trimble's background was regarded as newsworthy. Daphne says the speech was an example of her husband putting their family first:

> I think if it hadn't been for Vicky's position David probably wouldn't have thought about same-sex marriage. It wouldn't have been one of the things he felt passionately about. But, you know, if your daughter goes down that route, well, you have to support your daughter. That is it.[11]

Vicky Trimble accepts that her father changed his mind on same-sex marriage because of her personal situation, but also says he acknowledged there was an issue of equality:

> I think for him it may have been realising, you know, this is not fair, if you've got four kids and one of them is not allowed to do the same thing as the other three. It is not fair, is it? So that's where he came from.[12]

Trimble loved life in the Lords, but he also enjoyed getting away from Westminster. He and Daphne continued to spend time on the inland waterways of England, which they had been doing for many years. They had initially purchased a large narrowboat with six berths with its original name, *Doodley*, which the Trimbles were not keen on. This boat was large enough for the family, but they had recently downsized and purchased a smaller boat, which they called *Sine Nomine*. It had a double meaning for the new owners. The name was Latin and meant 'without a name', but it was also the title of a hymn tune written by Vaughan Williams, who was one of David's favourite composers. It was while she was on *Sine Nomine* that Daphne first noticed that David's memory and ability to do certain tasks were not what they once were.

In August 2019, the couple were negotiating the Hatton Flight in Warwickshire, which is a series of 21 locks on the Grand Union Canal. Daphne thought that David was not his normal self and had a 'lack of sharpness'. The next month, the couple travelled to the Mexican city of Mérida for a world summit of Nobel Peace laureates. They were away for seven days, and again Daphne spotted that her husband found the events 'a bit of a struggle', whereas normally he would have enjoyed such occasions. She also thought he was 'a wee bit withdrawn'.[13]

After the summer recess, Boris Johnson promised that he would defy 'the doubters, the doomsters and the gloomsters' by completing Brexit by 31 October. His optimism would be tested, and he would quickly discover that there was no such thing as a quick fix when it came to leaving the EU. He faced opposition not just from the Labour Party but also from a number of high-profile Tory rebels. This meant that his plans to leave the EU by October were quickly defeated, and eventually a new Brexit extension was agreed for 31 January 2020.

A deal was done with the EU, and it meant the transition period would last until the end of 2020, and then the UK would leave both the EU Single Market and the Customs Union. The deal Johnson agreed included a Northern Ireland protocol which would keep Northern Ireland in the EU's Single Market for goods. This was introduced to avoid checks at the border between Northern Ireland and the Republic.

It meant that, on 1 January 2021, after the transition period, a new Irish sea border would come into effect. The protocol understandably angered unionists: they felt betrayed by Johnson, who was heavily criticised. However, December brought the Tory leader an early Christmas present when he won a majority in the general election, and he promised again to 'get Brexit done'.

In January 2020, the Trimbles were off on their travels again. David had been invited to speak in Saudi Arabia and Daphne joined him to make sure everything went as planned. After observing changes in her husband on their narrow boat, and in Mexico, she was keen to be with him. Again, Daphne noticed that David did not appear to be 'as sharp as normal'.[14]

Back in Northern Ireland, there was a political breakthrough when a deal involving Sinn Féin and the DUP helped to see devolution return to Stormont. A new Executive was formed, with the two larger parties joined by Alliance, the UUP and the SDLP. For the DUP's Arlene Foster and Sinn Féin's Michelle O'Neill, it was an opportunity to start afresh after a three-year break.

As O'Neill settled into her new role as deputy first minister, the life of one of her predecessors captured the news agenda. Seamus Mallon, who had been in the role with Trimble from 1998 to 2001, died on 24 January after a short illness. Days before, Trimble had visited him at his home in Markethill in County Armagh. He described the former SDLP MP as someone who was 'committed to peaceful democratic politics – that was why he was such good parliamentarian'.[15]

In February 2020, the Trimbles were back overseas. They flew to Luxor and then went to explore Ancient Egypt with a cruise on the Nile. Daphne recalls that her husband was in 'good form'. However, passengers began to get anxious about the news that a dangerous new strain of the coronavirus, which had begun in China, was now spreading quickly to other countries.

Covid-19, as it came to be known, was now in many places, including the UK, Australia, Japan, Singapore and the United States, and the Trimbles and their fellow passengers were encouraged to use hand sanitisers and exercise caution. Within days, the UK was dealing with the biggest public health challenge it had ever faced. On 23 March, Boris Johnson took to the airwaves and announced a national lockdown. It meant that people could only leave their homes for limited reasons.

Life came to a crashing halt as schools and offices and restaurants were closed and people got used to working from home remotely. Everyone was urged to practise social distancing, regularly wash their hands and wear a mask. Like millions of other families, the Trimbles (who returned from their cruise just before lockdown) stayed at home and self-isolated. As a peer, David tried to contribute to the House of Lords by using remote online technology, but he often found it difficult to operate, impersonal and rather cumbersome. He much preferred visiting the Palace of Westminster in person when he was allowed to do so.

Politically, Trimble was concentrating on one thing: Brexit and the protocol. He was deeply concerned that the new arrangements would undermine the Good Friday Agreement that he had negotiated. There was much reflection on the 1998 deal when John Hume died in August 2020. Hume, who had dementia, spent his final days in a care home just outside his native Derry, and his funeral on 5 August was conducted under Covid guidelines. According to Trimble:

> Right at the outset of our Troubles, John made it clear he was committed to democratic means and peaceful means.[16]

The Brexit debate continued in the autumn of 2020, but it was conducted in the surreal atmosphere of the global pandemic. In November 2020, a second lockdown was introduced, and all non-essential shops and leisure and entertainment venues were shut. Much attention then focused on how people would spend Christmas, and initially Johnson asked people to keep their celebrations 'short' and 'small'.

Then the rules changed, and much tighter regulations were introduced. The Trimbles had originally planned to spend Christmas in Nottingham with their daughter Sarah and her family, but the rule change meant that David, Daphne and Vicky stayed in London.

Daphne recalls that, ultimately, their celebrations over Christmas were low key and 'a bit miserable'.[17] Their experience was repeated across the country, as families were split up during Christmas in a bid to stop Covid spreading.

The beginning of 2021 marked a major landmark in the Brexit story. The transition period ended on 1 January, and the EU and UK trade deal came into operation. The agreement included the Northern Ireland Protocol, much to the continued anger of many unionists. In February, the DUP leader and first minister, Arlene Foster, called on Johnson to scrap the protocol and urged him to take on board their concerns:

> I hope they're listening to the voice of David Trimble and me as first minister because I'm really concerned about where the unionist community is at present.[18]

In April 1998, when it came to the Good Friday Agreement, they had been on different sides, but now Foster and Trimble were united – on the issue of Brexit. Trimble began working with other like-minded unionists and launched a legal challenge against the UK government over the implementation of the protocol. The group included the UUP leader, Steve Aiken; the Traditional Unionist Voice (TUV) leader, Jim Allister; the DUP's Nigel Dodds and his colleagues Sammy Wilson and Sir Jeffrey Donaldson. They were joined by Baroness Hoey and former MEP Ben Habib.

When it was possible, Trimble travelled to Westminster at the start of most weeks and spent a number of days in the Lords before returning home to Northern Ireland. As a seasoned traveller, he knew London's underground system well, but on one occasion on the Tube he became disorientated and did not know where he was. He told Daphne about the incident and, understandably, she was very concerned. It was another indication that all was not well.

By the spring of 2021, Trimble's children were also beginning to notice that their father had changed. Richard says he spotted changes when he was chatting to his dad:

> After one of the lockdowns was lifted, I was just catching up with Dad again. I was thinking that he was making mistakes in his speech, and he was not quite as sharp as he was before, and that was a bad moment.[19]

Vicky also felt that her father's behaviour seemed different:

> He was just doing strange things, and we all noticed. But none of us were able to tell him, to say, 'Can you go to the doctor?' Because he wasn't the sort of person to go to the doctor. I think what really made him go was I went to the flat in London and it had been vacant for several months. There had been nobody there and the front door was open, unlocked and open.[20]

Trimble had forgotten to secure his London apartment and had returned to Northern Ireland. Aware that he needed a medical opinion, in April 2021 he went to see a specialist in a Belfast hospital. The news was not unexpected, but it was still deeply upsetting. He was diagnosed with mixed dementia, which is a combination of Alzheimer's disease and vascular dementia. He was put on a drug called rivastigmine, which is a patch applied to the skin, and this appeared to stabilise his condition.

A scan in June revealed the full extent of the disease, but the medics and the family remained hopeful that the continued use of the patches would slow its progression. Iain Trimble remembers his brother confiding in him that he had Alzheimer's:

> I started to notice that he was missing the odd word in telephone conversations a few years before I discovered what it was. I discovered what it was in 2021. That is when he took me to one side in the garden of his house and told me. He said, 'I have a bit of an issue'. I said, 'What is that?' And he said, 'I have dementia.' So, I said, 'What? Alzheimer's?' And he said, 'Yes.'[21]

In the autumn Trimble began to experience eating difficulties, and he had several scans and bronchoscopies. He had been losing weight, but he told Daphne that it was intentional, and he was happy about being lighter. In October the couple went on a cruise to the Canaries, and on his return to Westminster, Trimble continued with his campaign to have the protocol scrapped. However, his parliamentary colleagues noticed he had changed, and they spotted he was getting confused. It was suggested that he should consider retiring from the House of Lords, but he would not entertain the idea. In fact, he felt hurt by the suggestions.

Around this time in Belfast, Queen's University began to consider how best to mark the 25th anniversary of the Good Friday Agreement, which would occur in April 2023. The university wanted to mark Trimble's role in securing the agreement and ensure his legacy was celebrated. Senior figures at the university wanted to forge a better relationship with the former UUP leader after years of distance. Daphne and David met with the vice-chancellor, Professor Ian Greer, and the vice-president of governance and external affairs, Ryan Feeney, and over lunch a series of initiatives was agreed. Trimble agreed to accept a professorship from the university, and there would also be a lecture series in his name.

Queen's also wanted to commission a portrait of the former first minister which would hang in the Great Hall. Colin Davidson, a Northern Irish painter who had an international reputation, was commissioned to create the portrait. Davidson had previously painted figures including Queen Elizabeth and the former US president Bill Clinton, and he had also painted Trimble's fellow Nobel laureate John Hume.

The original plan was to have an unveiling of Trimble's portrait in the autumn of 2022 at the inaugural Professor Lord David Trimble lecture. However, that date would soon be revised, as it was clear Trimble was not well. As 2021 ended, the Trimbles were determined to have an enjoyable family Christmas to make up for the previous year. Although Trimble was not well, he did not want to spoil the festive spirit.

Richard remembers his father coming to the dinner table:

Dad was really quite unwell. And on Christmas Day he really should have been in bed, but he came down for Christmas dinner in his suit with a waistcoat on. And then he went and got the best bottle of bubbly out of the garage [and] he was popping it off and saying, 'Let's fill your glass up.' He was just trying to have Christmas dinner the way it always was. He really made it, in retrospect, you know. He was really pushing himself to do that, to be together as a family at Christmas time. And he really just wanted family time the same way as it would normally be.[22]

Nicky remembers that time very well, and wondering if it would be their last Christmas together:

> I remember sort of thinking, 'I'm not sure he'll even make it to next Christmas.' It turned out he didn't make it to the next Christmas. That was the last Christmas. And I think Dad must have felt that that was a real possibility.[23]

In the New Year, Colin Davidson got to work on his portrait of Lord Trimble. He was under pressure, as it was a tight deadline, and he was keen to make progress. He began the process by visiting the Trimbles at their home:

> I wanted to see David Trimble behind the façade, so it was important it was in his house, and it was important he talked about what he wanted to talk about. But immediately he started to talk about the music. He was surrounded by an immense collection of classical music. He talked about the operas. It seemed like hundreds of operas that Daphne and he had gone to over the years. He had a passion for it. He was visibly and deeply moved by a lot of music, because we had the music on in the background, and he was transported. He was in another

realm. He was truly himself, and I think that's the David Trimble that I wanted to paint.[24]

Early 2022 brought the Trimbles devastating news. David had gone through a series of tests, and the latest scan had revealed that he had a worrying shadow on his chest. His daughter Sarah, who worked as a pharmacist, feared the worst:

> When they saw a shadow on his chest, that was maybe a bit tough for me, because I kind of knew where it was probably going to be headed before we got the confirmation that it was cancer. Working in a hospital, from what I knew his scans had been like, it sounded quite likely that's what it was going to be. But we hadn't actually had the diagnosis at that point. That was a bit tough when he did finally get it. I think he was always a bit of a reluctant patient. I think at heart my dad was very much an optimist. And I think he just assumed that whatever it was, he would be fine.[25]

Trimble had lung cancer, but it was decided he was not well enough for surgery, as the cancer was too far advanced. He began chemotherapy in February 2022, and as Daphne recalls, 'he made light of it. As far as he was concerned everything was fine'.

Richard says that, although his father put on a brave face, he was well aware what having lung cancer meant:

> I think for us we were terrified of the dementia. But Dad was actually more terrified of the lung cancer, because lung cancer is what took his dad – my grandfather. He was dead before I was born, so I never met him. Dad was terrified because of having watched his dad die of lung cancer in quite a lot of agony, because end-of-life care in those days was not as good as it is today.[26]

In March, Trimble travelled to Westminster, accompanied by Vicky. He went to the House of Lords and spent some time at the Athenaeum Club, which was an important part of his life in London. He enjoyed being back amongst his fellow peers, but the trip came with a heavy price. When he and Vicky returned to Northern Ireland, they had Covid, and as a result David was later admitted to the Royal Victoria Hospital in Belfast.

By mid-May he had recovered well enough to go on another cruise. Daphne was determined to seize every opportunity to travel. She says her husband never talked about death:

> He wasn't for dying. We had holidays. The doctors never said to him, 'This is a death sentence.' They talked about 'Do you want to do the chemotherapy?' And he said, 'Yes.' And they never talked about time scale. David and I never talked about time scale. I don't know what was in his mind or what he thought. But the chemotherapy was actually starting, and they had reduced the size of the tumour.[27]

The Trimbles took a Baltic cruise and visited Copenhagen, Tallinn and Helsinki. They were initially supposed to go to St Petersburg, but that was cancelled because of the war in Ukraine. However, they did get to Oslo, which gave the couple the opportunity to revisit some of the places they first saw when David was awarded the Nobel Peace Prize in 1998.

As they made their way to the Nobel Museum it started to rain, and they arrived only to discover that the museum is always shut on a Monday. They were naturally disappointed and sheltered from the thunderstorm before heading to the Grand Hotel – where they had stayed back in 1998. They went inside the hotel to get some lunch, and, as Daphne recalls, the staff looked after them wonderfully:

> They made a fuss of us, and it was lovely. The waiter came and spoke to us, and then one of the managers said how nice it was to have us back again. A fellow diner who chatted to us paid for our lunch, which was most generous.

Then the hotel organised a taxi back to the ship. It was a great way to end the day in Oslo.[28]

It was quite the return to the Norwegian capital for the Trimbles, after a gap of nearly 24 years. At the end of the cruise – which was their last together – they returned to the UK and attended a series of social events in London. They were invited to take part in the celebrations for the Queen's platinum jubilee, and there was a family day at the Athenaeum Club, which they enjoyed with some of their grandchildren.

The Trimbles then came back to Northern Ireland, as they had an important appointment at Queen's University. Colin Davidson had finished David's portrait, and they were understandably very keen to see it.

25

PORTRAIT OF A PEACEMAKER

'History will be exceedingly kind to David.'
Reverend Dr Charles McMullan at the funeral of Lord Trimble

On a spring day in 2022, Daphne and David Trimble made their way to South Belfast. They were both returning to their alma mater – a place that meant a great deal to them. It was where they had studied and where they met and took the first steps in their relationship.

Queen's University was part of their story. For David it was a place of mixed emotion. He loved his time teaching there but felt his potential as an academic was never recognised by the authorities. He had been overlooked for promotion three times and would have loved to have been a professor. He also believed his time as a politician and peacemaker had never been fully acknowledged. That was about to change.

Colin Davidson had finished the portrait, and before it was publicly unveiled the Trimbles were given a private viewing. They were joined by Davidson and Lord Bew, and also by Sir Ian Greer and Ryan Feeney from Queen's University.

The portrait was initially covered, and Davidson remembers revealing his work:

> It was a very informal unveiling. I think I said a few words and just pulled the velvet cloth off. And they were both visibly moved, really visibly moved at that point. And they got what the painting was about. Because the painting for me captured the human being in that room that day

in February, talking to me passionately about the things that he loved.[1]

Thrilled by what they had been shown, the Trimbles then joined the others in the room for some lunch. Feeney remembers the conversation:

> During the lunch I was struck by how emotional David had become, often pausing to collect himself as Paul [Lord Bew] and Daphne stepped in to continue the conversation. As we planned the event, David made four requests: that Paul Bew delivered the first lecture; that Arlene Foster be invited to the lecture and dinner; that the participants from the Good Friday Agreement talks, including Bertie Ahern, be present; and finally, that he had to sign off the guest list.[2]

On 27 June 2022, the portrait was publicly unveiled at Queen's University in front of the Trimble family, invited guests and the media. It was a star-studded affair which attracted much coverage. There were video messages from former US president Bill Clinton, former prime minister Sir Tony Blair and Prime Minister Boris Johnson.

Richard Trimble was there that night and says that, although his dad was clearly not well, he was determined to enjoy the moment:

> I think for that evening he was just pulling out all his energy, really, just to enjoy that and lap that up. And you know his eyes were just so bright, you know, that evening. He was absolutely loving it and just relishing it, and why not?[3]

The event at Riddel Hall was attended by numerous politicians, including former UUP leaders Robin Swann, Mike Nesbitt and Steve Aiken and the ex-SDLP leader Mark Durkan. Former taoiseach Bertie Ahern was also there and got to spend some time with Trimble that evening. Ahern sensed he was coming to say goodbye to an old friend:

I said, 'David, you've given your life, a good part of your life, to politics. You showed huge leadership, huge strength. We wouldn't have been able to bring peace to Northern Ireland and bring peace to the island without you, and whatever about the ups and downs that we all have in politics, you showed really outstanding leadership.' He wasn't able to respond or talk much at that stage, but he really appreciated it, and I was delighted to be able to do that. He told me straight that day – not that I didn't know, because I was told to come – but he told me straight he had cancer, and he was gone. I thanked him for his friendship over the years and he thanked me for sticking with him. It was kind of sad, but it was nice at the same time.[4]

As Trimble had requested, the DUP leader Baroness Foster was invited to the event, which she says 'was most gracious of him'. The Queen's University graduate, who had also served as first minister and spent a lifetime in unionist politics, had much in common with the man being honoured:

It was a very emotional night, because we could all see he wasn't well, and it was really important for him that he was recognised in the place that meant so much to him, because he'd been a law lecturer there and because of his friendship with Edgar Graham. I think it was a really emotional night for him and the family.[5]

Others who had worked with David Trimble over the years were also invited, including former civil servant Colin Ross, who had been Trimble's principal press officer when he was first minister. Ross waited until Trimble had posed for some photographs and then spoke to him:

I said to him, 'I just want you to know that, if I could do it all again, if it was all possible, if we could roll back time and I could be there for you again, I would 100 times over. I loved every minute of it. Thank you and God bless you', and he nodded.[6]

David Kerr who had worked for Trimble for six years was there that night. At a dinner that evening he paid his own personal tribute:

> I believe history will be kind to you, David. You aren't the first politician to be under-appreciated in your lifetime and you won't be the last. Those of us who served alongside you know how tough the journey was. When we came to that fork in the road in April 1998, you took the road less travelled and that has made all the difference. Northern Ireland is an immeasurably better place today because of it.[7]

For the Trimble family the portrait unveiling helped to finally mark David's long association with Queen's University and recognise his political record. As Nicky Trimble remarked, it was about the university hierarchy wanting to 'take steps to acknowledge Dad. I think that healed an old sore for him.' The unveiling was poignant and understandably emotional, and there was a sense that people were saying goodbye to David Trimble.

No one knew at the time, but it would be his last public appearance. After the excitement of that June evening, Trimble's health worsened and the family were very concerned, as his daughter Sarah recalled:

> He had a little bit of a cough whilst I was there, and he had a temperature. He was trying to say, 'Oh, I'm absolutely fine, I don't need to go into hospital.' And I was saying, 'You need to go in.' Because basically, once you have chemo, if you have a temperature it can lead to an infection and can take hold quickly. So, I was the one that forced Mum to take him into hospital to get checked

over. Because I thought, 'If he's got a temperature there's something brewing.'[8]

Trimble was admitted to hospital, and even though he was not well his spirits were high. He believed his stay was temporary, and he and Daphne talked about a holiday:

> On the day that he died we had decided on a cruise in the Med for December. So, he had no notion of dying, but he had an infection, and they just couldn't get antibiotics strong enough to kill the infection.[9]

On Monday 25 July 2022, his condition deteriorated, and he died.

The Trimble children had not expected him to die so quickly. Vicky thought at one stage her dad would be around for some time: 'I thought he was going to be running up and down the Lords until his late eighties or early nineties.'[10]

Richard says his dad was convinced that he was going to recover:

> His mindset was definitely not 'I am about to die.' He was very much 'I've been in hospital and I'm going to come out again.'[11]

As they coped with their grief, the family were tasked with organising a funeral that they knew would be attended by leading figures from the British and Irish establishment. They understood it would be a massive news story, and it required much thought and organisation. The plan was that the congregation would be a mix of public figures alongside their neighbours, friends and church members. Afterwards all the mourners would gather for refreshments in the church hall.

However, a representative of the UK government wanted special treatment for high-ranking politicians, and the Trimble family said no, as Richard recalls:

> They wanted to have a separate room afterwards for all the dignitaries. And I said, 'This is a Presbyterian Church. You can be in the church hall with everyone else.'[12]

Daphne remembers hearing about the request for senior figures to be given their own private space:

> We weren't going to have the prime minister stuck in a wee room when people would have wanted to see him, so we said no to that. It is not us. It is not what we would have wanted. Everybody is there to take part in the funeral and treat everybody the same.[13]

A week after Trimble's death was announced, hundreds of mourners gathered at Harmony Hill Presbyterian Church in Lisburn for a service of thanksgiving. The family were joined by friends and David's former colleagues in the UUP and the Conservative Party and there were many politicians from other parties. Irish President Michael D. Higgins was there along with Taoiseach Micheál Martin and Bertie Ahern. Sinn Féin's Gerry Adams attended, as did the SDLP leader, Colum Eastwood, and Alliance's Stephen Farry. DUP leader, Sir Jeffrey Donaldson – once Trimble's severest critic in the UUP – was also there to pay his respects. Prime Minister Boris Johnson, in his final days in office, came with other ministers, and they were treated the same as the other mourners.

During the service, all four Trimble children gave bible readings, and the Reverend Dr Charles McMullen spoke of Lord Trimble's legacy:

> The reward for all of us has been a radically changed landscape here in Northern Ireland, which has saved many lives and allowed a generation to grow up in relative peace. As so many have said over these past few days, history will be exceedingly kind to David.[14]

The peer and Trimble biographer Lord Godson also addressed the congregation. He told mourners:

> David Trimble, whose earthly remains lie before us today, was the most prestigious and substantial figure thrown up by unionism since the foundation of Northern Ireland. The first to enjoy a global reputation.

He concluded his remarks by saying:

> David was not cold and uncaring. He cared more, loved more, than any politician I have ever known, but critically, like his religious faith, he rarely showed it. The Psalms of King David and the sayings of the Prophets, which was so much part of his faith and culture, have been read beautifully today by his children and others. He also knew the Book of Proverbs, and these timeless words are a fitting end for William David Trimble: 'a good name is more desirable than great riches, to be esteemed is better than silver or gold'. David leaves this world with the blessing of a good name here on earth.[15]

So, what should we make of David Trimble's contribution to public life in Northern Ireland, and how should we assess his legacy?

He was the 12th leader of the Ulster Unionist Party, and as Lord Godson declared at his thanksgiving service, he was the first to enjoy a reputation that went around the world. The Upper Bann MP was the first person to hold the title of first minister and the only unionist leader to be a Nobel laureate.

He took the unionist cause to parts of the globe that, before him, pro-union politicians either had deliberately stayed away from or were never invited to. He was no stranger to the United States and was keen to promote an alternative view of Northern Ireland to an audience more familiar with the Irish nationalist argument. He had watched John Hume successfully cultivate Irish America, and Trimble believed the unionist position had been largely abandoned in the United States. He established an office there whose sole task was to present the unionist case to American policymakers and the US media. Nancy Soderberg, who worked in the White House as deputy national security adviser, observed Trimble on his visits to the United States:

> I watched him emerge from a position of obstinacy in his early visits to the White House, to one who took real risks for peace. His good humour, stubborn determination to get to yes, and commitment to ensure the rights of the unionist community were protected made his place in history secure.[16]

When Trimble became the youngest leader of the UUP in 1995 he wanted to make the party more professional, and he approached his early days at the helm with much energy. He was the most talented of the leadership candidates and was best placed to take the party into the twenty-first century. It became clear under Trimble's leadership that he wanted all-party talks to work and that an essential part of any deal was an elected body with an attached power-sharing government. He had long accepted that unionists could not run Northern Ireland by themselves, and that nationalists were an essential part of any new dispensation. He believed majority rule did not work in a divided society.

On Good Friday 1998, Trimble was able to tick off much of his wish list. He negotiated the amendment of Articles 2 and 3 of the Irish Constitution, secured a new North–South relationship and established the adoption of the consent principle, and a new Assembly and Executive were created. Baroness Hoey, who was born in Northern Ireland and canvassed for the Good Friday Agreement, says Trimble's place in history is assured: 'He will not be someone who, as time goes by, will be forgotten. And what he did will outlast many of the people who have criticised him.'[17]

So, was Trimble a unique UUP leader? Could any other unionist leader have endorsed such changes and then later faced down critics in his own party at the numerous UUC meetings? Lord Empey says only Trimble had the character and ability to do that:

> There was nobody else on the scene at that stage who could have ridden the charger towards the enemy lines the way he did. And he made it clear to me and to others that as long as he could get a majority of one at each stage he was going to continue. And if he couldn't get them there, he'd go to the council, so he was determined to find a way.[18]

The SDLP's Dolores Kelly, who stood against Trimble in Upper Bann, agrees with Lord Empey's analysis:

> I think Trimble may well have been the only one that could have done it, and probably in part because of Drumcree and how he came forward. He had the street cred of being a hardliner in Vanguard, and he'd been on that journey, and he was able to bring others with him, but I think the governments and the IRA in particular let him down.[19]

Trimble always insisted that he secured much at Castle Buildings in 1998 – but what about the parts of the deal that caused him the most problems, notably decommissioning, policing and the early release of prisoners? These were the most contentious issues that created the greatest friction within the unionist community, and ultimately led to the collapse of the UUP.

Lee Reynolds, who began life in the UUP and once ran for the party leadership, was a critic of the Good Friday Agreement. He later joined the DUP and firmly believes the deal was bad for unionism and believes Trimble was a poor negotiator:

> He thought once he had something negotiated down on paper then a series of things flowed from it in the implementation stage, which isn't the way politics worked. You

know the thing that [Peter] Robinson got is you negotiate before a deal, during a deal and after a deal. Trimble never did the after, and then it's back to a whole series of little mini deals. He kept making mini deals that weren't particularly good.[20]

Other critics of Trimble argue that the building blocks of the Good Friday Agreement were flawed and suggest the deal cannot produce good government. Philip Black was once a colleague of Trimble's in the Ulster Clubs. He has consistently opposed the 1998 deal:

It institutionalises sectarianism, prevents normal politics developing and keeps us at each other's throats in that sense, until the only point, which is envisaged in that agreement, which is a united Ireland takes place. So, I mean, looking at it from the overall point of view it was a complete disaster.[21]

Baroness Foster insists Trimble got key parts of the 1998 deal right regarding Northern Ireland's status with the UK. She says he was correct to secure the consent principle concerning any change to Northern Ireland's status – but feels there were other issues which Trimble failed to deal with properly:

David got the constitutional issue right, and the consent principle, that was the one big thing, absolutely, he got it right. I've always said that, right through it. But what he didn't understand was the significance of letting prisoners out and the victims, how they would feel about it. The legacy issue, which is still around today, is as a result of that.[22]

Should Trimble have held out for a better deal on prisoners? Had such a deal been linked to decommissioning, could that have prevented the endless delays to devolution and stopped Stormont collapsing? Could it also have strengthened Trimble's position within unionism? The former prime minister Sir Tony Blair insists that any linkage between prisoners and guns back in 1998 would not have secured a deal:

> [Sir Tony Blair:] I could have said to the republicans, 'You're not getting the prisoners out until there is full decommissioning', but I can absolutely assure you we would not have had the Good Friday Agreement.
>
> [Stephen Walker:] You're convinced by that?
>
> [Sir Tony Blair:] Yes, I'm sure of it. Because I got to know Adams and McGuinness reasonably well by then, and, by the way, I always felt (and this used to enrage David when I would say this), but I always felt with them that they were pretty straight with me.[23]

Bertie Ahern recalls how the issue of decommissioning hung over the political process for years. Looking back, he thinks there should have been a time limit for decommissioning contained in the Good Friday deal:

> [Bertie Ahern:] There didn't have to be linkage. What should have happened is when we said all prisoners will be released in two years, we should have equally said on decommissioning that decommissioning will take place in two years. That is all we needed to do. And if we had done that, it would have made life so much easier for David afterwards.
>
> [Stephen Walker:] Because decommissioning ended up damaging him and his party, didn't it?
>
> [Bertie Ahern:] Oh, totally, and particularly him. I mean, decommissioning was always going to happen, but it was the fact that we had to drag it out.[24]

Gerry Adams, the former Sinn Féin president, insists that IRA decommissioning could not have happened any sooner:

> At his [Trimble's] funeral, I was walking out with a guy who introduced himself to me, he was from County Down, he was a friend of David's, and he said to me: 'You know wasn't it an awful pity that decommissioning could not have been done sooner?' And I said, 'Well, it couldn't have been. It was just not possible to get it done, except the way it was eventually done.'[25]

For years during his UUP leadership Trimble's negotiating hand was guided by votes at the UUC. The unwieldy decision-making body of the UUP often gave him a slim majority to carry on. Made up of ordinary party members from across Northern Ireland, they were in many ways the unsung heroes of the peace process, as they kept backing their leader and kept the political prospect alive when at times it looked finished.

In an interview in 2015, Trimble admitted that those meetings were necessary but meant that he neglected other parts of his job:

> I probably spent too much time on the party when I should have been spending it on the public. We knew we were going to have these challenges, and we knew we were going to have to win them, and I had to spend a lot of time and internal meetings before each gathering of the UUC. That was important because again it was primarily the activists who were backing me and allowing me to win successive votes.[26]

Even though he had to spend much time on internal party debates, Trimble still fared much better than the last unionist to lead a power-sharing government. In 1974, Brian Faulkner did not have the level of party support that Trimble regularly secured, and ultimately, he parted ways with the UUP. Trimble got a much better deal than Faulkner regarding North–South arrangements. The referendum vote in 1998 gave the Good Friday Agreement a strong public endorsement – which was something Sunningdale never got.

So how does Trimble compare to other UUP leaders? From a middle-class background, he was far removed from some of the UUP's former leaders, such as James Chichester-Clark, Terence O'Neill and Viscount Brookeborough, who all came from land-owning stock. Trimble's leadership victory in 1995 was seen as a step change, and he initially talked about party reform – although little actually happened. As a risk-taker, he was a complete contrast to his immediate predecessor, the conservative and cautious Jim Molyneaux.

Throughout his time in charge of the party, Trimble showed a pragmatism that previous leaders had not displayed. He enjoyed Westminster and being an MP, but it is clear he found his time in the first minister's office frustrating due to the stop-start nature of devolution. He never seemed to really enjoy the position.

Lord Rogan, his long-time friend, thinks he was a reluctant office-holder:

> I'm not sure his mind was totally on it, to be honest with you. And I also think perhaps if things had turned out better or different he might not even have wanted it. He never struck me as someone who wanted power.[27]

Daphne Trimble has a very similar view:

> Being first minister of Northern Ireland was not his ambition in life. It was something that he had to do. He didn't enjoy the day-to-day first minister stuff. I mean, he didn't do the whole thing so he could be first minister.[28]

Shortly before Trimble died, Mark Durkan, the former SDLP leader, visited him in his Lisburn home. They talked about the times they shared and the pressures of leadership, and Durkan joked about the large number of UUC meetings Trimble had to deal with, telling him that:

> 'On Catholic terms that was a novena. And we were praying for you on every one of them.' So, he had at best a mild chuckle at that. And then he went off into some pensive distance somewhere and I just thought, 'He's thinking about that series of pressurised tightropes he walked in that period.' Because he just stared. He seemed to be just lost in a bit of deep thought. And then he just spoke, and he didn't look at me fully when he was speaking. He just said, 'All those hundreds of ordinary unionists showed judgement and took risks, and nobody else has really given them credit for it.' And he turned round, and he looked at me, and the eyes widened, and the eyebrows raised, and that was his way of [saying,] 'Take that point'.[29]

Trimble acknowledged he made tactical mistakes. He believed the party should have been more astute about and cognisant of the changes to policing. He admitted they should have kept a closer eye on the Patten commission to try to minimise the hurt felt by RUC families over the name and badge changes. In terms of going into government without decommissioning in November 1999, Trimble accepted that there were strong arguments that the party should have been tougher:

> And that I think is probably the point at which you would have a significant number of people in the party saying, 'No, we should have toughed that out.' And then of course the other big point is when you come to the autumn of 2003. Was it wise to engage with republicans on a sequence there? [When a decommissioning sequence broke down] that is one point where I have to say that given the opportunity, I would have done things differently.[30]

Trimble also accepted that he made errors on some party matters. He said he should have tried harder to persuade Ken Maginnis and John Taylor to stay on as MPs in 2001 in an attempt to keep crucial seats in UUP hands. He also felt he should have stood down as UUP leader in 2003.

Trimble often approached politics the same way he had viewed his time in academia and would use the law and legal precedent to back up his argument or position. He would often say things as a constitutional lawyer rather than a party leader. There would be occasions when he had worked out the consequences of a decision way ahead of his colleagues.

David Kerr, who worked closely with Trimble, said his ability to be far-sighted was very impressive:

> You have to understand the man that he was. He was highly intelligent, probably on the spectrum in terms of his level of intelligence, a highly intelligent man. He was able to read documents faster than anybody. He was able to properly process information and see through issues and see beyond issues further and faster than anybody.[31]

Dr Graham Gudgin was another who was in awe of Trimble's ability to remember detail and read documents:

> He was a difficult man to like because he wasn't communicating. I think he was on some sort of autistic spectrum. He had a phenomenal memory, better than anybody I met in Cambridge.[32]

His long-time supporter Ruth Dudley Edwards says he was a 'most obliging, kind friend' but 'never got signals'. She said a number of colleagues had told Trimble they thought he was neurodivergent:

> David said to me in later years, 'They tell me I'm autistic and I probably am, rather.'[33]

His critics would say this intellectual approach meant he was at times cerebral when he should have been a more 'hands on' leader – but that was not Trimble's personality. He was shy and awkward to the point that some initially found him rude and standoffish. He could be visionary, reactionary, charming and combative, all in the one day. He could be stubborn – or, to use a good Ulster word, he could be *thran*, meaning obstinate or cranky.

However, he developed as a politician and became able to relax in company, even though it was not something that came naturally to him. He was an untypical political leader, as Alastair Campbell recalled:

> In many ways he was an odd guy. He wasn't a natural politician. You know, you look at his background, you look at his lifestyle: he was a very odd peacemaker. He could be unbelievably infuriating and difficult and complicated, but he could be warm, funny and self-deprecating.[34]

Trimble's greatest qualities were his courage and persistence. He took big decisions that other leaders would have baulked at. He also had a desire to see the political process through, even when the easier option would have been to step aside. As an elected representative he felt a sense of duty to his constituents, which perhaps explains why he did not quit earlier.

Mark Fullbrook, who worked with the UUP on campaigning and elections, says Trimble took decisions based on what was right for the country rather than what gave him a political advantage:

> He had a choice. He could do what was good for his career or he could do what would destroy his career but what was the right thing to do. And sadly, I would say that 95 cent of the politicians I've met would take what's best for their career.[35]

The political architecture that Trimble agreed to in 1998 remains in place today. Northern Ireland enjoys an imperfect peace, and Sinn

Féin and the DUP, as the two largest parties, command the lion's share of Executive posts. The UUP is a shadow of the party Trimble inherited when he took over the leadership in 1995.

Some 30 years on, the Ulster Unionist Party is a diminished force, particularly in urban areas like Belfast, and for a movement that once dominated Northern Ireland politics it is in poor health. Over the last two decades it has tried different leaders, but the party's fortunes have not dramatically improved. Many voters who deserted the UUP for the DUP have simply not returned. Many young unionist voters find the DUP a more attractive option. Trimble's critics say he must bear responsibility for the party's fall in fortunes. John Hunter, who was once a close friend of Trimble's, says his strategy killed the party: 'He was a disaster for unionism. He was responsible for the destruction of the UUP and the weakening of the union.'[36]

Despite the decline of unionism's oldest party, Sir Tony Blair says Trimble will always be remembered as the unionist who took the biggest risks:

> The most important thing for David and his legacy is just to understand that, ultimately, he delivered this thing. Ian Paisley didn't. David did it. Ultimately, I mean, Ian Paisley did in the end, because he believed his own community wanted to do the deal with [Martin] McGuinness. But the risks were taken by David. You know, he was the person that put his whole career on the line. He won the Nobel Peace Prize.[37]

So, did Trimble really deserve the ultimate peace prize alongside John Hume? The SDLP's Bríd Rodgers, who served as an Executive minister and ran in Upper Bann against Trimble, is in no doubt:

> He absolutely deserved the Nobel Peace Prize, because he did what many political leaders would never do. He sacrificed his own political future for the good of the people.[38]

While politically Trimble was poles apart from his fellow Nobel laureate John Hume, the two men had similar lives. Both were single-minded and determined to take certain routes despite internal and external pressure. Both had vision and an ability to think strategically and understood the need for compromise. Hume persisted with the peace process and his talks with Gerry Adams despite endless criticism and some vitriolic news coverage. Trimble stuck with the Good Friday Agreement and devolution, despite intense pressure from the DUP and internal party dissent. Both political leaders had staying power, or what Mark Durkan famously coined 'stickability'. Hume and Trimble were far-sighted and could appreciate the bigger picture.

The two laureates also had strong, influential and independent wives who played a big role in their political lives. Pat Hume and Daphne Trimble were each a crucial part of their husband's political journey, and they became good friends after the Nobel Peace Prize ceremony in Oslo. Daphne was an essential sounding board during difficult times. She was the origin of the so-called 'Daphne Principle' – when she observed that, at UUC meetings, all David needed was a majority, no matter how small, and then he should keep going to the next vote.

The influence of Daphne, now Lady Trimble, is key to the David Trimble story. Mary McAleese, who first encountered the couple in the 1970s, agrees:

> I have to say, that arc of change for someone like him was really quite remarkable, and so there must have been someone quite remarkable in his life. Who was helping him along that journey? And I credit Daphne with a lot of that.[39]

Others have observed the role Daphne Trimble played in shaping her husband's views and behaviour. Sinn Féin's Mitchel McLaughlin, who went on to be speaker at the Assembly, noted her influence during key political moments:

> It became evident over a period of time, I think, because sometimes she was just there, maybe in the background. There was an influence that was taking a more considered kind of view. I also think that David was smart enough, because he was very smart, that there was an enormous prize here. But you know, there were no freebies, there were going to have to be exchanges. And there were going to have to be gains for everybody.[40]

Trimble's political journey spanned the Troubles, and he watched the various attempts to secure peace sometimes as an observer and sometimes as a player. From an activist who opposed Sunningdale to a Nobel laureate, his story is a remarkable one. He was an unlikely politician. An outsider who became part of the establishment. A serial protester who turned into a world statesman. The most significant unionist leader since the creation of Northern Ireland.

Like his fellow laureate John Hume, he was a man of contradictions. His legacy is perhaps best summed up by his daughter Vicky: 'Without my dad we might not have peace in Northern Ireland.'[41]

George Mitchell famously observed that there would been no peace process without John Hume and no Good Friday Agreement without David Trimble. The former US senator is correct. Without Trimble's consent, the 1998 talks process would have ended in failure.

On a snowy April afternoon on the Stormont Estate, as the leader of unionism he was faced with a simple yet crucial question. Would the people of Northern Ireland be better off or worse off with this deal? His decision split opinion, as it still does today. It strained relationships and ended friendships and divided the party he led.

As his political rivals waited, Trimble finally reached for his phone and rang Mitchell, a call that ended years of violence, saved lives and changed Irish and British history. Good Friday 1998: the day William David Trimble became a peacemaker.

ACKNOWLEDGEMENTS

In 2023, shortly after publication of *John Hume: The Persuader*, I met Lady Trimble, and we talked about the possibility of a biography about her husband, Lord Trimble. She was enthusiastic about the project and kindly agreed to be interviewed, along with family members Richard, Vicky, Nicky and Sarah. I am very grateful for their honesty, openness and ongoing kindness. They have opened up the private world of David Trimble away from the public spotlight.

David's brother, Iain, his sister, Rosemary, and his nephew David were also willing to provide me with their unique insights. I appreciate their candour and patience in answering my endless questions.

The Trimble family are the people who knew David best, and their memories have enriched this book. Their reflections have meant that I have been able to chronicle David Trimble's personal story alongside the narrative of his political career. It was a most remarkable life, the story of a Bangor schoolboy who became a Nobel laureate. The street protester who delivered peace and created history.

Yet, this is not a sugar-coated version of David Trimble the academic and politician. It is a critical analysis of his leadership, reveals his character and personality, and in detail chronicles the strains and stresses of his time in office.

Over the last two years, I have interviewed over 100 people, including friends of Lord Trimble's, party colleagues, rival politicians, critics, diplomats and journalists. Key players including Sir Tony Blair, Bertie Ahern, George Mitchell, Mary McAleese, Baroness Foster and Gerry Adams have all shared their memories of working with Trimble. Former party leaders Lord Alderdice, Mark Durkan, David Ford and Lord Empey have also been supportive. Lord Rogan has been helpful finding documents and photographs, and Barry White has provided much support laced with his trademark humour.

I am grateful to all those who wanted to contribute to this book. Many of my interviewees shared their stories for the first time, and I am conscious of the trust that they have placed in me.

The problem with interviewing so many people is that it generates the need for dozens of transcriptions. I was blessed to have a small team of transcribers who listened to hours of interviews. Thank you to Helen Williams, Maureen Moran, Callum Roberts, Dan Flattery, Wendy Wilson and Jeremy Shields, who also helped with research.

I would also like to thank the great staff at the Linen Hall Library in Belfast, Peter Stewart at BBC Northern Ireland and Ryan Feeney and Conor Kerr at Queen's University, who kindly gave me access to Trimble-related material, which is part of the Quill Project.

I am also indebted to the staff at Gill, who have enthusiastically backed this project, in particular Patrick O'Donoghue, Margaret Farrelly, Iollann Ó Murchú, Graham Thew and Charlie Lawlor. I am also grateful to Barry Greenaway and Trevor Gray, who helped me research Trimble's time at Bangor Grammar School. Thank you to Mark Carruthers, who has the distinction of having proofread all my books. He has been a great supporter of this biography, and I am lucky to have his wise counsel and friendship. My readers included my journalist friends Alex Kane, Mark Devenport, Hugh Jordan, Sam McBride and Freya McClements.

Other reporting colleagues who have been most helpful are Mark Simpson, Gerry Moriarty, Vincent Kearney, Denis Murray, Gareth Gordon, David Blevins and Martina Purdy. Sadly missed are Ken Reid and Stephen Grimason, who knew Trimble well and who reported on the twists and turns of his leadership.

However, I was able to talk to both men before they died in 2024. I am also indebted to two of Trimble's colleagues, David Kerr and Lady Hermon, for their helpful observations on a version of this book.

Much of this biography was written away from Northern Ireland. I spent time in County Kerry and am grateful to the Irish Writers Centre, which awarded me a bursary to go to the wonderful clifftop surroundings of Cill Rialaig overlooking the Atlantic Ocean.

ACKNOWLEDGEMENTS

I enjoyed many happy weeks at the Tyrone Guthrie Centre at Annaghmakerrig in County Monaghan, which has always been one of my favourite places to write. I am constantly blown away by its peace and quiet and the kindness and support of the wonderful staff there.

Finally, to my friends and family, a big thank you for sustaining me over the past two years. Writing a book is never easy, and this one was particularly tough. It would not have happened without Katrin, Grace, Jack and Gabriel. My team. Thank you for your endless support, love and encouragement.

Stephen Walker
County Down
8 May 2025

SOURCES

1. Interviews conducted by Stephen Walker for this book

Daphne Trimble (1), 30 November 2023
Vicky Trimble, 1 December 2023
Richard Trimble (1), 8 December 2023
Sarah Trimble, 26 February 2024
Richard Trimble (2), 6 March 2024
Nicky Trimble, 7 March 2024
Daphne Trimble (2), 14 March 2024
Colin Davidson, 22 March 2024
Lady Hermon, 27 March 2024
Iain Trimble, 11 June 2024
Lord Rogan, 11 June 2024
Mark Neale, 11 June 2024
Jim Nicholson, 12 June 2024
Lord Empey, 12 June 2024
Michael McGimpsey, 12 June 2024
Barry White (UUP staff), 13 June 2024
Lord Alderdice, 14 June 2024
David Kerr (1), 18 June 2024
Chris McGimpsey, 19 June 2024
Esmond Birnie, 20 June 2024
Bertie Ahern, 20 June 2024
Lord Caine, 21 June 2024
David Montgomery (1), 21 June 2024
Leslie Cree, 24 June 2024
Alan McFarland, 25 June 2024
Judith Eve, 26 June 2024
Jane Wells, 2 July 2024
Dr Graham Gudgin, 7 July 2024
Rosemary Steele, 8 July 2024
Maura Quinn, 9 July 2024
Ray Hayden, 9 July 2024
David Burnside, 9 July 2024
Denis Murray, 9 July 2024
David Ford, 9 July 2024
Danny Kennedy, 10 July 2024
Arnold Hatch, 10 July 2024
Mary McAleese, 10 July 2024
Lord Murphy, 15 July 2024
David McNarry, 16 July 2024
Tim O'Connor, 16 July 2024
Alban Maginness, 17 July 2024
Ruth Dudley Edwards, 19 July 2024
Ken Reid, 22 July 2024
Vincent Kearney, 22 July 2024
Herb Wallace, 22 July 2024
Mary Madden, 23 July 2024
James Cooper, 23 July 2024
Dolores Kelly, 23 July 2024
Dermot Nesbitt, 25 July 2024
Lord Donoughue, 26 July 2024
Gerry Adams, 29 July 2024
Hugh Jordan, 30 July 2024
Lord Bew, 30 July 2024
Jim Rodgers, 7 August 2024
Baroness Hoey, 7 August 2024
Philip Black, 8 August 2024
Alex Kane, 9 August 2024
Baroness Foster, 9 August 2024
Alastair Campbell, 12 August 2024
Sam Beattie, 14 August 2024
Lord Weir, 14 August 2024
Bríd Rodgers, 14 August 2024
Mitchel McLaughlin, 15 August 2024
Jack Allen, 15 August 2024
Terry Wright, 15 August 2024
Mark Durkan, 15 August 2024
Trevor Low, 16 August 2024
Terry Neill, 16 August 2024
Joan Carson, 16 August 2024
David Montgomery (2), 19 August 2024

David Adams, 20 August 2024
Professor Thomas Hennessey, 2 September 2024
Felicity Huston, 3 September 2024
Ray Bassett, 3 September 2024
Noel Thompson, 3 September 2024
Liz O'Donnell, 3 September 2024
Gordon Lucy, 4 September 2024
Lee Reynolds, 4 September 2024
Dawn Purvis, 5 September 2024
Mary Kelly, 5 September 2024
Jane Morrice, 6 September 2024
Hugh Logue, 6 September 2024
Anne Logue, 6 September 2024
Baroness O'Loan, 6 September 2024
Mark Fullbrook, 9 September 2024
Eileen Bell, 9 September 2024
Iain Duncan Smith, 10 September 2024
Martina Purdy, 10 September 2024
Alex Benjamin, 11 September 2024
Mark Devenport, 11 September 2024
Gareth Gordon, 11 September 2024
Rodney McCune, 12 September 2024
Kate Fearon, 13 September 2024
Philip Robinson, 13 September 2024
Jim Wilson, 14 September 2024
Mark Simpson, 14 September 2024
Colin Ross, 17 September 2024
Jason McCue, 18 September 2024
Aubrene Willis, 19 September 2024
Stephanie Roderick, 19 September 2024
George Mitchell, 23 September 2024
David Blevins, 27 September 2024

Tony Blair, 22 October 2024
Lady Trimble (3), 9 November 2024
Lady Trimble (4), 14 March 2025
Clifford Smyth, 2 April 2025
John Hunter, 2 April 2025
Gary Kennedy, 3 April 2025
John Dobson, 4 April 2025
David Kerr, (2) 29 April 2025

2. Author's correspondence

Ryan Feeney
Ken Hambly
Eoghan Harris
Sir John Major
Nancy Soderberg

3. Official records

Dáil Proceedings
Hansard, House of Commons
Hansard, Northern Ireland Assembly
National Archives, London
Public Record Office of Northern Ireland
Quill Project, Queen's University, Belfast

4. Publications

Banbridge Chronicle
Belfast Telegraph
Birmingham Post
County Down Spectator
Daily Mail
Daily Mirror
Daily Telegraph
Derry Journal
Economist
Guardian
House Magazine
Independent

SOURCES

Irish Examiner
Irish Independent
Irish News
Irish Times
Journal
Kent Evening Post
Lurgan Mail
News Letter
New Statesman
New York Times
Observer
Portadown Times
Times
Sunday Life
Sunday Times
Sunday Tribune
Sunday World
Washington Post

Western Evening Herald
West Lancashire Evening Gazette

5. Television/radio/online

BBC News NI
BBC Northern Ireland
BBC Radio 4
BBC Radio Foyle
BBC Radio Ulster
ConservativeHome.com
Channel 4
ITV
Politico.com
RTÉ
Sky News
UTV

BIBLIOGRAPHY

Aitken, Jonathan, *Margaret Thatcher: Power and Personality* (Bloomsbury, 2013)

Anderson, Don, *Fourteen May Days: The Inside Story of the Loyalist Strike of 1974* (Gill & Macmillan, 1994)

Bardon, Jonathan, *A History of Ulster* (Blackstaff Press, 1992)

Beresford, David, *Ten Men Dead: The Story of the 1981 Irish Hunger Strike* (Grafton Books, 1987)

Bew, Paul, and Gordon Gillespie, *Northern Ireland: A Chronology of the Troubles* (Gill and Macmillan, 1993)

Blair, Tony, *A Journey* (Hutchinson, Random House, 2010)

Bloomfield, Ken, *Stormont in Crisis: A Memoir* (Blackstaff Press, 1994)

Campbell, Alastair, *The Blair Years* (Hutchinson, 2007)

Cochrane, Feargal, *Northern Ireland: The Fragile Peace* (Yale University Press, 2013)

Cochrane, Feargal, *Unionist Politics and the Politics of Unionism since the Anglo-Irish Agreement* (Cork University Press, 1997)

De Bréadún, Deaglán, *The Far Side of Revenge* (Collins Press, 2001)

Donoghue, David, *One Good Day: My Journey to the Good Friday Agreement* (Gill Books 2022)

Elliott, Sydney, and W.D. Flackes, *Northern Ireland: A Political Directory 1968–1999* (Blackstaff Press, 1999)

Faulkner, Brian, *Memoirs of a Statesman* (Weidenfeld & Nicolson, 1978)

Gillespie, Gordon, *Years of Darkness: The Troubles Remembered* (Gill & Macmillan, 2008)

Godson, Dean, *Himself Alone: David Trimble and the Ordeal of Unionism* (Harper, 2004)

Hennessey, Thomas, *Hunger Strike: Margaret Thatcher's Battle with the IRA, 1980–1981* (Irish Academic Press, 2014)

Kerr, Michael, *Transforming Unionism: David Trimble and the 2005 General Election* (Irish Academic Press, 2005)

McDonald, Henry, *Trimble* (Bloomsbury, 2000)

McKittrick, David, *Despatches from Belfast* (Blackstaff Press, 1989)

McKittrick, David, and David McVea, *Making Sense of the Troubles: A History of the Northern Ireland Conflict* (Viking, 2012)

McKittrick, David, Seamus Kelters, Brian Feeney and Chris Thornton, *Lost Lives: The Stories of the Men, Women and Children Who Died as a Result of the Northern Ireland Troubles* (Mainstream Publishing, 1999)

Mallie, Eamonn and David McKittrick, *The Fight for Peace: The Secret Story Behind the Irish Peace Process* (Heinemann, 1996)

Mallon, Seamus with Andy Pollak, *A Shared Home Place* (Lilliput Press, 2019)
Millar, Frank, *David Trimble: The Price of Peace* (Liffey Press, 2008)
Mowlam, Mo, *Momentum: The Struggle for Peace, Politics and the People* (Hodder & Stoughton, 2002)
Porter, Norman, *Rethinking Unionism: An Alternative Vision for Northern Ireland* (Blackstaff Press, 1996)
Powell, Jonathan, *Great Hatred, Little Room: Making Peace in Northern Ireland* (Bodley Head, 2008)
Purdy, Martina, *Room 21: Stormont – Behind Closed Doors* (Brehon, 2005)
Trimble, David, *The Foundations of Northern Ireland* (Ulster Society, 1991)
Trimble, David, *To Raise Up a New Northern Ireland: Articles and Speeches 1998–2000 by David Trimble* (Belfast Press, 2001)
Walker, Graham, *A History of the Ulster Unionist Party: Protest, Pragmatism and Pessimism* (Manchester University Press, 2004)
Walker, Stephen, *John Hume: The Persuader* (Gill, 2023)
White, Barry, *John Hume: Statesman of the Troubles* (Blackstaff Press, 1984)

ENDNOTES

1: Bangor Boy

1. Trimble, Iain. Interview conducted by Stephen Walker. 11 June 2024.
2. Trimble, Iain. Interview conducted by Stephen Walker. 11 June 2024.
3. Millar, Frank. *David Trimble: The Price of Peace*, Liffey Press, 2008.
4. Trimble, Iain. Interview conducted by Stephen Walker. 11 June 2024.
5. Trimble, Iain. Interview conducted by Stephen Walker. 11 June 2024.
6. Steele, Rosemary. Interview conducted by Stephen Walker. 8 July 2024.
7. Steele, Rosemary. Interview conducted by Stephen Walker. 8 July 2024.
8. Trimble, Iain. Interview conducted by Stephen Walker. 11 June 2024.
9. Trimble, David, *Meeting Myself Coming Back*, BBC Radio 4. 3 August 2013.
10. Steele, Rosemary. Interview conducted by Stephen Walker. 8 July 2024.
11. *On the Ropes*. BBC Radio 4. 12 July 2005.
12. Montgomery, David. Interview conducted by Stephen Walker. 21 June 2024.
13. Trimble family archives.
14. Trimble family archives.
15. Trimble family archives.
16. Correspondence with Ken Hambly.
17. Correspondence with Ken Hambly.
18. Low, Trevor. Interview conducted by Stephen Walker. 16 August 2024.
19. Low, Trevor. Interview conducted by Stephen Walker. 16 August 2024.
20. Correspondence with Ken Hambly.
21. Neill, Terry. Interview conducted by Stephen Walker. 16 August 2024.
22. McDonald, Henry. *Trimble*, Bloomsbury, 2000.
23. Trimble family archives.
24. Trimble, Iain. Interview conducted by Stephen Walker. 11 June 2024.
25. McDonald, Henry. *Trimble*, Bloomsbury, 2000.
26. Cree, Leslie. Interview conducted by Stephen Walker. 24 June 2024.
27. Cree, Leslie. Interview conducted by Stephen Walker. 24 June 2024.
28. Trimble, Iain. Interview conducted by Stephen Walker. 11 June 2024.
29. Trimble, Iain. Interview conducted by Stephen Walker. 11 June 2024.
30. Trimble, Iain. Interview conducted by Stephen Walker. 11 June 2024.
31. Steele, Rosemary. Interview conducted by Stephen Walker. 8 July 2024.
32. Frank Millar, *David Trimble: The Price of Peace*, Liffey Press, 2008.
33. Trimble, Iain. Interview conducted by Stephen Walker. 11 June 2024
34. Millar, Frank. *David Trimble: The Price of Peace*, Liffey Press, 2008.
35. Steele, Rosemary. Interview conducted by Stephen Walker. 8 July 2024.
36. Trimble family archives.
37. Trimble, Iain. Interview conducted by Stephen Walker. 11 June 2024.
38. Cree, Leslie. Interview conducted by Stephen Walker. 24 June 2024.

2: First among Equals

1. Trimble family archives.
2. Trimble family archives.
3. Trimble family archives.
4. Low, Trevor. Interview conducted by Stephen Walker. 16 August 2024.
5. Cree, Leslie. Interview conducted by Stephen Walker. 24 June 2024.
6. Trimble, David. *Meeting Myself Coming Back*, BBC Radio 4. 3 August 2013.
7. Wallace, Herb. Interview conducted by Stephen Walker. 22 July 2024.
8. Wallace, Herb. Interview conducted by Stephen Walker. 22 July 2024.
9. Wallace, Herb. Interview conducted by Stephen Walker. 22 July 2024.
10. Beattie, Sam. Interview conducted by Stephen Walker. 14 August 2024.
11. Wallace, Herb. Interview conducted by Stephen Walker. 22 July 2024.
12. Trimble, Iain. Interview conducted by Stephen Walker. 11 June 2024.
13. Wallace, Herb. Interview conducted by Stephen Walker. 22 July 2024.
14. *County Down Spectator*, 5 July 1968.
15. *Meeting Myself Coming Back*, BBC Radio 4. 3 August 2013.
16. *On the Ropes*, BBC Radio 4, 12 July 2005.
17. Eve, Judith. Interview conducted by Stephen Walker. 26 June 2024.
18. McAleese, Mary. Interview conducted by Stephen Walker. 10 July 2024.
19. Cooper, James. Interview conducted by Stephen Walker. 23 July 2024.
20. Logue, Anne. Interview conducted by Stephen Walker. 6 September 2024.
21. Madden, Mary. Interview conducted by Stephen Walker. 23 July 2024.
22. Wallace, Herb. Interview conducted by Stephen Walker. 22 July 2024.
23. McDonald, Henry, *Trimble*, Bloomsbury, 2000.
24. Beattie, Sam. Interview conducted by Stephen Walker. 14 August 2024.
25. Beattie, Sam. Interview conducted by Stephen Walker. 14 August 2024.

3: Vote Trimble

1. McAleese, Mary. Interview conducted by Stephen Walker. 10 July 2024.
2. McAleese, Mary. Interview conducted by Stephen Walker. 10 July 2024.
3. McAleese, Mary. Interview conducted by Stephen Walker. 10 July 2024.
4. Maginness, Alban. Interview conducted by Stephen Walker. 17 July 2024.
5. Maginness, Alban. Interview conducted by Stephen Walker. 17 July 2024.
6. Hansard. House of Commons. 29 January 1998.
7. McAleese, Mary. Interview conducted by Stephen Walker. 10 July 2024.
8. Trimble, David. *On the Ropes*, BBC Radio 4. 12 July 2005.
9. *New York Times*. 29 March 1972.
10. *Irish Times*. 8 May 2007.
11. Burnside, David. Interview conducted by Stephen Walker. 9 July 2024.
12. *Irish Times*. 8 May 2007.
13. Empey, Lord. Interview conducted by Stephen Walker. 12 June 2024.
14. Rodgers, Jim. Interview conducted by Stephen Walker. 7 August 2024.
15. McGimpsey, Michael. Interview conducted by Stephen Walker. 12 June 2024.
16. McDonald, Henry, *Trimble*, Bloomsbury, 2000.

17 Smyth, Clifford. Interview conducted by Stephen Walker. 2 April 2025.
18 Eve, Judith. Interview conducted by Stephen Walker. 26 June 2024.
19 Wallace, Herb. Interview conducted by Stephen Walker. 22 July 2024.
20 Eve, Judith. Interview conducted by Stephen Walker. 26 June 2024.
21 Faulkner, Brian, *Memoirs of a Statesman*, Weidenfeld & Nicolson. 1978.

4: Bringing Down the House

1 Maginness, Alban. Interview conducted by Stephen Walker. 17 July 2024.
2 Hatch, Arnold. Interview conducted by Stephen Walker. 10 July 2024.
3 Wallace, Herb. Interview conducted by Stephen Walker. 22 July 2024.
4 BBC TV. 25 May 1974.
5 Madden, Mary. Interview conducted by Stephen Walker. 23 July 2024.

5: Breaking the Convention

1 Maginness, Alban. Interview conducted by Stephen Walker. 17 July 2024.
2 Craig, Bill. Interview conducted by Richard Deutsch. Irish Studies. 1976.
3 McDonald, Henry, *Trimble*, Bloomsbury, 2000.
4 Logue, Hugh. Interview conducted by Stephen Walker. 6 September 2024.
5 Empey, Lord. Interview conducted by Stephen Walker. 12 June 2024.
6 Burnside, David. Interview conducted by Stephen Walker. 9 July 2024.
7 White, Barry, *Statesman of the Troubles*, Blackstaff Press, 1984.

6: Hello, Daphne

1 Trimble, Lady. Interview conducted by Stephen Walker. 30 November 2023.
2 Trimble, Lady. Interview conducted by Stephen Walker. 30 November 2023.
3 Trimble, Lady. Interview conducted by Stephen Walker. 30 November 2023.
4 McAleese, Mary. Interview conducted by Stephen Walker. 10 July 2024.
5 Trimble, Lady. Interview conducted by Stephen Walker. 30 November 2023.
6 Trimble family archives.
7 Trimble family archives.
8 Trimble family archives.
9 Trimble, Lady. Interview conducted by Stephen Walker. 30 November 2023.
10 Trimble family archives.
11 Trimble family archives.
12 Trimble family archives.
13 Trimble, Lady. Interview conducted by Stephen Walker. 30 November 2023.
14 Madden, Mary. Interview conducted by Stephen Walker. 23 July 2024.
15 Hansard. Northern Ireland Convention. 3 March 1976.
16 Hansard. Northern Ireland Convention. 3 March 1976.
17 Hansard. Northern Ireland Convention. 3 March 1976.
18 Hansard. Northern Ireland Convention. 3 March 1976.
19 Trimble, Lady. Interview conducted by Stephen Walker. 9 November 2024.
20 Wallace, Herb. Interview conducted by Stephen Walker. 22 July 2024.
21 Wallace, Herb. Interview conducted by Stephen Walker. 22 July 2024.

22 Beattie, Sam. Interview conducted by Stephen Walker. 14 August 2024.
23 Wallace, Herb. Interview conducted by Stephen Walker. 22 July 2024.

7: *To Have and to Hold*

1 *On the Ropes,* BBC Radio 4. 12 July 2005.
2 McGimpsey, Michael. Interview conducted by Stephen Walker. 12 June 2024.
3 McGimpsey, Michael. Interview conducted by Stephen Walker. 12 June 2024.
4 Trimble, Lady. Interview conducted by Stephen Walker. 9 November 2024.
5 Trimble, Lady. Interview conducted by Stephen Walker. 30 November 2023.
6 Trimble, Richard. Interview conducted by Stephen Walker. 6 March 2024.
7 Trimble, David (nephew). Interview conducted by Stephen Walker. 12 March 2024.
8 Trimble, David (nephew). Interview conducted by Stephen Walker. 12 March 2024.
9 Trimble, David (nephew). Interview conducted by Stephen Walker. 12 March 2024.
10 Trimble, David (nephew). Interview conducted by Stephen Walker. 12 March 2024.
11 McGimpsey, Chris. Interview conducted by Stephen Walker. 19 June 2024.
12 McNarry, David. Interview conducted by Stephen Walker. 16 July 2024.
13 McNarry, David. Interview conducted by Stephen Walker. 16 July 2024.
14 Hermon, Lady. Interview conducted by Stephen Walker. 27 March 2024.
15 *Belfast Telegraph.* 2 November 1981.

8: *Murder in the Morning*

1 Nesbitt, Dermot. Interview conducted by Stephen Walker. 25 July 2024.
2 BelTel documentary podcast. December 2023.
3 Eve, Judith. Interview conducted by Stephen Walker. 26 June 2024.
4 Wallace, Herb. Interview conducted by Stephen Walker. 22 July 2024.
5 Nesbitt, Dermot. Interview conducted by Stephen Walker. 25 July 2024.
6 *Meeting Myself Coming Back*, BBC Radio 4. 3 August 2013.
7 Hermon, Lady. Interview conducted by Stephen Walker. 27 March 2024.
8 *News Letter.* 8 December 1983.
9 *Meeting Myself Coming Back*, BBC Radio 4. 3 August 2013.
10 Eve, Judith. Interview conducted by Stephen Walker. 26 June 2024.
11 *Meeting Myself Coming Back*, BBC Radio 4. 3 August 2013.
12 *News Letter.* 20 November 1984.
13 Lucy, Gordon. Interview conducted by Stephen Walker. 4 September 2024.
14 Lucy, Gordon. Interview conducted by Stephen Walker. 4 September 2024.
15 Speech to Young Unionist conference. 3 October 1998.

9: *The Wilderness Years*

1 BBC TV. 23 November 1985.
2 Cochrane, Fergal, *Unionist Politics and the Politics of Unionism*, Cork University Press. 1997.

ENDNOTES

3. Black, Philip. Interview conducted by Stephen Walker. 8 August 2024.
4. Murray, Denis. Interview conducted by Stephen Walker. 9 July 2024.
5. Murray, Denis. Interview conducted by Stephen Walker. 9 July 2024.
6. Cochrane, Fergal, *Unionist Politics and the Politics of Unionism*, Cork University Press. 1997.
7. Eve, Judith. Interview conducted by Stephen Walker. 26 June 2024.
8. Eve, Judith. Interview conducted by Stephen Walker. 26 June 2024.
9. Eve, Judith. Interview conducted by Stephen Walker. 26 June 2024.
10. Wallace, Herb. Interview conducted by Stephen Walker. 22 July 2024.
11. Hermon, Lady. Interview conducted by Stephen Walker. 27 March 2024.
12. Wallace, Herb. Interview conducted by Stephen Walker. 22 July 2024.
13. Hermon, Lady. Interview conducted by Stephen Walker. 27 March 2024.
14. Eve, Judith. Interview conducted by Stephen Walker. 26 June 2024.
15. Wallace, Herb. Interview conducted by Stephen Walker. 22 July 2024.
16. McAleese, Mary. Interview conducted by Stephen Walker. 10 July 2024.
17. Devenport, Mark. Interview conducted by Stephen Walker. 11 September 2024.
18. Hayden, Ray. Interview conducted by Stephen Walker. 9 July 2024.
19. Dudley Edwards, Ruth. Interview conducted by Stephen Walker. 19 July 2024.
20. Smith, Marion. Interview conducted by Stephen Walker. 11 September 2024.
21. Wallace, Herb. Interview conducted by Stephen Walker. 22 July 2024.

10: *Goodbye, Queen's*

1. Weir, Lord. Interview conducted by Stephen Walker. 14 August 2024.
2. Lucy, Gordon. Interview conducted by Stephen Walker. 4 September 2024.
3. *Banbridge Chronicle*. 26 April 1990.
4. *Meeting Myself Coming Back*, BBC Radio 4. 3 August 2013.
5. Kennedy, Gary. Interview conducted by Stephen Walker. 3 April 2025.
6. Trimble, Richard. Interview conducted by Stephen Walker. 8 December 2023.
7. Kane, Alex. Interview conducted by Stephen Walker. 9 August 2024.
8. Kennedy, Danny. Interview conducted by Stephen Walker. 10 July 2024.
9. Kane, Alex. Interview conducted by Stephen Walker. 9 August 2024.
10. Kennedy, Gary. Interview conducted by Stephen Walker. 3 April 2025.
11. Dobson, John. Interview conducted by Stephen Walker. 4 April 2025.
12. Caine, Lord. Interview conducted by Stephen Walker. 21 June 2024.
13. Trimble, Vicky. Interview conducted by Stephen Walker. 1 December 2023.
14. UUP source.
15. Roderick, Stephanie. Interview conducted by Stephen Walker. 19 September 2024.
16. Hermon, Lady. Interview conducted by Stephen Walker. 27 March 2024.
17. Hoey, Baroness. Interview conducted by Stephen Walker. 7 August 2024.
18. *On the Ropes*, BBC Radio 4. 12 July 2005.
19. Blevins, David. Interview conducted by Stephen Walker. 27 September 2024.
20. Millar, Frank. *The Price of Peace*, Liffey Press, 2008.
21. Trimble, Nicky. Interview conducted by Stephen Walker. 7 March 2024.

22 Trimble, Richard. Interview conducted by Stephen Walker. 8 December 2023.
23 Trimble, Vicky. Interview conducted by Stephen Walker. 1 December 2023.
24 Trimble, Nicky. Interview conducted by Stephen Walker. 7 March 2024.
25 Purdy, Martina. Interview conducted by Stephen Walker. 10 September 2024.

11: *Snowballs and Secret Talks*

1 Trimble, Lady. Interview conducted by Stephen Walker. 14 March 2023.
2 Trimble, Lady. Interview conducted by Stephen Walker. 14 March 2023.
3 BBC Northern Ireland. 16 September 1993.
4 Correspondence between Sir John Major and Stephen Walker.
5 *Irish Independent*. 18 September 1993.
6 Millar, Frank. *David Trimble: The Price of Peace*, Liffey Press, 2008.
7 Hansard. House of Commons. 25 October 1993.
8 Hansard. House of Commons. 1 November 1993.
9 *Hume*. BBC Northern Ireland documentary. 19 September 2011.
10 *News Letter*. 21 December 1993.
11 *News Letter*. 21 December 1993.
12 *News Letter*. 4 January 1994.
13 CAIN archive – Conflict and politics in Northern Ireland.
14 BBC Radio Ulster. 31 August 1994.
15 BBC News NI website. 31 August 1994.

12: *Stalking and Walking*

1 Trimble, David. Interview conducted by Alex Kane. 14 August 2015.
2 Reid, Ken. Interview conducted by Stephen Walker. 22 July 2024.
3 Confidential source.
4 Kane, Alex. Interview conducted by Stephen Walker. 9 August 2024.
5 *Kent Evening Post*. 23 September 1994.
6 *Portadown Times*. 24 February 1995.
7 McFarland, Alan. Interview conducted by Stephen Walker. 25 June 2024.
8 Reynolds, Lee. Interview conducted by Stephen Walker. 4 September 2024.
9 Reynolds, Lee. Interview conducted by Stephen Walker. 4 September 2024.
10 *Sunday Life*. 19 March 1985.
11 *Irish Independent*. 17 June 1995.
12 Confidential source.
13 BBC News. 11 July 1995.
14 Maginness, Alban. Interview conducted by Stephen Walker. 17 July 2024.
15 McLaughlin, Mitchel. Interview conducted by Stephen Walker. 15 August 2024.
16 *Meeting Myself Coming Back*, BBC Radio 4. 3 August 2013.
17 PRONI. State papers.
18 PRONI. State papers.
19 Trimble, Lady. Interview conducted by Stephen Walker. 30 November 2023.
20 Trimble, Lady. Interview conducted by Stephen Walker. 30 November 2023.
21 Trimble, David. Interview conducted by Alex Kane. 14 August 2015.

13: Follow the Leader

1 Kearney, Vincent. Interview conducted by Stephen Walker. 22 July 2024.
2 Simpson, Mark. Interview conducted by Stephen Walker. 14 September 2024.
3 Gordon, Gareth. Interview conducted by Stephen Walker. 11 September 2024.
4 McNarry, David. Interview conducted by Stephen Walker. 16 July 2024.
5 Nesbitt, Dermot. Interview conducted by Stephen Walker. 25 July 2024.
6 Weir, Lord. Interview conducted by Stephen Walker. 14 August 2024.
7 Weir, Lord. Interview conducted by Stephen Walker. 14 August 2024.
8 Kennedy, Danny. Interview conducted by Stephen Walker. 10 July 2024.
9 Lucy, Gordon. Interview conducted by Stephen Walker. 4 September 2024.
10 Trimble, Vicky. Interview conducted by Stephen Walker. 1 December 2023.
11 *Portadown Times*. 1 September 1995.
12 *News Letter*. 8 September 1995.
13 Wallace, Herb. Interview conducted by Stephen Walker. 22 July 2024.
14 Murray, Denis. Interview conducted by Stephen Walker. 9 July 2024.
15 Empey, Lord. Interview conducted by Stephen Walker. 12 June 2024.
16 Burnside, David. Interview conducted by Stephen Walker. 9 July 2024.
17 Trimble, Lady. Interview conducted by Stephen Walker. 30 November 2023.
18 Trimble, David. Interview conducted by Alex Kane. 14 August 2015.
19 Neale, Mark. Interview conducted by Stephen Walker. 11 June 2024.
20 Empey, Lord. Interview conducted by Stephen Walker. 12 June 2024.
21 Wilson, Jim. Interview conducted by Stephen Walker. 14 September 2024.
22 Bew, Lord. Interview conducted by Stephen Walker. 30 July 2024.
23 Trimble, Vicky. Interview conducted by Stephen Walker. 1 December 2023.
24 RTÉ. 9 September 1995.
25 RTÉ. 9 September 1995.
26 RTÉ. 9 September 1995.
27 *Sunday Tribune*. 10 September 1995.
28 *Derry Journal*. 12 September 1995.
29 McGimpsey, Michael. Interview conducted by Stephen Walker. 12 June 2024.
30 McGimpsey, Chris. Interview conducted by Stephen Walker. 19 June 2024.
31 Dudley Edwards, Ruth. Interview conducted by Stephen Walker. 19 July 2024.
32 Alderdice, Lord. Interview conducted by Stephen Walker. 14 June 2024.
33 Durkan, Mark. Interview conducted by Stephen Walker. 15 August 2024.
34 Ahern, Bertie. Interview conducted by Stephen Walker. 20 June 2024.
35 O'Connor, Tim. Interview conducted by Stephen Walker. 16 July 2024.
36 Dudley Edwards, Ruth. Interview conducted by Stephen Walker. 19 July 2024.

14: New Labour, New Ideas

1 Kerr, David. Interview conducted by Stephen Walker. 18 June 2024.
2 Kerr, David. Interview conducted by Stephen Walker. 18 June 2024.
3 Kerr, David. Interview conducted by Stephen Walker. 26 January 2021.
4 Kerr, David. Interview conducted by Stephen Walker. 26 January 2021.
5 Kerr, David. Interview conducted by Stephen Walker. 26 January 2021.

6 Hansard. House of Commons. 24 January 1996.
7 *The Guardian*. 10 February 1996.
8 *Western Evening Herald*. 10 February 1996.
9 Mitchell, George. Interview conducted by Stephen Walker. 23 September 2024.
10 *Portadown Times*, 19 July 1996.
11 McGimpsey, Chris. Interview conducted by Stephen Walker. 19 June 2024.
12 Jordan, Hugh. Interview conducted by Stephen Walker. 30 July 2024.
13 Jordan, Hugh. Interview conducted by Stephen Walker. 30 July 2024.
14 Jordan, Hugh. Interview conducted by Stephen Walker. 30 July 2024.
15 Montgomery, David. Interview conducted by Stephen Walker. 21 June 2024.
16 Rogan, Lord. Interview conducted by Stephen Walker. 11 June 2024.
17 Blair, Sir Tony. Interview conducted by Stephen Walker. 22 October 2024.
18 Blair, Sir Tony. Interview conducted by Stephen Walker. 22 October 2024.
19 Blair, Sir Tony. Interview conducted by Stephen Walker. 22 October 2024.
20 Campbell, Alastair. Interview conducted by Stephen Walker. 12 August 2024.
21 Bell, Eileen. Interview conducted by Stephen Walker. 9 September 2024.
22 Blair, Sir Tony. Interview conducted by Stephen Walker. 22 October 2024.
23 CAIN archive – Conflict and politics in Northern Ireland.
24 Blair, Sir Tony. Interview conducted by Stephen Walker. 22 October 2024.

15: *The Final Countdown*

1 *Meeting Myself Coming Back*, BBC Radio 4. 3 August 2013.
2 *Meeting Myself Coming Back*, BBC Radio 4. 3 August 2013.
3 Purvis, Dawn. Interview conducted by Stephen Walker. 5 September 2024.
4 Adams, David. Interview conducted by Stephen Walker. 20 August 2024.
5 Adams, David. Interview conducted by Stephen Walker. 20 August 2024.
6 Cooper, James. Interview conducted by Stephen Walker. 23 July 2024.
7 Mitchell, George. Interview conducted by Stephen Walker. 23 September 2024.
8 Mitchell, George. Interview conducted by Stephen Walker. 23 September 2024.
9 *West Lancashire Evening Gazette*. 16 February 1998.
10 Fearon, Kate. Interview conducted by Stephen Walker. 13 September 2024.
11 *Birmingham Post*. 5 March 1998.
12 Mallon, Seamus, with Andy Pollak, *A Shared Home Place*, Lilliput Press, 2019.
13 Willis, Aubrene. Interview conducted by Stephen Walker. 19 September 2024.
14 *Belfast Telegraph*. 5 April 2023.
15 *Belfast Telegraph*. 5 April 2023.
16 Speech to UUP AGM. 21 March 1998.
17 Speech to UUP AGM. 21 March 1998.
18 Trimble, David. Interview conducted by Alex Kane. 14 August 2015.
19 Mitchell, George. Interview conducted by Stephen Walker. 23 September 2024.
20 Mitchell, George. Interview conducted by Stephen Walker. 23 September 2024.

21 Mitchell, George. Interview conducted by Stephen Walker. 23 September 2024.
22 Ahern, Bertie. Interview conducted by Stephen Walker. 20 June 2024.
23 Durkan, Mark. Interview conducted by Stephen Walker. 15 August 2024.
24 Kerr, David. Interview conducted by Stephen Walker. 29 April 2025.

16: Deal or No Deal

1 RTÉ. 10 April 1998.
2 Foster, Baroness. Interview conducted by Stephen Walker. 9 August 2024.
3 Foster, Baroness. Interview conducted by Stephen Walker. 9 August 2024.
4 *Irish Independent*. 8 April 1998.
5 Empey, Lord. Interview conducted by Stephen Walker. 12 June 2024.
6 Nicholson, Jim. Interview conducted by Stephen Walker. 12 June 2024.
7 Alderdice, Lord. Interview conducted by Stephen Walker. 14 June 2024.
8 Allen, Jack. Interview conducted by Stephen Walker. 15 August 2024.
9 O'Donnell, Liz. Interview conducted by Stephen Walker. 3 September 2024.
10 Hennessey, Thomas. Interview conducted by Stephen Walker. 2 September 2024.
11 Montgomery, David. Interview conducted by Stephen Walker. 19 August 2024.
12 Montgomery, David. Interview conducted by Stephen Walker. 19 August 2024.
13 Powell, Jonathan, *Great Hatred, Little Room*, Bodley Head, 2008.
14 Lord Trimble archives. Quill Project. Queen's University, Belfast.
15 Rodgers, Jim. Interview conducted by Stephen Walker. 7 August 2024.
16 Mitchell, George. Interview conducted by Stephen Walker. 23 September 2024.
17 Empey, Lord. Interview conducted by Stephen Walker. 12 June 2024.
18 Kennedy, Danny. Interview conducted by Stephen Walker. 10 July 2024.
19 Durkan, Mark. Interview conducted by Stephen Walker. 15 August 2024.
20 Bassett, Ray. Interview conducted by Stephen Walker. 3 September 2024.
21 Reid, Ken. Interview conducted by Stephen Walker. 22 July 2024.
22 Kerr, David. Interview conducted by Stephen Walker. 26 January 2021.
23 BBC. 10 April 1998.
24 Hunter, John. Interview conducted by Stephen Walker. 2 April 2025.
25 Mallon, Seamus, with Andy Pollak, *A Shared Home Place*, Lilliput Press, 2019.
26 Mitchell, George. Interview conducted by Stephen Walker. 23 September 2024.

17: Just Say Yes

1 Hayden, Ray. Interview conducted by Stephen Walker. 9 July 2024.
2 Trimble, David. Interview conducted by Alex Kane. 14 August 2015.
3 O'Donnell, Liz. Interview conducted by Stephen Walker. 3 September 2024.
4 *Hero or Traitor*. Channel 4 documentary. 1999.
5 Hoey, Baroness. Interview conducted by Stephen Walker. 7 August 2024.

6 Attwood, Tim. Interview conducted by Stephen Walker. 18 December 2020.
7 Kerr, David. Interview conducted by Stephen Walker. 26 January 2021.
8 Kerr, David. Interview conducted by Stephen Walker. 29 April 2025.
9 Kerr, David. Interview conducted by Stephen Walker. 26 January 2021.
10 Hoey, Baroness. Interview conducted by Stephen Walker. 7 August 2024.
11 Fullbrook, Mark. Interview conducted by Stephen Walker. 9 September 2024.
12 Kerr, David. Interview conducted by Stephen Walker. 26 January 2021.
13 Trimble, Lady. Interview conducted by Stephen Walker. 30 November 2023.
14 Trimble, Richard. Interview conducted by Stephen Walker. 8 December 2023.
15 Trimble, Lady. Interview conducted by Stephen Walker. 30 November 2023.
16 Trimble, Sarah. Interview conducted by Stephen Walker. 26 February 2024.
17 Trimble, Nicky. Interview conducted by Stephen Walker. 7 March 2024.
18 Trimble, Sarah. Interview conducted by Stephen Walker. 26 February 2024.
19 Wells, Jane. Interview conducted by Stephen Walker. 2 July 2024.
20 Wells, Jane. Interview conducted by Stephen Walker. 2 July 2024.
21 Wells, Jane. Interview conducted by Stephen Walker. 2 July 2024.
22 Hayden, Ray. Interview conducted by Stephen Walker. 9 July 2024.
23 Hayden, Ray. Interview conducted by Stephen Walker. 9 July 2024.
24 Mallon, Seamus, with Andy Pollak, *A Shared Home Place*, Lilliput Press, 2019.
25 Hansard. Assembly proceedings. 1 July 1998.
26 Hansard. Assembly proceedings. 1 July 1998.
27 Hayden, Ray. Interview conducted by Stephen Walker. 9 July 2024.

18: From Omagh to Oslo

1 Trimble, Nicky. Interview conducted by Stephen Walker. 7 March 2024.
2 Trimble, Lady. Interview conducted by Stephen Walker. 14 March 2024.
3 Trimble, Vicky. Interview conducted by Stephen Walker. 1 December 2023.
4 Trimble, Lady. Interview conducted by Stephen Walker. 14 March 2024.
5 *Irish Times*. 20 August 1998.
6 McAleese, Mary. Interview conducted by Stephen Walker. 10 July 2024.
7 *Belfast Telegraph*. 26 April 1999.
8 BBC. 12 July 1998.
9 CAIN archive – Conflict and politics in Northern Ireland.
10 BBC. 3 September 1998.
11 BBC. 3 September 1998.
12 *Breakfast with Frost*. BBC. 6 September 1998.
13 Adams, Gerry. Interview conducted by Stephen Walker. 29 July 2024.
14 Adams, Gerry. Interview conducted by Stephen Walker. 29 July 2024.
15 Bew, Lord. Interview conducted by Stephen Walker. 30 July 2024.
16 Adams, Gerry. Interview conducted by Stephen Walker. 29 July 2024.
17 Gudgin, Graham. Interview conducted by Stephen Walker. 7 July 2024.
18 Campbell, Alastair. Interview conducted by Stephen Walker. 12 August 2024.
19 Montgomery, David. Interview conducted by Stephen Walker. 19 August 2024.

ENDNOTES

20 Empey, Lord. Interview conducted by Stephen Walker. 12 June 2024.
21 Montgomery, David. Interview conducted by Stephen Walker. 19 August 2024.
22 Quinn, Maura. Interview conducted by Stephen Walker. 9 July 2024.
23 Gudgin, Graham. Interview conducted by Stephen Walker. 7 July 2024.
24 Gudgin, Graham. Interview conducted by Stephen Walker. 7 July 2024.
25 Logue, Hugh. Interview conducted by Stephen Walker. 6 September 2024.
26 Huston, Felicity. Interview conducted by Stephen Walker. 3 September 2024.
27 Conversation between Seamus Mallon and author.
28 Kerr, David. Interview conducted by Stephen Walker. 26 January 2021.
29 Mallon, Seamus, with Andy Pollak, *A Shared Home Place*, Lilliput Press, 2019.
30 Quinn, Maura. Interview conducted by Stephen Walker. 9 July 2024.
31 Kerr, David. Interview conducted by Stephen Walker. 26 January 2021.
32 Trimble, Sarah. Interview conducted by Stephen Walker. 26 February 2024.
33 Trimble, Lady. Interview conducted by Stephen Walker. 14 March 2024.
34 Harris, Eoghan. Commumication with the author. 25 July 2024.
35 Speech at Nobel Peace Prize. 10 December 1998.
36 Speech at Nobel Peace Prize. 10 December 1998.
37 Speech at Nobel Peace Prize. 10 December 1998.

19: Guns and Government

1 Logue, Hugh. Interview conducted by Stephen Walker. 6 September 2024.
2 Weir, Lord. Interview conducted by Stephen Walker. 14 August 2024.
3 Kane, Alex. Interview conducted by Stephen Walker. 9 August 2024.
4 Foster, Baroness. Interview conducted by Stephen Walker. 9 August 2024.
5 Carson, Joan. Interview conducted by Stephen Walker. 16 August 2024.
6 Cooper, James. Interview conducted by Stephen Walker. 23 July 2024.
7 McLaughlin, Mitchel. Interview conducted by Stephen Walker. 15 August 2024.
8 Quinn, Maura. Interview conducted by Stephen Walker. 9 July 2024.
9 Kerr, David. Interview conducted by Stephen Walker. 29 April 2025.
10 White, Barry. Interview conducted by Stephen Walker. 13 June 2024.
11 Reid, Ken. Interview conducted by Stephen Walker. 22 July 2024.
12 Birnie, Esmond. Interview conducted by Stephen Walker. 20 June 2024.
13 Hansard. Assembly proceedings. 15 July 1999.
14 Hansard. Assembly proceedings. 15 July 1999.
15 Mowlam, Mo, *Momentum*, Hodder & Stoughton, 2002.
16 BBC. 9 September 1999.
17 Neale, Mark. Interview conducted by Stephen Walker. 11 June 2024.
18 Mitchell, George. Interview conducted by Stephen Walker. 23 September 2024.
19 Mitchell, George. Interview conducted by Stephen Walker. 23 September 2024.
20 McCune, Rodney. Interview conducted by Stephen Walker. 12 September 2024.

21 Bew, Lord. Interview conducted by Stephen Walker. 30 July 2024.
22 Godson, Dean, *Himself Alone*, Harper Perennial, 2004.
23 *Observer*. 28 November 1999.
24 Trimble, Lady. Interview conducted by Stephen Walker. 14 March 2024.
25 CAIN archive – Conflict and politics in Northern Ireland

20: Stop Start Stormont

1 Trimble, Vicky. Interview conducted by Stephen Walker. 1 December 2023.
2 Trimble, Richard. Interview conducted by Stephen Walker. 8 December 2023.
3 Trimble, Nicky. Interview conducted by Stephen Walker. 7 March 2024.
4 *The Guardian*. 12 February 2000.
5 *The Guardian*. 8 April 2001.
6 Birnie, Esmond. Interview conducted by Stephen Walker. 20 June 2024.
7 *Belfast Telegraph*. 29 May 2000.
8 BBC Northern Ireland. 28 May 2000.
9 Ross, Colin. Interview conducted by Stephen Walker. 17 September 2024.
10 Trimble, Lady. Interview conducted by Stephen Walker. 14 March 2024.
11 Kelly, Dolores. Interview conducted by Stephen Walker. 23 July 2024.
12 Robinson, Philip. Interview conducted by Stephen Walker. 13 September 2024.
13 Murray, Denis. Interview conducted by Stephen Walker. 9 July 2024.
14 Trimble, David. Interview conducted by Alex Kane. 14 August 2015.
15 Hayden, Ray. Interview conducted by Stephen Walker. 9 July 2024.
16 Cooper, James. Interview conducted by Stephen Walker. 23 July 2024.
17 Blevins, David. Interview conducted by Stephen Walker. 27 September 2024.

21: Hearts and Minds

1 BBC. 23 October 2001.
2 Morrice, Jane. Interview conducted by Stephen Walker. 6 September 2024.
3 Ford, David. Interview conducted by Stephen Walker. 9 July 2024.
4 Durkan, Mark. Interview conducted by Stephen Walker. 15 August 2024.
5 Durkan, Mark. Interview conducted by Stephen Walker. 15 August 2024.
6 Madden, Mary. Interview conducted by Stephen Walker. 23 July 2024.
7 Durkan, Mark. Interview conducted by Stephen Walker. 15 August 2024.
8 *The Guardian*. 10 March 2002.
9 *News Letter*. 12 March 2002.
10 Gerry Adams. Interview conducted by Stephen Walker. 29 July 2024.
11 Neale, Mark. Interview conducted by Stephen Walker. 11 June 2024.
12 Kelly, Mary. Interview conducted by Stephen Walker. 5 September 2024.
13 Kelly, Mary. Interview conducted by Stephen Walker. 5 September 2024.
14 BBC Northern Ireland. *Hearts and Minds* programme. 27 June 2002.
15 Thompson, Noel. Interview conducted by Stephen Walker. 3 September 2024.
16 Kelly, Mary. Interview conducted by Stephen Walker. 5 September 2024.
17 Kerr, David. Interview conducted by Stephen Walker. 18 June 2024.

22: Spies, Splits and Suspensions

1 *Daily Mail.* 8 October 2002.
2 BBC. 8 October 2002.
3 CAIN archive – Conflict and politics in Northern Ireland.
4 Murphy, Lord. Interview conducted by Stephen Walker. 15 July 2024.
5 *Irish Examiner.* 1 May 2003.
6 BBC. 12 July 2003.
7 CAIN archive – Conflict and politics in Northern Ireland.
8 *Belfast Telegraph.* 22 October 2003.
9 Ahern, Bertie. Interview conducted by Stephen Walker. 20 June 2024.
10 *Meeting Myself Coming Back*, BBC Radio 4. 3 August 2013.
11 BBC. 18 November 2003.
12 *Meeting Myself Coming Back*, BBC Radio 4. 3 August 2013.
13 *Meeting Myself Coming Back*, BBC Radio 4. 3 August 2013.
14 Burnside, David. Interview conducted by Stephen Walker. 9 July 2024.
15 Kennedy, Danny. Interview conducted by Stephen Walker. 10 July 2024.
16 Empey, Lord. Statement to author. 7 April 2025.
17 Bew, Lord. Interview conducted by Stephen Walker. 30 July 2024.
18 Foster, Baroness. Interview conducted by Stephen Walker. 9 August 2024.
19 Hermon, Lady. Interview conducted by Stephen Walker. 27 March 2024.
20 *Meeting Myself Coming Back*, BBC Radio 4. 3 August 2013.
21 BBC. 5 January 2005.
22 Ford, David. Interview conducted by Stephen Walker. 9 July 2024.
23 *Irish News.* 21 April 2005.
24 Benjamin, Alex. Interview conducted by Stephen Walker. 11 September 2024.

23: A Good Innings

1 BBC Northern Ireland. *Election 2005.* 6 May 2005.
2 BBC Northern Ireland. *Election 2005.* 6 May 2005.
3 BBC Northern Ireland. *Election 2005.* 6 May 2005.
4 BBC Radio Ulster. 6 May 2005.
5 Hermon, Lady. Interview conducted by Stephen Walker. 27 March 2024.
6 Trimble, Nicky. Interview conducted by Stephen Walker. 7 March 2024.
7 Trimble, Lady. Interview conducted by Stephen Walker. 14 March 2024.
8 Benjamin, Alex. Interview conducted by Stephen Walker. 11 September 2024.
9 BBC. 9 May 2005.
10 Trimble, Richard. Interview conducted by Stephen Walker. 6 March 2024.
11 Wright, Terry. Interview conducted by Terry Wright. 15 August 2024.
12 BBC. 26 September 2005.
13 Trimble, Lady. Interview conducted by Stephen Walker. 14 March 2024.
14 Murphy, Lord. Interview conducted by Stephen Walker. 15 July 2024.
15 Trimble, Richard. Interview conducted by Stephen Walker. 6 March 2024.
16 Donoughue, Lord. Interview conducted by Stephen Walker. 26 July 2024.
17 Politico website. 19 December 2001.

18 Duncan Smith, Iain. Interview conducted by Stephen Walker. 10 September 2024.
19 Hermon, Lady. Interview conducted by Stephen Walker. 27 March 2024.
20 BBC Radio Ulster. 17 April 2007.
21 BBC Radio Ulster. 17 April 2007.
22 White, Barry. Interview conducted by Stephen Walker. 13 June 2024.
23 Empey, Lord. Interview conducted by Stephen Walker. 12 June 2024.
24 Trimble, Lady. Interview conducted by Stephen Walker. 14 March 2024.
25 McCue, Jason. Interview conducted by Stephen Walker. 18 September 2024.
26 BBC. 19 September 2014.
27 BBC. 19 September 2014.
28 BBC. 9 June 2016.
29 BBC. 18 June 2016.

24: The Final Days

1 *Derry Journal.* 21 March 2017.
2 Hansard. House of Commons. 18 December 2017.
3 *The Guardian.* 6 April 2018.
4 *Policy Exchange* report. July 2019.
5 *BBC Newsline.* 16 July 2019.
6 *Belfast Telegraph.* 17 July 2019.
7 *BBC Newsline.* 16 July 2019.
8 O'Loan, Baroness. Interview conducted by Stephen Walker. 6 September 2024.
9 Murphy, Lord. Interview conducted by Stephen Walker. 15 July 2024.
10 Trimble, Vicky. Interview conducted by Stephen Walker. 1 December 2023.
11 Trimble, Lady. Interview conducted by Stephen Walker. 14 March 2024.
12 Trimble, Vicky. Interview conducted by Stephen Walker. 1 December 2023.
13 Trimble, Lady. Interview conducted by Stephen Walker. 9 November 2024.
14 Trimble, Lady. Interview conducted by Stephen Walker. 9 November 2024.
15 BBC. 24 January 2020.
16 *Irish Examiner.* 3 August 2020.
17 Trimble, Lady. Interview conducted by Stephen Walker. 9 November 2024.
18 BBC. 12 February 2021.
19 Trimble, Richard. Interview conducted by Stephen Walker. 6 March 2024.
20 Trimble, Vicky. Interview conducted by Stephen Walker. 1 December 2023.
21 Trimble, Iain. Interview conducted by Stephen Walker. 11 June 2024.
22 Trimble, Richard. Interview conducted by Stephen Walker. 6 March 2024.
23 Trimble, Nicky. Interview conducted by Stephen Walker. 7 March 2024.
24 Davidson, Colin. Interview conducted by Stephen Walker. 22 March 2024.
25 Trimble, Sarah. Interview conducted by Stephen Walker. 26 February 2024.
26 Trimble, Richard. Interview conducted by Stephen Walker. 6 March 2024.
27 Trimble, Lady. Interview conducted by Stephen Walker. 9 November 2024.
28 Trimble, Lady. Interview conducted by Stephen Walker. 14 March 2025.

ENDNOTES

25: Portrait of a Peacemaker

1. Davidson, Colin. Interview conducted by Stephen Walker. 22 March 2024.
2. Correspondence with Ryan Feeney. 4 October 2024.
3. Trimble, Richard. Interview conducted by Stephen Walker. 6 March 2024.
4. Ahern, Bertie. Interview conducted by Stephen Walker. 20 June 2024.
5. Foster, Baroness. Interview conducted by Stephen Walker. 9 August 2024.
6. Ross, Colin. Interview conducted by Stephen Walker. 17 September 2024.
7. Kerr, David. Speech at Lord Trimble portrait unveiling. 27 June 2022.
8. Trimble, Sarah. Interview conducted by Stephen Walker. 26 February 2024.
9. Trimble, Lady. Interview conducted by Stephen Walker. 9 November 2024.
10. Trimble, Vicky. Interview conducted by Stephen Walker. 1 December 2023.
11. Trimble, Richard. Interview conducted by Stephen Walker. 6 March 2024.
12. Trimble, Richard. Interview conducted by Stephen Walker. 6 March 2024.
13. Trimble, Lady. Interview conducted by Stephen Walker. 14 March 2025.
14. BBC. 1 August 2022.
15. *Conservative Home*. 5 August 2022.
16. Correspondence with Nancy Soderberg. 4 May 2025.
17. Hoey, Baroness. Interview conducted by Stephen Walker. 7 August 2024.
18. Empey, Lord. Interview conducted by Stephen Walker. 12 June 2024.
19. Kelly, Dolores. Interview conducted by Stephen Walker. 23 July 2024.
20. Reynolds, Lee. Interview conducted by Stephen Walker. 4 September 2024.
21. Black, Philip. Interview conducted by Stephen Walker. 8 August 2024.
22. Foster, Baroness. Interview conducted by Stephen Walker. 9 August 2024.
23. Blair, Sir Tony. Interview conducted by Stephen Walker. 22 October 2024.
24. Ahern, Bertie. Interview conducted by Stephen Walker. 20 June 2024.
25. Adams, Gerry. Interview conducted by Stephen Walker. 29 July 2024.
26. Trimble, David. Interview conducted by Alex Kane. 14 August 2015.
27. Rogan, Lord. Interview conducted by Stephen Walker. 11 June 2024.
28. Trimble, Lady. Interview conducted by Stephen Walker. 14 March 2025.
29. Durkan, Mark. Interview conducted by Stephen Walker. 15 August 2024.
30. Millar, Frank, *The Price of Peace*, Liffey Press, 2008.
31. Kerr, David. Interview conducted by Stephen Walker. 18 June 2024.
32. Gudgin, Graham. Interview conducted by Stephen Walker. 7 July 2024.
33. Dudley Edwards, Ruth. Interview conducted by Stephen Walker. 19 July 2024.
34. Campbell, Alastair. Interview conducted by Stephen Walker. 12 August 2024.
35. Fullbrook, Mark. Interview conducted by Stephen Walker. 9 September 2024.
36. Hunter, John. Interview conducted by Stephen Walker. 2 April 2025.
37. Blair, Sir Tony. Interview conducted by Stephen Walker. 22 October 2024.
38. Rodgers, Bríd. Interview conducted by Stephen Walker. 14 August 2024.
39. McAleese, Mary. Interview conducted by Stephen Walker. 10 July 2024.
40. McLaughlin, Mitchel. Interview conducted by Stephen Walker. 15 August 2024.
41. Trimble, Vicky. Interview conducted by Stephen Walker. 1 December 2023.

INDEX

Adams, Gerry
  attends Omagh victim funerals, 266
  calls for decommissioning, 323, 401–2
  Canary Wharf bombing, 197
  describes Trimble, 213, 271
  excessive influence of Trimble, 216–7
  lauds Balcombe Street gang, 248
  meetings with Trimble, 269–70, 331–2
  reluctant Belfast visit, 344–5
  renegotiates, saves peace talks, 223–6
  talks with Hume, 147
  tells IRA to embrace democracy, 353
  Trimble's antipathy, 270–1
  Trimble's funeral, 396
  Trimble's leadership, 187
  violence 'over', 268
  welcomes IRA ceasefire, 155
Achnagairn Castle, 378
Adams, David, 212–3
Ahern, Bertie
  decommissioning, 401
  dismisses sectarian tag, 329–30
  good relationship with Trimble, 271–2, 392–3
  mother's death, 224, 225
  opinion of Trimble, 190
  similarity to Blair, 208–9
  support for power-sharing, ix
  supports Mitchell, 216
  Trimble's funeral, 396
Ahern, Julia, 224
Ahtisaari, Martii, 310
Aiken, Steve, 392
Alderdice, John, 190, 224, 230–1
Allen, Jack, 129, 232
Allen, Philip, 218
Alliance Party, 33–4, 50, 76
Allister, Jim, 352
Altnagelvin Hospital, 5
Andersonstown, 32
Andrews, David, 224, 225, 228
Anglo-Irish Agreement
  aims, 109–10
  declaration, 109
  focus of Upper Bann election, 135, 136
  origins, 106
  unionist opposition, 111–5
Anglo-Irish Division, Foreign Affairs, 191
Armitage, Pauline, 324
Articles 2 and 3, Irish Constitution, 227–8, 241, 398
Assembly election results, 260
Athenaeum Club, 389, 390
Attwood, Tim, 252
Autism, Trimble's belief he was autistic, 405

backstop plan, 376–7
Baird, Ernest, 69, 83, 107
Baker, Kenneth, 132
Balcombe Street gang, 248
Ballyholme Primary School, 8
Banbridge Chronicle, 139
Bangor Grammar School
   contemporaries, 7
   Trimble enters, 9–12
   Trimble's academic record, 15–6, 19
   Trimble's last days, 20
   Trimble unsporty, 20
Bar, Trimble called to, 31
Barker, James, 266
Barr, Glenn, 57, 58
Barry, Peter, 118
Bassett, Ray, 240
Beare, Norah, 350, 352
Beattie, Sam, 23, 37, 81
Beggs, Roy, 355
Begley, Thomas, 149
Belfast Telegraph, 142, 173
Bell, Eileen, 206
Benjamin, Alex, 354, 360
Bevins, Anthony, 152
Bew, Paul, (later Lord Bew), 185–6, 221, 270–1, 391, 392
Bingham, Rev. William, 268
Birnie, Esmond, 290–1, 307–8
Black, Philip, 113, 400
Blair, Tony
   asks Clinton to pressure Trimble, 238
   at Balmoral Show, 250
   backs Framework and Mitchell Principles, 207

   backs decommissioning, xi;, 207–8
   backs remain vote, 370–1
   opinion of Trimble, 204–5
   overawes Trimble, 290–1
   prisoner release, 400–1
   pushes devolution, 291–2
   pushes Trimble towards Good Friday Agreement, 235–7
   sets up Saville inquiry, 42
   supports Mitchell, 216
   tribute to Trimble, 407
   Trimble peerage, 363
   urges support for power-sharing, ix
   visits Balmoral Show, 207
   visits Omagh bomb victims, 265
Blevins, David, 139, 318
Bloody Friday, xii
Bloody Sunday, xii, 39, 40–1
Boal, Dessie, 43
Bono, 252–4, 278
Boyne, Battle of, 17
Bradford, Hazel, 91
Bradford, Nora, 299–300
Bradford, Robert, 97, 299
Bratty, Joe, 154
Breen, Harry, 319
Brexit, 364, 370–1, 375–6, 381–2
British Embassy, Dublin, 43
British-Irish Association, 123, 189
Brooke, Peter, 132, 140, 146
Brownlow House, Lurgan, 107, 128
Bruton, John, 196
Buchanan, Bob, 319
Bulletin, The, 57

INDEX

Burnside, David, 46, 68, 310–1, 342, 348–9, 355
Burntollet Bridge attack, 32
Bush, George W., 321

Caine, Jonathan, 136
Callaghan, Jim, 29
Cameron, David, 364–6, 367, 369, 370, 371
Campbell College, 9
Campbell, Alistair, 205, 272, 406
Campbell, David, 264
Campbell, Kenneth, 97
Campbell, Sheena, 132
Canary Wharf bombing, 196–8
Carson, Joan, 286
Chequers, 223
Chichester-Clark, James, 33, 34–5
'Chuckle Brothers' (McGuinness and Paisley), 366
civil rights campaign, 27
Clarke, Randall, 9, 10–11, 19
Clinton, President Bill
    McGuinness funeral, 374
    urges Trimble to sign peace agreement, xi, 238
    visits to NI, 268–9, 312
Colhoun, Jack, 5–6
Collins, Michael, 108, 269
Combined Loyalist Military Command, 160
common travel area, 375
Connolly House, Belfast, 155
Constitutional Convention, 61, 63, 79
Continuity IRA, 215–6, 218
Cooper, Bob, 78
Cooper, James, 30, 214, 286, 314, 360

Coulter, Phil, 282
Council of Ireland, 48, 54
County Down Spectator, 19, 25
Covid-19, 382–4, 389
Cowen, Brian, 345
Craig, Bill
    ambitions, 35
    influences Trimble, 29, 44, 51
    liquidation call, 45
    opposes Faulkner, 43
    opposes reforms, 29, 49, 55
    political career, 43–4
    RAF service, 43
    Trimble's high opinion, 44
    voluntary coalition collapses, 65–6
Craig, James, 108–9, 269
Cranbourne, Viscount, 251
Cree, Leslie, 13, 16–7, 20
Cunningham House, 358
Cunningham, Josias, 181–2

D'Hondt, Victor, 292
Dáil Éireann, 6
Daily Mirror, 203, 205
Daly, Bishop Edward, 282
Darling, Alistair, 203
Davidson, Colin, 386, 387–8, 390–2
Davidson, John Biggs, 100
de Brún, Bairbre, 339, 352
de Chastelain, General John, 222–3, 289, 298, 305, 344–5
De Rossa, Proinsias, 192
de Valera, Éamon, 108
decommissioning
    Good Friday Agreement, 234–7
    interlocuter, 298

439

precondition, 284
scepticism, 109
Sinn Féin in government, x–xi
Derry Citizens Action Committee, 29
Derry Journal, 188
Derry Siege of, ix
Devenport, Mark, 122
Devolution Group, 93, 94
direct rule, 45–6, 60, 306, 340
Dobson, John, 132, 135, 177
Dodds, Nigel, 314, 384
Doherty, Oran, 266
Donaldson, Jeffrey
   joins DUP, 352
   opposes Good Friday Agreement, 230, 237, 240, 242–3
   opposes NI Protocol. 384
   opposes Trimble, 228, 286
   resignation, 350
   seeks to replace Taylor, 125
   suspension, 342
   Trimble's funeral, 396
   Trimble's high opinion, 240–1
Donoughue, Lord, 364
Dougal, Jim, 147
Downing Street Declaration, 153
Drumcree church, 166–70, 172, 183, 190, 198, 267–8
Dublin and Monaghan bombings, 59
Durkan, Mark
   assesses Trimble, 326–7
   background, 325–6
   deputy first minister, 324–5
   Hume and Trimble in Poyntzpass, 220
   Trimble's image, 190–1
   Trimble portrait, 392

UUP dissenters, 240
visits Trimble at home, 403–4

Eagles, The, 317
Easter Rising, 108, 123
Eastwood, Colum, 376, 396
Edwards, Ruth Dudley, 123–4, 189–90, 192, 405
Elder, Raymond, 154
Elliott, Tom, 368
Empey, Reg, (later Lord Empey)
   backs Good Friday Agreement, 230
   Bill Craig assessment, 67
   leadership ballot, 181–2, 184
   Trimble in Lords, 367
   UUP leader, 362, 366
   Trimble assessment, 47, 398–9
Enniskillen bombing, xii
Europa Hotel, Belfast, 125, 174, 179, 245
European Commission of Human Rights, 94
Eve, Judith
   dean of Law faculty, 116–8
   rivalry with Trimble, 116–20
   shootings at Queen's University, 101, 104
   student of Trimble's, 30
   Trimble's marriage, 51, 52

FARC guerillas, 321
Farry, Stephen, 396
Faulkner, Brian
   backs Sunningdale, 52
   blames protestors for Bloody Sunday, 40

INDEX

heads NI Executive, 54
limited party support, 402
NI prime minister, 35
opposes power-sharing, 45
resignation, 45–6
summoned to Downing St, 29
Fearon, Kate, 217
Feeney, Ryan, 386, 391
Finucane, Pat, 319
Fitt, Gerry, 54, 55
FitzGerald, Garret, 106, 109
Ford, David, 324–5, 353–4
Fortnight, 95
Foster, Arlene, (later Baroness Foster)
    first minister, 373
    joins DUP, 352
    McGuinness funeral, 374
    opposes NI Protocol, 384
    prisoner release, 228–9
    resignation, 350–1
    RUC reforms, 228–9
    Trimble assessment, 285, 400
    Trimble portrait unveiling, 393
Framework Document, 160, 161
Free Derry Corner, 39
Free Presbyterian Church, 65
French, Tom, 132
Frizzell's shop bombing, 149–50
Fullbrook, Mark, 253, 406
'Fuss on the Bus', 346–7

Gardiner, Sam, 128–9, 130
Garvaghy Road, Portadown
    protests end, 267–8
    RUC block then allow Orange march, 198–9
    Trimble intervention, 166–7, 170
    Trimble refuses to engage with residents, 199
Godson, Dean, 34
Godson, Lord, 396–7
Good Friday Agreement
    details, 240–1
    impact of Brexit, 383
    long negotiation, ix–xi, 227–9
    preparatory discussions, 194–5
    prisoner release, 228–9, 230, 242, 400–1
    RUC reforms, 228–9, 241
    referenda to approve, 242, 244, 255
    Trimble's response, 109
    unionist opposition, 242
    violence threats against Trimble, 255–7
Gordon, Gareth, 175
Gracey, Harold, 167
Graham, Edgar
    murdered by IRA, 99–104, 261
    rising star, 96
    Trimble colleague at Queen's University, 94
    Trimble portrait unveiling, 393
    Trimble recalls, 299
Grand Hotel, Brighton, 105
Grand Hotel, Oslo, 389
Grand Union Canal, 381
Green, George, 46–7, 49, 69
Greer, Ian, 386, 391
Greysteel atrocity, xii, 150–1
Grimason, Stephen, 241
Gudgin, Dr Graham, 271–2, 275

Haass, Richard, 321
Habib, Ben, 384
Hadden, Tom, 95
Hambly, Ken, 10
Hamill, Robert, 319
Harmony Hill Presbyterian church, 178, 396
Harris, Eoghan, 280
Hatch, Arnold, 57, 129, 130
Hayden, Ray, 123, 259, 260, 317
Heads of Agreement paper, 216
Heath, Edward, 34, 45, 55
Hegarty, Bishop Seamus, 266
Hennessey, Thomas, 234
Hermon, Sir Jack, 96
Higgins, Michael D., 374, 396
Highcliff Hotel, Bournemouth, 157
Hillsborough Castle, 109, 118–9
Hoey, Kate, 138–9, 251–2
Holkeri, Harri, 222–3
Holland, Mary, 152
Holy Cross school dispute, 327–8, 329
Hourican, Liam, 123–4
House of Commons: Trimble's early experience, 137;
Hume, John
  appears with Trimble at U2 concert, 253–4
  background, 33
  backs coalition with Craig, 68
  bust in Leinster House, 7
  declines to be deputy first minister, 261
  Downing St Declaration, 153
  final illness, funeral, 383
  forms Derry Citizens Action Committee, 29
  input to Good Friday deal, 244
  MEP, 105
  negotiations with Trimble, 195
  New Ireland Forum, 106
  Nobel Peace Prize with Trimble, 277–82
  'petty people', 281
  poor relations with Trimble, 148–9, 195, 226
  presses unionists to accept peace deal, 232
  proposes Executive Commission, 146
  resigns leadership, 322
  talks with Adams, 147
  Trimble's opinion, 383
  welcomes IRA ceasefire, 155
Hume, Pat, 408
Humphrys, John, 28, 139
hunger strikes, 97
Hunter, John, 243, 407
Huston, Felicity, 276–7

Independent Commission on Policing in NI, 294–5
Independent International Commisson on Decommissioning, 213, 287, 310, 323, 362
Inside Politics, 123
Institute for Professional Legal Studies, 120–1
International Decommissioning Commission, 268
internment without trial, 35, 36–7
Irish Civil War, 108

INDEX

Irish Republican Army (IRA)
    attacks on UDA, 154
    border campaign, 28
    Brighton hotel bombing, 105
    confirms decommissioning, 323
    declares ceasefire, 155, 160
    Docklands bombing impact, 196
    ends war, 362
    Graham murder, 100–3
    kill Campbell and Bradford, 97
    raid Special Branch HQ, 330
    recruits after Bloody Sunday, 40
    reinstates ceasefire, 213
    secret contact with UK government, 149
    Trimble calls for total surrender, 150
    Trimble legitimate target, 53
    weapons dump inspections, 309

Jack, Captain William, Trimble's grandfather, 4
Jack, Ida, Trimble's grandmother, 4–5
John Paul II, Pope, 288
Johnson, Boris, 377, 381–2, 396
Jones, Colette, 132, 135
Jordan, Hugh, 201–2

Kane, Alex, 133–5, 160, 285, 316
Kearney, Vincent, 173–4
Keenan, Brian, 287
Kelly, Dolores, 315, 399
Kelly, Gerry, 339
Kelly, Mary, 332–3, 334–5
Kennedy, Danny, 134, 177, 239–10, 349
Kennedy, Gary, 131, 135
Kennedy, Jane, 327–8
Kerr, Bertie, 193, 194
Kerr, David
    calls on Trimble to resign, 335–6
    impressed by Maginnis, 233–4
    interviewed by Trimble, 193–4
    North–South bodies, 226
    Trimble tribute, 394, 405
    U2 concert, 254
    weather omen, 242
Khrushchev, Nikita, 20
Kilfedder, Jim, 50, 91–2, 164
King, Tom, 113
Kinnock, Neil: election 1992, 145
Kirwan, Wally, 232

Labour Party Conference, Blackpool, 200–4
Laird, John, 257
Land Registry, 21–3
Leckey, Ken, 49
Leeds Castle, 352
Legge, J.M., 170
Leneghan, Paddy, 72
Logue, Anne, 31
Logue, Hugh, 67, 275–6
Longford, Trimble links, 6, 7
Loughinisland bar attack, 154
Low, Trevor, 20
Lowry, Sir Robert, 61, 64–5
Loyalist Volunteer Force, 216
Lucy, Gordon, 130, 177–8
Lucy, Graham, 107–8
Lundy, Robert, ix, 4
Lurgan Mail, 129

Madden, Mary, 31, 59, 78, 327–8
Maginness, Alban, 42, 56, 62, 168
Maginnis, Ken, 171, 176, 187–8, 233, 257–8
Major, John
  backs EU remain vote, 370
  denies contacts with IRA, 149, 151–2
  Canary Wharf bombing, 196
  election 1992, 145
  Hume–Adams initiative, 147–8, 151
  meetings with Trimble, 157–8
  reliance on unionist MPs, 151
Mallie, Eamonn, 152
Mallon, Seamus
  deputy first minister, 261, 277
  Poyntzpass visit with Trimble, 218–9
  relationship with Trimble, 283, 382
  resignation, 293–4
  takes Nicholson's seat, 112
  Trimble assessment, 243
  Trimble's moodiness, 277
Mandelson, Peter, 297–8, 306, 313
Markethill, 211, 219
marriage equality, 378–80
Martin, Micheál, 396
Martin, Miss, Trimble's teacher, 8–9
Maryfield secretariat, 110, 235
Mason, Amanda, 357
Mason, Roy, 83
Mates, Michael, 100
May, Theresa, 371, 375–7
Mayhew, Sir Patrick, 146, 152, 154
Maze prison, 94

McAleese, Mary
  attends Omagh victim funerals, 266–7
  beats Trimble for top legal job, 120–1
  hugs Trimble in Buncrana, 266–7
  meets Trimble and Daphne in Rostrevor, 72
  opinion of Daphne Trimble, 408;
  opinion of Trimble, 30, 42
  President of Ireland, 266
  staff member at Queen's, 42–3
  Trimble's sectarian nature, 39, 40–1
McBride, Sam, 100
McCammick, Jim, 129
McCann, Eamonn, music promoter, 252
McCartney, Bob, 164–5, 214, 229, 353
McCombe, Heather
  different personality, 26
  honeymoon in Wicklow, 26
  joins UDR, 36
  marries Trimble, 26;
  separates from Trimble, 51–2
McCrea, Willie, 311, 355
McCue, Jason, 369
McCune, Rodney, 297–8
McCusker, Harold, 127
McCusker, Jennifer, 127–8
McDonald, Henry, 12, 201
McFarland, Alan, 162, 165
McGimpsey, Chris, 91, 189, 200
McGimpsey, Michael, 49–50, 86–7, 189, 317
McGoldrick, Michael, 198–9, 385

INDEX

McGuinness, Martin
   Education Minister, 301
   final illness, 373–4
   meets Queen Elizabeth, 374
   praise from Trimble, 374
   relations with Paisley, 366
   resignation, 373
   Trimble prefers him to Adams, 270
   works with IDC, 268, 269
McIvor, Basil, 32–3
McLaughlin, Mitchel, 168, 228, 287, 408–9
McLoughlin, Sean, 266
McMaster, Stanley, 55
McMichael, Gary, 132
McMichael, John, 132
McMullan, Rev. Charles, 396
McNamara, Kevin, 204
McNarry, David, 93–5, 175–6, 358–9
McWilliams, Monica, 324
Methodist College Belfast, 89
MI6, 152
Millar, Frank, 149
Mitchell Principles, 196, 197, 199, 207, 214, 216
Mitchell, Senator George
   assesses unionist divisions, 214–5
   background, 196
   chairs peace talks, xi
   challenges of role, 215–;
   deals with unionist opposition, 224–5
   Decommissioning Report, 196
   friend of Clinton, 196
   negotiates between Ahern and Trimble, 224–6
   opera joke, 296–7
   praises Trimble, 243–4
   reconciliation dinners, 217
   reviews Good Friday Agreement, 294–6
   sets ground rules for talks, 195–6
   timetable and end point for talks, 222–3
   Trimble criticism, 198
   Trimble's essential role, 409
   urges support for power-sharing, x;
   verified disarmament essential, 196
Molyneaux, Jim
   cautious nature, 403
   difficult relationship with Trimble, 124–5
   IRA ceasefire, 155
   integrationist, 92–3
   leadership challenged, 162–4
   lone operator, 158–9
   resignation pressure, 165–6
   response to Downing St Declaration, 153–4
   Trimble opens his mail, 159
   Trimble's low opinion, 158–60
   trusts Thatcher, 106, 162
Montgomery, David, 7–8, 203, 235–6
Morrice, Jane, 324
Morrison, Danny, 97
Mowlam, Mo
   brain tumour, 273
   D'Hondt procedure, 292–3

poor relationship with Trimble,
  249, 271–4, 294
replaces McNamara, 204, 207
standing ovation at party
  conference, 273
temporary release of prisoners,
  249, 273
visits loyalist prisoners, 273
works well with Mitchell, 224
Murphy, Paul, (later Lord Murphy),
  340–1, 363, 379–80
Murray, Denis, 114, 180–1, 315

Napier, Oliver, 54, 91–2
National Press Club, Washington,
  307
Neale, Mark, 183, 295, 331–2
Neill, Terry, 10–11
Nelson, Rosemary, 319
Nesbitt, Dermot, 99–102, 176
Nesbitt, Mike, 392
New Ireland Forum, 105–6
New Labour, 206
New Ulster Movement, 76
Newry, 76–7
News Letter: Trimble's hard line
  interview, 122
Newsnight, 200
Nicholson, Jim, 112, 125, 230–1, 282,
  291, 352
Nobel Museum, Oslo, 389
Nobel Peace Prize
  Adams speculation, 277
  award ceremony, 279
  financial benefits, 281
  Hume–Trimble award, 7, 277–8,
    407–8
  laureates summit, Mérida, 381
  Trimble recognition, 407
North–South bodies, 161, 283–4
North–South Ministerial Council,
  226, 234, 241, 298
Northern Bank robbery, 353
Northern Ireland Civil Rights
  Association: Trimble's hostility, 28
Northern Ireland Economic
  Research Centre, 275
Northern Ireland Forum for Political
  Dialogue, 197
Northern Ireland Protocol, 381–2,
  383, 384

O'Connor, Tim, 191–2
O'Donnell, Liz, 232–3, 250
O'Loan, Baroness, 379
O'Malley, Padraig, 214
O'Neill, Michelle, 382
O'Neill, Terence
  crossroads election, 32
  Harold Wilson confronts, 29
  leadership threatened, 32
  resignation, 33
  sacks Bill Craig, 29
Observer, The, 152
Official Sinn Féin, 192
Omagh bombing atrocity, 264–7,
  369
Orange Order, 16–7
Orr, Daphne (later Trimble)
  childhood, 74–5
  'Daphne principle', 300, 408
  faces violence, 314–5
  friendship with Pat Hume, 408
  legal career, 82

INDEX

Longford connections, 7
meets Trimble, 70-1, 73
Nobel ceremony, 279-82
peerage announcement, 362-3
schooling, 75-6
strong influence on Trimble, 42, 408-9
student days, 71, 77-8
supports Trimble's party leadership, 178
threats to Trimble, 255-6
Trimble's personal appearance, 257-8
Trimble's DIY failings, 88
Trimble's funeral, 396
Trimble's second wife, 2, 42, 87-8
Trimble's side arm incident, 79-82
Wallace's opinion, 82-3
Orr, Gerry and Barbara, 71-2, 73-4, 76

Paisley, Ian
  attacks Faulkner, 43
  calls Mayhew a liar, 152
  coalition U turn, 65-6, 68
  'dances' with Trimble in Portadown, 167-9
  'Dr No', 9
  early links with Trimble, xi
  hostility to Trimble, 83-4, 301
  first minister, 366
  MEP, 92, 105
  mocks Trimble in Stormont, 79-80
  opposes Anglo-Irish Agreement, 111-2

opposes Downing St Declaration, 153
opposes Good Friday Agreement, ix
opposes power-sharing, 55
personality, 43
rejects IRA ceasefire, 155
Paisley, Sylvia, (later Lady Hermon) 351
  hears Graham shooting, 102-3
  interviewed by Trimble, 95-6
  law lecturer, 95
  on Trimble's seat loss, 359
  opinion of Trimble, 351
  retains seat, 355
  speech-making technique, 138
  Trimble joins Conservatives, 366, 368
  Trimble's Hillsborough stunt, 118-9
  urges Trimble not to resign, 351
Parachute Regiment, 39
partition, 108
Patten, Chris, 132, 294-5, 404
Pearl Harbor, 321
Pearse, Pádraig, 123, 124
People's Democracy, 32
Police Service of Northern Ireland, 330, 339-40
Policy Exchange, 377
Poots, Charles, 50
Powell, Enoch, 66
Powell, Jonathan, xi, 235-6
Power-sharing Executive, 48-9
Poyntzpass, 218-20
Presley, Elvis, 15, 90

Purdy, Martina, 142–3
Purvis, Dawn, 212

Queen's Court Hotel, Bangor, 15
Queen's University Belfast
   contest for Dean of Law Faculty, 116–20
   honours Trimble, 386
   Trimble's academic ambitions, 31–2, 34
   Trimble assistant law lecturer, 26, 30
   Trimble 'boring' lecturer, 30
   Trimble considers history degree, 21
   Trimble distant from his students, 30–1
   Trimble portrait, 386, 387–8, 390–2
   Trimble studies law, 21–5
   Trimble takes leave of absence, 140–1
Quinn, Maura, 274–5, 278, 288

Railway Bar, Pontzpass, 218
Ramaphosa, Cyril, 310
Real IRA bombings, 264–7, 313
Reid, John, 313, 318, 340
Reid, Ken, 158, 240, 290
Renewable Heat Incentive, 373
'Reservoir Prods', 212
Reynolds, Albert, 152
Reynolds, Lee, 163–4, 399
Riddell Hall, 392
Robinson, Iris, 314
Robinson, Peter, 91, 366, 399
Robinson, Philip, 315

Roderick, Stephanie, 137–8
Rodgers, Brid, 132, 135, 227, 407
Rodgers, Jim, 47–8, 237–8
Rogan, Denis, (later Lord Rogan), 204, 266, 360, 361, 403
Ross, Colin, 311, 393–4
Ross, Hugh, 132
Ross, Willie, 161, 171
Rostrevor, 72
Royal Air Force, 12–3
Royal Black Institution, 92
Royal Inniskilling Fusiliers, 4
Royal Irish Constabulary, 6
Royal Irish Fusiliers, 107
Royal Irish Regiment, 4
Royal Irish Rifles, 107
Royal Ulster Constabulary
   confronts protesters in Derry, 27
   name change, 295, 404
   reform proposals, 228, 294–5
   Trimble family connections, 6
Royal Victoria Hospital, Belfast, 389

Salmond, Alex, 369
Sands, Bobby, 313
Savage, George, 129, 130
Saville inquiry, 42
Scottish independence, 369–70
Scottish National Party, 369
Sheridan, Lee, 23–4
Simpson, David, 357–8
Simpson, Mark, 173, 174–5
Sinn Féin
   arrests in Colombia, 321–2
   Downing St Declaration, 153–4
   excluded from meetings, 196, 197

INDEX

Frizell shop bombing, 150
in government, xi
'not house trained', 309–10
RDS Ard Fheis, 248–9
signs up to Mitchell Principles, 214
US visas, 322
Smallwoods, Ray, 154
Smith, Iain Duncan, 364–5
Smith, Marion, 11, 124
Smyth, Clifford, 51, 91
Smyth, Rev. Martin, 63, 160, 162, 171, 308, 342
Social Democratic and Labour Party, 34, 64, 146
Soderberg, Nancy, 398
Solzhenitsyn, Alexandr, 79
Somme, Battle of, 318
Spence, Gusty, 160
Spotlight, 122
Spring, Dick, 154
St Mary's church, Buncrana, 266
St Patrick's Day in US, 307
Steele, John, 170
Steele, May, 262
Stephens, Rosalind, 378
Stone, Michael, 250
Stranmillis College, 291
Sunday Tribune, The, 129, 188
Sunningdale Agreement, xi, 52, 55, 60
supergrass system, 94
Swann, Robin, 391

Tarantino, Quentin, 212
Taylor, John
   backs peace agreement, xi
   calls on Trimble to resign, 358
   helps Trimble in Commons, 137
   issues with peace deal, 229–30, 284
   Lord Kilclooney, 358
   possible party leader, 170–2, 181–2
   resigns as MEP, 125
   Trimble his EU election agent, 105
Thatcher, Margaret, 92, 105, 106, 109
Thompson, Noel, 333–5, 357
Times, The, 160
Trainor, Damien, 218
Trimble, Billy, David's father
   background 6
   death, 26
   distance from David, 14
   drinker, smoker, 14
   lung cancer, 24, 25–6
   moves to Bangor, 7
   urges David to join civil service, 21
Trimble, David, David's nephew, 89–90
Trimble, George, David's grandfather, 6
Trimble, Iain, David's brother
   brother's illness, 385
   church-going, 13–4
   David's car accident, 16
   joins ATC, RAF, 13, 26
   Orangeman, 17
   relationship with siblings, 1–2
   schooling, 2
Trimble, Ivy, David's mother, 3–4, 14

Trimble, Nicky, David's son
   family holidays, 263
   father's illness, 387
   father in Commons, 141
   father preferred academia, 142
   house protests, 256
   pressure on father, 304
   recognition from Queen's University, 394
Trimble, Richard, David's son
   family meal routine, 141–2
   father becomes MP, 133
   father's cooking skills, 88
   father's funeral, 395
   father's illness, 384–5, 386–7, 388, 392, 395
   meets King of Norway, 304
   phone threats, 255
   seat loss, 361
   Trimble peerage, 363
Trimble, Rosemary, David's sister, 2–3
Trimble, Sarah, David's daughter, 145, 257, 279, 388, 394
Trimble, Thomas, David's grand-uncle, 17
Trimble, Vicky, David's daughter
   comes out as gay, 378–9
   fails to meet Blair, 303–4
   father becomes MP, 136–7
   father's peace-making legacy, 409
   father's illness, 385, 395
   father's leadership ambitions, 178, 186
   marries Rosalind Stephens, 378–9
   mentioned in Lords, 380

Trinity Presbyterian church, Bangor, 13–4
Turkel Commission, 368
Twining, William, 23–4

U2, 252–3
Ukraine war, 389
Ulster Clubs, 113–5, 121
Ulster Conservatives and Unionists New Force (UCUNF), 366–7
Ulster Covenant, 4;
Ulster Defence Association, 44, 150–1
Ulster Defence Regiment, 36
Ulster Freedom Fighters, 44, 261
Ulster Hall, 180
Ulster Society, 107–8, 128
Ulster Special Constabulary, 76
Ulster Vanguard, 43–5, 50–1, 56, 64–5, 84
Ulster Volunteer Force, 154
Ulster Workers Council, 56, 57–9
United Ulster Unionist Council, 55–6, 61–2, 69
United Unionist Action Council strike, 83–4

Wagner, Richard, 201
Walker, Samuel, 129, 130
Wallace, Herb
   beats Trimble to law chair, 125–6
   friendship with Trimble, 22–3
   Graham murder, 101
   Hillsborough stunt, 118–9
   opinion of Trimble, 22–3
   Queens student with Trimble, 22–4

INDEX

Frizell shop bombing, 150
  in government, xi
  'not house trained', 309–10
  RDS Ard Fheis, 248–9
  signs up to Mitchell Principles, 214
  US visas, 322
Smallwoods, Ray, 154
Smith, Iain Duncan, 364–5
Smith, Marion, 11, 124
Smyth, Clifford, 51, 91
Smyth, Rev. Martin, 63, 160, 162, 171, 308, 342
Social Democratic and Labour Party, 34, 64, 146
Soderberg, Nancy, 398
Solzhenitsyn, Alexandr, 79
Somme, Battle of, 318
Spence, Gusty, 160
Spotlight, 122
Spring, Dick, 154
St Mary's church, Buncrana, 266
St Patrick's Day in US, 307
Steele, John, 170
Steele, May, 262
Stephens, Rosalind, 378
Stone, Michael, 250
Stranmillis College, 291
Sunday Tribune, The, 129, 188
Sunningdale Agreement, xi, 52, 55, 60
supergrass system, 94
Swann, Robin, 391

Tarantino, Quentin, 212
Taylor, John
  backs peace agreement, xi
  calls on Trimble to resign, 358
  helps Trimble in Commons, 137
  issues with peace deal, 229–30, 284
  Lord Kilclooney, 358
  possible party leader, 170–2, 181–2
  resigns as MEP, 125
  Trimble his EU election agent, 105
Thatcher, Margaret, 92, 105, 106, 109
Thompson, Noel, 333–5, 357
Times, The, 160
Trainor, Damien, 218
Trimble, Billy, David's father
  background 6
  death, 26
  distance from David, 14
  drinker, smoker, 14
  lung cancer, 24, 25–6
  moves to Bangor, 7
  urges David to join civil service, 21
Trimble, David, David's nephew, 89–90
Trimble, George, David's grandfather, 6
Trimble, Iain, David's brother
  brother's illness, 385
  church-going, 13–4
  David's car accident, 16
  joins ATC, RAF, 13, 26
  Orangeman, 17
  relationship with siblings, 1–2
  schooling, 2
Trimble, Ivy, David's mother, 3–4, 14

Trimble, Nicky, David's son
   family holidays, 263
   father's illness, 387
   father in Commons, 141
   father preferred academia, 142
   house protests, 256
   pressure on father, 304
   recognition from Queen's University, 394
Trimble, Richard, David's son
   family meal routine, 141–2
   father becomes MP, 133
   father's cooking skills, 88
   father's funeral, 395
   father's illness, 384–5, 386–7, 388, 392, 395
   meets King of Norway, 304
   phone threats, 255
   seat loss, 361
   Trimble peerage, 363
Trimble, Rosemary, David's sister, 2–3
Trimble, Sarah, David's daughter, 145, 257, 279, 388, 394
Trimble, Thomas, David's grand-uncle, 17
Trimble, Vicky, David's daughter
   comes out as gay, 378–9
   fails to meet Blair, 303–4
   father becomes MP, 136–7
   father's peace-making legacy, 409
   father's illness, 385, 395
   father's leadership ambitions, 178, 186
   marries Rosalind Stephens, 378–9
   mentioned in Lords, 380

Trinity Presbyterian church, Bangor, 13–4
Turkel Commission, 368
Twining, William, 23–4

U2, 252–3
Ukraine war, 389
Ulster Clubs, 113–5, 121
Ulster Conservatives and Unionists New Force (UCUNF), 366–7
Ulster Covenant, 4;
Ulster Defence Association, 44, 150–1
Ulster Defence Regiment, 36
Ulster Freedom Fighters, 44, 261
Ulster Hall, 180
Ulster Society, 107–8, 128
Ulster Special Constabulary, 76
Ulster Vanguard, 43–5, 50–1, 56, 64–5, 84
Ulster Volunteer Force, 154
Ulster Workers Council, 56, 57–9
United Ulster Unionist Council, 55–6, 61–2, 69
United Unionist Action Council strike, 83–4

Wagner, Richard, 201
Walker, Samuel, 129, 130
Wallace, Herb
   beats Trimble to law chair, 125–6
   friendship with Trimble, 22–3
   Graham murder, 101
   Hillsborough stunt, 118–9
   opinion of Trimble, 22–3
   Queens student with Trimble, 22–4

surprise at Trimble's first marriage, 26
Trimble backs UWC strike, 57–8
Trimble's First Class Honours, 24–5
Trimble gun incidents, 81
Trimble's marriage fails, 52
Trimble visits interned students, 36–7
Ward, William, 129, 130
Warrenpoint Methodist church, 76, 87
Waterfront Hall, 253–4, 299–300
Weir, Peter, 129, 176, 228, 284–5, 324, 328
Wells, Jane, 257–8
West, Harry, 55, 69, 87, 92
Weston Park talks, 318
Wharton, Nelson, 125
White, Barry, 276, 290, 367
Widgery report, 42
William, King, 17
Willis, Aubrene, 219
Wilson, Harold, 29, 33, 58
Wilson, Jim, 185
Wilson, John, BBC, 25
Wilson, Sammy, 355, 384
Winfield House meetings, 296–7
Women's Coalition, 217, 324
World Trade Center attacks, 321
Wright, Billy, 199, 215, 319
Wright, Terry, 361–2

Telegraph

YOUNG BRITAIN

Inside your
BUMPER ISSUE
All the day's sport

Maggie's final push

SPECIAL LATE
THE PEOPLE
IT'S

NEW YORK
CLASH CAN
LIFT SCOTS

Massive poll gives
resounding res